LOST SOUND

LOST SOUND

The Forgotten Art of Radio Storytelling

JEFF PORTER

The University of North Carolina Press *Chapel Hill*

© 2016 The University of North Carolina Press
All rights reserved
Designed by Alyssa D'Avanzo
Set in Calluna by codeMantra, Inc.

The University of North Carolina Press has been a member of the
Green Press Initiative since 2003.

Cover illustrations: *Radio Talent*, by Miguel Covarrubias (1938), courtesy
of the National Portrait Gallery, Smithsonian Institution / Art Resource, N.Y.;
digital equalizer display, © iStockphoto.com/sky_max.

Library of Congress Cataloging-in-Publication Data
Names: Porter, Jeffrey Lyn, 1951– author.
Title: Lost sound : the forgotten art of radio storytelling / Jeff Porter.
Description: Chapel Hill : The University of North Carolina Press, [2016] |
Includes bibliographical references and index.
Identifiers: LCCN 2015041084 |
ISBN 9781469627779 (pbk : alk. paper) | ISBN 9781469627786 (ebook)
Subjects: LCSH: Radio and literature. | Storytelling in mass media.
Classification: LCC PN1991.8.L5 P67 2016 | DDC 791.4402/8—dc23
LC record available at http://lccn.loc.gov/2015041084

Contents

Acknowledgments ix

Introduction 1

1 Acoustic Drift
Radio and the Literary Imagination 15

2 Prestige Radio
The Columbia Workshop and the Poetics of Sound 37

3 Mercury Rising
Orson Welles and the Master's Voice 62

4 You Are There
Edward R. Murrow and the Proximity Effect 83

5 The Screaming Woman 104

6 The Museum of Jurassic Radio
Sonic Excess in Dylan Thomas and Samuel Beckett 128

7 Radio as Music
Glenn Gould's Contrapuntal Sound 155

8 All Things Reconsidered
The Promise of NPR 182

Notes 211

Bibliography 253

Index 269

Illustrations

Nina Klowden with Virginia Payne as Ma Perkins 28

Norman Corwin, circa 1940 38

Orson Welles, Archibald MacLeish, and William Robson, 1938 56

Orson Welles, early 1940s 67

Edward R. Murrow, 1939 84

Agnes Moorehead 112

Dylan Thomas, 1953 129

Samuel Beckett, mid-1980s 142

Glenn Gould, circa 1970 157

Susan Stamberg, 1970s 184

Acknowledgments

This project benefited from the support of many individuals and institutions. Its early stages were fueled by a fellowship from the Arts & Humanities Initiative at the University of Iowa, which assisted with travel and other expenses. The project received a significant boost thanks to a Smithsonian Institute Senior Fellowship, which allowed me access to the resources of the Smithsonian as well as other archives in the area. While I was engaged in research in Washington, D.C., Dwight Bowers of the National Museum of American History, Amy Henderson of the National Portrait Gallery, and Susan Stamberg of NPR all provided especially valuable support and encouragement. I would also like to thank the librarians and curators at the Recorded Sound Reference Center at the Library of Congress, the Sound Archive at the British Library, the Lilly Library at Indiana University, the Paley Center, the New York Public Library, the Canadian Broadcasting Centre, and Photofest. Special thanks also to the University of Iowa Office of the Vice President for Research for supporting this project with a generous subvention.

A number of experts in radio studies offered timely advice and assistance, particularly Susan Squier, Michael Keith, and Gerald Zahavi. A special note of thanks is due to Kathy Newman, who read the manuscript with exceptional care and insight, and to the second, anonymous, reader for the University of North Carolina Press, whose enthusiasm for the project buoyed the final laps. From a different angle, Claire Sponsler shared her way with words at crucial stages of the project.

Without the editorial wisdom of Joe Parsons, this project could never have moved so smoothly to its final form. Alison Shay, Mary Carley Caviness, and Dorothea Anderson, also with the University of North Carolina Press, are likewise owed a hearty thanks for their help.

The students in my radio courses at the University of Iowa and at Grinnell College have earned a special thanks for happily serving as guinea pigs for my research, listening and responding to many of the radio programs and texts that have made their way into this book. Jessica Lawson, a Ph.D. student at the University of Iowa, provided much-needed help as my research assistant during one year in which she helped transcribe a number of the radio plays I analyze.

Parts of this book have appeared in different form elsewhere, and I am grateful to the editors of *Modern Drama* and to Carl Klaus and Ned Stuckey-French for offering a venue for preliminary work on this project. Readers who wish to see those versions can consult "Samuel Beckett and the Radiophonic Body," *Modern Drama* 53, no. 4 (Winter 2010): 431–46; and "Essay on the Radio Essay," in *Essayists on the Essay: Montaigne to Our Time*, edited by Carl Klaus and Ned Stuckey-French, 185–92 (Iowa City: University of Iowa Press, 2012).

Finally, friends and colleagues too numerous to name (but you know who you are) have shaped my thinking and encouraged my work. Among them I especially want to thank Phillip Lopate, Ralph Savarese, David Lazar, Leighton Pierce, Karl Klaus, Perry Howell, Judith Pascoe, and Patricia Foster.

LOST SOUND

Introduction

In 1941, John Cage received a commission from CBS to write a score to accompany a radio play by poet Kenneth Patchen, *The City Wears a Slouch Hat*, a surreal tale that follows the urban wanderings of a mysterious man called "The Voice."[1] Divided into thirteen scenes, the play chronicles the various encounters "The Voice" has with city dwellers, including a panhandler, thief, nightclub goers, bartender, cabdriver, street vendors, thugs, sobbing woman, and random phone callers. Like radio's "Shadow," "The Voice" has psychic powers he calls upon to disarm gun-toting thugs and predict the future. The play concludes with "The Voice's" retreat to a rock in the ocean, where he encounters another man who has left the noise of the city behind for the beating rhythm of the ocean waves. Both join in howling and laughing to the sound of the sea.

With its many sound cues, Patchen's script was rich in acoustic opportunities for sonic experiment, and when Cage was told by CBS that anything was possible, he let his imagination run free, producing a 250-page score written exclusively for electronic sound effects intended to be treated as musical instruments.[2] When that ambitious attempt proved unworkable, Cage quickly rewrote his score, scaling back his original ideas, using only percussive instruments (tin cans, gongs, alarm bells, whistles, bass drum, Chinese tom-tom, maracas, foghorn, thundersheet) and various acoustic effects.[3] Still, Cage was able to match many of Patchen's sonic cues with live and recorded sounds. The resulting score is a musical cacophony of percussive bangs and knocks that defines the chaotic energy and unrest of the urban landscape. Some listeners were baffled by what they heard, but others found *The City Wears a Slouch Hat* profound and moving.[4] Whatever their response, listeners understood that Cage and Patchen's avant-garde collaboration fit an emergent tradition that we are only dimly aware of today. *The City Wears a Slouch Hat* may have been an extreme example, but it stood alongside a panoply of literary radio art that had flooded the airwaves since the mid-1930s.

This is a book about a literary tradition that, while now seldom noted, was a vital part of broadcast radio in the 1930s and 1940s. Tracking that tradition's high points in American radio, the following chapters focus on the prestige movement sparked by CBS radio and then pursue postwar traces of the literary in British and Canadian programming. The story concludes with a return to American public radio and its brief but striking romance with sound art in the 1970s, as well as more recent developments such as the independent-radio movement and podcasts. The question this study tries to answer is how literary sensibilities—however fleetingly—radicalized a broadcast medium and were in turn energized by it.

A remarkable feature of broadcast history is that radio was at its most innovative in its earliest years. Until the late 1920s, American radio was a fledgling operation, largely restricted to regional transmitter towers, each independent and competing with the other. There was no such thing as a network. Radio audiences were small and the quality of programming (mostly popular music and variety shows) was limited. During radio's early period, less than half a million radios were in use, most of them owned by hobbyists and enthusiasts with the wherewithal to assemble their own sets. A well-known sociological study of a city called Middletown showed that in 1924 only one out of every eight families owned a radio set.[5]

Radio expanded faster than anyone could have foreseen. The proof was in the sales figures. Between 1930 and 1940, the number of radios in the United States grew by more than 100 percent. By 1937, over 50 percent of radio sets worldwide were owned by Americans.[6] By 1941, more families were equipped with radios than with cars and telephones.

For average Americans, radio had become an integral part of daily life. Listeners tuned in, on average, for five hours a day, embracing the new medium with gusto. The appetite for radio was enormous. Thirty million listeners—nearly 25 percent of the total population—listened to such popular programs as the *Amos 'n' Andy Show* and *The Chase and Sanborn Hour*. Forty million Americans heard President Roosevelt address the nation during his fireside chats.[7] Advertising revenues steadily rose: daytime sales were up 500 percent at CBS alone, according to *Time* magazine.[8] Radio was America's Internet.

As radio grew in popularity, a nationwide broadcasting system developed, with NBC and CBS controlling 30 percent of the nation's radio stations. The clout of those stations was enough to give the two networks the lion's share of broadcasting power in America. Unlike the assorted mix of local radio stations that characterized the early stages of radio, the new broadcasters stabilized their holdings around a wired network system and lucrative strategies for selling time to sponsors.

CBS flourished the most. As a fledgling company, the network had nineteen stations in 1928. Just seven years later, it had ninety-seven. While these numbers impressed economic observers, profits were slim since nearly two-thirds of CBS's broadcast time was unsponsored.[9] The network struggled to fill that time with educational programming (the newly proposed *American School of the Air*, for instance, recently staffed by novice radioman Edward R. Murrow) or by booking orchestral music. To fill unsponsored time, networks also created "sustaining" or prestige programs, which could be operated on the cheap.

William Paley, the chief of CBS, intuited that supporting highbrow literature would be an advantageous tonic for radio, especially for CBS, which lagged behind NBC and its lineup of popular performers (Jack Benny, Edgar Bergen, Bob Hope, Fred Allen, and Al Jolson, not to mention Arturo Toscanini). If CBS could not compete with Toscanini and the NBC Symphony Orchestra, it could nonetheless provide airtime for top-tier literature. From 1935 to 1938, an outburst of literary broadcasts changed the sound of American radio.[10] Excerpts from Shakespeare were suddenly heard on CBS (Burgess Meredith as Hamlet, Walter Huston as Henry IV, Edward G. Robinson as Petruchio, Orson Welles as Macbeth, John Barrymore as Richard III), as were the poems of Walt Whitman, Carl Sandburg, Stephen Vincent Benet, and Thomas Wolfe, which were adapted for broadcast by Norman Corwin on CBS's *Norman Corwin's Words without Music*. Not to be outdone, NBC commissioned its own poetry show (*Fables in Verse*), featuring the modernist poet, novelist, and editor Alfred Kreymborg. For the Mutual Broadcasting System, Orson Welles adapted Victor Hugo's *Les Misérables* in a seven-part broadcast in the summer of 1937.

Introducing upscale literary programming at the very moment that the broadcast medium was taking off in popularity was not only shrewd—it put off commercial radio's critics—but formative. "Prestige" was radio-speak for programming that had elitist literary content and was often used to refer to serious broadcast drama. Pressured by the success of *The Columbia Workshop*, CBS's 1936 experimental radio drama series, NBC moved quickly to establish its own highbrow drama series; its *Great Plays* debuted in 1938 with Aristophanes' *The Birds*, soon followed by Marlowe's *Tamburlaine* and adaptations of Euripides, Corneille, Shaw, Sheridan, Synge, and Ibsen. If radio began to sound like the Penguin Classics, this was not an accident but a clever move by broadcast culture.

Radio would have an enormous impact on the cultural lives of Americans throughout the 1930s and 1940s. It was a revolutionary medium,

Introduction 3

streaming a new symbolic language into homes across the country. The airwaves delivered jazz and classical music, entertained millions with serial comedies, and provided international news and commentary. Above all, radio told stories, not just to a handful of listeners around the proverbial campfire but to a mass audience. As *Time* magazine wrote in 1937, "The radio, which conveys only sound, is science's gift to poetry and poetic drama," and, "In the hands of a master a $10 receiving set can become a living theatre, its loudspeaker a national proscenium."[11]

The aesthetics behind the loudspeaker were at heart modernist. Modernism, in fact, seemed to shadow radio, as Jane Lewty notes.[12] Modernity's essence—disruptive, innovative, interiorized, complex, plural—found a home in the indeterminate forms and shifting tropes of radio in these decades, especially to the extent that CBS and NBC not only tolerated but encouraged inventive and even avant-garde experiments in radio storytelling. As a "decentralizing" and "pluralistic force," in Marshall McLuhan's words, radio seemed to offer a technological equivalent to the habits and obsessions of literary modernism, including a preoccupation with absence, disembodiment, and mediated subjectivities.[13] Just as modernist writers and artists were exploring the art of noise, complex vocalities, and the dynamics of what Walter Ong called "secondary orality," so too did radio.

The modernist interest in the acoustical imagination extended across the arts, prompting the emergence of a new sonic regime.[14] The broadcast studio was not just a hideaway for audio engineers, announcers, actors, band musicians, and advertisers. It also became a temporary haven for cutting-edge writers and artists and performers. That crossover was helped along by a significant number of modernist luminaries in the United States and abroad who were drawn to the potentialities of broadcasting, from Archibald MacLeish, Arthur Miller, and Samuel Beckett to W. H. Auden, T. S. Eliot, and Antonin Artaud. For these artists, radio offered an alluring medium that promised expanded audiences as well as a chance to explore the interface of writing and broadcast technology. Radio itself was a modernist invention that had already brought forth a new kind of user, the *listener*, who was simultaneously isolated and absorbed into an imaginary acoustic community. The listener and his auditory organs would pose new challenges to modernist writing—especially the challenge of sound. Because radio happens in the ear, the artist would have to extend the modernist mandate for innovation to new modes of aural experience; more than anything else, this effort would reshape the literary practices of modernist writers at the same time as it transformed radio.

Despite its importance, the story of radio's cultural impact has long gone untold. With the advent of television in the 1950s, radio receded quickly into the background of American thought, as if the victim of collective amnesia. It was no longer part of a larger conversation. Not only did listeners tune out, but so did critics. As the stepchild of media studies, radio was for years one of the most marginalized areas of modern academic research.[15] It's only recently that, despite this "massive act of public forgetting," as Michele Hilmes writes, a new generation of critics and artists has rediscovered the decisive role played by radio in the life of cultural forms.[16]

In a welcome turn of events, scholarship on sound culture and radio history has surged. Crucial to the new interest in sound was the 1992 publication of Douglas Kahn and Gregory Whitehead's *Wireless Imagination*, which redressed widespread ignorance of the role of sound in the experiments of the international avant-garde between 1880 and 1960. This seminal work was followed by two important studies, *Sound States* (1997), edited by Adelaide Morris, which applied the study of acoustics to twentieth-century Anglo-American poetry and experimental literature, and Kahn's *Noise, Water, Meat* (1999), which demonstrated how the production of sound was integral to the programs of radical modernist artists such as the Dadaists, the Constructivists, and the Surrealists.[17] Studies of literary acoustics such as these profited from the broader exploration of sonic properties and the cultural aesthetics of electrically mediated sounds by such scholars as Jean-François Augoyard and Henry Torgue, R. Murray Schafer, Rick Altman, Michel Chion, Jonathan Sterne, and Steven Connor. Equally influential has been the growth of work in sound theory and the phenomenology of listening, led by Pierre Schaeffer, John Cage, Don Ihde, Adriana Cavarero, Mladen Dolar, Jean-Luc Nancy, and Salomé Voegelin.[18]

Other studies bearing more directly on the history of radio took off in the 1990s as well, with a succession of scholarly inquiries targeting broadcast sound as a modern technology shaped by complex social and political histories, such as Hilmes's *Radio Voices* (1997), Susan Douglas's *Listening In* (1999), Susan Squire's *Communities of the Air* (2003), and Kathy Newman's *Radio Active* (2004). What these studies told us, broadly speaking, was that radio held the nation together during the Depression years by offering listeners a shared experience. Beamed into households across the country, radio programming constructed "imagined communities" and had a constitutive effect on its audiences that, contrary to the warnings of the Frankfurt School, was not always unfavorable. These studies also told us that radio has a complicated history, particularly in terms of the ideological conflict over network radio's economic prerogatives, its public responsibilities, and its racial and gendered exclusivity.[19] Collectively, the work of these critics showed that radio's so-called missing decades of the 1930s and 1940s were essential for understanding the social history of the twentieth century.

I take these studies further by examining the impact of *literary* practices on broadcast history, looking specifically at radio's embrace of modernist literature. In a way that now seems remarkable, modernist textual practices were adapted by radio auteurs to produce an auditory art that not only complicated radio storytelling but also remained accessible to large audiences. The result was a period of radiophonic experimentation that shaped a kind of acoustic ordering of modern experience.

The successful cross-fertilization of radio storytelling and modernist literature was in part due to their mutual ability to circulate widely, unfettered by geographical boundaries. In print or on the air, modernism unfolded as a transnational movement with an extensive reach. In its early years, for instance, the American magazine *Little Review* was the first to publish Joyce's *Ulysses*, while the British magazine *Blast* was printing the work of Ezra Pound. Pound himself was an aggressive marketer of the new borderless literature, introducing literary modernism to Chicago and New York while residing in London. Marianne Moore, Mina Loy, Gertrude Stein, D. H. Lawrence, and W. H. Auden likewise shuttled back and forth between London, Paris, and New York, turning their transatlantic experience into a commonplace of modernism. With the arrival of highbrow radio programming on both sides of the Atlantic, literary modernism reached even larger audiences, through the ears as well as the eyes. Given this border crossing, any study of literary modernism and radio has to take a wide-angled view.

In focusing on the interplay between literary modernism and broadcast radio, I build on a handful of recent studies. The contributors to *Broadcasting Modernism* (2009)—edited by Debra Rae Cohen, Michael Coyle, and Jane Lewty—for instance, examine how modernist writers of all stripes not only incorporated radio as a device into their fiction but also embraced the emerging medium by producing works exclusively for the ear. In narrower-gauge studies, Todd Avery's *Radio Modernism: Literature, Ethics, and the BBC, 1922–1938* (2006) looks at the Bloomsbury group in relation to BBC cultural programming, while Timothy C. Campbell's *Wireless Writing in the Age of Marconi* (2006) seeks to reinterpret Ezra Pound's

Cantos and his Italian radio broadcasts in terms of wireless inscription.[20] Although taking seriously the connection between broadcast and print, this scholarship tends to focus on radio's impact on literature rather than, as my book does, on the literary properties of radiophonic content.

Lost Sound explores the way modernism was absorbed by radio and seeks to understand how literary textualities contributed to the prestige movement in radio during the mid-1930s through the 1940s and beyond. For a brief spell, a door opened in broadcast culture that allowed sophisticated forms of storytelling to mix with prevailing forms of popular radio. The prestige movement's demand for noncommercial programming was met by a marked increase in literary-savvy productions, which in turn posed new aesthetic challenges for broadcasting. Previously limited to sirens and gunshots, radiophonic practices were stretched so as to broaden the spectrum of sound representation and thus accommodate the demands writers were placing on broadcast forms by adapting modernist motifs (dissonance, fragmentation, and interiority) to the new medium. With the success of the *Columbia Workshop* in 1936 and similar programming efforts, network radio was forced to embrace experimentation, whether it liked to or not.

The following chapters chart the give-and-take between evolving radiophonic techniques and shifting modernist textual practices in the growth of radio storytelling. While the customary approach to radio content during its oft-hailed "golden age" has been largely descriptive rather than interpretive, my analysis of radio's literary past views descriptions of broadcast culture as inseparable from a close reading of radio's acoustic texts. In line with that assumption, each chapter pairs discussion of broadcasting's commercial and institutional pressures with in-depth interpretation of the literary programming that was filling airtime.

Radio may have returned the modernist writer to the roots of literature in the aurality of language, but the new medium was not limited to speech. The spoken word was merely one sound that vied with others—music, acoustic effects, voice—and increasingly so the more radio prospered and stretched its auditory range. One of the more interesting tensions that marks the history of literary radio, I argue, is triggered by the friction between word-centered and sound-centered storytelling. When sound calls attention to itself it evokes a capacity to transcend its referent, resonating in ways that are closer to music than language. Such sound-centeredness ushers in other meanings, including unintended associations, and therefore possesses the power to disturb word-meaning, thus upsetting the semantic order of language. The destabilizing potential of pure aurality has historically provoked various kinds of phonophobia. Plato's antipathy to Homer, akin to the banning by Socrates of poetry from the Republic, is a notorious example, as is the destruction of the pipe organ by Puritans in seventeenth-century England. In his study of opera, Michel Poizat termed such efforts to control aurality the *mastering effect*, whereby voice is made to conform to the signifying regime, thanks to vesting in the primacy of the spoken word—or what Antonin Artaud called "the dictatorship of speech." The mastering effect fixes the voice to the order of discourse so as to curb its disruptive effects and dispel its native *différance*.[21]

During the heyday of radio, the mastering effect revealed itself in subtle and not-so-subtle ways. Edward R. Murrow faced stiff resistance from CBS in his efforts to mix recorded music and sound effects with his reports from the London Blitz, as network radio forbade the use of "taped" sounds in broadcasts (a ban that was not lifted until the late 1940s). Similar constraints were placed on daytime serial drama to guard the message of the spoken word from the sound and fury of music and acoustic effects. The most prolific of the "soap opera" studios, for instance, set up a virtual embargo on extraverbal sound production.

In mid-century radio, the mastering effect is a modern offshoot of a phonophobia that, at least since the time of Plato, reinforced the linkage between the spoken word and semantic meaning. The aim was always to restrict aurality to the letter of language in order to preempt any slippage between sound and sense. The concern was that such slippage, or what I call *acoustic drift*, would interfere with the perception of a message. In radio, the mastering effect was called upon to ensure that broadcast sound, even if not transparent, at least seemed so. The point of the mastering effect was to impose a kind of noise reduction on radio's storytelling by ensuring the supremacy of the spoken word, in opposition to the tendency of acoustic drift to derail the signifying process in favor of sonic *jouissance*.

Modernist programming vitalized radio. It elevated drama and introduced other genres to broadcast culture, such as the literary essay and narrative poetry. The movement also encouraged experiments with narrative form and provoked interest in radiophonic techniques that pushed the boundaries of music and sound effects. As a consequence, its storytelling acquired an acoustic depth and density that called attention to the nature of the medium itself. In certain cases, radio would become its own story, lending itself to modernist tropes of self-referentiality with an implied critique of broadcast practices. What emerged from this multiplicity of voices and sounds—from aural complexity—was a radio modernism that in its more avant-garde manifestations explored the recalcitrance of sound in the signifying process.

A central point of *Lost Sound* is that radio, as an acoustic medium, operates at the border of sound and sense, continually creating (and adapting to) the tension between word-meaning and sound-meaning. This tension has been for the most part productive, especially during broadcasting's boom years when new radiophonic practices stirred up a surplus of acoustic signs that challenged customary modes of listening.

The outburst of aurality that triggered a new sonic regime inspired by modernist literature and that untethered sound from linguistic meaning cleared the way for more radical forms of radio art but also provoked cultural nervousness about the status of sound. Critics worried that if sound did not always coincide with meaning, then listeners might stray from radio's message, caught up in a tide of acoustic drift. As the first chapter of this book shows, while the literary turn in radio would prove itself willing to embrace the disruptive side of sound, acoustic drift was not entirely welcome in network programming. In their quest to dominate the market, creators of soap operas, such as Anne and Frank Hummert, developed a form of sound-averse melodrama that attempted to curb radio's sonic exuberance. Despite the Hummerts' commercial success, however, innovative experiments with sound effects—such as the Martian "hum" that occurs halfway through *The War of the Worlds* or the evocative soundscape of Lucille Fletcher's *The Hitch-Hiker*—made it clear that acoustic drift would be the key to unlocking the hidden power of sound.

Although wireless storytelling was still in its early stages, it didn't take long for radio to mature, as Chapter 2 argues. Vital to the literary turn in radio was the prestige movement launched by the underdog CBS network, which became a haven for inventive radio auteurs whose creative output rescued broadcast culture (at least for a spell) from the pull of daytime soaps and for-profit programming. American network radio was barely ten years old when CBS debuted the *Columbia Workshop* in the summer of 1936.[22] The aim of the *Workshop* was to produce serious radio literature by pushing the envelope of playwriting as well as broadcast technology. Not only Orson Welles but other writers who moved into radio—including Norman Corwin, Arch Oboler, and Archibald MacLeish (whose *The Fall of the City* went further than any other program in adapting a modernist literary style to radio)—were invited to press the boundaries of radiophonic storytelling. During the course of its eight-year run (1936–43; 1946–47), the *Workshop* aired nearly 400 works for radio, many of them (like *Broadway Evening* and *Meridian 7-1212*) bold and experimental exceptions to what listeners ordinarily heard.[23]

Prestige radio contributed to what many saw as a novel body of enduring literature, a virtual public library that allowed CBS to characterize itself not just as a broadcaster but as a publisher.[24] To some, it seemed as though a new cultural form had emerged, something less ephemeral than nighttime variety shows or daytime serials. When CBS realized that prestige drama was earning points for the network, it began searching for even more literary luster, a search that led the network to approach the wonder boy of theater, Orson Welles, to produce a new weekly show, *Mercury Theatre on the Air*.[25] Chapter 3 examines Welles's subversive radio genius, which lay in creating narrators who fragmented the authorial perspective into multiple voices. As his radio adaptations of *Dracula* and *War of the Worlds* show, Welles embraced the premise of a dominant narratorial presence, only to deconstruct it. Teasing listeners with the prospect of discursive mastery, he denied them the comfortable certainty of one monologic perspective.

In the late 1930s and early 1940s, nearly all of America was listening to the voice of Edward R. Murrow, which, thanks to the illusion of proximity, seemed to be right there in the living room, the voice of an intimate friend. His keen attention to the acoustic effects of the London Blitz was one of the signature marks of Murrow's reports, and this sound bias distinguished his essays from such rival broadcasts as the radio commentary. Though rarely viewed as an essayist, Murrow achieved a style that was essentially a literary feat, Chapter 4 argues, the function of which was to evoke a participatory sense of history that would infiltrate the collective mind of a United States filled with deep-seated isolationist prejudices. To achieve this, Murrow constructed a new voice for radio, one that could not be mistaken for that of the traditional commentator, the reigning king of radio news. Ironically enough, Murrow devised a form of broadcast that had as much in common with CBS's *Columbia Workshop* as with print journalism, inventing a hybrid genre that borrowed equally from the modernist literary essay (exemplified by Stephan Crane and George Orwell) and from American radio drama.

CBS may have earned prestige for Murrow's widely admired enunciative mastery, but someone would have to pay for that discursive power.

Betty Wason was one reporter who apparently did. Her expulsion from the airwaves was a small case that reflected a much larger concern for network radio and is the subject of Chapter 5: the problem of the speaking woman. If radio was inhospitable to the female voice in nonperforming roles, that bias was not confined to network policy. A similar kind of vocal erasure found its way into radio's story lines and was, in fact, thematized in fantasies of entrapment and suffocation throughout 1940s radio. CBS's long-running radio-noir anthology, *Suspense*, specialized in desperate and hysterical female subjects whose traumatized voices echoed the profound discursive impotency of women enforced by the networks.[26] The dilemma of the screaming woman, hauntingly vocalized by Agnes Moorehead in Lucille Fletcher's *Sorry, Wrong Number*—the single most popular episode of *Suspense*—reproduces the predicament of the female voice in radio. The female voice was radio's outsider—its pariah—no less alien than *Mercury Theatre's* Martians. The screaming woman took radio beyond the symbolic order of the word, disturbing the apparently natural relations between language and meaning.[27]

Whatever their aesthetic differences, Dylan Thomas and Samuel Beckett shared, as Chapter 6 makes clear, an interest in defying radio's ontological borders (between being and nonbeing, embodiment and disembodiment) by flirting with the disruptive properties of sound. For Thomas and Beckett, the voice is not speech but sound, and their radio plays, especially *Under Milk Wood* and *All That Fall*, take extreme measures to liberate the word from speech—from the *logos*—destabilizing the codes of language. Using the incantatory power of voice, Thomas dramatizes the arbitrariness of signification through an excess of sound, while Beckett insists that spoken language is of the body, and in embodiment we find new ways to complicate, if not resist, the symbolic order of language and to take revenge on the *logos* for having devocalized language.[28]

As innovative as Thomas and Beckett were, there was room for more experimentation at the boundary of sound and sense. As Chapter 7 demonstrates, Glenn Gould radically redefined the experience of the listener by subverting the conventional aesthetics of documentary radio. Using modernist collage-like techniques, Gould interferes with the logocentric prerogatives of talk-based radio, moving a speech-centered genre in the direction of pure musicality. In the precarious balance between sound and sense that was increasingly typical of avant-garde radio, Gould's *Solitude Trilogy* went out of its way to sabotage the latter, all the better to liberate the acoustic side of radio from what Gould viewed as the tyranny of language. Gould saw in radio an opportunity to use the human voice as a kind of musical instrument, but this could only be achieved by complex editing in which documentary subjects are recast, thanks to an ambitious course of tape-splicing, as sonic types and tonalities rather than as linguistically individuated subjects. The result of Gould's "contrapuntal" approach to radio was a new mode of listening in which semantic listening gave way to tonal listening. Gould created a radical and subversive model for radio art that subsequent sound-makers, especially at National Public Radio in the 1970s and 1980s, would use to reshape the norms of institutional discursive authority.

NPR has always been a haven for people with brains, but in the beginning it was also a sanctuary for literate people with ears. As the final chapter explains, the "magazine" format adopted by *All Things Considered* and *Morning Edition* was a nod toward established literary publications like the *New Yorker*, with its mix of genres—commentary, fiction, poetry, essay, review, humor, portraiture—as a programming model. With ninety minutes at its disposal, *All Things Considered* could reasonably indulge its listeners with an inventive mix of news, commentaries, satire, essays, plays, and mini-documentaries that earned the program a cult following by 1978. Rather than featuring headline news, NPR revealed a preference for marginal stories, which fed its interest in pseudo-news radio genres, like commentaries, essays, and documentaries. NPR's was a quirky voice, long before quirkiness acquired cultural cachet, and its pursuit of offbeat topics allowed the network to sustain a commitment to sound as an artistic medium. In the 1970s, when NPR's producers made decisions without regard for Arbitron ratings, a sense of adventure informed the young network's attitude toward storytelling that harked back to the golden years of radio. During that time, NPR surprised even itself by hiring Joe Frank (1978) and by picking up Ken Nordine's eccentric *Word Jazz* (1980). Fabulists who later developed cult followings in the manner of Jean Shepherd, Frank and Nordine were a good match for NPR's experiment with novel forms of storytelling, which for a brief period in the 1970s and 1980s tested the boundaries of listening.

In an orthodox reading of broadcast history, television is the villain that finished off radio—or, as a pop-rock band said on MTV in 1979, "video killed the radio star." That radio was simply elbowed aside by a newer and more capable technology is in keeping with the displacement hypothesis, which has been a useful tool in plotting media histories.[29] Today, the Internet is said to be displacing traditional media, like television and cinema. In the late 1930s, radio itself was charged with threatening both movie-watching and news-reading. While it is certainly true on some level that the arrival of TV had a chilling effect on radio programming, a more nuanced reading of the fate of broadcast sound suggests that radio was as vulnerable to its own inner logic as to external technological change. American radio did not simply rise and fall, like Rome.[30] Its history is more wavelike, shaped by an inherent tension between sound and sense that defines radio as an acoustic medium and that set off pendulum swings between word-meaning and sound-meaning.

Even before the advent of television, both Edward R. Murrow and Archibald MacLeish backtracked on their earlier commitments to radio's innovative sonic regime. Looking ahead to the future of radio, Murrow told his audience in 1947, "I believe we will place more emphasis on the importance of the individual hearing and understanding what is said, rather than over-writing the voice with music or with sound effects of any kind."[31] In the late 1940s, sound gave way to word-meaning in a retrenchment that privileged speech above all else. The sudden loss of faith in radiophonic creativity signaled that the great period of sonic exuberance was over.

But not for good. In the 1960s, the free-form movement in radio, energized by the cult of the DJ and the arrival of stereophonic sound, fostered a renewed interest in close listening and acoustically complex programming.[32] A few years later, public broadcasting returned to sonic traditions that had prevailed during radio's best years, revitalizing broadcast sound as an acoustic medium. Suddenly, cutting-edge drama found its way back on the air after nearly twenty years of silence, as did avant-garde sound collages, personal essays, surrealistic narratives, and vérité sound documentaries. By the early 1990s, however, radio swung once more toward the right in the contest between sound and sense. Determined to become the *New York Times* of the airwaves, NPR found its way back to talk radio, a form of broadcast that depended on the power of the word to define its range of meaning, closing the door on twenty years of auditory adventures. Today, the legacy of radiophonic storytelling is found elsewhere, in podcasts and the independent-radio movement.

The eight chapters of this book rely on a methodology that brings together close readings of the canonical radio programs that comprise a forgotten literary movement in the history of broadcast radio. My "reading" of radio literature is grounded in what Charles Bernstein has called "close listening," in which the sonic dimension is regarded as a constitutive feature of an audio text. Close listening to radio requires a multitrack-like attention to the acoustic and nonacoustic layers that make up the "total" radio work—script, voice, music, sound effects, noise, ambience. As Bernstein observes, sound creates meaning as much as refers to something meant.[33] Sound is the bridge between text and auditor, physically connecting radio to its listeners.

Thanks to the fans of what is affectionately called "Old Time Radio," a large number of the radio broadcasts I discuss can still be heard today in digital copies available in electronic format. Many of the radio scripts I analyze are available in book form and are cited in the notes. Those that are not (such as Gould's "The Idea of North") appear in my own transcriptions.

Acoustic Drift
Radio and the Literary Imagination

Only ten years earlier, it was anyone's guess how to make money from broadcasting, but by 1936 the industry had stabilized itself around a wired network system and lucrative strategies for selling time to sponsors.¹ That year, the *Green Hornet* radio show first aired on Detroit's WXYZ. North of the border, the Canadian Broadcasting Corporation took to the airwaves, as did the New Zealand Broadcasting Service further away. From Windsor Castle, the BBC aired King Edward's abdication speech, heard by an estimated 20 million listeners. In the same year, CBS broadcast H. V. Kaltenborn's eyewitness account of Spanish Civil War combat from southern France, the first-ever live battle report. In Berlin, the Reichs-Rundfunk-Gesellschaft transmitted the Summer Olympics to forty countries in twenty-eight different languages. "What the press has been in the nineteenth century," Goebbels predicted in a 1933 speech, "radio will be for the twentieth century."² On a lighter note, from Radio City's studios in New York, ventriloquist Edgar Bergen introduced Charlie McCarthy to American listeners, not long after Fanny Brice launched her little-girl vocal routine as Baby Snooks.

The year 1936 was also when the German-born art and film theorist Rudolf Arnheim published radio's first serious study. In the opening pages of *Radio*, Arnheim was eager to recognize radio as an autonomous art form with its own unique aesthetic properties, a medium as compelling as painting and film.³ "Broadcasting," he wrote, "has constituted a new experience for the artist, his audience and the theoretician: for the first time it makes use of the aural only, without the almost invariable accompaniment of the visual which we find in nature as well as in art. The result of even the first few years' experiments with this new form of expression can only be called sensational." At the core of this new art was the material quality of sound. Arnheim defined sound not as a means to an end, a substance waiting to be made relevant by other devices, but as a medium with its own form of expressiveness. A work of radio art was thus capable of "creating an entire world complete in itself out of the sensory materials at its disposal—a world of its own which [did] not seem defective or to need the supplement of something external."[4]

So powerful was the aurality of radio, Arnheim argued, that it could never be limited to mere communication or to the realm of the spoken word. The impact of voice exceeded speech: "It should be realized that elementary forces lie in the sound, which affects everyone more directly than the meaning of the word, and all radio art must make this fact its starting point. The pure sound in the word is the mother-earth from which the spoken work of art must never break loose, even when it disappears into the far heights of word-meaning."[5]

Arnheim believed that as an art of sound, radio could not only hurdle space, abolishing territorial borders, but also test the boundaries of hearing, producing tensions between pure sound and the experience of meaning. On radio, the attentive listener hears words and, more importantly, acoustic properties such as intonation, timbre, pitch, resonance, tonality, and vocal intensities—what Arnheim called "tone-colours"—that do not always refer to the message. As Arnheim understood, sound and sense do not necessarily coincide in the mind of the listener. The word first comes to us as a sound, enveloped by other sounds. It is only later, on a higher level of abstraction, that we detach the word from its soundscape, parsing its meaning according to linguistic codes. For a brief moment, though, the spoken word and its noise are fused, merged in what Arnheim calls a "sensuous unity" exterior to language: "The aural world consists of sounds and noises. We are inclined to give the first place in this world to the spoken word. . . . We must not forget, however, especially when we are dealing with art, that mere sound has a more direct and powerful effect than the word. . . . It is difficult at first for most people to realize that, in the work of art, the sound of the word, because it is more elemental, should be of more importance than the meaning. But it is so."[6] Arnheim was asking readers to think of sound as a semiotically complex phenomenon in itself, detached from verbal meanings. As a statement about art, advancing the priority of sound over the law of meaning was consistent with avant-garde ideas—such as those associated with Luigi Russolo's Noise Art, F. T. Marinetti's Bruitism, Dada's sound poetry, Antonin Artaud's Theatre of Cruelty, and Pierre Schaeffer's *musique concrète*—even if it was not very amenable to an emergent radio industry that saw its future in the economics of sponsorship. Once sound was no longer tethered to linguistic meaning, a radical form of radio art was implied, as Douglas Kahn has noted, a possibility unlikely to please the guardians of American radio.[7]

Phonophobia

In fact, cultural nervousness about the psychodynamics of radio sound had already appeared. The worry was that if sound did not always coincide with meaning, then listeners might stray from radio's message. This anxiety was an early concern of radio research. As Hadley Cantril and Gordon W. Allport wrote in 1935, when Americans became mesmerized by a technology that exalted the "auditory sense" above all others, the sound of radio could become a source of distraction, interfering with chores and activities and even disrupting the content of radio itself, leaving programs half-heard.[8] Americans did housework, handicrafts, and farm work with the radio on; they drank, smoke, embroidered, talked, danced, played bridge, did homework, and made meals against the backdrop of daily broadcasts, presumably inattentively.

The problem of the distracted listener surfaced as a pressing theme in American public discourse during the 1930s, much the way Internet surfing worries today's cultural elite. Educators and reformers lamented that listeners were not giving radio programming their undivided attention. Surveys indicated that many Americans simply did not focus on radio shows. Young people in particular, it was thought, lacked sufficient concentration to give radio its proper due, failing to listen with discerning interest to radio's speaking voices and their messages. Without greater attentiveness, reformers feared, American listeners would lose their critical edge, becoming more passive, even lazy. To avoid bad habits, listeners were advised to consult with network guides in newspapers so as to make more deliberate programing choices. They were encouraged to organize attentiveness groups, and it was even suggested that "intelligent" listening habits be taught in the schools.[9]

In the view of the cultural elite, Americans were experiencing what I would describe as a kind of *acoustic drift*, straying from radio's message. If this was true, the cause was not so much that their minds were elsewhere but that, as Arnheim noted, it was the nature of sound to stray from the work of meaning. "Since sound follows the listener wherever he turns, radio tends to become the auditory foil of daily occupations, attracting sporadic attention, but not really commanding its audience. . . . Pure sound," he wrote, encourages the mind to "wander."[10]

America's cultural elite may have had radio's socioeconomic influence in mind when preaching against distracted listening, but the logocentric assumptions they brought to the medium—especially the assumption that radio's form should always be inseparable from its message-bearing content—were not necessarily in its best interests. As Jacques Derrida explained in his critique of Edmund Husserl in *Speech and Phenomena*, the assumed unity of thought and sound in the *logos* is a fundamental theme of philosophy, but that unity is a figment of the philosophical imagination. In particular, Derrida contested the teleological essence of speech and the idea that meaning (the signified) is made present, if not transcendent, in the spoken word. Such presence is possible, Derrida observed, only when the signifier is in absolute proximity to the signified. Only then are voice and thought one, combining to make what Aristotle called the *phone semantike* (the signifying voice/sound).

Should that unity be disturbed, such as when I see myself write (rather than hear myself speak), this proximity is broken and its integrity is dissolved, in which case meaning becomes that much more recalcitrant.[11] For Derrida, logocentrism depends on the absolute unity of various pairings: voice and thought, sound and sense, signifier and signified.[12] In their quest for unmediated meaning and for a signified that transcends its own making, logocentric systems crave the coherence of the sign and will do almost anything to protect it. In the aesthetics of radio, as in any art, these unities are inevitably compromised to a greater or lesser degree. The more ambitious radio became—the more it sought to exploit its own medium—the less respect it would pay to the coherence of the sign and the more it would seek out its own materiality. With its literary turn in the mid-1930s, broadcast storytelling acquired a sonic depth that often called attention to the nature of radio itself.

Sound has always presented certain challenges to the *logos*, as in the scream, or wordless music, or polyphony, or noise itself, which is often experienced, Jacques Attali claims, as an "aggression against the code-structuring messages."[13] Even in opera, the tension between language and voice is so great as to be threatening, since the voice beyond words is a thing not only of fascination but of great danger.[14] Sound may tell a story, as Salomé Voegelin points out, but it is often fleeting and uncertain: "Between my heard and the sonic object/phenomenon I will never know its truth but can only invent it, producing a knowing for me."[15]

Such uncertainty (what Julia Kristeva would call "negativity") reflects the recalcitrance of sound in the signifying process, which is perhaps the most important effect of what I am calling acoustic drift.[16] Acoustic drift refers to the uncoupling of sound from sense, to those moments when sound becomes unmoored from the anchor of language. In the most ordinary way, acoustic drift is common when we face unfamiliar sound structures, as in a foreign language. To a non-native speaker, the Proustian sentence—*Longtemps, je me suis couché de bonne heure*—will come nearer music than speech if heard rather than read.[17] When sonority takes a detour from the message, the listener will roam back and forth between a sound's sonic properties and its meaning, deferring the complex coding that turns acoustic information into meaningful words.[18] Typically, modes of listening oriented toward speech require the paring down of the sound stream to a linguistic unit, reducing noise and minimizing the expressive potential of the phonetic to discrete letters. Acoustic drift has the capacity to delay that process, suspending the coded interpretation of a message or what Michel Chion calls "semantic listening."[19]

Radio as an acoustic medium plays at the border of sound and sense, constantly producing (and adapting to) the tension between word-meaning and sound-meaning. This tension has been a productive one for radio, especially during its heyday when radiophonic practices provoked a surplus of acoustic signs that challenged modes of listening. Radio carried more voices and sounds into the ear, as Joe Milutis has suggested, than the mind could stand.[20] The radio listener had to sort through a head full of sound, parsing meaning from sound effects, music, voice, and spoken words. If the literary turn in radio confused the line between phonocentric and logocentric interpretive routines, that in itself was a kind of *noise* that interfered with the unity of sound and sense.

Radio may have been new, but phonophobia was old—as old as Socrates—and manifested itself as a preference for language-as-word over meaning-in-sound.[21] As Pope famously admonished: "The sound must be an echo to the sense."[22] Whether in music or voice, sound should not diverge from the word that certifies its meaning, for once it departs from its textual grounding, sound becomes senseless or threatening, all the more so, as Mladen Dolar notes, because of its alluring powers.[23] The voice should stick to the letter. Sound that does not contribute to making sense is, in this tradition, discarded as either frivolous or monstrous. For phonophobia, the work of sound is to support the bringing about of meaning: reduced to an acoustic signifier, sound should make utterance possible and then disappear in the signified.

Warnings such as Pope's have a long history. Similar concerns, especially those inspired by phonophobia, can be traced to Plato, who gives strongest expression to his logocentric zeal in his critique of the lyricism of Homer, the musical poet. Plato charged in *The Republic* that Homer was a "creator of phantoms," a mere imitator who, like the tragedians, produced images without knowledge of the truth. No one, for instance, should believe that Achilles, the son of a goddess, could have desecrated the body of Hector by dragging his corpse behind his chariot with such impiety.[24] Homer's *Iliad* is made up of such falsifications, Plato alleged, one after another. What most got under Plato's skin, however, was the poet's aurality, especially the musicality of the rhapsode's performance, which Plato called "the sweet influence which melody and rhythm by nature have." The seductive charm of Homer lay in the acoustic form of his dactylic verse, but that charm had little to do with the cognitive worth of his thought, Plato complained. In fact, deprived of its music, Homer's poetry would have little to show, since its effects rest on style not substance: "We shall say that the poet himself, knowing nothing but how to imitate, lays on with words and phrases the colors of the several arts in such fashion that others equally ignorant, who see things only through words, will deem his words most excellent, whether he speak in rhythm, meter, and harmony about cobbling or generalship or anything whatever. So mighty is the spell that these adornments naturally exercise, though when they are stripped bare of their musical coloring and taken by themselves, I think you know what sort of a showing these sayings of the poets make."[25]

Plato may have had little patience for Homer and his kithara (the lyre of Apollo), but the box-shaped four-string instrument was at the heart of Homer's poetic performances. During recitals, the instrument rested against the Homeric bard's shoulder, propped up by a sling that wrapped around his wrists. More likely than not, he improvised his four-note melody as he sang his tale, a melody that ran up and down the scale like dark ships rising and falling at sea. Every telling was different—he rarely kept to the same script. To adjust the beat of his phrases to the constraints of the dactylic hexameter line, a bard would run through his options, his stockpile of epithets (lord of the war cry, breaker of horses, sacker of cities, the great tactician, high-hearted, wide-ruling, bronze-armored, brazen-clad, gray-eyed, white-armed, lovely-haired, daughter of Zeus) and with lightning speed stitch in a tag that fit—all of this while sustaining the story's measure on his lyre.[26]

Plato's hostility toward Homer's vocality was matched by similar derision for the *aulos*, the flute-like wind instrument said to have been invented by the satyr Marsyas and identified with the sensuous sounds of the Phrygian double-pipe of Dionysus. The Athenians, we are told, were wary of its "soft lovely" tones.[27] In the *Symposium*, Eryximachus dismisses the flute-girl (*auletride*) so that the assembly can focus on the impending conversation without being distracted by the vulgar sounds of the aulist. The noise of the *aulos* should not drown out the voice of the *logos*.[28] Aristotle likewise raised questions about the value of *aulos*-playing, suggesting that performing on (or listening to) the instrument was not "conducive to virtue."[29]

The history of sound objects that have provoked phonophobia is not short. Consider the lute. In its capacity to arouse the listener, the lute was a kind of early modern *aulos*, seductive and ecstatic, and for that reason it was often described as a "woman's instrument."[30] Unsurprisingly, female lute players were associated with Homer's Sirens, famous for their danger to male self-control. The lute, as Katherine Butler notes, was eroticized in early modern portraiture, thanks in part to the musicianship of Venetian courtesans, who carried a lute as a badge of their trade.[31] Richard III's complaint that grim-visaged war "now capers nimbly in a lady's chamber / To the lascivious pleasing of a lute" resonates with the phonophobia of Plato, who warned that excessive sonority would weaken the warrior's virility, but also reminds us how sonority, in this unwritten history, can be marginalized and feminized as a threat to male agency.[32] It was the work of logocentrism to contest the sensuality of musical sonority on the grounds of rationality, moderation, and masculinity. Richard III's preference for the "stern alarums" of combat fits well with the order of discourse, which he manipulates so cunningly.

From Homer to Shakespeare and beyond, outbreaks of phonophobia vex the arts like paranoid dreams, provoked by moments of radical auralism that refused to conform to the symbolic order. A literary history of the scream alone would present several examples, from the fearful shriek of Achilles that destroys twelve Trojans by the sheer force of its blast to the inflammatory outbursts of Antonin Artaud and the glass-shattering cries of Günter Grass's Oskar Matzerath in *The Tin Drum*.[33] Passing beyond language, these terrible voices (*deinos phone*), which are as amazing as they are disturbing, pose a profound threat to Aristotle's *phone semantike*. Such voices constitute a kind of counter-tradition, the dark side of the *logos*, encompassing the song of the Sirens, whose acoustic allure was irresistible, as well as the dangerous incantations of Shakespeare's Weird Sisters.[34]

Closer to radio's cultural moment, modernist sound artists confronted the phonophobia of neoclassicism head-on. Kurt Schwitters's classic Dada sound poem "Ursonate" (1922–32) is a notorious example of the avant-garde's quest to musicalize the voice. Schwitters developed "Ursonate" as a half-hour performance that relied on invented vocalizations ("Rinn zekete bee bee") that, no matter how nonsensical, rigorously abided by a classical sonata form, with rondo, largo, scherzo, and finale movements. The poem's sonorous rigor contrasts ironically with its apparent lack of meaning. Like other Dada sound poets, Schwitters went so far as to suggest that the voice—even speech itself—could operate beyond the banality of sense.

Historically, efforts to protect the territory of the spoken word against such acoustic misbehavior occasionally led to the policing of sounds, from banning varieties of music that obscured the intelligibility of words (such as polyphony) to the prohibition of public singing by castrati. In the modern period, radio censorship would play a similar role by determining what was permissible within the representational limits of broadcasting. Such was the case when Artaud's commissioned sound piece *To Have Done with the Judgment of God*, scheduled to air in early 1948, was cancelled at the last moment by the director of French Radio. It was feared that Artaud's radio play, composed of absurdist poetry (recited by the author) and various sound effects, including drum, xylophone, gong, inarticulate screams, grunts, shrieks, and nonsense words, would create a scandal by violating broadcast rules of decorum.[35]

Acoustic Deviance

Even such an abbreviated history of acoustic deviance indicates to what extent auditory departures from the rule of meaning produce tension between language-as-word and meaning-as-sound, to borrow Don Ihde's distinction, a strong effect of which is the disturbance of the message.[36] Acoustic drift is at the center of such interference. Such drift is a fundamental condition of radio and is set in motion by the multiplicity of voices and sounds produced by radiophony.

An example from radio's early years appears halfway through *The War of the Worlds*. Orson Welles's interest in eccentric sound effects in radio drama is well known. To evoke the scene of Jean Valjean's escape through the sewers of Paris in his 1937 adaptation of Victor Hugo's *Les Misérables*, for instance, Welles placed microphones in a lavatory at floor level in order to create the muted echoes of voices in a damp and stony setting.[37] In *War of the Worlds*, Welles instructed his sound effects crew to revisit the washroom, this time with an empty mayonnaise jar whose lid was slowly unscrewed from inside the toilet.[38] This odd technique produced a strange sound that takes center stage at Grover's Mill, bewildering all, including the on-site reporter Carl Phillips and the astronomer Professor Pierson:

> PHILLIPS: Now, ladies and gentlemen, there's something I haven't mentioned in all this excitement, but now it's becoming more distinct. Perhaps you've caught it already on your radio. Listen please:
>
> (*long pause*)
>
> (*faint humming sound*)
>
> Do you hear it? It's a curious humming sound that seems to come from inside the object. I'll move the microphone nearer. (*pause*) Now we're not more than twenty-five feet away. Can you hear it now? Oh, Professor Pierson!
>
> PIERSON: Yes, Mr. Phillips?
>
> PHILLIPS: Can you tell us the meaning of that scraping noise inside the thing?
>
> PIERSON: Possibly the unequal cooling of its surface.
>
> PHILLIPS: I see; do you still think it's a meteor, Professor?
>
> PIERSON: I don't know what to think.[39]

Authorities (police, reporter, astronomer) struggle to make sense of the humming sound, just as, presumably, do radio listeners. Pierson, the professional astronomer, resigns himself to uncertainty, an unusual gesture for the expert, while Phillips, anticipating what will become a classic Edward R. Murrow trope, inches nearer to the mysterious sound source, planting his microphone as close as possible to the humming sphere. "Listen," he instructs his audience, "I'll move the microphone nearer." The odd "humming sound," in a significant figure-ground reversal, is no longer a secondary feature, as in ambience, but the salient narrative meme, the thing itself. In other words, the "humming" is a modernist *noise* because it refuses to be reduced to word-sense and instead arrives with the force of a disturbance.

As a trope, the humming would be viewed as a synecdoche, where the part (resonance) stands in for the whole (alien invasion). It is owing to Phillips's acoustic vigilance that the listener is aware of this anomalous sound as a sign of strangeness, as a mysterious "perceptual 'something,'" despite Pierson's efforts to banalize its significance. Illustrating the claim of Maurice Merleau-Ponty that "each part arouses the expectation of more than it contains, and this elementary perception is therefore already charged with a meaning," the humming is an ominous portent of something yet to come.[40]

By creeping closer to the source of the humming with his microphone, Phillips hopes to localize its meaning, as if language were not up to the task. In doing so, he casts meaning as a function of presence—the presence of sound. Startlingly, that presence turns out to be fatal.

> PHILLIPS: Wait! Something's happening!
> (*hissing sound followed by a humming that increases in intensity*)
> PHILLIPS: A humped shape is rising out of the pit. I can make out a small beam of light against a mirror. What's that? There's a jet of flame springing from the mirror, and it leaps right at the advancing men. It strikes them head on! Good Lord, they're turning into flame!
> (*screams and unearthly shrieks*)
> (*crash of microphone . . . then dead silence*)

The "curious humming sound" is an unsolved mystery that will be clarified only after the listener confronts the arrival of hostile aliens. The incineration of the radio reporter (Carl Phillips) and everyone else in the vicinity coincides with the revelation of the sound's secret. Acoustic drift will come to an end, but only in an apocalyptic message bearing destruction—and silence (the famous "dead air"). That this message—as a prequel to the Martian death ray—should also herald the collapse of radio (with the "crash of microphone," forecasting the fall of the CBS studio in New York) adds a layer of irony that points to the dangerous power of sound. The less we know about the meaning of this hum, the safer we are.

"To be listening," as Jean-Luc Nancy writes, "is always to be on the edge of meaning."[41] The sphere's hum vibrates on the edge of a meaning that comes from elsewhere. It is the sound of outré space. On this fringe is where acoustic drift is most intense, where meaning has not (yet) been fixed and signification waits to be stabilized.[42] As in opera, where sound manifests itself as a surplus, radio's sonic effects are not always dissipated by the signifying order. When sound does not exhaust itself in the message, its surplus is evoked as meaning-in-sound, which lies outside language-as-word.

That the Martian hum might be outside of language fills the reporter Phillips with the excitement of discovery. Sensing a good story, Phillips resists Pierson's efforts to normalize the sound (the professor suggests it was possibly caused by "the unequal cooling of its surface"). Instead, Phillips insists on the hum's acoustic drift, its *undecidability*—"Still think it's a meteor, Professor?" Unlike the message-oriented scientist, Phillips is attracted to the absent signified that shrouds the sound object in mystery. He seeks not an answer but a story. As the mysterious vibration indicates, it did not take much for sound and sense to part ways, as would happen increasingly with the new direction radio was taking. By straying from the explication of the "learn'd astronomer," the Martian hum points away from signification and toward event, its force the result of its disruptive function. In doing so, it resembles modernist noise of the sort advanced by the Dadaists, among others, whose function was to complicate literary meaning by interrupting the message and calling attention to the materiality of representation. Although Professor Pierson did not realize it, the force of the hum had more to do with the possibilities of radio—and with the subversive nature of sound—than with anything in H. G. Wells's novel.[43]

The analysis of acoustic drift, which is as intrinsic to radio as the vibration of waves, is made possible by recent trends in sound theory that have rescued the idea of sound from the logocentric monopoly of the spoken word. Countering the long-standing tendency, harking back to Plato and Aristotle, to relegate sound (*phone*) to the abstract realm of thought (*semantike*), current interest in voice and vocal expression has sought to restore a degree of concreteness (including embodiment) to the sonorous. Often this comes at the expense of patriarchy and the symbolic order. Rather than being silenced by thought, *phone* is now understood by many sound theorists to be the material, physical element of language that enables its worldliness. As a result, sound as sound, free of the traditional privileging of its relationship with language, has become analyzable as a source of meaning-making on its own.

As Adriana Cavarero argues in *For More Than One Voice*, language is not a voice's primary destiny. The voice is sound, not speech, even when it utters words. For that reason, sound can never really be grasped the ways words are, if only because the sonorous, as Jean-Luc Nancy notes in *Listening*, exceeds form.[44] And so the problem, as Dolar in *A Voice and Nothing More* states, is that sound always produces a remainder that does not disappear in meaning—a remainder that doesn't make sense. The will of the *logos* might be to capture sound in a complex system that subordinates the acoustic sphere to the realm of sight, but Dolar reminds us that there will always be a remnant (the Derridean supplement) that does not vanish in meaning, a remainder that doesn't make sense but exists as a leftover or a castoff.[45] What to do with that supplement would become the defining challenge for radio.

The Mastering Effect

While the literary turn in radio would prove itself willing to embrace the disruptive side of sound, acoustic drift was not entirely welcome in network programming, least of all in the wordy realm of soap operas. Nine years after the broadcast of the first soap in 1932, serials had captured 90 percent of daytime programming. They enjoyed an audience of 20 million listeners, for whose attention Oxol, Procter and Gamble, Lever Brothers, General Mills, Kellogg, A&P, Borax, General Foods, Pillsbury, and others vied with great eagerness. Soaps were criticized throughout the 1930s and 1940s by news columnists, psychologists, media critics, magazine writers, and consumer advocates.[46] The popular humorist James Thurber described the domain of daytime serials in a string of *New Yorker* articles as "soapland," a world produced by "factory-made wordage" that conformed to a narrowly defined pattern in the service of merchandizing rather than art. Having listened to countless soaps for a full year, Thurber was stunned by the untiring predictability of daytime serial drama. "A soap opera is an endless sequence of narratives," he wrote, "whose only cohesive element is the eternal presence of its bedeviled and beleaguered principal characters."[47]

Driven by the commercial imperatives of uniformity and frequency, the soap relied on a form of narrative discourse that was reluctant to compromise its clarity. The soap was radio's hear-through genre. To maintain its transparency, the producers of serial drama had to foil acoustic drift by regulating sound-making. To do so, soaps would have to tap into what Michel Poizat has called the "mastering effect," which emphasized the primacy of word-meaning over sound-meaning. In opera, Poizat argues, the mastering effect made sure that the voice of the diva did not free itself from the spoken word and remained bound to a narrative instance.[48] The aim was, as Dolar observes, to pin the voice down to the letter in order to curb its disruptive effects.[49] As with the *aulos* in antiquity, acoustic drift in modernist radio would have to be restrained in order to protect speech from sonic deviance.

A remarkable case in point is the prolific output of the Hummerts, the husband-and-wife team credited with inventing the daytime soap opera. Frank and Anne Hummert alone cranked out 125 serialized melodramas in their Park Avenue "radio factory" over the course of thirty years. The longest-running Hummert soap opera, *The Romance of Helen Trent*, debuted in 1933 on CBS and aired until 1960, featuring a middle-aged woman still searching for romance. (Absurdly, Ms. Trent remained the same age for the length of the series.) The twenty-seven-year-old show ran for well over 7,000 episodes before the network pulled the plug. At the peak of their career, the Hummerts had nearly forty different shows on the air simultaneously. In the years 1932–37, the Hummerts produced 46 percent of network daytime serials. The couple claimed to manufacture, thanks to their assembly-line approach to writing, over one hundred scripts per week. This they said with unequivocal pride.[50]

The Hummerts treated radio as a blank sheet of paper, as if the *logos* could be transferred from script to airwaves without a hitch. Such transparency required rigorous codes, privileging the semantic over the auditory, to guide the spoken word from its source in voice to its fruition in the message and to assure, as Robert Allen writes, the stability of the relationship of listener to text.[51] Any deviation from soapland's horizon of expectations would be startling and might break the listener-program contract. Avant-garde narrative techniques, including radiophonic experiments with sound, of course would be unthinkable, as would be literary modernism's unreliable narrators, shifting voices, interior monologues, trust in collage, and hostility toward bourgeois values. Such tactics would be welcome in prestige programming. With modernism, the soap opera may have shared an avoidance of closure but not much else.

As a pop-narrative form, the daytime serial promised to take radio down a narrow path lined with cereal ads, toothpaste, and cleaning products. In the case of the Hummerts, who approached storytelling like car manufacturing, the secret lay in engineering a repeatable formula that could be rigorously followed. As reported by *Time* magazine in 1939, the couple assembled innumerable scripts per week, many of which were produced as fifteen- and thirty-minute radio dramas in their propriety studio (Air Features). While the Hummerts employed a bevy of ghostwriters to crank out story after story, the hired hands served primarily as dialogue writers, not as "authors," and were isolated from Air Features, where the script was later duly massaged and broadcast live. *Time* compared the Hummerts' process to a "factory" or "mill," an analogy that stuck.[52]

Nina Klowden (*on left*) with Virginia Payne as Ma Perkins, reading for *Ma Perkins*, CBS radio, 1940s. (Courtesy of Photofest)

The Hummerts managed not only to produce an unlikely quantity of radio scripts but also to maintain control over nearly every phase of the process. Remarkably, the duo had more or less cornered the daytime serial market; more interestingly, they did so by implementing a series of constraints to ensure clarity of word-meaning. Behind these constraints was a concerted effort to maintain, in Thurber's words, "conformity to the pattern."[53] As the radio actress Mary Jane Higby remembers, "an actor could spot an Air Features script across the room." Not only was it written in lavender ink, but it was ringed by rigid rules. The Hummerts did not permit their directors to interpret the script but insisted that they follow its words literally and faithfully. Nor were directors permitted to embellish the story with expressive sounds, for that might detract from the readability of the language. "Art effects—unessential sound, background music—that might obscure one word of dialogue" were rigorously banned, Higby notes. What mattered most was the articulation of language. The Hummerts, recalls Higby, demanded that "each vowel and consonant be enunciated with painful precision" and strictly ruled out the overlapping of speeches.

The writing staff was held in check by a long list of regulations, all aimed, as Higby remembers, at making sure listeners knew at every moment exactly who was speaking to whom and why.[54]

In their quest to dominate the market, the Hummerts developed a form of melodrama that attempted to curb radio's sonic exuberance. Narratively, Hummert-produced soap operas were marked by an effort to limit polysemy. In the case of the long-running *Ma Perkins* (1933–60), written and produced by the Hummerts and sponsored by Procter and Gamble, the ideal of transparency manifests itself in a stenographic code that narrowly restricts the acoustic play of voice. *Ma Perkins* tells the story of a feisty widow whose children and friends continually call upon her guidance when tackling life's varied difficulties.[55] Owner of a small-town lumberyard, Ma presides over a family of three, doling out wisdom to townsfolk and keeping her children out of trouble. Like other soaps, each fifteen-minute episode of *Ma Perkins* was carefully framed by an announcer who not only summarized the storyline but kept the sponsor's "message" up front ("For a wash that's white without bleaching, use Oxydol with its lively, active, Hustle Bubble suds"). The announcer's narratological role also included mediating the characters and plot in ways that nudged the exegesis in a conventional direction. As a voice of authority, the announcer managed the "message" on all levels.[56]

> ANNOUNCER: And now for Ma Perkins! Well, the mystery surrounding the strange explosion in Ma's lumberyard is still unsolved! All anyone knows is that Ma's son-in-law, Willy Fitz, had built a shack at the far end of the lumberyard, had been spending quite a lot of time there—when suddenly the whole thing blew up! Willy was injured and taken to the hospital. Ma refused to let Chief of Police Tookey question Willy yesterday. But you can be sure Ma herself is wondering what caused this terrible explosion. Here she is visiting Willy at the hospital. Dr. Stevens is there with her.
>
> STEVENS: (*brightly*) Yes, Willy. I'm happy to tell you that you're doing fine!
>
> MA: (*brightly*) Oh, that's jest th' best news a body could want—Doc Stevens! Ain't it, Willy?
>
> WILLY: (*weak, but not nearly so much as before*) Yeah, it—it sure is, Doc Stevens!
>
> STEVENS: Yes, sir! You'll be out of the hospital in a week sure!

WILLY: (*sadly*) Do I—have to—stay here that long?
MA: (*gently*) Land o' Goshen, ya hafta git th' proper rest 'n' attention, Willy!
STEVENS: (*easily*) Oh, of course, Willy! You must remember that piece of timber that struck you on the head gave you a pretty bad concussion! (*Ma affirms*)
WILLY: (*thinking*) Yeah—my head sure does—feel sore! Gee, I know that![57]

A typical *Ma Perkins* script furnished few if any sound cues but supplied a catalog of delivery prompts: brightly, sadly, gently, easily, firmly, soberly, resignedly, warmly, wearily—and so on. Like emoticons for sound actors, *Ma Perkins*'s "parentheticals" left little room for interpretation, limiting the emotional vocabulary of the show to two dozen adverbs. In contrast, the *Mercury Theatre*'s broadcast of *Dracula*, from the same period, is a riot of noise. *Dracula*'s script features no delivery prompts, only sound cues: Thunder, Rapid hoof beats, Dog howls, Wind arises, Wolves bay, Horses whinny, Footsteps, Music rises, Breaking glass, Door slam, Whip cracks, Wagon wheels over cobblestone, Chain rattles.

With over eighty delivery prompts in one fifteen-minute episode of *Ma Perkins*, the voice of the actor was fixed by writing, instructed by the word. Between the normalizing role of the announcer and the excess number of delivery cues—not to mention the minimizing of music and sound effects—*Ma Perkins* was obviously the work of an overdetermined system of meaning-making, engineered to produce a "message."

Avant-garde radio this was not, but soap operas like *Ma Perkins* made tremendous profits for both sponsors and the broadcast industry. Ironic as it may seem, soaps subsidized the rest of radio, as Kathy Newman points out, including the highbrow literary fare that aired in the evening.[58]

That the Hummerts' factory model thrived so well—the couple was netting $300,000 annually from radio in 1940 (equal to $4 million in 2012 dollars)—revealed to what extent aurality could be minimalized in radio drama and contained within a system of signification that subordinated sound to language. The Hummerts were maestros of the mastering effect. In the sonic economy of the soap, spoken words would always have primacy over sound events. If voice could be wielded as an instrument, then meaning was its goal. For the Hummerts, it was crucial to safeguard the stability of meaning in a medium capable of driving a wedge between voice and the signified, vital to hold in check the destabilizing effects of acoustic drift. Embracing the transparency of language-as-word, the Hummerts hoped to prevent the voice from straying away from sense, ensuring the congruity of sound event and meaning. In this way, the spoken text of daytime serials was reduced to, as Steven Connor would say, the condition of the written word.[59] In soaps and similar broadcast shows, the sonorous was to be avoided at all costs.[60]

I am exaggerating the Hummerts' case, although only slightly, to illustrate the presence of the mastering effect in an economically powerful genre at a key moment in radio history. Not all soaps betray the kind of phonophobia we find in the Hummerts' production model, but given the Hummerts' programming dominance, their efforts to impede radio's material core—*sound*—is significant. Ironically, the commercials that aired during soap operas, with their catchy jingles ("I'm Chiquita Banana and I've come to say"), slogans, and goofy puns, relied more heavily on sound effects and music than did the feature narrative.[61]

Who or what controlled the discourse of radio was a question that surfaced repeatedly. The broadcast system could turn one speaker into a wizard of Oz with just a microphone and a switch, projecting a disembodied voice into millions of homes around the country. That mastery cast a spell not only on demagogues but on radio storytellers. As later chapters will show, attaining enunciative mastery—and losing it—was a recurrent theme in radio that cut across genres and genders.

Radio's Literary Turn

Profitable and influential, the Hummerts' radio model may have dominated daytime programming during the formative period of broadcasting, but evening was a different matter. By 1936, nighttime hours were increasingly filled with music, comedy, variety shows, and "serious" drama, the latter opening the door to highbrow literary content.[62] The debut of CBS's *Columbia Workshop* in 1936 made an immediate impact on broadcast culture, introducing the idea of radio literature with much fanfare. Thanks to the *Columbia Workshop*, literature-based radio would be at the center of the "prestige" movement.[63]

What made the literary turn in radio so welcome in some circles was fear that radio, as the cutting-edge playwright Arch Oboler warned, might be usurped by soap operas. Quality programming, it was hoped, would reclaim radio for serious literature. Not only did radio literature boost network esteem, drawing distinguished titles and prominent talent to idle time slots, but it was for the most part inexpensive. With the *Workshop*'s early success, CBS initiated a "history-making" series of eight Shakespeare plays the following year, produced by Brewster Morgan (former director of the Oxford Theatre in England) and starring well-known celebrities in leading roles (John Barrymore, Walter Huston, Edward G. Robinson, Tallulah Bankhead, and Burgess Meredith). Not to be outdone, NBC announced a rival Shakespeare series, to be produced by John Barrymore. Both networks commenced their series with adaptations of *Hamlet*. News of CBS's "ambitious" *Shakespeare Cycle* traveled fast. A headline in the *Lincoln Journal and Star* in Nebraska proclaimed on 11 July 1937: "CBS Shakespeare Cycle to Open Monday with Meredith in Leading Role of Hamlet: Noted Series to Present Eight of Bard's Plays Directed by Brewster Morgan; Famed Talent List Scheduled." Thomas Archer wrote on 24 July 1937 in the *Montreal Gazette*: "Shakespeare, by way of radio, must still be regarded as experimental, albeit a very hopeful experiment. . . . Radio excels as a medium for Shakespeare because it appeals to the ear and not to the eye."[64]

Radio's dueling Hamlets (Meredith versus Barrymore) highlighted the summer of 1937, but network rivalry did not stop here. The fact that the *Columbia Workshop* drew both critical and popular acclaim—it set the standard for "prestige" programming—vexed NBC. Feeling pressure from upstart CBS, NBC debuted an experimentalist of its own, signing Arch Oboler—the Edgar Allen Poe of radio—to take over the weekly horror show *Lights Out*. Like the *Workshop*, Oboler's *Lights Out* ("It is later than you think") flirted with modernist practices, such as his trademark stream-of-consciousness technique, and also experimented at the boundaries of storytelling and sound design. Oboler delighted in the grotesque, deploying unusual effects to intensify the listener's terror. In one play, *The Dark*, the body of a man turns inside out shortly after a deadly black fog is accidently let loose on an unsuspecting town. A challenge to the sound effects department, this disaster to human flesh was evoked by noisily removing a surgeon's rubber glove close to the microphone, while at the same time crushing a berry basket—to the accompaniment of the cackling laughter of a madwoman. Oboler's surreal sense of horror manifested itself in a variety of memorable ways: making bacon sizzle to suggest a condemned man's electrocution, beating noodles with a plunger to evoke the sound of eating human flesh (used alongside Peter Lorre as human brain eater in *I'm Hungry*).[65] Stephen King called Oboler horror's premier auteur. On the CBS side, Welles's radiophonic efforts were no less clever than Oboler's morbid sound effects for NBC. From the emergence of the otherworldly Tripod and the firing of the Martian death ray to the panic of witnesses and the anxious shrieks of the reporter, the Grover's Mill sequence in *The War of the Worlds* achieves its thrill less by speech than by sound. In the *Mercury Theatre*'s inaugural broadcast of *Dracula*, both scene and action are evoked by a salvo of sounds aired simultaneously—hoof beats, thunder, wind, wolf howls, the neighing of horses, the coach's clatter—as Jonathan Harker wends his hazardous way through the eerie Borgo Pass.

In these and other productions, Oboler and Welles pointed the way to prestige radio's integration of innovative radiophony into its stories. Before long, the appeal of radio's sonic uprising spread across network boundaries, and sometimes even contested the primacy of the spoken word. Rarely did a *Columbia Workshop* program rely solely on words for its impact. Instead, producers preferred an acoustic chorus: voice, ambience, musical motifs, and effects. The *Workshop* saw sound-making as part of its mandate to be "experimental" and vital to the "magic of radio," as the show's announcer promised each week. While prestige radio was by no means uniform in its approach to sound design, many programs, like the *Workshop*, *Lights Out*, and *Mercury Theatre on the Air*, exploited acoustic devices new to radio (parabolic microphones, equalization filters, and echo chambers) to create soundscapes that expressed a modernist interest in the tormented subjectivity of narrative characters.

The force of such innovations, especially during evening shows, provoked changes in the voice of broadcast radio.[66] Leading the way, the *Columbia Workshop* escalated music and sound effects in many of its productions, even when that compromised the audibility of the spoken word. By trebling the acoustics of radio's voice (adding music and ambience to speech), the *Workshop*'s innovations split the acoustic field in two: focused (speech) and fringe (background) sounds. With such a split came the suggestion of sonic depth and the possibility of distraction from the message—more occasion for acoustic drift. As Irving Reis explained in a CBS press release, the *Columbia Workshop* did "not plan to abide by any preordained concept of radio drama" but intended to try almost anything that might "lend itself to unique treatment and interesting experiments with sound effects and voices."[67] These experiments introduced a degree of polyphony that would deepen the experience of listening, steering radio literature in a more sonically adventurous direction.

Music and sound effects would become vital to nighttime radio drama. In the gothic features on *Suspense* (1942–62), storylines were scored from start to finish with expressive music that reinterpreted the elements of narrative distress in auditory terms, while sound effects were used extensively to build a complex acoustic space. In the famous episode of Lucille Fletcher's *The Hitch-Hiker*, first performed by Orson Welles and his *Mercury Theatre* on 17 November 1941, Ronald Adams (played by Welles) is stalked while driving cross-country by a mysterious man repeatedly appearing on the side of the road. In Pennsylvania, Ohio, Missouri, and New Mexico, Adams sees the same man again and again. Adams becomes obsessed with the eerie figure, even trying to run the hitchhiker down with his Buick in a fit of paranoia. At wit's end, Adams phones home to Brooklyn, hoping to speak with his mother—by this point he is barely clinging to normality—only to learn that she has suffered a nervous breakdown on learning of her son's death in an auto accident days earlier. Ronald Adams, he is informed by the stranger who picks up the phone, died six days ago on the Brooklyn Bridge.

Although the startling fact that we are listening to a posthumous narrator is saved for the plot twist at the end, the show's radiophonic motifs indicate much sooner that Ronald Adams is not of this world. In addition to Bernard Hermann's mournful score, the drone of motoring sounds (which run the length of the play and evoke a sense of stasis), the chiming of church bells, the ringing of a gas pump, the haunting "Hellooo!" of the hitchhiker, the jangle of change in a coin-operated pay phone, all produce a woebegone mood, a for-whom-the-bell-tolls gloom, that haunts listeners. The play's sound mix is complex but compelling, evoking a chilling sense of isolation and displacement, and what seems at first simply one man's neurosis, the result of a paranoid mind playing itself out, is transformed by sound into a nightmarish reality, with every auditory signal we hear tolling a kind of death knell.

Alone at the end of the play, Adams reflects on the strangeness of his dilemma: "And so—so I'm sitting here in this deserted auto camp in—Gallup, New Mexico. I'm trying to think. Trying to get hold of myself. Otherwise, I—I'm going to go crazy. Outside, it's night. The vast, soulless night of New Mexico. A million stars are in the sky. Ahead of me stretch a thousand miles of empty mesa—mountains, prairies, desert. Somewhere among them, he's waiting for me. Somewhere I shall know—who he is—and who I am."[68] The trustworthiness of the narrator is in question throughout the story, simply because we are, much like the female hitcher later offered a ride, doubtful of the driver's state of mind. From the beginning of the tale, the listener is made to wonder about the narrator's stability:

> My name is Ronald Adams. I'm thirty-six years of age, unmarried, tall, dark with a black moustache. I drive a 1940 Buick, license number 6Y175189. I was born in Brooklyn. All this I know. I know that I'm at this moment perfectly sane, that it's not me who's gone mad—but something else, something utterly beyond my control. I've got to speak quickly. At any minute the link may break. This may be the last thing I ever tell on earth—the last night I ever see the stars.

Is he losing his mind or is he lost in some other way? Ronald Adams does indeed turn out to be an unreliable narrator, not because (as listeners suspect) he is going crazy, but because he is dead and thus disconnected from physical space. As Neil Verma observes, Adams's road trip ends far from his intended target (Los Angeles) but close to the continental divide, an evocative threshold of sorts. In this tale, the idea of journey's end is an elaborate joke, a pun that occurs at the expense of both Adams and the listener.[69] Just as the "divide" between this world and another eliminates the relevance of geography, so the boundary between interior and exterior space vanishes by the end. The church bell (and its many proxy chiming sounds) that intermittently rings throughout the story is part of a sonic strategy that moves the listener from a realist landscape into a surrealist space of nonbeing in which the stability of identity and the signs of reality cease to signify.[70] The bell sounds, which are initially diegetic (such as the railway warning), become increasingly ambiguous as the story unfolds, their referents more and more evasive. When Adams in panic calls home from New Mexico, the coins he drops into the pay phone ring as loud as church bells. Not the sound of change, the repeated chimes refer to something else, though we don't know this until the end. The deferral of the referent, which is at the heart of the story's suspense, depends on radio's unique ability to convey two different streams of auditory meaning. Although the story's more pronounced subject may be cross-country travel, *The Hitch-Hiker*'s implicit theme is tied to a subtle but elaborate interest in acoustic drift.

Fletcher herself attributed the spine-chilling effect of *The Hitch-Hiker* to a particular style of sound she envisioned when shaping the narrative. She explained that the script was written primarily for the voice of Orson Welles, playing Ronald Adams, the haunted traveler, but the script also drew on the *Mercury Theatre*'s innovative sound effects and their expressive power.[71] "*The Hitch-Hiker* was written for Orson Welles in the days when he was one of the master producers and actors in radio," Fletcher wrote in her preface to the story. "It was designed to provide a vehicle not only for his famous voice, but for the original techniques of sound which became associated with his radio presentations." And so, Fletcher added, it was "Orson Welles and his group of Mercury Players that made of this script a haunting study of the supernatural, which can still raise hackles along my own spine."[72]

The year 1936 was seminal but also a crossroads for radio. In one direction lay pop-narrative serials and the lucrative daytime soaps, a mode of production that largely worked against radio's sonic nature but inflated the economic bottom line. In an entirely different direction lay literary radio, the aesthetics of which were radically open. If daytime serials were overdetermined and heavily commodified, nighttime radio literature was given over to hybridity and experimentation and pressed programming beyond the existing popular genres. Captivated by sound, politically and artistically sophisticated writers and producers of the mid-1930s engaged in radiophonic practices that redefined the ways in which narratives could be heard on the airwaves. The emergence of ambitious narratives constituted a literary turn in radio that leveraged the medium's material basis and sound technologies. Prestige radio would thrive on good writing, but that work would be empty without the radiophonic innovations of Orson Welles, Arch Oboler, Norman Corwin, the *Columbia Workshop*, and others who mined the tension between sound and sense. Their intuitive understanding of how to exploit radio's semiotic quirks, particularly the slippage between words and nonverbal signs, opened up radio as an artistic form. As they glimpsed, acoustic drift would be the key to unlocking the hidden power of radio.

Prestige Radio
The Columbia Workshop and the Poetics of Sound

On 8 May 1945, 60 million Americans (nearly half the nation) tuned in to hear *On a Note of Triumph*, Norman Corwin's masterpiece marking the end of World War II. The play opens with Bernard Hermann's brassy score and the brusque words of the narrator, played by Martin Gabel: "So they've given up? They're finally done in, and the rat is dead in an alley back of the Wilhelmstrasse. Take a bow, GI. Take a bow, little guy. The superman of tomorrow lies at the feet of you common men of this afternoon. This is It, kid, this is The Day, all the way from Newburyport to Vladivostock."[1] A landmark in radio, the hour-long program saluted America's GIs in high colloquial style and then went on to raise questions about the larger meaning of victory. As expressed by the Everyman character of the GI, these questions ("Who did we beat, how much did it cost, what have we learned, what do we know now, what do we do now, is it going to happen again?") are delivered in an earnest, humble voice that contrasts markedly with the booming accents of the narrator. The play is memorable for such oppositions and mood swings, progressing by sudden turns that transformed the exhilaration of victory into something more emotionally fraught and intellectually challenging. Corwin did not allow the listener the luxury of forgetting, in the joy of the moment, the human cost of war or the reluctance of Americans to get involved in the first place.

The play's mosaic form deepens the commemorative work it undertakes while complicating its reception in a typically modernist way. A mix of newsreel, commentary, narration, drama, and poetry, *On a Note of Triumph* conjures up the entire history of radio in its broad effort to imagine the enormity of a war the likes of which no one had seen before. Its hybridity keeps listeners guessing about its mode of address, just as much as its shifting tonalities prevent any kind of categorical resolve. Corwin's ability to hover between "triumph" and doubt

Norman Corwin directing a radio play in the CBS control room, circa 1940. (Courtesy of Photofest)

prevents the predictable signifieds from lining up in the end.[2] The play concludes not with cheers and confetti but with a secular prayer ("Lord God of Trajectory and blast whose terrible sword has laid open the serpent so it withers in the sun for the just to see, sheathe now the swift avenging blade with the names of nations writ on it, and assist in the preparation of the ploughshare"), a burst of neobiblical prose reminiscent of the heightened writings of Walt Whitman, James Agee, and Pare Lorentz.[3]

What held all of this together was not only the vernacular lyricism of Corwin's script but also the heart-stirring zeal of Martin Gabel's remarkable narration. The voice of the narrator, rising and falling from panoramic heights to close-up intimacy, is the strong force that contains and unifies all the disparate parts of the play. It was an "unflinching voice," as Philip Roth remembers it in his novel *I Married a Communist*, the voice of "common man's collective conscience," an image of the national character inscribed in sound.[4]

Where did this voice come from?

With few rules or well-defined conventions, radio storytelling was something of a frontier in its early days, akin to the theatrical scene in Elizabethan England in the 1580s when Shakespeare first arrived in London. But it did not take long for radio to develop its own literary voice, and around that sensibility an "adaptive" culture emerged that (in the Elizabethan spirit) begged, borrowed, and stole. Critical to the new trend was not only Corwin but two additional inventive radio auteurs, Archibald MacLeish and Orson Welles, whose creative intelligence made Corwin's Whitmanesque narrator possible and helped rescue radio from the economic pull of the daytime soaps.

By the late 1930s, nearly 90 percent of all American households had radios. Even with the economic hardships of the Depression, families had found ways to scrape a few dollars together for a radio. As movie theaters closed their doors (attendance dropped by 33 percent between 1929 and 1935), radio picked up the slack. At the end of the decade, Americans reportedly preferred listening to radio over moviegoing and reading.[5] The print world could not help but take notice. *Fortune*, *Time*, and *Popular Mechanics* ran feature articles on the sudden success of network radio. "Nobody could deny," *Time* magazine wrote with parental respect, "that as a business proposition, radio was indeed a thriving youngster."[6] Only once in the last ten years, the magazine observed, had radio failed to pile up huge revenues to top previous years. Sales of radio time were soaring. In 1938, radio was doing $140 million worth of business ($2.2 billion in 2013 dollars), rivaling the revenues of other media, such as magazine advertising ($166 million) and newspapers ($595 million).[7]

While it had relied on music recitals and discussion shows early on, in the 1930s radio embraced short fiction and drama, taking its lead from pulp magazines and other serial genres that fed popular culture. Americans clung to their radios as if they were the one thing they could not do without. "If we lost the radio, I'd be willing to dig my own grave," said one listener. "I tell you, the only time it isn't on is when I'm out of the house," said another.[8] Americans listened to their radios around the clock and from room to room. "We have one radio—but we move it all around; wherever we are, the radio is!" explained a typical "housewife." "Oh, I always can hear it," said another. "I have two in my bedroom, and my husband has one in his bedroom, and we have one in the kitchen and one in here (the dining room) and one in the sitting room. And when I go inside to make the beds I just turn it on in there, and when I go back I switch it on out here."[9] For these listeners, nothing could take the place of radio.

Gathering around a large tabletop radio each evening had become a national ritual. As families tuned in to *The Jack Benny Show*, *Burns and Allen*, *I Bet Your Life* with Groucho Marx, and *The Firestone Hour*, they embraced their radios as prized objects. The radio set itself was regarded as a piece of furniture, especially the large and expensive wooden consoles made by Zenith, whose cabinets featured a stylish mix of multicolored woods, Greek Revival inlaid trim, imported marquetry, and fine fluting for dramatic effect. The company's Stratosphere model, introduced in 1935, stood over four-feet tall, had two twelve-inch speakers, used fifty watts of power, and sold for $750 (equivalent to $13,000 in today's dollars). A new Buick was cheaper.[10] More readily available were the less expensive sets, like the "tombstone" and "cathedral" radios marketed by Philco, Emerson, and Silvertone, but even these were made of fine walnut, with decorative fluting on the sides and a cloth grille behind cut-out woodwork.

Its technology hidden behind an Art Deco facade, the radio had become the new symbolic center of the home. But all was not well in radioland. As the decade went on, serial melodramas and soaps ("tune in next time") were increasingly underwriting the capitalization of radio as a business.[11] This daytime babble prompted new concerns about the quality of broadcast programming and provoked, as David Goodman explains, anxieties about radio's effects on public and civic life.[12] The new medium's perennial critic, James Rorty (once an adman himself), wrote that radio, in its dependence on advertising dollars, was essentially "drunk and disorderly."[13] Radio was simply "a new and noisy method of letting peddlers into your home," as another listener grumbled.[14] By selling the minds and ears of listeners to the highest bidder, radio had become a dealer in consumerist propaganda—and that was not a good thing.[15] H. L. Mencken wondered why American radio could not be more like the BBC, a government agency that broadcast "nothing shabby, cheap or vulgar onto the air. There is no bad music by bad performers; there is no pestilence of oratory by ignoramuses; there is no sordid touting of tooth-pastes, automobile oils, soaps, breakfast foods, soft drinks and patent medicines. In America, of course, the radio program costs nothing. But it is worth precisely the same."[16]

Such criticism had come to a head in the mid-1930s in a series of legislative scuffles between broadcast radio and its detractors—a coalition of liberals, academics, politicians, and various nonprofit groups that campaigned to curb the growing commercialization of the airwaves. As one activist complained to Congress, radio suffered from an "overlordship of mere commercialists whose dominant purpose is to accumulate wealth even at the cost of human decay." As a consequence, there was, Norman Corwin observed, "about as much creative genius in radio today as there was in a convention of plasterers."[17] Not only had radio sold out to commercial sponsors, critics said, but its actual programming was a "cultural disaster." Radio was "pollution of the air," as Senator Henry Hatfield decried on Capitol Hill.[18] The radio reform movement objected that education, religious, and labor groups had been squeezed out of the publically owned airwaves by corporate interests and lobbied Roosevelt's Federal Radio Commission to restructure the allotment of channels. With momentum briefly on its side, the reform movement proposed radical new legislation (the Wagner-Hatfield amendment), which would have redistributed 25 percent of existing radio channels to the nonprofit sector.

The perceived threat to network control of the airwaves galvanized radio's ownership class into action. Educators may have wanted a slice of the broadcast spectrum but the networks were not about to give anything away. Having closed ranks, network owners lobbied to make sure the Wagner-Hatfield amendment did not succeed. Nor did the newly minted Communications Act of 1934 challenge the networks' economic model or alter the broadcast structure. As Susan Smulyan observes, the growing influence of "broadcasting in politics and the huge profits made by broadcasters during difficult times gave the networks and the radio industry enormous leverage with legislators and federal officials."[19] Nevertheless, the national debate over the quality of radio served notice that critics would be paying attention. Network leaders were suddenly nervous, afraid that New Deal activism might include a plan for a national public broadcast system. The demand for educational programming, to which the networks had turned a deaf ear, could not be ignored much longer, not if the networks wished to avoid government regulation. As Rorty complained, radio was contributing little that was "qualitative to the culture."[20]

The Demand for New Programming

What was bad for the nonprofit camp was good for radio's prestige movement.[21] Broadcast reform may have failed politically, but it generated such wide-ranging criticism of commercial radio that the desire to ward off potential government reform reshaped broadcasting practices for some time to come. "In this battle for prestige," wrote NBC programs vice president John Royal in 1937, "we are probably going to do a lot of things we ordinarily wouldn't do." Wary of intervention, broadcasters understood they had to burnish their brand or face regulation.[22] Just two years after the Wagner-Hatfield amendment died on the House floor, CBS tried something new. Network radio was barely ten years old when CBS debuted the *Columbia Workshop* in the summer of 1936.[23] The aim of the new program was to produce serious radio literature by pushing the envelope of not only playwriting but of broadcast technology as well. No more melodrama, slapstick comedy, or variety shows—this would be a venue for serious literature. Writers were encouraged to compose for the ear, to experiment with new conventions, and sound designers were urged to work with new techniques.[24] Because network radio was thriving on advertising dollars, it could afford to take such artistic risks. Not only Welles but other writers who moved into radio, like Archibald MacLeish, Norman Corwin, and Arch Oboler, were invited to press the limits of radiophonic storytelling, and their efforts with CBS's cutting-edge series did not go unnoticed.

The impact of the *Columbia Workshop* on radio culture is hard to overstate. Soon CBS was commissioning scripts from other artistically ambitious writers, including Stephen Vincent Benet, Arthur Miller, Dorothy Parker, Pare Lorentz, John Cage, Kenneth Patchen, Alan Lomax, Thornton Wilder, Alfred Kreymborg, William Saroyan, W. H. Auden, and Lucille Fletcher—not to mention the thousands of unsolicited manuscripts the program received each week. The *Workshop*, which became known to insiders as a "writer's theater," was particularly interested in sound effects and in educating the listening public about the expertise behind the sound design of radio drama.[25] To Irving Reis, the program's first director, the public would best be served not just by listening to provocative radio but by learning its inside story. During his two-year term at the *Workshop*, Reis framed several broadcasts with instructional demonstrations and presentations. These included stodgy lectures on acoustics, but also artful dramatizations of "behind-the-scenes" radio practices. A playwright, Reis was also a studio engineer whose hands-on relationship with broadcast technology gave shape to his idea of the *Workshop* as an experimental "laboratory" for radio drama.[26] In the *Workshop*'s inaugural episode, which aired in July 1936, parabolic microphones were used to track actors walking around the studio as though on stage. Not tethered to microphones, the cast of *The Finger of God* moved freely about rather than remaining fixed in place. The new amplification strategy, which was "never attempted in radio before" (according to the announcer), evoked a narrative space in which the listener might wander. This was a departure from the flat sound typical of word-based storytelling.[27] Manipulating spatial cues for aesthetic effect would become an effective way for radio to exploit acoustic drift.

A similar "experiment," as the *Workshop* liked to call its efforts, was introduced the following week with *Broadway Evening*, a documentary-like play that follows a couple on their evening walk through the New York theater district. The work does not tell a story so much as capture the myriad sounds of the city: clanking subway, gathering crowds, street peddlers, ambulance sirens, stray conversations. An urban soundscape, *Broadway Evening* has more in common with the sound collages of European avant-garde radio, such as Walter Ruttman's *Weekend* (1930), than with conventional Anglo-American radio drama.[28] What mattered most was the *Workshop*'s ability to produce a multilayered sonic experience based on acoustic realism. "Although all the voices you heard performing in the script come from the *Workshop* studio, practically all sound effects were actually taking place during this past half hour on Broadway and were picked up by our microphones to furnish an authentic background to this play," the announcer explained in the epilogue.

In *Broadway Evening*, the *Workshop* wasted no time in confronting radio listeners with innovative sound-making. Leopold Prosser's acoustic snapshot of urban nightlife was impressionistic, noisy, and jarring. Above all, it was non-narrative, deliberately challenging listeners to rethink their assumptions about the hierarchy of the spoken word on radio. "Here is its voice," intones the narrator, gesturing to a multitude of street sounds, the clamor of trains, the hubbub of pedestrians, trolleys, and car horns. That the story was plotless or that the voices of the ambling protagonists were lost in a cacophony of urban noise seemed in part to be the point. Underneath the couple's end-of-day walk down Broadway is an underlying social frenzy of hustling voices, including those of aggressive peddlers and hawkers, which contrast sharply with the middle-class protagonists, who are forced to yell at the tops of their lungs to be heard over the rattle and roar of the ambient sound. Over and above the racket of the street is the larger drama that plays out between the human voice and the jarring noise of the machine (train, subway, bus, ambulance). The piece documents the contest between language and the background sounds that threaten to drown it out. True to its modernist ambitions, the *Workshop* gives the machine the last "word," as if agreeing with the Futurist Luigi

Russolo that "today, Noise is triumphant and reigns sovereign over the sensibility of men."[29]

Nothing could be more foreign to the creed of daytime radio serials than a collage-like *Broadway Evening*, in which the dialogue of the leading actors is overwhelmed by the heteroglossia of modernity. Reis later acknowledged that capturing live sound from the streets of New York for *Broadway Evening* may have created a "chaotic" background, as he confessed to *Popular Mechanics* magazine two years later.[30] Noise, Jacques Attali explains, is a resonance that interferes with the perception of a message in the process of emission.[31] As interference, noise was an effective way to escalate acoustic drift at the expense of the mastering effect. In *Broadway Evening* there was no story, a fact that might seem appalling on daytime radio. If anything, the program was about its own sound. It was an affirmation of noise, of radio's own substance, and, as such, it was a subversive poke at the production codes of pop-narrative daytime programming. Radio had become a commodity, a means of making money, based on a tight economy of signs achieved through the mastery of sound by words. The *Workshop*'s ambitious efforts to redefine the radiophonic practices of broadcast drama challenged the logocentric bias of conventional radio programming.[32] And yet CBS, which produced a constant flow of internal memos vowing not to puzzle or offend listeners, not only tolerated the *Workshop*'s experimental spirit but taunted rival NBC with its critical and popular success. The contest to create and define "prestige" radio had begun, and the *Columbia Workshop* unmistakably led the way.[33]

The following week, the *Workshop* broadcast a short work by Vic Knight that showed off the *Workshop*'s interest in innovative programming as well as its desire to turn audiences into knowledgeable listeners. Knight's *Cartwheel* was a fourteen-minute play with thirty-four characters and twenty-three sections that followed the history of a rare set of silver dollars over a period of fifty years. With so many voices and so many scene changes, producing *Cartwheel* would seem a daunting task, but the technical difficulty posed by such ambitious demands fit the *Workshop*'s penchant for experimental drama. (The following year, Reis would produce MacLeish's *The Fall of the City*, which would call for a crowd of 10,000 people.) The *Workshop*'s predilection for difficult radio productions had a didactic side that entailed technical demonstrations on the craft of radio. Before the airing of *Cartwheel*, for instance, CBS's radio audience first had to listen to an elaborate lecture on advances in microphone technology, which included the actor Ray Collins reciting Hamlet's third soliloquy

("To be or not to be"), while a *Workshop* engineer cut back and forth from an old carbon microphone (late-nineteenth-century technology) to a modern "velocity" (or ribbon) microphone. The differences are startling. Compared with the old microphone, the new technology brought *Hamlet* into the living rooms of listeners.

Although the technical demonstration took up almost half of the program's allotted time, it was nearly as engaging as the featured work of the evening, Knight's *Cartwheel*. The *Workshop* wanted listeners to know that radio was on the cutting edge of technology, but it also wanted to emphasize the idea of radiophonic presence, the capacity of radio, as Arnheim had just written, to abolish distance, which would soon become one of the dominant tropes of radio.[34] That presence, according to Paul Fussell's recollection of 1940s radio, conferred "intimacy and authority" on the spoken word.[35] If the medium wasn't the message, it is difficult to know what else was.

During its first year under the direction of Reis, the *Columbia Workshop*'s interest in sound became a regular feature of the show, with lectures and demonstrations about pitch recognition, the structure of the ear, scene acoustics, and high- and low-pass filters. Listeners soon became familiar with the *Workshop*'s discursive announcers and their penchant for digressing to comment on "exciting moments behind the scene in radio." On these occasions, the show's announcer would behave much like the intrusive narrator of the early novel, postponing the story in order to talk shop with the listener. These intrusions can best be understood as interventions on behalf of a radio art that sought to test the boundaries of hearing; they serve as an acoustic bridge between the listener and the new radiophony advocated by the *Workshop*, in which the radio play was conceived more as a "sound drama" (in Arnheim's words) than anything else.[36]

As didactic as some of these technical talks might seem today, the *Columbia Workshop*'s acoustic lab caught on with listeners. In its January 1938 issue, *Popular Mechanics* magazine took notice of the *Workshop*'s innovative approach to radio art, running an article on Reis's unique handling of sound effects. It was very much a fan article that went into elaborate detail describing the *Workshop*'s unorthodox sound designs. For a scene in a mine shaft (*A Comedy of Danger*, 1936), as the magazine noted, Reis created an echo chamber to evoke the illusion that actors were speaking at the bottom of a mine pit. In order to make the sound of a nagging wife as shrill as possible in *The Downbeat on Murder* (1936), Reis relayed the actress's voice (Adelaide Klein) through a high-pass filter, attenuating the lower frequencies in favor of a sharper and more annoying tone. The article was especially struck by the sound of the beating heart in the *Workshop*'s adaptation of Poe's short story *The Tell-Tale Heart* (1937). The effect was achieved, the article explained, by strapping a stethoscope to an athlete lying on a couch to which a microphone was attached. The sound of the heartbeat was amplified by a loudspeaker for the broadcast; during the finale the sound grew "louder and louder until it resembled the pounding of an orchestral timpani." A photo of the reclining donor shows the airborne heartbeat, wires and all.[37]

When Reis left CBS for Hollywood at the close of 1937, the *Workshop*'s digressions on radio production tapered off. *Time* magazine, which frequently ran reviews of "prestige" programs on CBS and NBC, made light of Reis (now that he was gone) and his apparent obsession with radio technology but acknowledged his significance. The original head of the *Workshop*, he was a director who "thought the production, not the play, was the thing, and who sweated with oscillators, electrical filters, echo chambers to produce some of the most exciting sounds ever put on the air—Gulliver's voice, the witches in Macbeth, footsteps of gods, the sound of fog, a nuts-driving dissonance of bells, the feeling of going under ether."[38]

Under Reis's direction, the *Columbia Workshop*'s craft-based discussions moved the program in a self-referential direction. On many occasions, the evening's broadcast was presented as reflexive artwork, with its codes openly on display. Listeners could not help but be aware that what they heard was a sophisticated narrative fabricated for radio broadcast. In its seventh episode, for example, the *Workshop* combined its behind-the-scenes exhibition with the featured drama of the night, *The San Quentin Breakout*, which originally aired on *Calling All Cars*, a West Coast cop series. Written by William N. Robson, the crime story drew upon an actual prison break that had occurred a year earlier, in which four convicts escaped from San Quentin with prison officials as hostages. The escapees were caught shortly after an intense police chase. The audacity of the prison break made the story big news, but even more sensational was the fact that Robson's dramatization went on the air less than three hours after the event happened. The radio play scooped the newspapers. The *Workshop* invited Robson to reconstruct the unusual story behind his radio script and conduct a behind-the-scenes dramatization of the original West Coast radio production.

As Robson explains, he was sitting in Hollywood working on a script while listening to the radio in the background. Robson's voice fades out as a news flash fades up. "Stand by for a special news bulletin," says a radio newscaster. A fictionalized Bill Robson asks his wife to turn the volume up on the radio. We have entered the mimetic space of the *Workshop*'s drama, in which a make-believe Los Angeles radio studio has only an hour and a half (rather than six days) to write and produce a play based on a prison break unfolding in real time. The drama's suspense hinges on the writer's ignorance of how his script will end, since the real police are still chasing the real convicts. He won't find out until just minutes before the show goes on the air. As the play progresses, the real Robson stands by, just outside of the mimetic space of the story, serving as storyteller: "The race between the tapping of the typewriter keys and the ticking of the red second hand on the clock began. But that red second hand—the tyrant of radio, the implacable timekeeper of the networks, swings slowly, ruthlessly around the bland face of the studio clock—kept gaining. Conflicting reports, contradictory rumors, sheaves of messages, at each moment a new flash coming in describing the mad dash of the convict-laden car. On opening night, excitement gripped the studio, as they got their instructions word by word."[39] As a behind-the-scenes voice, Robson interacts with the *Workshop*'s live drama, providing a commentary on a story that is less about the real-world getaway than about the making of the original radio play. His role is a meta-narrative, one that interprets the process of radio theater while adding his own stagy flourish ("the mad dash of the convict-laden car") to the pseudo-fictional text. As Robson observes, actors are rehearsing their lines in the studio, the composer is arranging music, the soundman is organizing his effects, all while the real convicts are being pursued by the police. What we hear, in other words, is a dramatization of a dramatization. The actual breakout itself was far less interesting to the *Workshop* than how the event was mediated by radio. The *Workshop* was clearly fascinated by the way radio transformed reality into fiction—and vice versa—and it seemed delighted in its ability to blur the line between these two modalities. Radio's effort to wrest the breaking news from a rival medium was itself news, as far as the *Workshop*'s announcer was concerned. The shrewd movement among the various registers of storytelling (from announcer spiel to guest narration and then back and forth between diegesis and mimesis) suggests how interested the *Workshop* was in the mediatory nature of narrative frames, a lesson not lost on Orson Welles. The *Workshop* was proving that by working at the boundary of fiction and nonfiction one could produce interesting radio. In such broadcasts, the *Columbia Workshop* sought to defer the willing suspension of disbelief on which more conventional programming (such as serial melodrama) relied.

Before the first year of weekly broadcasts ran its course, you could hardly listen to a radio work without being aware of the apparatus, aware that the unfolding drama was made possible only by elaborate broadcast technology and complex narrative practices. If there was an implied culprit in this equation it was the anti-radiophonic standard set by the formulaic soap opera. Nothing could be further in form and content from the daytime serial than the *Columbia Workshop*.

The educational spin *Workshop* announcers placed on the new drama series reflected CBS's sensitivity to the criticism network radio received for heavily commercialized programming. For the *Workshop*'s part, it promised to serve the public by offering instruction on broadcast technology and the inner workings of dramatic radio. The eagerness of the series to indulge in radio pedagogy, at the risk of storytelling, distinguished CBS's experiment from other ventures in prestige programming. The *Workshop* viewed the story behind the story as being fully as compelling as the featured play, and it seemed to have been largely right.[40] To our ears, these digressions might seem like procrastination, but most radio programs created generous "space" for border rituals (that is, everything that goes on before the fiction unfolds) in which hosts, announcers, and narrators played the roles of gatekeeper and impresario, while reaffirming their programs' formal properties.

The *Workshop* gave the announcer an unusually broad stage for exhibiting the sorcery of a new technology. He came to embody the agency of radio, circling the week's entertainment digressively. Behind the "magic of radio" were a lot of wires and gizmos. It was the announcer's job to remind audiences that the fictional world of radio was an elaborate construction made possible by ingenious devices and cunning men, and that radio stories were constructed through a self-conscious process of deferral and mediation.

The sense of delay was repeatedly evoked by the frequency with which the announcer assigned narrative roles to other speakers, including celebrities who helped with technical demos, as well as writers, directors, officials, and experts who described this or that technique (including a scientist from Bell Labs who lectured on the physics of sound and the nature of hearing).[41] Accomplices in delaying the evening's entertainment, the *Workshop*'s guest presenters replicated the work of the announcer. Within this "chain of supplements," as Derrida would put it, the *Workshop* invented an exteriority that existed outside the world of the *Workshop*'s main event (the fiction).[42] Always consulting others, the *Workshop*'s announcer dispersed the narrative function across multiple layers of the spoken, perfecting what Roland Barthes in *S/Z* called a "dilatory space," the place of postponement.[43] The more elaborate this dilatory space became, the greater the evening's sense of suspension.

As such self-referential maneuvers created new listening demands, the challenge to a "sustaining" (noncommercial) show like CBS's *Columbia Workshop* was to find an audience for unconventional programming. The *Workshop* saw itself as an important twist in the literary turn of broadcast culture and deliberately staged its programs so as to tutor American listeners in the skills needed to appreciate a complex kind of radio storytelling. The *Workshop*'s efforts did not go unnoticed. "Little by little, with gingerly audacity, CBS has been edging toward a radio revolution," *Time* magazine wrote, citing the *Columbia Workshop* among radio's most significant innovations.[44] According to the literary critic Carl Van Doren, the new works broadcast by ambitious radio programming created an opening for a "literature of the air."[45] The critical respect and public interest aroused by the *Workshop*'s output during its first three years reassured the network that it was moving in the right direction. As CBS vice president Douglas Coulter wrote in the first printed collection of *Workshop* plays, "One of the important things [we] set out to do was to develop a new crop of writers who would turn out original material created specifically for the medium of radio." Perhaps not all 140 airings were big hits, but many of its broadcasts "were milestones on the path of creative thinking and writing in radio."[46]

Literature of the Air: MacLeish and Corwin

During the course of its eight-year run (1936–43, 1946–47) the *Workshop* aired nearly 400 works for radio, many of them (like *Broadway Evening* and *Meridian 7-1212*) bold and experimental exceptions to what listeners ordinarily heard.[47] But no *Workshop* program went further in adapting a modernist literary style to radio than Archibald MacLeish's *The Fall of the City*, broadcast in April 1937, near the end of the *Workshop*'s inaugural season. The Pulitzer Prize–winning MacLeish wrote two critically acclaimed plays in verse for radio. Both plays address the rise of fascism in Europe and are alike in their interest in radiophonic communication and the machinery of broadcasting. CBS's *Columbia Workshop* aired both works, *The Fall of the City* in 1937 and *Air Raid* the following year.

The Fall of the City turned out to be an exceptional literary event of mid-1930s radio. Written against the background of rising international conflict and the abrupt downfall of several European cities, the play explores the psychology of freedom in the face of menacing tyranny. It boldly internalized the *Workshop*'s new radiophony, transforming "the paraphernalia of radio," in MacLeish's words, into the structure of the play. MacLeish saw what was most innovative about *The Fall of the City* in radio's own terms: "The really inventive technical development is the use of the natural paraphernalia of the ordinary broadcast, that is to say, an announcer in the studio and a reporter in the field. I used that in both *Fall of the City* and in *Air Raid*, and a very successful device it turned out to be. It gives you the Greek chorus without the rather ridiculous self-consciousness involved in carting a chorus in and standing them against the wall and have them recite. These people have a function; they are recognized by large audiences of nonliterary people as being proper participants."[48] As it already had done in many *Workshop* broadcasts, radio itself would intrude into the stylized world of MacLeish's narrative with its technology and enunciatory power. Its mediatory presence would become part of the story, not just a framing device.[49]

Set in a central plaza of an unnamed city, the play opens with the appearance of a prophetess, just risen from the dead, warning of future peril. A great crowd gathers to hear her prediction. One after another, influential figures address the increasingly anxious assembly—all of this conveyed by a radio announcer reporting into a microphone. The narrative itself, in a deft move by MacLeish, takes the form of a radio broadcast—as did the *San Quentin Prison Breakout* aired six months earlier by the *Workshop*. Although MacLeish's play was literally based on the conquest of the Aztec city of Tenochtitlan by Hernán Cortés in 1521, he acknowledged that he had in mind the much-anticipated Nazi annexation of Austria (the *Anschluss*) when writing, which would occur in another year, in March 1938. Within a few months of its production, several European cities did indeed fall to the Nazis, investing MacLeish's work with an eerie sense of foresight, which was noted by several reviews at the time.

The technical challenges posed by *The Fall of the City* were considerable, since the play called for a throng of 10,000 people. Irving Reis, who directed the program, moved the production out of CBS's New York studio into the drill hall of the Seventh Regiment Armory on Park Avenue. During rehearsal, Reis recorded the shouts and cries of the 200 students he cast for the crowd (mostly from New York and New Jersey) and then played back four copies of the recording over loudspeakers during the performance--1,000 voices would have to do. *Time* magazine hailed the result as "the most ambitious radio play ever attempted in the US."[50]

"Ladies and gentlemen," the story opens, "this broadcast comes to you from the city. . . . We take you now to the great square of [that] city."[51] Residents of an allegorical town—it could be Rome, or Vienna, or Prague—anxiously await the fateful arrival of a conqueror as prophesied by the sibyl: "The city of masterless men / Will take a master. / There will be shouting then: / Blood after!" The Voice of the Dead Woman, as this ghostly character is called, speaks with a Cassandra-like dismay, giving voice to a deep and troubled foreboding that runs throughout the work. She casts a pall over the city that is never lifted, and although her resurrection remains a riddle, the Announcer provides an anthropological reading of her bizarre presence. As he explains (channeling his inner Shakespeare), the return of the dead is an omen that signals an impending disaster: "Small wonder they [the Crowd] feel fear. / Before the murders of the famous kings, / Before imperial cities burned and fell, / The dead were said to show themselves and speak. / When dead men came disaster came. Presentiments / That let the living on their beds sleep on / Woke dead men out of death and gave them voices."[52] Despite the portentous mood, the lead character in *The Fall of the City* is not a sibylline presence from the past but a radioman—a figure of the future. The Announcer, played by the then little-known Orson Welles, reports on events with continual attentiveness, guiding the work's point of view from start to finish. He may speak in pentameter verse, but he describes the behavior of the urban populace much like a commentator in a newscast might. He is the man on location providing a blow-by-blow account of the scene as the conqueror draws nearer the city: "They are milling around us like cattle that smell death. The whole square is whirling and turning and shouting. One of the ministers raises his arms on the platform. No one is listening: now they are sounding drums: Trying to quiet them likely: No! No! Something is happening: there in the far corner."[53]

The Announcer's eyewitness narration, supported by vivid crowd sounds, dominates the play, framing most of the dialogue and action as the story moves inevitably toward the doom of the city. Microphone in hand, he looks on as one speech-maker after another (messengers, orator, priests, General) advances to interpret the significance of the mystifying prophecy or to warn of the Conqueror's progress. To each oration, the crowd listens anxiously, as if spellbound, but only after the Announcer has framed the moment of speech: "There's a voice over the crowd somewhere. They hear it: they're quieting down.... It's the priests! We see them now: it's the priests on the pyramid! There might be ten of them: black with their hair tangled.... Listen!"[54] The command to "listen" is issued repeatedly by the Announcer—an appeal to the power of aurality—but after a succession of speeches, some full of appeasement, others filled with paranoia, the crowd loses focus and disintegrates just as violence breaks out on the edges of the city. Like the funeral orations delivered long ago in the Athenian agora, the speeches in *The Fall of the City* are public performances grounded in democratic rhetoric. Their outcome, however, is not civic solidarity but complete chaos. The Crowd "won't listen," reports the Announcer near the end: "They're shouting and screaming and circling." Microphone in hand, MacLeish's radio Announcer looks on as the Crowd surrenders to a fantasy of the political unconscious: "The city of masterless men has found a master!" citizens cry triumphantly, conceding autonomy to something else, behaving as if they had just won a victory. "You'd say it was they were the conquerors," the Announcer adds ironically under the swelling roar of voices: you would think it was "they that had conquered."

That the Crowd is complicit in the fall of the city is plain to see (and hear). As MacLeish later explained, his story was largely about the "proneness of men to accept their own conqueror, accept the loss of their rights because it will in some way solve their problems."[55] But why the city should be so eager to embrace a tyrant, imaginary or real, is not clear. There is a Dostoyevsky-like sense that humans cannot bear the burden of freedom, but there is also evidence that the order of discourse (the Athenian speech-making) has somehow failed. What survives the sermonizing, demagoguery, and oratory is the chorus-like irony of the radioman. At first just a reportorial bystander who cannot see past the commotion stirred by the prophecy, Welles's Announcer is turned by necessity into an interpreter, a perceptive commentator whose point of view ("the people invent their oppressors") coincides with the radio text's authorial irony.[56]

Beyond the antifascist politics of *The Fall of the City*, MacLeish's interest in history's mediation by radio, a new media, is complicated by the story's reliance on older media—especially oratory and prophecy, ancient systems of communication anachronistically framed by broadcast technology. As the play ends, it is the radioman, Welles's Announcer, who bears witness to the failure of the *polis* and the futility of speech-making. Oration is no match for the pathology of fascism, since the order of discourse produces only civic noise.

What is striking about this play is the way MacLeish integrated current events, radiophonic expression, and Greek tragedy. MacLeish collapses together two very different traditions, combining the ancient convention of the Greek chorus with the newly emerging one of the radio commentator. As MacLeish explained in the foreword to *The Fall of the City*, the problem with most plays written for radio stems from their reliance on the conventions of the stage. The trick was to adopt techniques from the medium itself, the most interesting of which was the radio announcer. "The Announcer," MacLeish wrote, "is the most useful dramatic personage since the Greek chorus: "For years modern poets writing for the stage have felt the necessity of contriving some sort of chorus, some sort of commentator.... But how justify its existence dramatically? How get it on? How get it off again? In radio this difficulty is removed before it occurs. The commentator is an integral part of radio technique. His presence is as natural as it is familiar. And his presence, without more, restores to the poet that obliquity, that perspective, that three-dimensional depth without which great poetic drama cannot exist."[57] As MacLeish noted, the disembodied nature of radio offered an opportunity for rehabilitating a dramatic technique that had fallen out of use in realist theater.

MacLeish's blending of the classical with the contemporary was, of course, a typically modernist habit, and in his radio plays this mix helped him find a unique way to plumb the depths of current events: Hitler's *Anschluss* in *The Fall of the City* and the Czechoslovakian crisis in *Air Raid*. Like Auden, MacLeish was drawn to classical drama (*Oedipus* was the model for his first stage play, *Panic*, in 1935) as a way of exploring the trauma and tragic disorder of history. "Ancient history repeats itself with us," MacLeish said.[58] But by situating the "paraphernalia of the ordinary broadcast" within both of his radio plays, MacLeish also called attention to the complicated ways in which history was mediated not only by art (in this case, dramatic verse) but by broadcast technology as well. One semiotic system borrowed from antiquity was embedded in another newer system that hadn't yet been codified. While the medium certainly wasn't the message in either *The Fall of the City* or *Air Raid*, it came surprisingly close to being so.[59]

A voice in a studio and an announcer in the field—this is how MacLeish described his modification of drama written for radio. Imagine placing a CBS news crew at the scene of Aeschylus's *Agamemnon*, complete with a short-wave radio and microphones. Gone are the Watchman and Chorus of Elders; in their place, Edward R. Murrow.[60] "This is Mycenae.

I am speaking from the Citadel of Argos, under the starry conclave of the midnight sky. Down to my right is the Odeion, one of two Greek theatres, this one carved into the lower rocky slopes of the Larisa. It is now nearly 2:30 in the morning and still no sign of the signal-flame, the balefire bright indicating that the city of Troy has fallen."[61] MacLeish's radiophonic innovation was to modernize Greek tragedy on the eve of World War II by turning this most essayistic of broadcast conventions—the radio announcer or commentator—into a trope of radio, a move that lent the *Anschluss* and Hitler's invasion of the Sudetenland a kind of transhistorical resonance, à la Yeats.

MacLeish's *The Fall of the City* enjoyed widespread critical acclaim in the press. In the words of *Newsweek*, MacLeish had shown that radio drama "was something radically different from the drama of the stage and screen," if only because, as a reviewer for *Time* magazine explained, MacLeish had found a way to exploit "one of the most accepted public spokesmen in 20th-century life, the radio announcer . . . who could describe events in a way that would make them immediately believed."[62] MacLeish had demonstrated how relevant radio drama could be, even when drawing on something as remote as Aeschylean tragedy.[63] That a radio play could also reflect on its own mode of production was perfectly in tune with the *Workshop*'s sound aesthetic.[64] Moreover, by adopting radio's announcer role, MacLeish was able to exploit the practice of deferral as a way of complicating the narratological dynamics of his play through placement of a narrating voice in a mimetic story space. Welles's Announcer not only describes the events unfolding in the city—"We are here on the central plaza . . . the crowd is enormous: there might be ten thousand"—but cues up the various speakers (the Messenger, the Orator, the Priests, the General) who enact oratorical functions ("Listen! He's here by the ministers now [the Messenger]! He's speaking"). The back-and-forth movement from narration to enactment, as demonstrated by the *Workshop* any number of times, called attention to the kinds of discursive breaks and thresholds that the literary turn brought to radio. Like other works produced by the *Workshop*, MacLeish's *The Fall of the City* seemed to be feeling out the rules of discursive formation in an expanded enunciative field.

This was radio modernism in all of its acoustic intricacy, and strangely enough it was sponsored by CBS's network managers. Without the *Workshop*, MacLeish's play probably would not have been produced. There was simply no prior place for it, as Merrill Denison noted at the time.[65]

With the broadcast of MacLeish's *Fall of the City*, the *Columbia Workshop* became the undisputed leader of avant-garde radio in America. The enthusiastic public heralded the arrival of serious radio drama. "Aside from the beauty of its speech and the power of its story," wrote *Time* magazine, "*The Fall of the City* proved to most listeners that the radio, which conveys only sound, is science's gift to poetry and poetic drama . . . that artistically radio is ready to come of age, for in the hands of a master a $10 receiving set can become a living theatre, its loudspeaker a national proscenium."[66] Writing in the *Hollywood Quarterly* a few years later, William Matthews identified the essence of MacLeish's achievement: "Apart from the beat of the drum, the shrilling of the flute, and the roaring and whispering of the crowd, it is the spoken word chiefly that MacLeish uses to get effects that are as spacious and moving as any that are dreamed of by users of noisemaking instruments and machines."[67]

MacLeish himself must have sensed something of the significance of the *Workshop*'s production of his play. In the first printed edition of *The Fall of the City*, he added a foreword that was in effect a call-out to poets to write for radio. MacLeish reminded his fellow writers that because "the ear is already half poet," radio is the writer's perfect audience. Writers should be "storming the studios," he suggested, for "what poet ever lived who was really satisfied with writing the thin little books to lie on the front parlor tables?"[68]

The Fall of the City was produced for less than $500. Compared to the $17,000 budget lavished on *Lux Radio Theatre*'s broadcast of *The Legionnaire and the Lady* that same year, *Workshop* production costs were piddling.[69] When W. H. Auden submitted a script to the *Workshop*, he received $100, which is what MacLeish earned for his radio writing. MacLeish's call to poets did not fall on deaf ears. Soon, the *Workshop* would receive over 7,000 unsolicited manuscripts each year, many of which were invasion narratives. As CBS itself observed, "We have been flooded with scripts about bombing planes—not entirely, we believe, because of the success of MacLeish's *Air Raid* or Corwin's *They Fly through the Air*, but because of the fact that people are conscious of bombing planes these days. The *Workshop* is merely reflecting the popular mind."[70] The gratuitous bombing of Guernica by Nazi planes in 1937 was partly responsible for this trend. Hitler's sudden acts of aggression in Europe seemed only to add real-life evidence to what looked more and more like clairvoyance on the part of the *Workshop*.

Orson Welles, Archibald MacLeish, and William Robson rehearsing the radio drama *Air Raid*, 1938. (Courtesy of the New York Public Library, the Library for the Performing Arts, Billy Rose Theater Collection)

MacLeish's *Air Raid* was broadcast in October 1938 and focused on the impassivity of the mostly female inhabitants of a small European border town about to be blitzed by a fleet of bombers. It is about a war not waged by armies but by distant machines in "the blindness of the skies." Again, MacLeish incorporated radio itself as a trope into his play (deploying a studio director, announcer, and short-wave transmission).[71] "One moment now we'll take you through," says the Studio Director. "The town is in those mountains: you are there"—anticipating, once again, the voice of the iconic 1940s newsman.[72]

An antifascist work, *Air Raid* describes the horror of aerial bombing in the form of a vicious attack on the women and children of a small European village. The women assume the planes will simply fly over, because their village is not a military threat, but as they discover, in modern total war that assumption no longer holds. In the play, a Murrow-like radio announcer is stationed on the roof of a tenement building, waiting for enemy planes to arrive. Broadcasting his report via shortwave radio, the

Announcer captures on microphone, as Murrow would a year later, the peaceful sounds of civilians, along with the more violent noise of bombers and antiaircraft guns: "There's the siren: the signal: / They've picked them up at the border" (111).[73]

MacLeish's collaboration with the *Workshop* had a marked impact on his conception of radio drama. We can glimpse this in the sound design of *Air Raid*, which is structurally more sophisticated than that of his earlier radio play. The text is crammed with sound cues, many of which contribute to the clashing mix of pacific female voices and brutal war machines. As the play's sound scheme reveals, MacLeish developed an intricate series of sonic cues to express this tension: "*Under the Announcer's words, the voices of women have been rising: gay: laughing: the words indistinguishable*" (103); "*Over the laughter and the voices a woman's voice, very high and clear and pure, singing a scale—Ah! Ah! Ah! Ah!*" (105); "*Under the murmur of the women in the courtyard comes the slow: low: barely audible pulsing of a plane swelling and lapsing*" (109); "*Over the voices of the lovers and the faint lapsing drone of the plane comes the Singing Woman's voice in a high clear scale: rising: descending*" (111); "*A siren sounds at a distance like a hoarse parody of the Singing woman's voice: rising, shrieking, descending. It is repeated under the voices, nearer and louder*" (111).

As the bombers near their civilian targets, the Announcer warns that spotters have heard the approaching planes. "We hear them: we can't see them. / We hear the shearing metal: / We hear the tearing air" (120). Announced by their "roar," the aircraft arrive with not just bombs but with sonic weapons that are nearly as fatal as explosives: "*The pitch of the roar opens: the sound is huge, brutal, close*" (122). MacLeish's acoustic effects build to a climax when the domestic sounds of female voices, laughing and singing, mix with sirens, evoking a dissonant and increasingly ominous cacophony: "*For an instant the shrieking voices of the women, the shattering noise of the guns and the huge scream of the planes are mingled, then the voices are gone and the guns are gone and the scream of the planes closes to a deep sustained music note level and long as silence. . . . The diminishing music note again. Over it the voice of the Singing Woman rising in a slow screaming scale of the purest agony broken at last on the unbearably highest note. The diminishing drone of the planes fades into actual silence*" (123).

The note of dissonance steadily escalates as siren sounds are joined by the clamor of roaring planes and guns. Ironically, the discordant mix produces its own kind of music: "*The scream of the planes closes to a deep sustained music note,*" one so harsh that it blots out the voice of song. The arrival of the bombers is a disaster, not only for the town but for the spoken word, just as the assault is also an attack on the listeners' ears. In what is essentially an atonal sound montage, MacLeish plays the lyricism of the female voice (often heard singing) against the "brutal" noise of war machines. This scheme comes to a climax when the singing and shrieking of voices merge with the roar of the warplanes in a moment of chaos. The female voice is mutated by machine noise into an apocalyptic scream, and as it becomes indistinguishable from the screaming sounds of bombers the singing voice is no longer an affirmation of life but a Cassandra-like sign of doom. The boundary between signal and noise breaks down completely. Is the scream of bombers music or noise—and what of the Singing Woman's operatic note of "purest agony"? As these questions suggest, the ambitious sound design of *Air Raid* confounds the conventional codes of radio listeners by playing up the indeterminacy of sound and sense.[74] By the play's end, we seem to have stepped outside of language.

In the winter of 1939, the *Columbia Workshop* aired another invasion narrative in the air-raid genre, Norman Corwin's *They Fly through the Air*.[75] The genesis of the radio play, according to Corwin, was a remark made by Mussolini's son, an air force pilot who had described the explosion of a bomb on the ground below as a thing of beauty, "like a budding rose unfolding." Corwin's play recounts the cold-blooded indifference of a bomber crew performing a devastating hit on a civilian target, destroying homes and strafing fleeing women and children. It is dominated by a semi-omniscient ironic narrator who stands above the action and derides the flight crew's unconscionable act. The play moves in and out of the plane, panning from the kitchens of homes below back up to the cockpit of Plane Number Six, as the Narrator speaks to the crew with irrepressible sarcasm:

> O Winged Victory!
> The Spartans would have coveted
> The courage of your combat!
> Just think:
> Ten thousand savage roof tops, tarred and tiled,
> Against a single plane!
> And you, three men and half a dozen bombs
> Against the regiments of tenements, arrayed between the banners of
>   their wet wash,
> The bed sheets and the shirts and pillow slips
> Snapping defiance in the fresh-sprung breeze.[76]

The crew members' lack of valor is as disturbing as their lack of voice. The triteness of Plane Number Six ("Let's call it a day. Getting on toward lunch time anyway") only confirms the criminal banality of machine-based war. Appalled by such disinterest, the Narrator derides the crew's airborne aloofness ("O. K. Man the guns"—says the pilot—"No point letting any of the rest get away") as a technologized indifference to the lived position of men and women.

In the biting twist of the play's finale, the bomber itself is taken out by a fighter plane, another machine. Corwin's sound cues capture the expressive shriek of the plunging bomber, which runs slowly underneath the Narrator's closing taunt:

> SOUND: *Sharp burst of filter gun. Scream of anguish. Firing out. Motors begin to cough. Effect of spinning uncontrolled. This builds into a long, slow crescendo until the crash at the conclusion of the following speech of the narrator.*
>
> NARRATOR: This is humiliating, gentlemen, to reel so drunkenly in sight of all the sober earth. There's apoplexy in your motors now and they will not recover.... Be calm; sit back. There still is time to see a final symmetry. The spiral of your spinning is a corkscrew in the sky....
>
> SOUND: *Terrific crash. Absolute silence.*[77]

The war machine now reels "drunkenly" in the sky like a boozer, its engines belching smoke and fuel. In his satiric finale, the Narrator derides the nose-diving bomber and its doomed crew. He sees "apoplexy" in its motors, as if the machine were a victim of stroke. The personifying metaphors are delivered in mockery of the bomber's "monstrous machinations." In contrast to the crew's mechanized nihilism, the Narrator's uncompromising sarcasm signals a reassertion of the embodied voice as being-in-language. The Narrator's outrage is provoked not only by the loss of innocent life but by the detachment of the pilots and their distance from common experience. The pilots, disconnected from the domestic lives of civilians below, reveal little affect when releasing their bombs and strafing women and children. Mere operators of a machine, they are portrayed by Corwin as agents of a mechanical form of cruelty.

Corwin takes satisfaction not only in the doomed fate of Bomber Number Six, as the invader is called, but in the "absolute silence" that follows its "tremendous crash." The clamor of its motors, its guns, and bombs—its machine noise—is portrayed as an encroachment on human language throughout the play (the civilians who are bombed and strafed are often in the middle of conversation). Behind his narrator's persistent irony, Corwin plots revenge on noise that interferes with the primacy of the spoken word. The more radical the *Columbia Workshop*'s sound aesthetic became, the closer it veered toward modernist radiophony and the art of noise. The extensive work produced by Corwin for CBS created an informal system of checks and balances that maintained the poetic imperatives of the spoken word against the hubbub of music and sound effects and thus slowed the movement toward radically experimental radio. Corwin was no less enthusiastic than anyone else at the *Columbia Workshop* about innovative radiophony, but unlike Welles and MacLeish he resisted the modernist indeterminacies that might subvert the enunciative mastery of his narrators.

Despite its radical breakthroughs, prestige radio was a pragmatic solution to a problem. The simple fact was that the networks had vacant airtime to fill, and because production costs for highbrow radio were relatively low William Paley quickly calculated that CBS had much to gain and little to lose by broadcasting programs affiliated, in one way or another, with serious literature and bold writing.[78] After three years of blistering criticism for airing rubbish, the networks were, with reason, fearful that government watchdogs would step in at any moment and regulate the airwaves. Under the guise of public uplift, the networks hoped to acquire the necessary cultural prestige to forestall such an event.

While the networks took a literary turn partly to keep the critics at bay, corporate heads like Paley of CBS and M. H. Aylesworth of NBC understood as well as their critics that radio hadn't gone very far in developing its own voice. Even though radio had become a dominant player in the American scene, beyond ever-popular light entertainment (such as *Amos 'n' Andy* and *The Shadow*) it did not have much to show for itself.

And then, suddenly, it did. The effects of the *Columbia Workshop* can be gauged by its impact on other radio artists. When Alan Lomax was asked by CBS to produce a series on American folk music in the mid-1930s, he at first declined. Lomax thought that radio, overrun by soaps, was not a place for serious work. "I thought this was a joke," he said. "I didn't know that anybody could be seriously interested in working on the radio, a pile of crap." But his attitude changed, thanks to the *Workshop*'s programming: "Then I heard Corwin's broadcasts and I did a flip, I realized that radio was a great art of the time."[79]

Lomax was not the only one whose ears had been opened by the drama of MacLeish and Corwin. The unprecedented outpouring of radio art on the *Columbia Workshop*'s weekly broadcasts was changing the way listeners in general approached American radio. Magazines and newspapers around the country began tracking radio drama; *Time* magazine ran periodic reviews of prestige drama as part of its radio coverage. It seemed as though a new cultural form had emerged, something less ephemeral than nighttime variety shows or daytime serials.

As the critic Carl Van Doren wrote in 1941, Norman Corwin was "to American radio what Marlowe was to the Elizabethan stage." In Van Doren's view, prestige radio contributed to a "gradually accumulating body of permanent literature."[80] CBS did not waste much time taking credit itself for this new body of literature. In an ad placed in the trade magazine *Broadcasting*, the network reminded readers how vital its noncommercial programming had become to a literary turn in radio: "More and more, publishers are turning to the *literature of the air* for source material. This may not be a trend. But we think it writes this story: *the literature of the air has come of age*. Day in, day out, the air is full of first editions . . . printed in decibels instead of type, signed by our advertisers and ourselves. CBS sustaining programs *alone* would fill a five-foot shelf each week. And in any one year, CBS builds for its millions of listeners a well-stocked, well-balanced library."[81] At a time when the literary possessed recognizable cultural value, CBS was quick to claim the glamour of the book for radio. The idea of a "literature of the air" conferred permanence on what was essentially an ephemeral art. Viewing radio as literature encouraged CBS to portray itself as a great publishing house, the Simon and Schuster of the airwaves. In its simplest form, the radio play constitutes an adaptation of printed words to sound. But the *Broadcasting* ad imagines a reversal: the converting of sound back to print. The values of literature were thus transferred to radio so thoroughly that airwaves became not just the purveyor but the source of cultural prestige. In the battle for cultural capital, radio was holding its own.

Mercury Rising
Orson Welles and the Master's Voice

The decision to stock unfilled airtime with "prestige" radio drama and other culturally attractive programs, such as the *Columbia Workshop*, had been made by William Paley because he saw radio as a new force in the delivery of ideas, or so he had said while testifying in 1934 before the Federal Communications Commission (FCC) on spectrum allocation, listing CBS's "cultural" programming as a significant network asset. Although only 29 percent of CBS's unsponsored time was dedicated to public affairs programming, Paley no doubt wished to play up his commitment to "mass education and culture," as he put it. Like other representatives of the industry, Paley was "loathe," he said, "to believe any legislative mandate" could improve American radio programming.[1]

The turn toward "quality" programming at CBS was, needless to say, not a Reithian move. The legendary founding father of the BBC was famous for his vision of public service, with an emphasis on educating and informing listeners. In John Reith's eyes, the BBC was the great custodian of culture and public taste. The business of radio, said Reith, was "to carry into the greatest possible number of homes everything that is best in every department of human knowledge, endeavor and achievement, and to avoid the things which are, or may be, hurtful." Nothing could be more Arnoldian and less American.[2] Paley had little interest in cultivating the higher sensibility of listeners, despite what he told the FCC. But he did hope to burnish the network's image, partly to keep the critics at bay and partly to get the jump on NBC, radio's dominant network.[3] As a result of Paley's bold strategy, CBS was turned from an upstart radio network into a creative hub of literary experiments in storytelling and drama.

From 1935 to 1938, an outburst of literary broadcasts changed the sound of radio. Arthur Miller, Norman Rosten, Carl Sandburg, Maxwell Anderson, and Robert Sherwood wrote for CBS's *The Cavalcade of America*, a historically based drama series, and *Theater Guild on the Air*.[4]

The *Columbia Workshop* adapted Stephen Vincent Benet's *John Brown's Body*, Lewis Carroll's *Alice in Wonderland*, T. S. Eliot's *The Four Quartets*, and Aldous Huxley's *Brave New World*. Pare Lorentz would soon write *Ecce Home* for radio broadcast, and John Cage and Kenneth Patchen would produce *The City Wears a Slouch Hat* for the *Workshop*.[5]

If Norman Corwin was radio's Marlowe, Orson Welles was its Shakespeare. When CBS realized that prestige drama was earning points for the network, it began searching for even more literary luster, a search that led the network to the wonder boy of theater, Orson Welles, who arrived on the broadcast scene just as radio was taking off in a new direction.[6] Welles was approached by CBS's William Lewis to launch a new drama series as a summer replacement for *Lux Radio Theatre*. The series would be up against NBC's popular *Chase and Sanborn Hour* with Edgar Bergen and Charlie McCarthy and funding would be limited, but Welles would have creative carte blanche. Lewis gave Welles a total budget of $50,000 for nine one-hour episodes, not quite one-quarter of the budget spent by *Lux Radio Theatre* on its radio adaptations. To CBS executives, Welles was a living embodiment of the avant-garde, whose shine might light up the network.

In his work for CBS, Welles's innovation was to pick up on Corwin's emphasis on narrative voice but then to disturb its authorial control. The Corwinesque narrator in *They Fly through the Air with the Greatest of Ease* or in *On a Note of Triumph* is an expansive speaker whose large poetic gestures ("Take a bow, GI, take a bow, little guy. The superman of tomorrow lies at the feet of you common men of this afternoon") add up to a comprehensive intelligence that illuminates all corners of the story world. His is a voice of principle whose authority is undivided. The voice of Corwin's master narrator is the strong force that contains and unifies all the disparate parts of his works. Welles's subversive radio genius lay in creating authorial narrators who fragmented the authorial perspective into multiple voices. As his radio adaptations of *Dracula* and *War of the Worlds* show, Welles created the promise of a dominant narratorial presence only to deconstruct it. He teased listeners with the prospect of discursive mastery but denied them the comfortable certainty of one monologic perspective.

Welles caught the eye of CBS thanks to his work on the stage and for radio, much of which was affiliated with the Popular Front movement, both politically and aesthetically. Like many modernist writers and artists with ties to radio in the 1930s and 1940s, Welles's creative agenda was shaped by antifascist and left-wing leanings.[7] His 1936 innovative production of *Macbeth* with the Negro Theater Federal Project in Harlem had featured an all-black cast and had relocated the play to nineteenth-century Haiti, with voodoo witches filling in for Shakespeare's Weird Sisters. Complete with beating drums and chanting priestesses, Welles's adaptation was a sensation that toured the country after opening in Harlem. One year later, Marc Blitzstein's "labor opera," *The Cradle Will Rock*, also directed by Welles, was cancelled by government agents just days before its debut in New York City. Locked out of their own venue, Welles and Blitzstein staged their play's opening night at an alternative theater in defiance of authorities. The entire cast and audience marched twenty-one blocks to the Venice Theatre, where the play ran for nearly three weeks to much fanfare. As *Time* magazine put it, Orson Welles had become the "brightest moon" rising over Broadway in years.[8]

Audiences encountered Welles on the air as well. They knew him from adaptations of *Hamlet* and *Macbeth* on the *Columbia Workshop* and as the Announcer in MacLeish's *The Fall of the City*. They also heard him every Sunday at 5:30 PM on the Mutual Network as Lamont Cranston in *The Shadow*, a role he assumed in 1937.

Welles's first real impact on literary radio had come with an adaptation of Victor Hugo's *Les Misérables*. Thanks in part to heady publicity surrounding *The Cradle Will Rock* and his growing fame on the New York theater scene, the Mutual Broadcasting System offered Welles a chance to produce, direct, and star in his own highbrow radio drama series. Welles chose *Les Misérables* for a seven-week summer series. In the theater, Welles would become notorious for overcomplicating the design and concept of productions in his ambitious drive for innovation. In radio, he went the other way. Often choosing complex works of literature, like *Dracula* or *A Tale of Two Cities*, and paring them down, he was at his narrative best when minimizing.

With *Les Misérables*, Welles managed to condense a rambling 1,500-page novel into a coherent broadcast, largely by focusing on the book's more obvious themes: the redemption of Valjean, the rescue of Cosette, and Javert's blind fixation on disciplinary justice. Hugo's narrator had cautioned readers that his story was not the tale of an ex-convict and Fantine's daughter but a drama in which the leading character is the "infinite."[9] Welles, however, paid little heed and reduced Hugo's "totalizing vision," as Mario Vargas Llosa terms the novel's point of view, to its narrative essentials.[10] Cut from the script were Hugo's elaborate detours (Hugo terms these "parentheses") on the Order of Perpetual Adoration and the battle of Waterloo, not to mention his long digressions on excrement and the history of Parisian sewers. Welles removed the more digressive materials from *Les Misérables* in favor of the simplest elements of a story: plot, character, scene. Doing so was necessary, required by the limitations of radio and the thirty-minute format of a summer series. But the Hugo cuts also revealed Welles's interest in manipulating the diegetic space of broadcast fiction.

CBS originally hoped to capitalize on the stage successes that Welles had achieved in collaboration with John Houseman at the *Mercury Theatre* in New York City.[11] Initially called *First Person Singular*, the name of the weekly broadcast was soon changed to *Mercury Theatre on the Air*. In a press release to *Newsweek*, Welles said that the new program would "bring to radio the experimental techniques which have proved so successful in another medium, and treat radio with the intelligence and respect such a beautiful and powerful medium deserves," but he also warned readers not to expect mere sound versions of theatrical works.[12] Welles thought of radio as a platform less for drama than for narrative. Radio was, in his view, at its best when following the laws of the novel: "The less radio drama resembles a play the better it is likely to be. This is not to indicate for one moment that radio drama is a lesser thing. It must be, howsoever, drastically different. This is because the nature of radio demands a form impossible to the stage. The images called up by a broadcast must be imagined, not seen. And so we find that radio drama is more akin to the form of the novel, to story telling, than to anything else of which it is convenient to think."[13] Welles recognized that the novel was an untapped "form" that might enrich radio's content, presumably by opening the door to narrative tropes, twists, and complications usually reserved for print. As Welles saw it, wireless was foremost a storytelling venue, and he was intent on novelizing radio. What's more, such a move would allow him to narrativize the role of the announcer, much as MacLeish had done in *The Fall of the City* and *Air Raid*. The announcer was a broadcast insider, someone whose commentary on the anticipated program carried the sanction of radio as a system. He was the network's spokesman. In MacLeish's radio work, the announcer—this agent of modernity—was seldom problematic; in Welles's hands, however, he most often was. That in itself was a serious plot twist.

Dracula and the Master's Voice

John Houseman was charged with producing a script each week for the new radio show, *Mercury Theatre on the Air*. "Being wholly without experience," Houseman confessed, he "did little more than extract, abbreviate, compress and paraphrase the most exciting sections" from whatever literary "classic" Welles had selected for broadcast that week. Adapting a work of literature to radio was mostly a cutting job. Welles would review Houseman's work and suggest changes.[14] *Mercury Theatre on the Air* was originally scheduled to open with Robert Louis Stevenson's *Treasure Island*, which Houseman had dutifully condensed. With just a few days before airtime, however, Welles swapped Stevenson's adventure yarn for Bram Stoker's *Dracula*. A favorite of Welles's, *Dracula* was a daring choice and a far more complicated narrative than *Treasure Island*. Time was running out, though. With a deadline looming, Houseman and Welles worked frantically for eighteen straight hours over steak, brandy, and coffee at Reuben's restaurant on Fifty-ninth Street, trimming Stoker's extravagant patchwork of a novel down to a sixty-minute radio play. Despite the chaos of last-minute changes and rehearsal disorder, the *Mercury Theatre*'s 1938 broadcast of *Dracula* was a critical success.[15] Although only a small audience had tuned in, the radio play was so compelling it soon became a landmark event.

Stoker's novel is anything but straightforward. In narrative structure, *Dracula* presents itself as a collation of assorted texts—letters, diaries, newspaper clippings, journals, case histories, ships' logs—all of which are conveyed by different characters in the story. Not only does the novel call emphatic attention to its own textuality, but it multiplies narrative points of view in a surprisingly modernist fashion.

Transferring the novel's complexity to radio was not easy. Welles could have avoided many difficulties simply by making Arthur Seward the authorial voice in the story. Welles does in fact privilege Seward with authorial presence at the start of the broadcast, but he then undercuts that maneuver by decentering Seward's narrative and by entangling his story in a web of documentary records, much in the spirit of Stoker's original text, which placed so much emphasis on the process of writing.[16] In Stoker's novel there is no master narrative. That Welles sought to capture a small share of the textuality of *Dracula* on the air—including what seemed most disorienting about the novel—reflects his interest in the kind of modernist experiments that would raise questions about the limits of radio's discursive mastery.

Welles's Arthur Seward, a collapsing of the novel's Arthur Holmwood (Lucy's fiancé) and Jack Seward (a scientist), is now engaged to Mina and assigned the job of narrating.[17] Seward manages the narrative for the first half of show but then gives way to other narrators (Mina, Harker, and Van

Orson Welles at the CBS microphone during one of his wartime broadcasts, early 1940s. (Courtesy of the Lilly Library, Indiana University)

Helsing) in the latter half, as if Welles wished to ease or guide his listeners into the decentralized zone of Stoker's patchwork narrative. Seward's pledge to represent the documentary evidence as "simple fact" is a false promise because the facts are not at all simple, nor does his possession of the evidence guarantee that he will master its meaning. In fact, Seward for the most part delegates his narrative task to others, as though deputizing the entire staff of *Mercury Theatre* to take on the harrowing job of bearing witness to the "truth" of a monster. Seward hands over passages from the documents as though performing the deferral ritual of the radio announcer that transfers the enunciative role to another speaker. "I present you, first, with excerpts from the private journal of Jonathan Harker," he says.

Welles endows Arthur (Author) Seward's opening narration with authority, but it is an authority borrowed from the proximity of Welles's own prefatory commentary at the top of the program marking the series debut:

> Good evening. The *Mercury Theatre* tonight faces a challenge, an opportunity for which we are grateful. We will present during the next nine weeks, many different kinds of stories, stories of romance and adventure, geography, mystery, and human emotion, stories by authors like Robert Louis Stevenson, Emile Zola, Dostoyevsky, Edgar Allen Poe, and PG Wodehouse.... We're starting off tonight with the best story of its kind ever written. You'll find it in every representative library of classic English narratives. It's Bram Stoker's *Dracula*. The next time I speak to you I'm Dr. Arthur Seward. George Coulouris plays Jonathan Harker and Martin Gabel plays Dr. Van Helsing. It is Dr. Seward who tells the story. And so for the moment, goodbye Ladies and gentlemen, I'll see you in Transylvania.

We are reminded in this speech that Welles's literary prestige stands behind tonight's story. Nor are we to forget that Arthur Seward is Orson Welles, who just spoke to us in his directorial persona. Seward stands guard over a mass of written testimony and documentary evidence, just as Welles presides over the *Mercury Theatre*'s production—all of which mediates the fantastical account of Dracula. "All needless matters have been eliminated," Seward assures us (even though they have not, considering the elaborate framework), and only the heart of the matter remains, the core of truth, its essence. As narrator, Seward affirms the correctness of his story, enacting what Gérard Genette would call the "testimonial function." His trust in the order of discourse, we soon learn, however, is poorly placed, given the reach of Dracula's powers (and his demonic voice). That misplaced faith in the truth's essence (the logocentric function of discourse) is partly the point of the radio play.[18]

That *Dracula* is a novel whose collaged form calls attention to the effects of mediation could not have been lost on Welles, who seems more interested in its narrative complexity than in its gothic thrills. Most of the novel's characters engage in extensive writing in one form or another. Nearly everything in the novel, in fact, is converted into writing. For Jonathan Harker, in particular, keeping a journal is crucial to remaining sane ("I must keep writing at every chance, for I dare not stop to think").[19] In the radio adaptation of *Dracula*, writing is necessarily converted to speaking. Even though a diary or a journal is credited as the source text, what the listener hears is the speaking voice: Harker voicing his private journal or the Captain relating the ship log of the *Demeter*, which Seward explains is taken from a newspaper clipping. Even Seward "quotes" from his "private journals." Writing can only be a rumor on radio.

The facts, then, are allowed to speak for themselves, but only in the most oblique of ways. The initial narrative space of the play is occupied by the extradiegetic Seward, reading aloud from his archive of papers, journals, diaries, and notes, presumably somewhere outside of the immediate story world. The implied space of enunciation is neither London nor Transylvania but a nebulous courtroom where Seward's documents are presented as evidence in an imaginary trial. Whether Seward is the prosecuting attorney or the defense one cannot say. All we know is that he has placed himself in a position of logocentric authority: he will stand behind the "truth" of his papers, however improbable their content might be.

In a way, this radio play is a one-man show: an actor sits at a desk with a stack of papers narrating alone before a microphone. Although Welles plays just two roles—Seward and Dracula—the entirety of the play is mediated by his narrative voice. All of the action, meanwhile, unfolds in the intradiegetic space contained within writing. Neither Harker nor Mina shares the broadcast microphone with Seward. As he insists, they exist only inside of their written texts. To tell the story of Dracula, he must cue them up. "I present you, first, with excerpts from the private journal of Harker." Note it is not Harker that is introduced to listeners but his journal. The characters in this tale can only speak on Seward's signal, as if he were positioned in the studio control room issuing cues. Even when Seward enters the story world himself, interacting with Van Helsing or Mina, it is only from within a text: "I'm still quoting from my own personal papers," he reminds us halfway through the play—lest listeners forget.

The story world remains offstage, so to speak, or at least off center. What is central is writing. On a certain level, Welles's broadcast of *Dracula* is an allegory of radio adaptation, recapitulating the process of turning text into voice as narrativized speech. But that process is deeply affected by persistent schemes of deferral that offset the story world of mimesis.

To adapt *Dracula* to radio, Welles had to disregard Stoker's own suspicion of recorded sound. He had, in fact, to reverse the novel's fetishizing of writing. In Stoker's telling, Seward is a gadget lover who owns the most up-to-date technology, including a phonograph machine. A man of science, Seward is a nonwriter who prefers the spoken over the written word, chronicling his thoughts into a new Edison phonographic recorder. In the novel, Seward behaves like a ham radio operator speaking into his microphone in the privacy of his bedroom, where he has compiled a stack of wax cylinders containing his notes and diary. For much of the novel, Seward's emotional distress is alleviated by the use of sound recording.

But Seward's obsession with the phonograph must be mastered by the written word. The determined Mina convinces the reluctant psychiatrist that, for the sake of "our knowledge of that terrible Being," it will be necessary to transcribe the wax cylinders using her typewriter. And so the voice of Seward travels from the phonograph through Mina's ears to her hands on the keys, moving from one medium to another, from wax to paper. Seward's notes now belong to the public record, part of the growing body of information that Mina is consolidating on the mystery of Dracula.

Stoker calls attention to the differences among written, recorded, and spoken language throughout the novel, all the while privileging Mina's agency as scribe. Unlike Mina's typescript, which is the work of a cutting-edge technology, human utterance in the novel is associated with mystification and the irrational. Even the phonographic voice of Dr. Seward is shrouded in secrecy until it is transcribed and edited by Mina and her typewriter. The archaic voice of Dracula, with its hypnotic force, is even more mysterious. Dracula's power over others, including animals, derives from the force of his voice to evoke submission. His is a voice, what's more, that can be communicated across time and space—like radio. It comes from a different order of being and is not of our world. When he warns Harker not to underestimate the uniqueness of his new setting, Dracula points to the ontological nonconformity between worlds. "We are in Transylvania; and Transylvania is not England. Our ways are not your ways, and there shall be to you many strange things."[20]

In Stoker's novel, the mastery of the bewitching voice is opposed by contemporary forms of inscription, from typewriting to telegraphy, which draw a heavy line between modernity and its discontents.[21] As Harker notes in his diary, "Unless my senses deceive me, the old centuries had, and have, powers of their own which mere 'modernity' cannot kill."[22] The madman Renfield refers to Dracula as the "Master," and the Master's Voice is one of the powers Harker describes. Later, Dracula's vampiric connection with a bitten Mina manifests itself through his disembodied words. Like a ventriloquist, Dracula casts his voice into the mannequin Mina becomes under his mesmerizing influence. The Count himself acquires a kind of radio presence in the voice that Mina hears—as disembodied sound. The same acousmatic voice, however, is used against the Count when Van Helsing realizes that Dracula's radio signal can be tracked through his connection to Mina. Once Van Helsing tunes in to Dracula's broadcast channel, he can triangulate his presence. The hypnotized Mina is manipulated by Van Helsing like a GPS device so as to learn Dracula's whereabouts. Tell me what he hears, Van Helsing commands the quasi-vampire: "Lapping waves and rushing water, darkness and favouring winds," Mina reports. "All is dark. I hear water swirling by, level with my ears, and the creaking of wood on wood. Cattle low far off."[23] The defeat of Dracula requires an ingenious act of eavesdropping, by means of which Van Helsing converts the Master's Voice into geographical coordinates.

Dracula's influence in the novel depends largely on the power of his voice, as a direct form of contact. It is a voice, in fact, that defies signification. There is no message, no semiosis—the sound is all. His is the voice of the radical other, fortified with the allure of the Sirens. That pure sound stands in contrast with Stoker's teeming text, which is a product of vast mediation and bureaucratic technology. Dracula's magic voice is disarmed not by putting wax in one's ears, but by turning the occult voice into information.

That the voice of Dracula proves to be his own undoing is an irony that testifies to the efficacy of the vampire hunters to create an information network, or what Friedrich Kittler calls the gadgetry of "mechanical discourse processing."[24] We see the triumph of modernity over voice in the character of Mina, who plays the role of editor, librarian, and archivist. She produces the typescript that is vital to the pursuit of the Count. It is her chosen task to transcribe and collate the assorted textual and oral documents that "bear witness," as Welles's Seward says, to the "truth" of Dracula. Of all the characters pursuing the vampire, Mina is the one most responsible, as "Recording Angel," for the production and circulation of written documents.[25] She comes the closest of any character to playing an authorial role. In laying such emphasis on the tools of information-gathering and writing, the novel stakes a claim for the priority of modern textuality at the expense of the Master's Voice. The pre-modern charisma of Dracula is no match for the modern secretary equipped with cutting-edge technology.

To the extent that *Dracula* as a novel relies on an improvised scribal circle for its narrativity, the book would seem to challenge, if not defy, radio. The novel is essentially anti-radiophonic, calling attention to its own textuality at every turn. Welles' adaptation counters this fact by changing Stoker's scribal gestures into radiophonic events. Early listeners noted the broadcast's heavy reliance on sound, even if they did not always appreciate what Welles was trying to accomplish. *Variety*, for example, called *Mercury's Dracula* "a confused and confusing jumble of frequently inaudible and unintelligible voices and a welter of sound effects."[26] At all narrative levels, Welles uses acoustic resources to drive his tale forward, manipulating the sounds of transportation (coach, steamship, train, horses) to hurry the listener through the plot, as well as to construct characters.

As each of Seward's testimonial documents in the radio play speaks out, as though a talking book, the entire *Mercury Theatre* cast begins more and more to resemble Stoker's own phonographic Dr. Seward, the man behind the microphone. If Seward, a secondary character in the source text, is chosen by Welles to preside over the narration, to serve as its conductor, it may be because it is Seward's repressed aurality (in the novel) that, now liberated on the radio, is free to collide with the rival voice of Dracula. On radio, Seward conjures up his co-characters like a magician, using the wizardry of narrative. He channels Harker, Van Helsing, Mina, the Captain, all who speak on his authorial command. This is a variation of the telepathy that connects Dracula and his women, especially Lucy and Mina. Dracula speaks through them.

In the radio play, Mina Harker's capacity to hear Dracula (her last name, with its echo of hearkening, signals this capacity) is doubly significant, as it not only allows Van Helsing to zero in on the vampire but also reproduces the central act of radio—listening to voice. "What do you hear, Mina?" Van Helsing asks repeatedly. The bewitched Mina, played by Agnes Moorehead, answers in a voice that is transfixed on the absent Master. "I can hear far off, confused sounds, as of men talking in strange tongues. Fierce, falling water and the howling of wolves. There is another sound—how queer a sound—like . . . like . . . ." Growing more desperate, Van Helsing urges Mina to be more attentive. "Like what? Speak, Mina! Speak, I command you! I command you to speak!" Mina is trapped between two masters, both of whom place great demands on her capacity to receive their signal, to heed the voice of patriarchy (in one form or another). That it should be Mina, and not Harker, who drives the stake through Dracula's heart in Welles's radio adaptation is not a terrible surprise. It is the only way to silence the uncanny voice of the vampire, and Mina knows that voice better than anyone. Moreover, by killing Dracula, depriving the monster of his voice, Mina regains her own voice, as she is no longer enthralled by the Master's Voice.

Welles also rescues Jack Seward from Stoker's silencing by casting him as the first narrator, the concertmaster. As narrator of the radio play, Seward recovers his voice. More extroverted than Stoker's timid version, Welles's Seward transmits his journal to thousands of listeners. The new Seward is considerably more broadcast worthy, quick to tell a story, eager to be heard. In place of the anachronistic Edison machine used in privacy by Stoker's Seward, Welles places Seward at the center of the corporate apparatus of radio itself, a broadcast system of unimaginable reach.

Narration, however, exacts a terrible price in *Mercury Theatre*'s adaptation, as the elaborate work of narrative polyphony takes its toll on Seward. His voice grows fainter with the progress of the show, as though vampirized by the narrative process itself, the task of channeling others. Eventually, as in much of Welles's radio work, the framing, no matter how complicated, dissolves into the story world, as if its intricacy were the condition of its disappearance. With the pursuit of the monster in the second half of the play, the voice of Welles as Seward will jump (like a virus) to another body—Dracula—leaving behind the muted Seward, now merely a trace of his authorial self. The reassuring first-person narrator ("Ladies and Gentlemen, my name is Arthur Seward") that opens the broadcast is by the end all but forgotten by listeners. It is replaced by the pitched-down demonic voice of Dracula, which seizes our attention, just as it captivates the mind of Mina.

In using this tactic, Welles draws on the modernist predilection for deferral. As in Kafka's writing, in which Joseph K. is beleaguered by forms of postponement that undermine his agency and paralyze his actions, Welles uses radio's own codes to destabilize Seward's narratorial presence. By subjecting Seward to a discursive network he cannot master, Welles flirts with modernism's habit of deferring and negating meaning, sharing its mistrust of representation as a means of knowing. In *Dracula*, the message never arrives, no matter how many channels it is sent through.

The War of the Worlds: Radio's Unreliable Narrators

On 30 October 1938, three months after the airing of *Dracula*, listeners tuning into CBS radio were greeted by the music of Ramon Raquello and his orchestra, broadcast live from the Park Plaza in New York City. Minutes into "La Cumparsita," a reporter broke into the show to deliver an important announcement concerning a disturbance on the surface of Mars. The broadcast returned to the music but was again interrupted by news that a meteor had crashed into a New Jersey farm. What radio listeners heard that night was Orson Welles's adaptation of *The War of the Worlds*, a radio play that had been written and performed to sound like a real news broadcast. Disguised as a normal radio program, the play's improbability (an invasion from Mars) slipped under the radar, provoking what newspaper reports described as "a tidal wave of terror that swept the nation."[27]

If countless listeners mistook the live entertainment for real news, that was because Welles, who knew how to use radio's emergent codes to blur the lines between fact and fiction, had ingeniously embedded an invented story within a documentary frame. In many respects, Welles's notorious broadcast was a modernist coup whose key critical strategy, the performance of radio vérité, not only constituted a genre-blurring parody of radio's own coverage of the Munich Crisis just months earlier, but also problematized the purpose of radio at a critical moment in its young history.

The Munich Crisis was a significant event in radio history, provoking the advent of broadcast news. Beginning with the Austrian *Anschluss* in March 1938, the diplomatic confrontation with Hitler was the first world predicament to be broadcast over the airwaves, every anxious moment of the seven-month-long ordeal. The crisis itself was a major media event marked by high drama: fear, suspense, and a war of words that was tracked by listeners worldwide with increasing concern. "Radio has our ears," the *Nation*'s media critic, James Rorty, wrote, and to the extent that it can convey "the sound of history" it will continue to command our undivided attention.[28] A tireless critic of broadcast's commercial interests, the left-leaning Rorty had become radio's gadfly, but now he was listening with renewed interest.[29] If in Rorty's ears radio had come of age, it was the invention of the up-to-the-minute news broadcast that made the difference. It was during the Munich Crisis that CBS and NBC invented a news format that relied on nonstop coverage and the evening news roundup—practices that banked increasingly on news bulletins ("We interrupt this broadcast"). The news bulletin quickly became the newest form of deferral on the radio.

Americans listened to the entire crisis on the radio.[30] To cover these developments, radio networks had sent a flock of foreign correspondents to Europe. While transatlantic broadcasts had been rare in the past, news roundups were now coming out of European radio bureaus around the clock. The expanded news included commentaries and flash bulletins. By month's end, CBS and NBC, in particular, had produced over seventy-three hours of shortwave broadcasts from various cities, the wide use of which had made it possible to broadcast not historical impersonations in the style of *March of Time*, but the actual voices of the key actors in the Munich drama. By the time the crisis was over, Americans had heard Hitler, Mussolini, and Chamberlain firsthand and had tuned in to Hitler's Nuremberg address, as well as to Chamberlain's "Peace in Our Time" speech. As Erik Barnouw wrote, it was the greatest show yet heard on American radio.[31]

James Rorty was speaking for many when he praised radio's ability to immerse listeners in distant events: "During the past thirty days radio has been used in the attempt both to make war and to make peace, to rescue Western civilization and to push it over the abyss. The issue of life or death for millions of men, women, and children has hung, or seemed to hang, on the turn of sentence or on the inflection of a voice, while all over the planet those millions have listened in terror and anguish."[32] For Rorty, the isolated American radio listener had suddenly been reinvented in the image of history, and that history took the form of a crisis. For eighteen days in September, an anxious audience was transfixed by American radio networks as eyewitness reports on the aggressive moves of Hitler and the desperate diplomacy of Chamberlain streamed across the Atlantic. "It is scarcely too much to say that the future of civilization," Rorty concluded, "will be determined to a considerable degree by who rules radio and how." Americans had listened to Europe, and they would never forget.

Radio itself, as CBS commentator H. V. Kaltenborn wrote that same year, became one of the biggest stories of the Munich Crisis.[33] For liberals like Rorty and Kaltenborn, radio had awakened America from its isolationist sleep. Average citizens, in the collective posture of listening, had rediscovered their sense of nationhood and engagement with a troubled world at large. Marshall McLuhan's "tribal drum," as he would soon call radio, was beating loudly.[34]

Kaltenborn was widely regarded as one of the heroes of the eighteen-day crisis. At the height of the 1938 Munich predicament, he made headlines by providing three weeks of uninterrupted coverage, delivering commentaries on Hitler's and Mussolini's plans for Europe, famously pausing only to sleep on a cot in CBS's Studio Nine in New York City. So tireless and compelling were Kaltenborn's commentaries on each incoming bulletin from the news ticker that he became the embodiment of concentrated listening. Kaltenborn provided elaborate rundowns in one communiqué after another on the crisis. Stationed at his microphone, surrounded by notes and transcripts, headphones wrapped around his head, Kaltenborn was the premier radio announcer in America, an overnight celebrity. So popular were his commentaries that scheduled commercial programming was cancelled on the spot by CBS.

Writing in 1938, Kaltenborn, like Rorty before him, acknowledged the newfound power of radio. "When the crisis came, we had mastered a force of which we knew almost nothing in 1914. Through it, and because of it, the peoples of the world demanded and got an exact accounting of every important move by their leaders." The listeners demanded peace, which "even the most hardened dictator could not but obey. The medium was radio."[35]

The Munich Crisis turned the radio announcer into a cultural hero and created a bull market for commentators.[36] Before the outbreak of political tension in Europe, network radio employed only a handful of commentators, like Boake Carter and Floyd Gibbons, but afterward hundreds of new voices were heard around the country in this role. Along with Kaltenborn came Gram Swing, Dorothy Thompson, and Lowell Thomas. And of course there was Edward R. Murrow and his team (Bob Stout and William Shirer).[37]

The sudden demand for commentators was a result of radio's growing credibility. By the late 1930s, radio was preferred to newspapers as a source of information by a wide margin. One survey in October 1938 found that 70 percent of those questioned had relied on radio as their principal news source during the European crisis.[38] The human voice of the announcer is what mattered most to listeners, as if it held the promise of authenticity.[39] The commentator could be trusted.

Except when he couldn't be. Welles's *War of the Worlds* turned assumptions about the trustworthiness of radio news and authoritative commentators on their heads. The story of the broadcast and its aftermath is well known. Americans all over the country swallowed the preposterous tale that Martians had invaded Earth, that, armed with deadly heat rays, men from Mars were systematically destroying all life on this planet.[40] The *New York Times* received hundreds of phone calls (875, to be exact) from anxious listeners. Police stations were inundated by bewildered callers. All over the country, people were contacting authorities pleading for help. A mere thirty minutes into the broadcast, listeners in the Northeast packed their cars with belongings and raced frantically away from Philadelphia and New York, which were (it was "reported") already under attack. Americans left their homes to escape disaster, some in the direction of Canada, while others climbed on rooftops to get a view of the Martians, claiming to see the orange glow of Manhattan in flames.[41] In Indianapolis, an overwrought woman interrupted a church service bawling that the world was coming to an end—she had heard so on the radio. Some fashioned wet towels into protective facemasks to fend off the poisonous gas discharged by Martians. As one listener later reported, "We were getting more and more excited. We all felt the world was coming to an end. I kept saying over and over again to everybody I met: 'Don't you know New Jersey is destroyed by the Germans—it's on the radio.'"[42]

What could have provoked such credulity? Welles duped his audience by producing an authoritative framing narrative meant to hide the far-fetched story at the center of the broadcast. That authority was shrewdly borrowed from the respectability of radio commentators, which had risen so high after the Munich Crisis.

In *War of the Worlds*, Welles spread that authority across a cast of announcers, narrators, and commentators. The distribution of trustworthiness across multiple voices deepens the apparent legitimacy of the broadcast by echoing the now familiar form of the news bulletin, but also by reminding listeners, as the *Columbia Workshop* often did, that radio was a formidable broadcast apparatus:

> ANNOUNCER: The Columbia Broadcasting System and its affiliated stations present Orson Welles and the Mercury Theatre on the Air in "The War of the Worlds" by H. G. Wells.
> ANNOUNCER: Ladies and gentlemen, the director of the Mercury Theatre and star of these broadcasts, Orson Welles.
> ORSON WELLES: We know now that in the early years of the twentieth century this world was being watched closely by intelligences greater than man's, and yet as mortal as his own. . . .
> ANNOUNCER: (*fade in*) . . . for the next twenty-four hours not much change in temperature. . . . We take you now to the Meridian Room in the Hotel Park Plaza in downtown New York. . . .
> ANNOUNCER THREE: Good evening, ladies and gentlemen. From the Meridian Room in the Park Plaza Hotel in New York City, we bring you the music of Ramón Raquello and his orchestra. With a touch of the Spanish, Ramón Raquello leads off with "La Cumparsita."

ANNOUNCER TWO: Ladies and gentlemen, we interrupt our program of dance music to bring you a special bulletin from the Intercontinental Radio News. . . .

ANNOUNCER THREE: And now a tune that never loses favor, the ever-popular "Stardust." Ramón Raquello and his orchestra. . . .

CARL PHILLIPS: Good evening, ladies and gentlemen. This is Carl Phillips, speaking to you from the observatory of Princeton. I am standing in a large semi-circular room, pitch black except for an oblong split in the ceiling. Through this opening I can see a sprinkling of stars that cast a kind of frosty glow over the intricate mechanism of the huge telescope. The ticking sound you hear is the vibration of the clockwork.[43]

Before landing in Princeton, where the "action" really begins, the listener must pass from one announcer to another. In this moment, the narrative is really about radio's own network and the radiomen (three announcers, the director, and a reporter) who serve the needs of the broadcast system, if not the public interest. These two things, the needs of the system and the public interest, are indistinguishable. The medium remains the message until Carl Phillips takes the story over from the announcers.

As the broadcast continues, the unsettling multiplicity of announcers gives way to a focus on one voice. When we first meet him, Carl Phillips invites our trust, primarily because we are relieved to at last have someone in control. Phillips not only updates listeners with news of the mysterious meteor but also takes charge of the story by interviewing an expert and by reporting as an eyewitness from the field. At this stage in the story, he serves as the master narrator whom listeners have eagerly awaited, with the promise of providing interpretive authority that might make sense of the growing mystery.

It is not long, however, until Phillips's commanding presence as commentator breaks down. Frank Readick, who played Carl Phillips and was known for his impersonations in *The March of Time* and as Lamont Cranston in *The Shadow*, prepared for his role in *War of the Worlds* by reading the transcripts of Herb Morrison's recorded account of the *Hindenburg* disaster. A Chicago reporter, Morrison was sent to cover the Zeppelin's arrival in New Jersey in May 1937. Microphone in hand, Morrison was describing preparations for landing when the giant airship suddenly burst into flames in midair. Passengers and crew members leapt for their lives. Morrison and his sound engineer stayed on, recording the catastrophe in full detail. Morrison's commentary is famous for its unrestrained emotional response to the awful disaster, for his anguished cry as he watched the *Hindenburg* disintegrate in midair: "Oh, the humanity, the humanity!" What we hear in Morrison's halting, stricken voice-over is a man unable to control the situation, reduced to tears and mournful outbursts, his subjectivity on display. During their final rehearsals, Welles asked Readick to listen to the Morrison recording over and over, so that he could put the reporter's hysterical manner to use while playing the role of Phillips.[44]

Frank Readick's Herb Morrison moment arrives at the Wilmuth farm in Grover's Mill, New Jersey, where a huge cylinder had fallen, maybe a meteor. When the metal top of the alleged meteor twists off, revealing a creature inside, Phillips can barely tell the story:

> CARL PHILLIPS: Ladies and gentlemen, this is the most terrifying thing I have ever witnessed.... Wait a minute! Someone's crawling out of the hollow top. Someone or ... something. I can see peering out of that black hole two luminous disks.... Are they eyes? It might be a face. It might be ...
> (*Shout of awe from the crowd*)
> CARL PHILLIPS: Good heavens, something's wriggling out of the shadow like a gray snake. Now it's another one, and another one, and another one! They look like tentacles to me. I can see the thing's body now. It's large, large as a bear and it glistens like wet leather. But that face, it ... Ladies and gentlemen, it's indescribable. I can hardly force myself to keep looking at it, so awful. The eyes are black and gleam like a serpent. The mouth is V-shaped with saliva dripping from its rimless lips that seem to quiver and pulsate. The monster or whatever it is can hardly move. It seems weighed down by ... possibly gravity or something. The thing's ... rising up now, and the crowd falls back now. They've seen plenty. This is the most extraordinary experience, ladies and gentlemen. I can't find words.... I'll pull this microphone with me as I talk. I'll have to stop the description until I can take a new position. Hold on, will you please, I'll be right back in a minute....
> (*Fade into piano*).

Moments later, Phillips is killed by the Martian death ray as the invaders unleash their deadly weapon, destroying everything in their path. We hear Phillips's frightened commentary on the terrifying event—and then nothing. Complete silence. The transmission had been cut off. Welles cued up a six-second pause that seemed to last forever. Many have singled out the dead-air sequence as the most terrifying moment in the broadcast. By this point, only sixteen minutes into the production, *War of the Worlds* had already convinced many listeners that the end was near.

In his convincing impersonation of Herb Morrison, Readick captured the legendary reporter's unhinged commentary with near perfection. Overwhelmed by an event he could not understand, Carl Phillips lost all authorial control. His narration broke up, disrupted by something that did not belong on earth. The death of Phillips and the subsequent dead-air sequence signaled the collapse of a role that American listeners had come to expect, the trustworthy commentator. By silencing Phillips, Welles created a representational catastrophe that is perhaps as scary as anything else in the broadcast, even the Martians. Evidence suggests that listeners became hooked precisely at this point. And who could blame them. The Martians weren't the real threat—it was the prospect of radio's unreliability. Mars was a red herring.[45]

This destabilizing effect is continued at the close of the broadcast in what is supposed to be a moment of reassurance. In his sign-off, Welles addresses listeners in his role as host, informing his audience that the apocalyptic scenario just broadcast was an elaborate Halloween jest:

> This is Orson Welles, ladies and gentlemen, out of character to assure you that *The War of the Worlds* has no further significance than as the holiday offering it was intended to be. The *Mercury Theatre*'s own radio version of dressing up in a sheet and jumping out of a bush and saying Boo! Starting now, we couldn't soap all your windows and steal all your garden gates by tomorrow night . . . so we did the best next thing. We annihilated the world before your very ears, and utterly destroyed the C.B.S. You will be relieved, I hope, to learn that we didn't mean it, and that both institutions are still open for business.

Welles's disclaimer seems to cast the broadcast as a juvenile prank, a hoax that is not to be believed, but before we can take any comfort in his words, he undercuts his statement. CBS's New York studios were, he reminds us, "utterly destroyed before your very ears," leaving open the possibility that the invasion may not have been entirely fictional. Playing the part of the unreliable narrator, Welles in his sign-off treated the relationship between his story world and the listener's non–story world with calculated ambiguity, preferring to blur the line between what might be and what is. In so doing, the promise of closure stirred by radio's routine closing statement was compromised by Welles's afterthoughts. Welles used the same technique in *Dracula*, signing off by assuring listeners that vampires are little more than figments of the imagination, but then without warning cueing up a howling wolf sound and producing the low-pitched voice of the Count himself once more: "Ladies and Gentlemen, there are wolves, there are vampires!" The story world, without warning, erupts into the announcer's sign-off frame, an acoustic domain presumably outside of the story space. Welles's prank in both *Dracula* and *War of the Worlds* is just a gag, but it is also a serious exploration of the expressive boundaries of radio.[46]

In his radio plays, Welles was less interested in history than in the dynamics of representation. He had borrowed MacLeish's fictionalized radio announcer for *War of the Worlds*, but he placed a reverse spin on its use. By obliterating Carl Phillips and CBS's Studio One, Welles quite literally deconstructed the radio commentator. Through sleight of hand, Welles turned broadcast radio on its head. The FCC issued warnings, and the major networks promised to police the borderlines between fact and fiction more diligently in the future. Bulletins would be certified and radio commentators would be vetted. In the meantime, the *Mercury Theatre on the Air* was awarded a sponsorship from Campbell's Soup—and not from the DuPonts, as newspapers had joked—and acquired a growing fan base, in spite of Welles's acoustic misbehavior. If Welles had deliberately traumatized radio, he did so at perhaps its greatest moment of esteem, when CBS's self-proclaimed status as the "news network" enjoyed the kind of standing the BBC would acquire after World War II. Welles may have bitten the hand that fed him, but he also lived up to the modernist distrust of transparency.

The mastering effect was applied to radio primarily to stabilize the signifying order. Sound was a danger to word-meaning, but Welles's genius lay in his ability to exploit the tension between sound and sense. Using highbrow works of literature, Welles infiltrated the system of meaning only to create havoc. His radiophonic brilliance thrived in the gap between acoustic chaos and literary meaning-making. While MacLeish's project was the re-coding of classical tragedy through the internalization of radio as a communications metaphor, Welles's radio work derived its energy from un-coding. Instead of translating meaning from one medium to another as MacLeish did, Welles used literary antecedents in order to expose the naïveté of radio's representational codes that typically separated fiction from reality. Radio needs a master's voice, an enunciative position of power, in order to make sure no one mistakes fiction for reality. By challenging discursive mastery through the compromised voices of Seward and Dracula, as well as Phillips and the sign-off host, Welles denied any voice the final say. In so doing, he set radio on a new trajectory.

4

You Are There
Edward R. Murrow and the Proximity Effect

On a warm September afternoon in 1940, 1,000 German planes entered British airspace. The sky turned dark on what came to be called "Black Saturday." The Heinkels moved so slowly you could see the iron crosses on their underwings. It was said to be a terrifying sight, and the roar of the bombers was thunderous. "I'd never seen so many aircraft," wrote one RAF pilot. "As we broke through the haze, you could hardly believe it. As far as you could see, there was nothing but German aircraft coming in, wave after wave."[1] To an amazed Maurice Wood, in the vicinity of Big Ben, it was the "majestic orderliness" of the bomber formation that was most startling.[2]

A few minutes later, the East End went up in smoke. From a remote distance, London glowed a fiery red as enormous clouds of smoke rose up over the Thames. It was spectacular, even beautiful, said one observer four miles away from the first wave of bombs.[3] It was havoc closer in. You could hear the whistling and then the boom, thump, thump, thump of German bombs. As the air-raid sirens howled, fires sped through dockyards and factories and warehouses and apartments. The flames were like living monsters.[4] The streets were strewn with rubble, bricks, and broken glass and everything was black and yellow. Pedestrians lost their shirts and trousers in the suction of the bomb. Whole roads moved like ships at sea, rising and falling, and the bombers just kept coming.[5] The Luftwaffe pounded London, leaving over 1,000 dead and 200 injured. The Heinkels were back the next night, waves of them. They would return night after night for two straight months of relentless bombing. By the time the Blitz ended in May 1941, over 40,000 civilians had been killed and nearly 1 million houses had been wrecked in London alone. On average, 150 German bombers flew over London each evening in fifty-seven consecutive nights of bombing.

By the outbreak of war in Europe, nearly 62 percent of Americans were tuning in to news shows on a regular basis. Newspapers were not forgotten,

Edward R. Murrow seated behind the CBS microphone, 1939. (Courtesy of the Library of Congress, Prints and Photographs Division, New York World-Telegram and the Sun Newspaper Photograph Collection, LC-USZ62-126486)

but they struggled to keep pace. Radio had an obvious edge. It was quicker, free, and permitted multitasking. Moreover, radio transported listeners to the scene of the action.[6] The "great miracle" of radio, wrote Rudolf Arnheim, lay in its "overleaping of frontiers." This was radio's secret. Radio in effect became a giant ear that extended the range of hearing to distances never before imagined.[7] As Hadley Cantril and Gordon W. Allport wrote in a pioneering behaviorist study of radio in 1935, the listener was rarely confined to a single locale but could "jump through time and space with an alacrity that defied" other media. With the right sound effect, the listener could be placed in ancient Rome just as easily as in modern London.[8] In the end, it didn't matter where your Radiola was: radio took you there. *You Are There*, as CBS soon put it.

For many Americans, "there" was a London besieged by war. Edward R. Murrow covered the Battle of Britain and the nightly air raids on London with legendary brilliance, chronicling the bombardment in detail in his terse, highly descriptive style.[9] Amid the acrid smell of high explosives and the piercing sounds of sirens, Murrow found the perfect venue for what would become a new kind of aural literature. Although Murrow has long been known as the founding father of broadcast journalism, he made a less-noticed contribution to literature as the inventor of the radio essay.

During the Battle of Britain, Murrow's voice was listened to more than any other, and he was soon regarded as the eyes and ears of World War II. Surviving on coffee, cigarettes, and whiskey, Murrow became an icon almost overnight of a new kind of foreign correspondent. At a moment when broadcasting modes were being reinvented, Murrow's style became a model for other journalists at CBS, especially the so-called Murrow Boys—Eric Sevareid, Larry LeSueur, William Shirer, and even Mary Marvin Breckinridge—who embraced the Murrow style with its drama of the narrative "I," figurative language, conversational on-air persona, vivid imagery, short understated sentences, and bold sound effects, as an alternative to more conventional journalistic practices. As Eric Sevareid wrote at the time, Murrow was a Boswellian figure who threw out the strict, traditional formulae of news writing in order to achieve a more expressive, if not subjective, vision of wartime London. He was a "literary artist" trying to awaken American listeners to the urgency of the issue before them.[10]

Against Commentators

Though rarely viewed as an essayist, Murrow's style was essentially a literary feat, the function of which was to evoke a participatory sense of history that would infiltrate the collective mind of an American culture filled with deep-seated isolationist prejudices. While Murrow made no secret of his dread of Hitler, he avoided the kind of editorializing—network broadcast rules strictly forbade any direct expression of opinion—indulged in by radio commentators like Dorothy Thompson, H. V. Kaltenborn, or the BBC's own J. B. Priestley. Instead, Murrow hoped to re-create for listeners the visceral drama of a war that for many back home was, if not irrelevant, at least unimaginable. To achieve this, Murrow had to construct a new voice for radio, one that could not be mistaken for that of the news commentator, the reigning king of radio nonfiction. Ironically enough, Murrow devised a form of broadcast that had more in common with George Orwell's *Homage to Catalonia* and CBS's *Columbia Workshop* than with traditional print journalism. It was a hybrid genre that borrowed from the modernist tradition of literary journalism as well as the emergent form of American radio drama. Like his contemporaries in radio drama, Murrow understood how thematizing radio's own devices might lead to innovative broadcast work. If Orson Welles took advantage of the news commentator to blur fact and fiction, Murrow used that same figure to suggest a measure of false authority, which allowed him to redefine the terms of radio authenticity according to his own firsthand forays in and around ground zero. Like Archibald MacLeish and Norman Corwin, Murrow was not an adapter but worked with original material. His short, seemingly ephemeral essays in broadcast form were part of a broader literary continuum that, for a while, found a home in radio.

Like everyone else, Murrow took cover on that first day of the bombing of England. With two other journalists, he lay flat on the ground outside of London, as he explained in a CBS broadcast the following night (8 September 1940): "Before eight, the siren sounded again. We went back to the haystack near the airdrome. The fires up the river had turned the moon blood red. The smoke had drifted down till it formed a canopy over the Thames; the guns were working all around us, the bursts looking like fireflies in a southern summer night. The Germans were sending in two or three planes at a time. . . . They would pass overhead. The guns and lights would follow them, and in about five minutes we could hear the hollow grunt of the bombs. Huge pear shape bursts of flame would rise up into the smoke and disappear. The world was upside down."[11] After several months of a so-called Phony War (England waited nine months for the devastating bombardment to begin), there was finally action. Murrow's broadcast conveys the excitement of witnessing the first significant assault on England. There was no mistaking the meaning of Hitler's flying armada. War had finally come to England. Murrow's "report" is not only charged with the thrill of the instant, as if he were waiting for this moment since first arriving in London, but it is also ambitious in a literary sense.[12] As with most Murrow broadcasts, it went beyond the mere facts of an event and was rich in metaphor, irony, and high drama, exploring a range of emotions and experiences in subtle ways that surpassed the nightly analysis provided by America's most well-known commentators. Murrow's 8 September report describes the "blood red" of the moon, the smoke "canopy" over the river, the "fireflies" bursting from the big gun, "pear shaped" flames, and the "grunting" of bombs. It was not enough to limn each tableau in detail, however; Murrow also wanted to capture the immediacy of the scene, to evoke a you-are-there sensation for American listeners back home, which required a more purposeful use of figurative language. Murrow went out of his way to construct a radio-friendly mise-en-scène that would convey the nearness of war to an audience thousands of miles away.

The vivid picture of London in flames was not unlike the images described by other correspondents in London, such as Ernie Pyle, but Murrow's metaphors also conveyed important information about himself: his flights of fancy were equal to the menacing flights of the Luftwaffe and called attention to his authorial role. As poet of the rooftop, the bard of shrapnel, Murrow fashioned a persona whose literary ingenuity and on-air presence were constructed to offset the brute erasure of a fascist offensive in what seemed, especially to Americans, like the end of Old Europe. Murrow's literary persona was not that of the omniscient expert but shared with Orwell's—and modernism's—beleaguered narrators the struggle against the nightmare of history. Murrow's voice was that of a fallible man whose role as foreign correspondent was rendered perilous by the difficulties of knowing how to make sense of the unprecedented destruction caused by the London Blitz.

His literary deftness conveyed much more than information about war's grim realities to his audience. What Murrow sought to capture in his nightly broadcasts was the visceral (if not vicarious) experience of the upheaval suffered by the English in what was regarded as an extraordinary new phase of warfare, the sustained bombing of civilian targets. The novelty of the Blitz—of "terror bombing"—was as appalling as it was fascinating for many foreign correspondents. The Germans had utilized aerial bombardment before (on Guernica in the Spanish Civil War), but the intensity and duration of the London Blitz was unprecedented: fifty-seven nights of airborne violence. No one knew when or if a bomb would land nearby. It could happen at any moment. Murrow saw in Nazi aggression a threat not just to England but to all free people. The sense of common peril evoked by the imminent threat of bombing became a theme of his broadcasts. That such a danger could be endured was the implied promise of his intrepid on-air persona, which Murrow presented as the gutsy foreign correspondent roused to greatness by danger. The bombing of London brought out the best in Murrow, he wished his listeners to think, just as it brought out the best in Londoners.[13]

To an ear tuned to the verse plays for radio written by MacLeish and Corwin, Murrow's metaphors may have sounded familiar. Murrow's "blood red" moon, for instance, seemed a not-very-distant trace of the "bloody signs" of war described by the Studio Director in MacLeish's *Columbia Workshop* radio play *Air Raid* (1938).[14] Such echoes invested Murrow's persona with a "prestige" quality and helped him position this new genre—what Sevareid called a new kind of "contemporary essay"—on the literary side of nonfiction. As Sevareid saw it, the value and uniqueness of Murrow's radio essays lay in the fact that they were not radio commentaries, the form that had dominated the airwaves until now and the closest thing to nonfiction on radio.[15] The radio commentary—the nightly fifteen-minute sizing up of the day's events by authoritative radio personalities who enjoyed cult-like following—was, in fact, what the Murrow Boys, as Murrow's colleagues were called, were up against as CBS's fledgling news group scrambled to tell its stories.

The traditional radio commentator was a kind of aural columnist who rose to fame in the mid-1930s and remained a leading player in radio until 1950. As war broke out in Europe, twenty commentators broadcast regularly over the networks; by the end of the war that number had increased to an estimated 600.[16] The radio commentator made a living by expressing strong opinions and uttering bold turns of phrase (Father Coughlin on the DuPonts: "This family witnessed American liberty in its cradle and is seemingly happy to follow it to its grave").[17] The most popular commentators, like Boake Carter, were indeed "flamboyant and dramatic," as Sevareid suggested, and eventually got into trouble for being pretentious. Others, like Huey Long and Father Coughlin, were tub-thumpers who could easily (and did) fall into zealotry or demagoguery. Both Carter and Father Coughlin were forced off the air when concerned sponsors flew the coop.[18]

The more measured commentators, Raymond Gram Swing, Dorothy Thompson, Elmer Davis, and Lowell Thomas, enjoyed longer careers, offering listeners dignified voices to go along with their studious texts. Their broadcasts were often scholarly and worldly and could even resemble an academic lecture, along the lines of Elmer Davis, who favored an erudite style and liked to play the role of what Sevareid called the "public thinker." CBS's own H. V. Kaltenborn was by far the most celebrated radio commentator in America during the war, having been catapulted to fame during his exhaustive coverage of the Munich Crisis in 1938. Kaltenborn's forceful style, his ability to carve up the muddle of European politics into a coherent narrative, lent his voice a professorial authority.[19] His broadcasts were virtuoso performances, and his grasp of foreign affairs amazed many. His insistent and assertive, even if slightly overdetermined, manner fascinated listeners, as if Kaltenborn were imposing his American will on un-American material. Kaltenborn's commanding persona projected an irrefutable air. To some, he seemed omniscient. Like the voice of Oz, Kaltenborn was an oracle at a troubled and confusing moment in time. He saw what was coming and did not mince words when forecasting doom, even if that role seemed to lie outside his task as news analyst. By the conclusion of the Munich Pact, Kaltenborn had become a household name. *Radio Daily* voted him America's top commentator. He was awarded honorary doctorates. Hollywood even offered him a role in *Mr. Smith Goes to Washington* (he played himself).[20]

The Year of Living Dangerously

The commentator, an early exemplar of the talk-radio host, lived by the spoken word. Because his relationship to radio was determined primarily by words and their meanings, he cared little for sound as sound, which was not included in his métier. Not so for Murrow. Murrow's keen attention to the acoustic effects of the London Blitz was one of the special features of his reports. From the droning noise of the V-1 rocket to the tolling of Big Ben, Murrow's embrace of nonverbal sound distinguished his essays from the rival broadcasts of the radio commentator. Murrow was especially enamored of the radio close-up. Early on, radio researchers had noted that one distinctive advantage of radio over other media lay in its ability to produce "close-ups" of acoustic events, such as the pouring of a drink, the clack of high heels, or the creak of a door. Sound effects were convincing, researchers like Cantril and Allport suggested, because the focal capacities of the auditory imagination play such an important role in sound representation.[21] The sound-effects handbooks of the day took pride in describing scenes that could exist only in the listener's mind, such as a Parisian sewer in Welles's 1937 radio adaptation of *Les Misérables* (evoked by the "close-up" sound of Jean Valjean wading through water).[22]

For Murrow, the radio "close-up" was crucial to surmounting the great distance between continents, and for this reason he liked to imagine that his broadcasts would bring the war in Europe "much nearer to the wheat farmer in Kansas than any official communiqué."[23] Murrow relied heavily on what I call the *proximity effect* not only to close the gap between London and Kansas, but also to play out his idea of the radio essay. In radio, the proximity effect is a referential gesture that seeks spatial nearness to an acoustic source in order to localize meaning, as if language were not up to the task. When, for instance, Carl Phillips moves closer to the strange humming sound in the *War of the Worlds*, aiming his microphone at the sphere, he casts the meaning of the event as a function of the presence of sound. "Listen," he instructs his audience, "I'll move the microphone nearer." In sound representation, the proximity effect is a focal maneuver that plays up the acoustic signifier over the signified. "No one," Murrow reported in March 1941, "will ever describe adequately just what it feels like to sit in London with German bombs ripping in the air, shaking the buildings, and causing the lights to flicker, while you listen to the German radio broadcasting Wagner or Bavarian folk music." This is partly why Murrow and his followers insisted on the importance of the on-the-spot immediacy of CBS's new broadcasts.[24] The radio commentator was typically studio-bound—in his commentaries there was no there there. The Murrow Boys, however, were in the field, up to their ears in the wreckage of war, flying combat missions with RAF pilots, speeding though air raids in convertibles, ducking bombs on rooftops, watching and listening to the "little people," as Murrow liked to call ordinary English citizens, promising an unmediated glimpse of a besieged London. However naive, their belief in direct access to the action was part of their quest for presence, without which there could be no real understanding. To know the situation, one had to be there. As Murrow would say in his broadcasts, "Things must be experienced to be understood."[25]

From the beginning, Murrow took deliberate measures to promote the impression of immediacy in the CBS-style radio essay. It would need to sound a certain way, which meant it would not sound like Kaltenborn's or Gram Swing's or Dorothy Thompson's commentaries. "I want our programs," he avowed, "to be anything but intellectual." They would instead be "down to earth and comprehensible to the man in the street."[26] Murrow's cadre of reporters would "describe things in terms that make sense to the truck driver without insulting the intelligence of the professor."[27] The goal was to limit as much as possible the emotional distance between the broadcast text and the listener.[28]

To that end, Murrow fetishized reporting that evoked specific locations, the effect of which was to make Americans understand that the bombing of England was not a remote event, off in the distance and unrelated. His signature opening, "This is London," made famous by the emphatic "this," represented a kind of territorial claim on behalf of CBS, as if England were a new frontier and Murrow an explorer. The strategy was as compelling as it was successful.[29] In a relatively short time, Murrow came to embody the imperiled London in his broadcasts--was even called its "voice," as if he had physically merged with the besieged city. Murrow still talking was proof that London had not yet been bombed back to the Stone Age, as many in America half expected. Murrow's narrative presence was vital to this project, the promise of a participant observer who could not only see but hear what others could not. As an eyewitness to the destruction of London, Murrow pledged to live dangerously, to be near ground zero, documenting the everyday details of death and survival. More than any other foreign correspondent, Murrow relied on an immersive aesthetic that not only legitimized the radio essay as a new acoustic form but also recommended it as the most authentic genre for representing wartime London.

To friends and colleagues, Murrow's desire to be near or at the scene of a bombing was strange. He seemed to be courting disaster. His boss, William S. Paley, believed Murrow harbored a death wish and instructed him to avoid aerial combat missions.[30] Drawn by danger, Murrow presented his ground-zero adventures in his broadcasts as rites of passage, bringing him closer to some kind of indefinable reality that seemed, in the early surrealistic glow of war, difficult to find, especially during the so-called Phony War (as the delay of civilian bombing was called): "Yesterday afternoon I stood at a hotel window and watched the Germans bomb the naval base at Portland, two or three miles away. In the morning I had been through that naval base and dockyard and satisfied myself that the Admiralty communiqués reporting earlier bombings had been accurate."[31] If Murrow brought clarity to his listeners through a painstaking inspection of what he saw, these fact-checking tours often put him in harm's way, by placing him in the vicinity of falling bombs and flying shrapnel.

Such escapades were risky, but they also played well to listeners back home, as Murrow's sheer daring became an inseparable part of his broadcast persona. Ever the doubting Thomas in search of the "real," Murrow demanded to see for himself the damage done by German bombs, refusing to take official communiqués at face value. "I have a peasant's mind," Murrow wrote.[32] The following week, Murrow again returned to the coast of England on the lookout for bombs, racing over country roads in a convertible two-seater:

> The damage done by an exploding bomb to windows in a given area is a freakish sort of thing. A bomb may explode at an intersection and the blast will travel down two streets, shattering windows for a considerable distance, while big windows within a few yards of the bomb crater remain intact. The glass, incidentally, generally falls out into the street, rather than being blown inwards. During the last two weeks I spent a considerable amount of time wandering about the south and southeast coast in an open car. Much of the time was spent in that section which has been termed by some journalists, but not by the local inhabitants, as Hell's Corner. Now an open car is not to be recommended under normal conditions, for the weather isn't right, but it's helpful these days to be able to look and listen as you drive along.[33]

It was helpful indeed, so much so that firsthand looking and listening became Murrow's signature method of reportage, an at-the-scene style that distinguished him from his peers.

It is little wonder, then, that Murrow had no tolerance for commentaries on the Blitz from a far-off country.[34] In a report from 12 September 1940 (five days after the bombing of London began), Murrow summarized a broadcast by the popular radio commentator Dorothy Thompson. Her talk was sent by NBC from New York via shortwave radio and was a variation of an inspirational speech delivered by Thompson three months earlier in Montreal, also broadcast to London by the Canadian Broadcasting Corporation (CBC). In the Montreal talk, Thompson appealed to England's cultural tradition as a bulwark Hitler would never overcome, urging the British people to put their faith in Winston Churchill and in a history rich with spirits that hovered, in her view, around England: "Around you, Winston Churchill, is a gallant company of ghosts. Elizabeth is there, and sweetest Shakespeare, the man who made the English Renaissance the world's renaissance. Drake is there, and Raleigh, and Wellington. Burke is there, and Walpole, and Pitt. Byron is there, and Wordsworth and Shelley."[35] Murrow's criticism of Thompson's belletristic tropes gave him occasion to subtly pitch his understated and on-the-spot style as a better alternative to the overblown studio commentary. Far away from the bombing, Thompson couldn't possibly understand what Londoners suffered, Murrow seemed to suggest, not without firsthand experience:

> Miss Dorothy Thompson made a broadcast to Britain tonight. Her audience was somewhat reduced, since the air-raid siren sounded just after she started speaking. She informed the British that the poets of the world were lined up on their side. That, she said, was a matter of consequence. I'm not sure that Londoners agreed that the poets would be of much assistance, as they grabbed their blankets and headed for the air-raid shelters. I think these Londoners put more faith in their antiaircraft barrage, which seemed to splash blobs of daylight down the streets tonight. . . . I know something about these Londoners. They know that they're out on their own. Most of them expect little help from the poets and no effective defense by word of mouth. These black-faced men with bloodshot eyes who were fighting fires and the girls who cradled the steering wheel of a heavy ambulance in their arms, the policeman who stands guards over the unexploded bomb down at St. Paul's tonight—these people didn't hear Miss Thompson; they're busy, just doing a job of work, and they know that it all depends on them.[36]

Murrow stopped short of calling Thompson's broadcast corny, but his criticism is clear.

On one level, Murrow's short broadcast on this occasion saluted (as it often did) the resilience of ordinary people, the everyday scramble of working-class Londoners to survive the devastating bombing. The rescue workers, firemen, ambulance drivers, policemen, nameless parents huddling with children in the London Tube—these were the heroes of Murrow's broadcasts. On another level, Murrow took exception to Thompson's out-of-touch musings. To suggest that the good intentions of poets in New York or in Paris or in San Francisco could come to the aid of embattled Londoners seemed, in Murrow's view, silly. Thompson's fanciful optimism, Murrow implied, was no match for the reality of bombs and blankets and bloodshot eyes. Thompson's language was literary and distancing, if not patronizing. It reflected an Edwardian sensibility that sought cover from the Luftwaffe under a belletristic style that was hard for someone like Murrow, who harbored modernist misgivings about such idealism, to swallow. Murrow held to his hard-earned insights into the realities faced by war-bedeviled Londoners, repeatedly insisting that any real grasp of the bombing required immersion in the scene. You had to be there. To Murrow, Thompson's style of radio commentary seemed suspiciously aloof. Safe in her New York studio, Thompson did not bear witness (as Murrow had) to the suffering and courage of Londoners.[37] How could she possibly know their struggle unless she were there dodging shrapnel?[38] Murrow's allegiance to the victims of the Blitz—"I know something about these Londoners"—contained a large degree of moral empathy that could only arise from proximity to the tribulations of Londoners. As uttered by Murrow, the word "know" receives as much emphasis as the demonstrative pronoun in "This is London." In both discursive moves, Murrow takes ownership of the narrative, inserting himself between the listener and the scene as a mediating consciousness. "These things must be experienced to be understood," he often said.[39] Murrow, of course, was protecting his turf (bombed-out London) from rival broadcasters. He was also branding his own genre, the radio essay, by distinguishing it from commentaries as something unique and authentic.[40]

Murrow knew that sound was essential to this project, and he was eager to transmit the aural effects of battle back to listeners in Kansas and Missouri. But this was easier said than done. British censorship forbade live locative (scene-specific) broadcasts by foreign reporters for fear of betraying sensitive geographical information, while American network radio banned the use of prerecorded materials. Despite CBS's embargo on prerecorded sound, Murrow worked tirelessly with the BBC's liaison office and the British Ministry of Information to ease restrictions on live broadcasts.

Murrow's determination to feature "atmosphere" in his broadcasts—including the ambient sounds of planes, sirens, ambulances, and antiaircraft—followed the modernist practice of flirting with meaning at the border of sound and noise. He understood that nothing in print could rival the vivid acoustic uproar of recent American radio drama. In July 1940, Murrow witnessed such a moment when encountering a BBC mobile unit on the cliffs of Dover. The van was recording an afternoon skirmish between the RAF and German dive-bombers, which were attacking a British convoy in the English Channel. What caught Murrow's attention was the sonic dynamics of the BBC report broadcast later in the evening. In his own report that night (14 July 1940), Murrow conveyed his excitement about the ability of the BBC's audio engineer and reporter to compile a dramatic mix of ambient sound and narration that resembled a play-by-play analysis of a soccer match. The BBC: "You can hear our own guns going like anything now. . . . There's one coming down in flames. Someone's hit a German and he's coming down in a long streak of smoke, coming down completely out of control, a long streak of smoke. The pilot has bailed out by parachute. He's a Junkers 87 and he's going flat into the sea. There he goes! SMA-A-ASH! Terrific pummel on the water! ... There's a little burst, there's another bomb dropping."[41] What impressed Murrow most were the actual sounds of guns and planes. As Murrow explained in his own report that same night, British listeners (unlike American radio listeners, he may have thought) were able to hear the "cough of antiaircraft fire and the stutter of machine guns overhead." They also heard warplanes and bombs.

That the BBC commentator (Charles Gardner) had recorded the sound of war as background to his analysis must have stirred a sense of déjà vu in Murrow, as these were the same sound effects that had been cued up in the *Columbia Workshop*'s invasion plays. The astute listener might have recognized that two different genres, broadcast journalism and radio drama, were merging in an unexpected moment of radiophonic cross-breeding. As Murrow explained in his report of 19 July: "Roaring out of the loudspeakers of Britain tonight came the thunder of one-thousand-horsepower motors of British fighters as they swept out over the Channel in two flights—the first to engage the German fighter escort and the second to tackle the bombers. Later we heard a description of Spitfires and Hurricanes driving Messerschmitts back toward the French coast."[42] Of Gardner's commentary, Murrow had little to say other than to marvel at the "faintest trace of excitement in his voice." He was much more interested in the idea of mixing voice with ambient sound, so as to turn a radio text into a radio play.

How different this was from the standard radio commentary. Live coverage of exciting events was novel to radio listeners on both sides of the Atlantic, and few models existed. Hence it was no surprise that the BBC's Dover broadcast provoked controversy when some found "the hot little engagement" (as Gardner described the fight) too dramatic and sensational for "news."[43] If listeners had difficulty distinguishing between radio drama and a newscast, they could hardly be blamed. Such ambiguity was an occupational hazard of radio, whose representational codes were still in flux, especially in America, where air-raid dramas had blurred the line between fiction and reality. It is in fact hard to separate Murrow's eagerness to exploit ambient sounds in his reports from the success of invasion narratives recently made popular on CBS.

CBS executives had reason to be nervous about Murrow's use of sound effects.[44] Barely two years had passed since the network aired Orson Welles's *War of the Worlds*. For many, the panic revealed the powers and perils of radio. It wasn't the idea of Martians that frightened listeners in

1938 so much as the clever simulation of live locative broadcasting. When told by authorities of the prank, many shrugged off reassurances that what they heard was merely a *play*, a fantasy. As one listener in Brooklyn complained, "What do you mean it's just a play? We can hear the firing all the way here and I want a gas mask. I'm a taxpayer."[45] The dynamics of locative sound seemed to transcend realism. Sound was an influential medium, no one could deny.[46] As CBS executive Ed Klauber professed, "I think we've learned something from all this, and that is *not* to simulate news."[47]

Listening In

One of the early lessons of prestige programming, especially on CBS, was that wordless sounds could have a powerful impact. Sound effects in radio drama were illusions, but in London Murrow was surrounded by the racket of real battle and was vexed by the ban that prevented him from recording it. As one biographer put it, Murrow was "itching" for action and for the ability to capture that action for audiences.[48] After pressing the Ministry of Information for weeks, Murrow was finally cleared for a live remote broadcast—the first of which was the CBS program *London after Dark*, produced in partnership with the BBC and the CBC and featuring eyewitness accounts of bombing from different vantage points in London. The technical provisions of the program allowed Murrow to feature the soundscape of war-torn London, not as a sonic backdrop, but as the very subject of his broadcast. *London after Dark* took American listeners on a "sound-seeing tour" of blacked-out London. First there was Murrow at Trafalgar Square, then Eric Sevareid at Hammersmith Palais (in the middle of a dance floor while a band played "A Nightingale Sang in Berkeley Square" with air-raid sirens blaring in the background) and Vincent Sheean at Piccadilly Circus, followed by BBC interviews with train conductors at Euston Station. The program concluded with a J. B. Priestley commentary from Whitehall.

Murrow himself stood on the steps of St. Martin's-in-the-Fields, microphone in hand. Nearby was a BBC equipment van. "This is Trafalgar Square," he began in *London after Dark*. Murrow remained quiet for a moment, capturing ambient sounds with his microphone. "The noise that you hear at the moment is the sound of the air-raid sirens. I'm standing here just on the steps of St Martin-in-the-Fields. A searchlight just burst into action, off in the distance. One single beam, sweeping the sky above me now." Murrow raised his voice over the screaming ambulances and howling air-raid sirens. Double-decker buses growled by. "We're just at the entrance of an air-raid shelter here and I must move this cable over just a bit so people can walk in. I'll just let you listen to the traffic and the sound of the siren for a moment."[49]

In Murrow's radio work, the siren becomes much more than an indexical reference to danger.[50] Murrow suspends his own text so that listeners might concentrate better on the rising and falling noise of the air-raid siren, as if it were another voice whose importance called out for a moment of silent respect. Murrow will defer to the siren much the way Carl Phillips yielded to the Martian hum, extending his microphone in the charged air in *London after Dark*: "The noise that you hear at the moment is the sound of air-raid sirens.... I'll just let you listen to the traffic and the sound of the siren for a while." In the mind of the listener, the mournful howl of the siren becomes a psychoacoustic event with a wide symbolic spectrum; it conveys meaning beyond language and wordlessly captures the supreme terror of invasion. A year earlier, *Variety* magazine had warned readers of radio's power to overwhelm listeners with acoustic excitement: "While it does not create the tensions of the day, radio elongates the shadows of fear and frustration. We are scared by the mechanized columns of Hitler. We are twice-scared by the emotionalism of radio. Radio quickens the tempo of the alternative waves of confidence and defeatism which sweep the country and undermined judgment. Radio exposes nearly everybody in the country to a rapid, bewildering succession of emotional experiences."[51] In 1939, networks banned broadcast of an air-raid alert because it was "unneutral," meaning it was deemed sensational.[52]

As *London after Dark* continued, Murrow bent down and placed his microphone on the sidewalk in order to capture the sounds of civilians walking to the Underground shelter. This must have seemed odd to any Londoners passing by, the tall reporter in his formless raincoat squatting on the pavement with his instrument, tethered by a long cable to a BBC van. "I'll just ooze down in the darkness here along these steps and see if I can pick up the sounds of people's feet as they walk along," Murrow said. "One of the strangest sounds one can hear in London these days or rather these dark nights; just the sound of footsteps walking along the street. Like ghosts shod with steel shoes."

Murrow's interest in "footsteps"—rather than in the voices of passersby— is motivated by his attraction to acoustic signifiers, to the sound object (*l'objet sonore*, in Pierre Schaeffer's terms), as if by word of mouth alone he cannot capture the historical moment. In shifting the center of aural attention from the mouth of Londoners to their feet, Murrow turns away from the expected source of radiophonic meaning—speech and the logocentric—toward what Sevareid had called "the tap-tap-tap of Londoners' footsteps as they went determinedly about their business."[53] As if anticipating the ephemerality of this acoustic moment, Murrow does not let the sound object speak for itself but instead supplements it with a metaphor: "the sound of footsteps ... like ghosts shod with steel shoes."[54] It is a broadcast moment that will evoke Ezra Pound's haiku "In the Metro" (1913): "The apparition of these faces in the crowd; Petals on a wet, black bough." The contrast between the footsteps and the "grunt of bombs" is arresting. The warscape juxtaposes the noise of battle and civilian endurance. As it turns out, we cannot today detect those footsteps on recordings of the original broadcast—the inaudible footsteps are literally "hearsay." Luckily, Murrow adds a verbal sign: in this case speech is filling in for an absence Murrow himself could never have predicted.

Considering its technological demands, *London after Dark* was an ambitious broadcast. But even more noteworthy were Murrow's novel twists on reporting. By isolating one small part of London's soundscape, Murrow engages in an act of selective listening that valorizes a single precise element, the footsteps. Jean-François Augoyard and Henry Torgue relate such acts of sonic valorizing to what they call the "synecdoche effect," the use of intentional listening in organizing sound perception.[55] The synecdoche effect was an essayistic trick by Murrow, a swerve from the more spectacular sound of war that was in keeping with his interest in the "little incidents" of wartime London. Murrow imagined it was these small events that conveyed the deeper meaning of London's air war:

> The scale of this air war is so great that the reporting of it is not easy. Often we spend hours traveling about this sprawling city, viewing damage, talking with people, and occasionally listening to the bombs come down, and then more hours wondering what you'd like to hear about these people who are citizens of no mean city. We've told you about the bombs, the fires, the smashed houses, and the courage of the people. We've read you the communiqués and tried to give you an honest estimate of the wounds inflicted upon this, the best bombing target in the world. But the business of living and working in this city is very personal—the little incidents, the things the mind retains, are in themselves unimportant, but they somehow weld together to form the hard core of memories that will remain when the last "all-clear" has sounded.[56]

The idea that "little incidents" bore larger meaning accurately captured the spirit of Murrow's essayism and informed his strategy of selective listening. By isolating "little" sounds to tell a story, Murrow hoped to get around the representational difficulties (the problem of "scale," as he notes above) that complicated reporting on the war. Murrow's use of the proximity effect fit these tactics well. Murrow was putting America's ear to the pavement.[57] He could not, nor could his listeners, get any closer than this to wartime London. In such a way, he defined his own stance as a radio essayist as that of a master of acoustic vigilance.[58] Microphone in hand, he would draw nearer the temporal flow of the moment, which could be arrested only by bombing.

On 21 September 1940, Murrow made his first live rooftop broadcast from atop the BBC's Broadcasting House. "I'm standing on a rooftop looking out over London. At the moment everything is quiet."[59] Justly famous, Murrow's rooftop broadcast is curious for its "blindness." In the darkness of the blackout, Murrow could only guess where things were. The Blitz was something you could hear but not see—much like radio. When narrating the events of an air raid, Murrow rarely witnessed the source of his sounds. The planes were too high overhead to see, and the antiaircraft fire (despite its bursts of light) was as elusive as the falling bombs in the dark of night. These were disembodied sounds to which he gave a label, as though they were being described by a blindfolded man. "Sometimes when the Germans come over above the clouds," Murrow reported, "it is possible to hear the whisper of high-flying aircraft and the growl of fighters diving with full throttle, interspersed with bursts of machine-gun fire. But nothing can be seen."[60] Murrow marveled at the invisibility of German planes. There was something "unreal" about this air war. "Much of it you can't see," he wrote, "but the aircraft are up in the clouds, out of sight. Even when the Germans come down to dive-bomb an airfield it's all over in an incredibly short time. You just see a bomber slanting down toward his target; three or four little things that look like marbles fall out, and it seems to take a long time for those bombs to hit the ground."[61]

The Acoustic Close-Up

In Murrow's radio essays, the Blitz was a problematic event that defied common efforts to define its significance. Not only was the constant bombing of civilian targets—for fifty-seven consecutive nights—extraordinary, but the German assault posed perceptual challenges as well. To see in the dark under London's blackout rules was nearly impossible, and like the V-2 rocket, which arrived without warning, the bombs dropped by the Luftwaffe could not be pinpointed until their detonation (although, ominously, they could be heard). As Murrow told others, "I can't write about anything I haven't seen." But write he did. For Murrow, attentive listening was a critical way around these obstacles. This war was a modernist war, as Murrow intuited, and it required a modernist response. Acoustic vigilance was Murrow's variation on modernism's limited perspective.[62] In his most forceful broadcasts, Murrow conveyed what could be heard but not necessarily seen.

The screaming of bombs and howling of sirens were recognizable signs, and they were a persistent presence in Murrow's broadcasts. But even more interesting to Murrow were those sounds that were not so predictable, sounds that could be captured only in acoustic close-ups by selective listening. "One night I stood in front of a smashed grocery store and heard a dripping inside," he reported on 13 September 1940. "It was the only sound in all London. Two cans of peaches had been drilled clean through by flying glass and the juice was dripping down onto the floor."[63] The dripping juice, like the footsteps at Trafalgar Square, was another "little incident" significantly amplified to a larger magnitude: "the only sound in all London." Could anything be of less consequence in the midst of an apocalyptic war? If the footsteps (for Murrow) represented the persistence of Londoners in the face of annihilation, the pierced peach cans suggest a different story. Penetrated by flying glass, the slashed cans bleed, their juice dripping onto the floor. What exactly the moment might have conveyed to listeners back home is hard to say—the loss of life, human suffering, or just a destroyed can of fruit—but Murrow's representation of himself as the perceptive listener, attentive to the eccentricities of meaning, is perfectly clear. That a commonplace can of peaches might hold such significance required some manipulation. Once Murrow's small, quotidian sounds were isolated as the target of selective listening, they suddenly became bigger and more unusual, their reference points shifting under the literary work of suggestiveness. Murrow's figurative expressions completed the acoustic close-up by reconfiguring the sound object's meaning as something striking and uncanny (the footsteps of Londoners were "like ghosts shod with steel shoes"; the dripping juice "was the only sound in all London").

The closer Murrow brought his listeners to the ordinary objects and events of bombed-out London, the stranger the war became:

> The other night . . . I heard a sound as I stood on a street corner. . . . The sound that I heard was caused by the raindrops, but they were not hitting the pavement. It was a crisp, bouncing sound. Some of you have heard that sound as the rain drummed on a tent roof. Three people, old people they were, stood beside me in the rain and murk; they were on their way to the shelters. The bedding rolls were hunched high on their shoulders, and the blankets and pillows were wrapped in oilcloth. And a more chilling, brutal sound is not to be heard in London. As those three people squelched away in the darkness, looking like repugnant humpbacked monsters, I couldn't help thinking after all they're rather lucky—there are hundreds of thousands who haven't even oilcloth to wrap their bedding rolls. Sounds, as well as words, get all twisted in wartime. Familiar harmless sounds take on a sinister meaning. And, for me, the sound of raindrops hitting windowpanes, tar roofs, or tents will always bring back those three misshapen people on a London street corner on a wet November night.[64]

In this vivid tableau, Murrow isolates the aural signifier (sound of rain), quickly detaching its effect from the expected referent (rainy streets, city weather, wet night), which would reduce the sound of rain to local ambience, mere rainfall. Murrow's sound object is more peculiar than that. "The sound that I heard was caused by the raindrops, but they were not hitting the pavement." Instead, the sound of rain was marking off three refugees, making known their plight. The benign raindrops acquire a "sinister meaning" in Murrow's brooding meditation, just as the refugees come to resemble "humpbacked monsters." As described by Murrow, the raindrops evoke the pain of displacement, not merely a wet night. The raindrops stir a search for meaning not programmed by experience or by conventional usage. In this gap between the known and the unknown—between rainy weather and the insidious effects of war—the raindrops stray from the rule of expectancy. What we hear gets distorted in wartime, Murrow says. "Familiar harmless sounds take on a sinister meaning." These shifts in meaning were fundamental to Murrow's effort to valorize his broadcasts as grounded in a unique kind of modernist awareness—an awareness of something that transcended our usual modes of perception and feeling. Walking the streets of bombed-out London was a growing encounter with a disturbing otherness.

The acoustic alertness of Murrow's reports is what distinguished his project from the broadcasts of commentators, those studio-bound editorialists who pronounced from afar. Few of his reports were hard of hearing. Even when he could not capture live sound with a microphone, Murrow verbalized what he heard: The V-1 rockets, Murrow reported in 1943, "come over, sounding like a couple of dissatisfied washing machines hurtling though the air"; Berlin was "a kind of orchestrated hell—a terrible symphony of light and flame"; the bombers going out that night sounded like a "giant factory in the sky"; the tanks on the roads "sound like a huge sausage machine, grinding up sheets of corrugated iron."[65] Murrow's sonic images are rarely objective but instead are idiosyncratic and distinctly figurative, and they project the image of the world as off-kilter (washing machines should not be streaking through the sky). Listeners may have been startled by Murrow's metaphors, but such quirky imaginings were vital to his radio essays and cast the author as exemplary listener, one with an ear as acute as Poe's Roderick Usher.

Listening may be a subjective act, but Murrow wishes to turn it into a public event, as if he were a human microphone. Sound, for Murrow, was history's way of inscribing itself into the imagination of men and women. The sounds of this war—in Murrow's words, the "stutter of machine guns," "roaring fighter planes," "screaming sirens," "distant crump of bombs," and endless "clamor of ambulance bells"—had never been witnessed by civilians before. They were unprecedented, defying familiar codes. "Maybe the children who are now growing up," Murrow wrote, "will in future wars be able to associate the sound of bombs, the drone of engines, and the carrying sound of machine guns overhead with human tragedy and disaster."[66] But until then, Murrow would have to find his own meaning in the moment.

Murrow's subjective engagement with the warscape of London was unique on radio, and his first-person meditations on the bombing of London marked the arrival of the essay on broadcast radio. For Murrow, the essayistic voice, which is personal and explorative, was a more authentic solution to problems posed by reporting on an anomalous war than the voice of the commentator, aloof and authoritative. Murrow's broadcasts were at their essayistic best when in search of sound, especially when Murrow himself poked around the rubble of London for the telling sonic quotation.[67] In such scenes, Murrow's efforts to locate the significance of the moment were dependent on his sound-making skills, his ability to provide the eloquent acoustic close-up. Murrow demonstrated that even without a microphone the proximity effect was a powerful device in radio-making, since being close to the source of sound, Murrow seemed to think, was like being near the origin of meaning itself.

In unexpected ways, Murrow's interest in the proximity effect defined the experience of listening back home as well. As the unpredictability of shortwave radio broadcasts from Europe put the burden of hearing on listeners, this meant that listeners had to draw nearer their radios than ordinarily necessary. They literally had to give the radio their ear.[68]

The Screaming Woman

As described by Ovid, Echo was a wood nymph who loved the sound of her own voice. More precisely, she was a chatterbox. As described by Sophocles, she was "the girl with no door on her mouth."[1] Echo still had a body then, Ovid says, and was not merely a voice, as she would later become after an ill-fated encounter with Narcissus, the delicate youth who shunned all would-be lovers. "Nothing could have been worse / than falling in love / with Narcissus," writes the poet Allison Funk, "Unless they'd had children."[2] In Greek, Echo (*Ēkhō*) means "sound."

Like Scheherazade, who diverted the misogynistic king from cruelty against women, entertaining him night after night with distracting stories, Echo employed similar skills to distract Juno, the queen of the gods, while Jove played fast and loose with other nymphs. (Ironically, in popular adaptations of *The Arabian Nights*, Scheherazade is often absent, essentially silenced—or Echo-ed.) When Juno discovered this trickery, she punished the garrulous Echo by taking away her voice, allowing her only the smallest ability to speak. All Echo could do, being so cursed, was repeat the sound of another. Said Juno: "You shall forfeit the use of that tongue with which you have cheated me, except for that one purpose you are so fond of—reply. You shall still have the last word, but no power to speak first."[3] No longer able to initiate speech, Echo loses control over her own voice, while being excluded from language.[4] She tries her best to woo Narcissus but only produces fragments of his own speech ("Who is here," "Here!"). Scorned, Echo wanders in shame among the trees, hiding in lonely caves, her sad body wasting away. Only her bones and the sound of her voice survived, Ovid writes.[5]

In Ovid's cruel irony, Echo is disciplined for speaking too much, as if she has crossed some measurable threshold of female verbosity. No longer able to compose a thought, or to start or finish a sentence that is her own, Echo has suffered a kind of stroke, falling into the grip of a profound neurological disorder that cripples her linguistic abilities. That Juno should sentence Echo to a form of aphasia dooms the chatty nymph to an eternal servitude in which she is bound to the speech of others. Echo is in effect turned into a dummy for someone else's ventriloquism. In Ovid's story, it is Narcissus who plays the role of Edgar Bergen. His speech is copied comically by Echo, as if she were making fun of his vanity. She can utter only fragments of his discourse. He spurns her out of pride as well as a suspicion that she is mocking him in mimicry of his simple language ("Any one here?" "Here!"). Why didn't Jove offer the hapless nymph some kind of compensatory gift? Discursive deviance, it would seem, is an unpardonable transgression.

Narcissus had already become a hero of psychoanalysis by the time Marshall McLuhan wrote about him.[6] Like Freud, McLuhan focused on Narcissus rather than Echo, understanding the boy's infatuation with his own image as a visual extension of himself: "The youth mistook his own reflection in the water for another person. This extension of himself by mirror numbed his perceptions until he became the servomechanism of his own extended or repeated image. The nymph Echo tried to win his love with fragments of his own speech, but in vain. He was numb. He had adapted to his extension of himself and had become a closed system. Now the point of this myth is the fact that men at once become fascinated by any extension of themselves in any material other than themselves."[7] In McLuhan's reading of the myth, Echo has been left out of the story. Her voice does not seem to matter. What does matter is the visual projection of Narcissus followed by the boy's internalizing of that image: "To behold, use or perceive any extension of ourselves in technological form is necessarily to embrace it. . . . It is this continuous embrace of our own technology in daily use that puts us in the Narcissus role of subliminal awareness and numbness in relation to these images of ourselves. . . . Man in the normal use of technology (or his variously extended body) is perpetually modified by it and in turn finds ever new ways of modifying his technology."[8] McLuhan recognizes subliminally the uselessness of Echo in his theory of media. The extension of Narcissus, as someone who gazes into the mirror image, is implicitly matched by the attenuation of Echo as a once-upon-a-time speaking subject. He is lost in the gaze; she loses her voice. In the ecology of the human sensorium, something must give for Narcissus to complete his visual project. For McLuhan, it is the aurality of Echo (and the agency of sound) that loses ground and is consequently excluded from the story of *technics*.

McLuhan's omission is a reminder of the extent to which Echo has been marginalized by her displacement from the symbolic order. Echo plays the role of tape recorder, a very poor one at that, repeating the last sounds of others. "Alas," said Narcissus. "Alas," said Echo. "I am in love with my own reflection." "Reflection," sighed Echo.[9] She is what Kaja Silverman would call an "acoustic mirror."[10] Not only is the image of Narcissus repeated but so are his words. The tragedy of Narcissus is to be immersed in the repetition of himself, a fate from which Echo is spared.

McLuhan may have been biased toward Narcissus, but the sad story of Echo has served contemporary theory well, especially as a metaphor for the problem of the speaking woman.[11] Echo's cruel fate, as Adriana Cavarero has suggested, is the tale of women's own devocalization and disembodiment by patriarchy and the symbolic order.[12] The legacy of Echo is evident throughout the history of film and broadcast radio, especially in those cases where the voices of women are strictly forbidden. During radio's so-called golden years, most broadcast roles were reserved for men. Dorothy Thompson was a nationally syndicated commentator, but she was an exception to the rule. Mary Marvin Breckinridge, who worked for Edward R. Murrow as a foreign correspondent, aired stories from Europe for CBS during the war; but she had a deep voice, went by her middle name, and was wealthy. The networks subscribed to the usual gender inequities, but prejudices against the female voice ran high even among radio listeners. Unlike the male voice, which was deemed to be "well modulated," the female voice was thought to be "aggravating" and "monotonous." It was full of "personality" and "enthusiasm," listeners complained, and therefore unsuitable for "maintaining the necessary reserve and objectivity" demanded by radio's more serious tasks. Women were essentially banned from speaking on air in nonperforming roles.[13]

The brief radio career of Betty Wason, a CBS foreign correspondent, is a striking case in point. Though not a member of his inner circle, Betty Wason worked for Murrow during the war years in Europe and was regarded by many as a good writer and capable reporter. She had a knack for breaking timely stories and finding out where the action was. In one of her early reports from Stockholm, in April 1940, Wason went live with a report about women spies in Norway. Her report immediately raised concerns with CBS back in New York, not because of its content but because CBS was unhappy with the sound of Wason's voice. It was not forceful enough. Explained Wason: "I received a call saying my voice wasn't coming through, that it was too young and feminine for war news and that the public was objecting to it."[14] Wason was not a child. At twenty-eight, she was certainly older than twenty-one-year-old Russell Hill, whose Berlin broadcasts provoked no grumbling.

The network instructed Wason to find a male proxy and forbade her from speaking on her own. Reaching Athens just in time for the Italian invasion of Greece, Wason ignored the embargo on her voice and went on air with breaking news but was once again scolded by CBS officials in New York, who suggested that she find a man to speak for her. She needed a voice dummy.[15] Betty Wason had been to the front lines, had even survived to tell the tale. She escaped border guards, hitched rides across mountain passes, hid in the woods, and outlived air raids. But all that listeners back home heard, she feared, was a voice that was "frail and feminine." Said Betty: "It was frustrating because other people were quoting me." Radio was no place for the female voice.[16] On some level, Wason's loss of voice was little different from the curse of Echo. Wason too was a kind of chatterbox. She refused to keep silent and coveted the last word—holding forth at least twice without authorization—until network bosses banned her voice outright.[17]

The Screaming Point

If primetime radio was inhospitable to the female voice in nonperforming roles, that bias was not confined to network policy. A similar kind of vocal erasure found its way into radio's story lines and was, in fact, thematized in fantasies of entrapment and suffocation throughout the 1940s. CBS's long-running prestige anthology *Suspense*, one of the more sophisticated series dedicated to horror, repeatedly adopted radio noir themes, specializing in desperate and hysterical female subjects whose traumatized voices echoed the profound discursive impotency enforced by the networks.[18] Many of *Suspense*'s subjects are distressed women who are stalked (or ensnared) by homicidal men, including husbands and psychopaths. In *The Whole Town's Sleeping*, an intrepid Lavinia Nebbs (played by Agnes Moorehead) returns home by herself from the movies one night, despite recent unnerving events in which a serial killer known as "The Lonely One" has murdered several vulnerable women, including Lavinia's friend Eliza.[19] Against the advice of acquaintances and authorities, Lavinia shrugs off any worry, resolving to walk home alone through a dark and creepy ravine, just as the town bell chimes midnight. A Detective will offer protection—"I'll have one of my men walk you across the ravine," he says—which Lavinia brushes aside: "That won't be necessary, thank you very much." A strong-willed woman who prides herself on being immune to prevailing anxieties, Lavinia resists the caution of others. "I'm just not afraid, that's all," she tells a friend who is herself rather anxious. "And I'm curious, I suppose. Of course, I'm using my head. I mean, logically, the Lonely One can't be around. Not now, with the police discovering Eliza's body and all." Lavinia refuses to see herself as a damsel in distress and is not reluctant to speak her mind. "I'm not afraid of the dark," she tells the police. She does not want or need rescuing.

The listener knows, of course, that Lavinia will suffer for her defiance. She survives the scary walk home alone, although not without evident distress. Hearing footsteps, she lets out a small scream, overcome by paranoid imaginings. The self-reliant Lavinia is no longer so self-assured. "Shall I call Mr. Kennedy? Did he hear me scream? Or did I scream? Maybe I only thought I did. Then he didn't hear me at all. I'll go back up [the ravine]. Go to Helen's and sleep there tonight. No! It's nearer home now. Don't be silly. Wait." Lavinia makes a mad dash for home—"Only a little way! Across the bridge! Run! Run! Don't turn!"—promising her offended gods she will "never go out again alone," only to find the serial killer waiting for her inside her own home. Trapped by the murderer, Lavinia surrenders to terror, losing her voice:

> LAVINIA: *(terrified)* What—? *(swallows hard)* What—? *(with great effort)* Who—is it?
> SOUND: *A man's footsteps slowly approach.*
> LAVINIA: *(shudders in fear, whimpers)*
> SOUND: *Man's footsteps stop.*
> MAN: *(low, lovingly)* Beautiful. So beautiful.
> LAVINIA: *(beat, shudders, screams)*

The ravine-traversing Lavinia, who freely crosses boundaries, is punished for being willful. Even her friends are puzzled by her nerve. "You've acted so strangely tonight," says Helen, the last to see her alive. For having defied male authority—for being different—Lavinia is rendered speechless, duly throttled by a serial killer. In her final moment, she cannot even predicate her own sentences ("What—?"), the woman who said *no* to authority ("That won't be necessary"). Lavinia's strong-willed voice is, in the end, reduced to what Silverman calls the most exemplary of female sounds: the scream.[20]

Lavinia's scream signals her loss of enunciative power in the order of discourse. Outside of this order, the female voice is sentenced to a tongue-tied purgatory, where it is only permitted shudders, whimpers, screams, and cries. Like Echo, Lavinia's transgression is a side effect of her discursive competence. She, too, over-speaks.

Equally horrifying is the fate of Mrs. Nesbitt in Ray Bradbury's *The Screaming Woman*, broadcast by *Suspense* in 1948.[21] The story is told by Margaret, an imaginative young girl, who while on her way home one day takes a shortcut through Mr. Kelly's big lot where she encounters a mysterious voice. Mr. Kelly's lot is a kind of liminal space, a play zone full of possibility but also a dumping ground strewn with debris and waste. Margaret hears the voice of a woman in distress, screaming. Stunned, she stops to listen. The voice seems to come from beneath the ground. "Help me, help me!" cries the stifled voice.

Having borne witness to the primal scream of woman, Margaret runs home with her news, but is not taken seriously. "Listen, momma, there's a screaming woman in the lot!" cries Margaret (played by Margaret O'Brien). "She was screaming and screaming and screaming. Momma, listen to me! We've got to dig her out. She's buried under tons and tons of dirt." The hushing-up of the female voice is not a figurative turn in this late-1940s radio thriller but a literal fact that defines the story's terror. It is also a voice that will not go away, a voice that will, though smothered, not go unheard. Margaret overhears the muted sounds of Mrs. Nesbitt, which enthrall her, as if this strange voice were calling out to her alone. Because Margaret cannot locate its source—the entombed body—the voice of the screaming woman is for her an acoustic marvel, a cause of unexpected fascination, broadcasting her message through wood and dirt out of sheer desperation, a message that carries traces of its own censorship.[22]

The dilemma of the screaming woman reproduces the predicament of the female voice in radio, especially since Mrs. Nesbitt is constructed as what Michel Chion calls an "acousmêtre," a subject whose voice is heard but whose body is missing.[23] Helen Nesbitt has not been murdered but is buried alive by her husband. Her body is not so much absent as hidden, removed from the realm of inferred visibility by "junk and dirt and glass." To achieve this effect in broadcast, Helen Nesbitt—played by Agnes Moorehead—is not only distanced from the microphone but her voice is muffled artificially by sound-deadening materials. In an inversion of the proximity effect, Moorehead's screaming woman is literally hushed in the studio. If in the emerging codes of sound representation the construction of nearness conferred privilege on discernibly close sounds, sounds kept at a distance would be undervalued in the economy of narratorial signs. Distant radio voices rarely carry narrative agency. Mrs. Nesbitt is less a character than a discarded object lost in Mr. Kelly's scrap heap. What endows the play with such terror is the sound of that smothered scream, the Lazarus-like cry of someone who struggles to return from the dead. With so much emphasis on the stifled voice of Mrs. Nesbitt, the story seems mindful of how radio can deploy its codes to the disadvantage of speaking women. Helen Nesbitt's was a voice that emerged from radio's collective unconscious.

With the radio thriller, the horrifying cry represents the height of fear, and nothing is spared in order to reach the screaming point. That climax was vital to the genre, but not just as a sign of terror. What the scream embodies in radio or film, according to Chion, is an unthinkable moment that exists "outside of language, time, and the conscious subject." The "screaming point" is where "speech is suddenly extinct, a black hole, the exit of being."[24] The fact that Helen Nesbitt's missing body continues to radiate sound is far more unsettling than her murder could ever be, since a voice without a body, as Steven Connor reminds us, "suggests some prior act of mutilation." Associated with every ghostly voice is an often violently mutilated and "muted body," someone driven beyond the pale, past language.[25]

The scream took radio beyond the symbolic order of the word, signaling a disturbance in meaning. Antonin Artaud had already theorized the scream as radical expression in *The Theatre and Its Double* in 1938, in which he pressed the importance of replacing spoken language with gestures, cries, noise, and glossolalia.[26] The subordination of theater to speech, as Artaud saw it, was a grave misconception. Language—all representation, for that matter—betrays the "real voice of nature." In Artaud's "theater of cruelty," sonorization—rhythms, sounds, noises, resonances, twitterings, cries, onomatopoeia, and screams—played a crucial part in his attempt to reinvent theater. "I am adding another language to the spoken language, and I am trying to restore to the language of speech its old magic, its essential spellbinding power, for its mysterious possibilities have been forgotten."[27] The tradition of logocentrism found no greater foe than Artaud, who wished to liberate sound from the tyranny of speech—to speak without passing through words. For Artaud, theater became a contest between speech and noise, all in an attempt, as Mark Weiss notes, "to express the inexpressible, profound, chaotic essence of human existence."[28] As Artaud saw it, he spoke not for the avant-garde but for the dispossessed: "Let me be heard by coprophiliacs, aphasics, and in general by all those discredited in words and speech, the Pariahs of thought."[29]

The female voice was radio's outsider. It was a voice no one wished to hear. Margaret's fascination with the screaming woman is tied to their shared predicament, for no one listens to Margaret either. It takes one silenced female to hear another. Listening, in fact, is a derelict practice in this story. Mr. Kelly, who owns the empty lot, wonders why Margaret and her friend Dippy are digging around his property. Margaret repeats her mantra—"Mr. Kelly, there's a Screaming Woman." "I'm not interested," Mr. Kelly replies. But listen, Margaret insists. "Don't hear anything," he says dismissively. Margaret's parents are hardly more responsive. "Listen, momma, there's a screaming woman in the lot!" "I'm sure," Margaret's mother says complacently, "she can wait till after dinner." Margaret then appeals to her father—"Daddy, there's a screaming woman in the lot!"—but he too is flippant. "Well, I never knew a woman who didn't," he replies. Margaret's parents are no more interested than Mr. Kelly. Margaret, on the other hand, is in a state of emergency (she is trembling, her father observes), having been awakened by (or to) something she doesn't understand. Margaret's desperation mirrors that of the screaming woman—her narrative is hysterical—as though by listening to the strange woman's suffering she has been affected by it, has joined in. The parents, however, read their daughter's story as a tall tale, dismissing it as the work of an excitable child with an overactive imagination. They refuse to listen. Like Echo, Margaret is doomed to repetition.

We never learn why her husband has attempted to do away with Mrs. Nesbitt—there had been a quarrel (perhaps she over-spoke)—but we can imagine that this cry had meaning for listeners that went beyond the details of the buried woman's plight. Her scream could hardly not have reminded listeners of the sirens, shrieking bombs, squealing, and wailing of dying men and women of war reporting. MacLeish had concluded his 1937 radio play *Air Raid* by turning a singing woman (practicing scales) into a screaming woman, whose voice is drowned out by sirens and howling planes, and eleven years later *Suspense* reprises that scream in a postwar setting.[30]

Sorry, Wrong Number

Neither MacLeish's nor Bradbury's distressed women, however, captivated the American public as hauntingly as did Agnes Moorehead in Lucille Fletcher's *Sorry, Wrong Number*, the single most popular episode of *Suspense*.[31] Moorehead played an "invalid" (Mrs. Elbert Stevenson) who overhears a conversation on the phone between two men devising a

Agnes Moorehead at the CBS microphone in one of eight live broadcasts of Lucille Fletcher's *Sorry, Wrong Number* performed from 1943 to 1950. (Courtesy of Photofest)

murder. An inadvertent eavesdropper, Moorehead's character tries desperately to alert authorities to the impending crime: "I could hear them but they couldn't hear me," she tells the police. Growing more hysterical with every moment (the murder is to take place in thirty minutes), Mrs. Stevenson finds herself in the midst of a nightmare from which she cannot wake. That she is the intended victim of the murder only dawns on her in the closing minutes of the play, in a wicked plot twist that turns this female speaking subject into another helpless screaming woman.

The vocalized distress of Moorehead's Mrs. Stevenson apparently struck a chord. The play was in such demand that it was subsequently restaged seven times, each live broadcast performed by Moorehead, before being adapted for film by Paramount (a division of CBS) in 1948, with a screenplay by Fletcher and starring Barbara Stanwyck and Burt Lancaster. Two years later, the movie version returned to the wireless, with Stanwyck and Lancaster reprising their roles for a *Lux Radio Theatre* broadcast of the play. Rounding out the text's cross-media migrations, in 1954, NBC-TV broadcast a television version starring Shelley Winters. In recent years, the play has made its way onto the Internet via old-time radio websites and YouTube videos. It has been running almost continuously ever since its debut broadcast in 1943 and has been translated into fifteen languages, including Zulu; and two operas have been based on its story. Within ten years, *Sorry, Wrong Number* had infiltrated every available mode of representation, moving rapidly through the technological newness of radio, cinema, and TV.[32] Mrs. Stevenson fascinated the public; her agony transfixed listeners like an acoustic spell.

A clerk-typist for CBS radio in New York City, Lucille Fletcher prepared the manuscripts of other playwrights and soon realized that she could probably do better. Her first story was about a man who drove across the country while being stalked by the same hitchhiker everywhere. Fletcher's husband, the composer Bernard Hermann, showed the script to Orson Welles, whose *Mercury Theatre on the Air* produced the story in 1941 for *Campbell Playhouse*, featuring Welles himself as the lead character (Ron Adams). Welles later pitched the story to CBS's other popular show, *Suspense*, which aired *The Hitch-Hiker* in 1942, the year the thriller series debuted. The success of *The Hitch-Hiker* raised Fletcher's status at CBS from clerk-typist to scriptwriter. She didn't waste any time. Her next radio play, *Sorry, Wrong Number*, premiered in 1943 on *Suspense* and quickly became one of the most legendary radio plays of all time, second perhaps only to *The War of the Worlds*.

Sorry, Wrong Number concerns a bedridden neurotic who overhears two men plotting a murder. After making several calls to various parties, including the police, Mrs. Stevenson discovers that she herself is the unnamed victim. In between, she struggles desperately to communicate her warning to authorities. No one takes her seriously, however. Even the telephone operators remain unhelpful and indifferent. Marooned in her bedroom, Mrs. Stevenson attempts a kind of remote control over her narrowly confined world by telephone. Although Mrs. Stevenson reaches out

The Screaming Woman 113

to others, the unfriendly phone system refuses to provide her with a dialogic partner. She is trapped in a monologic system that not only isolates her but persecutes her for speaking.

The details of the story are interesting for several reasons but in particular for the way they call attention to the perversity of telephony. Mrs. Stevenson, who cannot reach her husband by phone, asks the operator to redial his office. "I don't see how [my husband's phone] could be busy all this time. . . . He's working late tonight, and I'm all alone here in the house. My health is very poor—and I've been feeling so nervous all day"—she says, providing the operator with more information than necessary.[33] A stranger appears on the other end of the line and can be heard speaking to another man in a conspiratorial tone. The two men are arranging the murder of an unnamed woman. "At 11:15," explains one man to the other (the murderer), "a subway train crosses the bridge. It makes a noise in case her window is open, and she should scream." Mrs. Stevenson tries to interrupt *but can't be heard*. The call is cut off just as the man is about to note the address. Alarmed, Mrs. Stevenson phones the operator back and demands to be reconnected with the mystery speaker, which of course is impossible since the overheard call was a glitch in the system. The wires literally got crossed. Mrs. Stevenson next tries the police. "I'm calling to report a murder," she says, "although the murder hasn't been committed yet. I just heard plans over the telephone." Telephones are "funny things," the officer says, noting there is not much the police can do, unless Mrs. Stevenson believes that someone may be planning to murder her. Of course not, she says. "I mean, why should anybody? My husband Elbert—he's crazy about me—adores me—waits on me hand and foot—he's scarcely left my side since I took sick twelve years ago," says Mrs. Stevenson, again revealing more about herself than necessary.

The police have better things to do, it seems, than listen to the whining of a neurotic lady. Mrs. Stevenson slams the phone down, frustrated by the officer's indifference, and begins talking to herself, "whimpering with self-pity," as the script explains. "Oh, why doesn't Elbert come home? Why doesn't he?" The phone then rings, but no one is on the line. Troubled and annoyed, she dials the operator and begins to rant: "Operator, I don't know what's the matter with this telephone tonight, but it's positively driving me crazy. I've never seen such inefficient, miserable service. Now, look. I'm an invalid, and I'm very nervous, and I'm not supposed to be annoyed. But if this keeps on much longer. . . . The whole world could be murdered, for all you people care. And now—my phone keeps ringing."

The claustrophobic world of Mrs. Stevenson seems only to grow smaller. The phone rings again. Frazzled, she lifts the receiver, screaming into the handset: "Hello. HELLO. Stop ringing, do you hear me? Answer me? What do you want? Do you realize you're driving me crazy?" This time it is a messenger from Western Union who delivers news of her husband Elbert's business trip to Boston. He won't be returning until tomorrow. Elbert has left his wife all alone, and on such a night. The terrifying implications push Mrs. Stevenson over the edge. *Breathlessly, aghast, to herself*, as the script instructs, Mrs. Stevenson begins to connect the dots. "No—No—it isn't true! He couldn't do it! Not when he knows I'll be all alone. It's some trick—some fiendish . . . ." As we hear the sound of the train roaring by outside across the bridge, Mrs. Stevenson realizes the terrifying irony of her predicament. The unthinkable is true. Growing increasingly hysterical, she picks up the receiver ("with trembling fingers," notes the script) and phones the hospital, pleading for help. She demands that a trained nurse be sent to her apartment immediately. "I'm a sick woman. I—I'm very upset. Very. I'm alone in this house—and I'm an invalid—and tonight I overheard a telephone conversation that upset me dreadfully. About a murder—a poor woman who was going to be murdered at eleven-fifteen tonight—in fact, if someone doesn't come at once—I'm afraid I'll go out of my mind." With that, Mrs. Stevenson hears a click on her line, the sound of the extension phone downstairs being lifted off the hook. Someone else is in the apartment. Mrs. Stevenson immediately hangs up, frozen in terror, listening, mirroring the posture of her radio audience. In a suffocated voice she says, "I won't pick it up. I won't let them hear me. I'll be quiet—and they'll think . . . ." The operator rings the police station, but it is too late. We hear a train pass by outside Mrs. Stevenson's window, drowning out her scream for help and the sounds of struggle with her killer. With the police on the other line, the play ends as the murderer picks up the receiver and answers Officer Duffy, "Sorry, wrong number."

Agnes Moorehead was widely praised for her performance in the story. The press admired the actress's ability to give voice to the "high-strung" personality of a woman who seemed at every moment to strain the limits of socially acceptable female behavior. Mrs. Stevenson is not only neurotic and paranoid but also irritable, sarcastic, ill-natured, and mean. ("I will try to check it for you, madam," replies the operator to Mrs. Stevenson's request to trace a phone call—to which she responds irritably: "Check it! Check it! That's all anybody can do. Of all the stupid, idiotic . . . !" She barks, slamming the receiver down.) She is an acoustic spectacle, an eruption of female hysteria, and Moorehead's ability to capture the unacceptable side of the female speaking subject seized the imaginations of listeners everywhere and spurred many to phone CBS requesting additional performances of the radio play.

Discursive Deviancy

What was it about Moorehead's voice that aroused such fascination? The suggestion that a woman cannot be safe even in her own home was certainly relevant and compelling; however, as Allison McCracken suggests, Mrs. Stevenson might be the victim of the story but she was also its "monster."[34] Moorehead, described by *Time* magazine as one of "Hollywood's best movie bitches," had turned the voice of Mrs. Stevenson into an abomination by representing the excessive female subjectivity of, in Lucille Fletcher's words, a "querulous, self-centered neurotic."[35] Mrs. Stevenson's character, thanks to Moorehead's voicing, is given an excess of subjectivity that is startling in the context of normative gender roles pervasive on the radio (especially in soaps). Together, Lucille Fletcher and Agnes Moorehead test the very limits of deviant female subjectivity with their hyperbolizing of Mrs. Stevenson as the madwoman in the attic, creating in the guise of a thirty-minute radio play the anatomy of a screaming woman.

Agnes Moorehead made a career of depicting, as Patricia White writes, "female difference."[36] While she was one of the most in-demand voice actresses throughout the 1930s and 1940s, portraying, for example, Margo Lane in *The Shadow* and Eleanor Roosevelt in *The March of Time*, Moorehead had a knack, as White notes, for a "deviant version of femininity": shrews, busybodies, hypochondriacs, nags, crones, and spinsters, not to mention witches, were her repertoire.[37] *Sorry, Wrong Number* was written specifically for Moorehead because Fletcher wanted an ornery voice for Mrs. Stevenson. Moorehead delivered. As the contemporary press noted with admiration, Moorehead's Mrs. Stevenson was an especially "vitriolic," "frustrated," and "bitter" woman.

That Mrs. Stevenson was an angry, unhappy married woman who refused to swallow her frustration might indicate what was both so compelling and, at the same time, so repugnant about her character for a national audience. Not only does she violate the convention of "The Good Wife" as someone who should speak in a low, soft, soothing, and pleasant voice, but Mrs. Stevenson also complicates the position of listeners by implicating them in her own predicament. As *Suspense*'s narrator explains during the program's introduction, *Sorry, Wrong Number* is a story of a woman who "overheard a conversation with death." Mrs. Stevenson herself, in other words, is a listener. She is engrossed by a mystery, a murder plot, much the same way the radio audience is tuned in to CBS's thriller. Mrs. Stevenson's "suspense" is ours in every respect.

This shared position, however, does not make the listener any more sympathetic to Moorehead's invalid. Fletcher's own remarks about Mrs. Stevenson, whom she calls a "lonely" and "neurotic" woman whose helplessness reveals the "empty thing" that her life has become, show surprisingly little compassion for her protagonist.[38] Mrs. Stevenson's world is no bigger than her bed, and her cries for sympathy ("I'm very nervous. I need soothing") are pathetic but not pitiful. If anything, our proximity to the victim makes us uncomfortably intimate with Mrs. Stevenson and her transgressive voice, and this probably compounds the audience's aversion to her. The not-so-secret wish of the listener in *Sorry, Wrong Number* is for the protagonist's demise and for that voice to be silenced. Mrs. Stevenson realizes this far too late: "I won't let them hear me. I'll be quiet—and they'll think . . . ." By then it's too late. The intruder is only footsteps away.

Chion's "screaming point" does not occur until the end of the play, but we have been waiting eagerly for it, for the cessation of the speaking woman's voice. The play triggers an unsettling ambivalence. We are vexed by the voice of Mrs. Stevenson but also can't help but recognize the misery she suffers at the hands of bad technology. Midway through the play, Mrs. Stevenson receives two mysterious phone calls. She picks up the receiver, eagerly expecting her husband, but hears no voice on the other end. "Hello. Hello. For heaven's sake, what's the matter with this phone?" She dials into the system, demanding clarification. "Hello. Operator. I don't know what's the matter with this telephone tonight, but it's positively driving me crazy. I've never seen such inefficient, miserable service. . . . My phone is ringing. Ringing, ringing, ringing every five seconds or so, and when I pick it up, there's no one there."

Mrs. Stevenson tries with increasing desperation to navigate a recalcitrant, if not errant, communications network, but rather than linking her with outside help, the system only aggravates her isolation and helplessness. It is a perverse technology that seems, in fact, strangely out to get her. The phone system is opaque and unresponsive, unable to provide the contact necessary to communicate her warning. "The system is automatic, madam," says the Operator. "If someone is trying to dial your number, there is no way to check whether the call is coming through the system or not." The tonality of Mrs. Stevenson's reply—"Well, of all the stupid, idiotic . . . ! (*she hangs up*)"—may be incorrect, yet the sense rings true. While the police admit that "telephones are funny things," they dismiss Mrs. Stevenson's call for help (with the listener's blessings). She nevertheless continues to pester the police with remarkable persistence. "We'll take care of it, lady," the policeman says, which is of course a lie. Mrs. Stevenson calls his bluff: "Will you broadcast it all over the city? And send out squads? And warn your radio cars to watch out—especially in suspicious neighborhoods like mine?"

Moorehead's voice might be annoying and shrill, but no one listens to her. In anticipating her doom, the listener is complicit with the phone network that persecutes Mrs. Stevenson and even seems to conspire in her murder. The killers can't hear her, and the phone operator and police ignore her. Her husband, by proxy, will apparently silence her. The audience, however, hears every word. Mrs. Stevenson is up against an information system that will not acknowledge her voice, as if she spoke the wrong language (which, of course, she does). Her distress is not only a result of patriarchy but also of telephony's refusal to admit her into its mediatory network.[39] This is not what Ma Bell ("The Voice with a Smile") promised. Period ads pitched the phone operator as "alert" and "courteous." "They're nice people to do business with," pledged a 1939 ad for Bell Telephone System. The phone operator with a "smiling voice" was an invitation to talk, someone expected to "exercise a soothing and calming effect" on callers, a woman on hand to help reduce the isolation of other women.[40] So much false advertising, as far as Mrs. Stevenson is concerned ("I haven't had one bit of satisfaction out of one phone call this evening," she fumes). When she asks the operator, "Why are you so stupid?" we cringe at her ill temper. But what she says is absolutely true. The system is deaf and dumb—or worse. Like Artaud, Mrs. Stevenson believes that she is a woman whose "spirit has greatly suffered, and by virtue of this I have the right to speak."[41]

Rarely do killers on the radio get away with murder, but Mrs. Stevenson's murderer goes scot-free. Although we do not know this exactly, we suspect that Elbert, Mrs. Stevenson's husband, has arranged the murder of his wife. Ironically, Elbert is absent from the story, never once appearing. To the extent that he stays "hidden in the system," as David Crane notes, Elbert's crime becomes more nefarious in proportion to his absence from the scene.[42] Elbert is a phantom villain, a villain who asserts his presence with neither body nor voice.

By grounding the story in a succession of telephone exchanges experienced by an isolated woman confined to her bedroom, Fletcher created a narrative that seems ideally suited to the uniqueness of radio drama. In a *Life* magazine review of the broadcast, *Sorry, Wrong Number* was called "radio's perfect script."[43] Fletcher herself had said that she "wanted to write something which by its very nature should, for maximum effectiveness, be heard rather than seen," a play that could only be performed on the air. In fact, it was originally designed, she wrote, "as an experiment in sound and not just as a murder story." The telephone was to be the "chief protagonist." And then along came Agnes Moorehead. "In the hands of a fine actress like Agnes Moorehead," Fletcher said, "the script turned out to be more the character study of a woman than a technical experiment, and the plot itself, with its O. Henry twist at the end, fell into the thriller category."[44]

It is impossible not to notice the workings of gender on voice, at a time when nearly all America was listening to Edward R. Murrow, who, thanks to the illusion of proximity, seemed to be right there in the living room, an intimate friend. Murrow was everything the abject Mrs. Stevenson is not. No one will listen to her, and the phone system refuses to grant her any narratorial weight. Unlike Murrow, who invented his own enunciative style, Mrs. Stevenson is reduced by telephony's indifference to a state of hysterical expression. The more desperate she is, the more fragmentary her discourse becomes, until, as with many of radio's screaming women, her speech is downgraded to nonsemantic sounds, the refuge of the abject. As the murderer approaches her bed, Mrs. Stevenson becomes "incoherent" with fear and begins to scream, but even this vocalization, which is erased by the "roar" of a passing train, will be lost to meaning. Mrs. Stevenson's "final say" is the "thump" of her lifeless body.

In his classic essay on music, Roland Barthes describes the "grain" of the voice as a form of bodily expression that evades the laws and limits of linguistic exchange. The grain is "the materiality of the body speaking its mother tongue . . . and forms a signifying play having nothing to do with communication, representation, expression."[45] Like gesture, which Barthes defines as the surplus of action, the grain of the voice is an excess that surpasses the message. In the case of Agnes Moorehead's portrayal of Mrs. Stevenson, the "grain" of her voice produces a surplus of uncoded meaning that evokes the imaginary, radicalizing the notion of woman as speaking subject. We hear what we should not hear, that which exceeds hearing, female abjection. While she has the power to speak, she does so not from a position of discursive mastery but from a problematic interiority. What is good for radio is bad for telephony.

The "grain" of Mrs. Stevenson's voice is so conspicuous that her speech becomes equated, in Silverman's words, with an "intractable materiality"—a corporeal presence that is cut off from meaning.[46] It does not help that Mrs. Stevenson repeatedly identifies herself as an "invalid," reminding listeners of a body that, in an acousmatic medium, presumably does not exist. Hers is what Connor calls the "vocalic body."[47] Mrs. Stevenson's vocalic body, as performed by Agnes Moorehead, generates an acoustic spectacle that disturbs the genre—the victim is not supposed to be the "bad guy" nor is the killer supposed to get away with murder—by exceeding the codes set in place to contain it. The real danger on radio is not the arrival of a nameless killer but the voice that, as Mladen Dolar writes, drifts free of the word and becomes "the voice beyond the logos."[48] The screaming woman is such a voice, a voice that exists outside signifying structures and has the capacity to disturb the apparently natural relations between language and meaning. Silencing the monstrosity that is Mrs. Stevenson requires unusual steps. Moorehead unlocked the terrific power of radio in the guise of aural deviance: the hysteria of the screaming woman. The silencing of Mrs. Stevenson is not so much a murder as it is a *devocalization*.

Mrs. Stevenson Goes to Hollywood

We may think of radio as older than film, but it is actually the younger technology. With its sudden and unexpected growth in the 1930s, radio made quite an impression on an already-established Hollywood. For some in the film business, the new medium was a competitor, threatening to capture cinema's moviegoing audiences. Newspapers and large theater owners in particular saw the popularity of radio as an imminent danger to their bottom lines. But others in Hollywood viewed radio as an opportunity to promote their industry. Opportunists like David Sarnoff, president of RCA, which owned both the NBC radio networks and RKO Pictures, and Adolph Zukor of Paramount Pictures, which owned a major stake in CBS radio, deliberately sought ways to build strong ties between radio and film.[49] Like a Steve Jobs or Eric Schmidt of their day, Sarnoff and Zukor had ambitions to create giant entertainment networks around the reciprocity of film and broadcasting.

The immediate effect of this was Hollywood's direct interest in radio programming. A case in point was the long-running *Lux Radio Theatre*, sponsored by Lever Soap. In the mid-1930s and 1940s, *Lux Radio Theatre* was the most popular anthology series on the air and remained so for almost twenty years, functioning as an effective interface between the cultures of cinema and radio and strengthening the economic and production interests of both. Broadcast from the West Coast, the show featured adaptations of popular films, along with their star-studded casts, and was hosted by Cecil B. De Mille ("Greetings from Hollywood, ladies and gentlemen"). The show's great popularity (an estimated 40 million listeners tuned in to *Lux* each week) relied on the glamour of its actors and featured as many of the big-name stars who appeared in the original films as possible. Most of the radio adaptations were broadcast soon after the film's first run, which helped to boost box office numbers.[50]

The film-radio connection, however, was a two-way street. Radio borrowed content and stars from Hollywood's studio system, but Hollywood borrowed from radio, too. Broadcast stars like Bing Crosby, George Burns, Gracie Allen, Agnes Moorehead, and Kate Smith were lured onto Hollywood sets, and in 1940 RKO signed Orson Welles (fresh off his *War of the Worlds* broadcast) to a two-picture deal. The most interesting transaction between cinema and radio during this period was the 1948 film adaptation of Fletcher's *Sorry, Wrong Number*, directed by Anatole Litvak and starring Barbara Stanwyck and Burt Lancaster.

By the time the film *Sorry, Wrong Number* was released by Paramount, the murder of Mrs. Stevenson was widely known from its repeated performances on the air. For Paramount, this was the point. It was *the* radio broadcast of the 1940s, and Paramount's marketing team said so without much restraint. Advertisements for the film stressed the popularity of the original radio play, described as "the prize-winning radio suspense drama that thrilled 40,000,000 people" and "the most famous radio drama of all time."

Like her counterpart in radio, Barbara Stanwyck's Leona Stevenson in the film is confined to her bed and telephone. But this Mrs. Stevenson is not invisible. She is, every bit, part of the extravagance that is her luxury apartment. Leona first appears to the viewer in a medium shot, sitting up in bed, clutching a large white phone receiver close to her head. It is evening. The clock on her bedside table reads 9:24. Stanwyck's Leona wears a nightgown that repeats the pattern of embroidery on the upholstered headboard and drapery, as if one with the interior design of the uptown penthouse room. On the phone, Leona complains to the operator that she cannot get through to her husband, that his line is invariably busy. Leona is portrayed as an imperious shrew, badgering the operator as though the busy signal were her fault. Bejeweled and in her nightgown, surrounded by lavish objects in her plush New York City apartment, Leona is a woman with a broad sense of entitlement, a character targeted for our loathing.

But why so tense? She has not yet overheard the murder plot. Stanwyck's body language betrays her distress, as if the surrounding luxury were a trap. She is bunched up in a king-size bed, clutching the phone while lighting up a cigarette in a spectacle of orality. The camera zooms in, scrutinizing the face of the famous actress, as if to take a closer look at her features. Leona is defined by the camera as a stationary subject who compensates for her immobility by overusing her mouth. A radio, a clock, the telephone, and an open cigarette case stand beside her on the night table, the radio a reminder of that other medium and source text. For a brief moment, the film will pay homage to the famous *Suspense* radio performance that paved the way for the movie: the woman, the bed, the phone, and the radio.

Stanwyck's Leona calls the operator in order to trace the "wrong number," but the operator, of course, is not omniscient and couldn't possibly locate a phone call that has ended. Leona does not take no for an answer and turns surly. "Oh, for heaven's sake! All of this idiotic red tape. You just sit there and let people die!" she says in the first of many bursts of exasperation. When she is rerouted to the "chief operator," the camera (as if to avoid Leona's retelling) begins snooping around the apartment. In a lengthy tracking shot, the camera pans away from the bed and slips down the spiral staircase, prowling around the chiaroscuro of the first floor and then fixing significantly on the downstairs phone switch. There is something conspiratorial about its slow, deliberate tracking as it surveys the apartment, as if it were collaborating in the planning of a crime. Though Leona is off camera during the tracking shot, her disembodied voice remains central to the sequence. The sound of Leona is not diminished even though we have moved some distance from its source. For a while, Leona's telephone voice becomes a radio voice that fills the entire apartment. The problem for Leona is that the film-noirish camera is plotting against her.

Every time the increasingly desperate Leona reaches for a cigarette, we see the radio on the nearby table. At one point, she turns it on and we hear loud classical music, which, swelling melodramatically, seems to comment (though not very subtly) on Leona's rising anxiety as she staggers across her bedroom, clutching her heart. The sound produced by the radio, momentarily serving as nondiegetic music track for the narrative, is reduced to an overwrought simulacra of the "real" film score. Radio, it is suggested, is no match for film.

While true to the gist of the radio play, the film adaptation of *Sorry, Wrong Number* departs from the original radio broadcast significantly. As in the radio play, Leona lives prosthetically through telephony. It is her link to the outside world. Leona's telephone calling, however, is responsible for narrativizing many events in the story. In the film, Leona is not merely a screaming woman—a spectacle of female hysteria—she is also the story's primary narrator, responsible, like Dr. Seward in *Mercury Theatre*'s *Dracula*, for organizing the story by linking her to other narrative voices.[51] Radio's Mrs. Stevenson may be thwarted repeatedly in her effort to obtain agency, but film's Leona is given directorial authority over the story. Each filmic event is triggered by her phone call, as if telephony were a remote technology. Leona's controlling voice, however, is at issue in the film and becomes increasingly problematic, as various forces and figures converge to deny her enunciative power.

Telephony is inseparable not only from narration but from death, as the film's prologue warns. Following the opening credits, onscreen text appears over a wide shot of a large switchboard and telephone operators, scrolling slowly upward as dramatic background music builds to a climax: "In the tangled networks of a great city, the telephone is the unseen link between a million lives. . . . It is the servant of our common needs—the confidante of our inmost secrets. . . . Life and happiness wait upon its ring . . . and horror . . . and loneliness . . . and *death!!!*" A kind of epigraph, the printed text casts a disturbing shadow over the film before it even begins. In this version of *Sorry, Wrong Number*, the phone system is not a harmless grid but a "tangled network" already placed under suspicion.

With its multiple flashbacks and numerous voices, *Sorry, Wrong Number* as a film is a "tangled network" itself, which reveals by degrees the conditions that have driven Henry Stevenson to arrange Leona's murder. The motives behind Mrs. Stevenson's murder in the radio play are left to the listener's imagination. Her husband, in fact, has no presence in the original play. He is significantly in absentia. The film, however, goes out of its way to provide an unequivocal rationale for Henry's crime. Henry (Burt Lancaster) is given a backstory and a point of view. By the end of the film, we know more about Henry than we really care to.

In contrast with the radio play, in which the telephone conveys Agnes Moorehead's deviant aurality but little else, the film uses the telephone to transmit narrative information. Leona calls Henry's secretary, Elizabeth Jennings, inquiring about her husband's whereabouts. Jennings has no idea, but—eager to let the cat out of the bag—she informs Leona that a woman (Sally Lord) met with her husband at the office during the afternoon. Jennings's narration switches to voice-over with the flashback of Sally Lord's arrival at Henry's office and their subsequent lunch together. Every phone call introduces a spoken narration that triggers at least one flashback. The effect of these returns to prior events is to privilege seeing over hearing. The acousmatic voice-over (a reminder of radio) is gradually absorbed by the image, clarifying what the eye sees. The point of the film adaptation of *Sorry, Wrong Number* is to reassert the authority of seeing over hearing.[52] The movie will put upstart radio in its place by silencing its voice.[53]

Stanwyck's Leona is essentially trapped at the intersection of three media systems: radio, telephony, and film. While her relationship to the phone is radiophonic—she uses her phone receiver as a microphone to broadcast her voice to others, her sole means of control—the logic of the film is to turn Leona's narrative stance, as Silverman writes, into a "condition of verbal and aural incompetence."[54] Stanwyck's Leona may acquire a discursive authority Agnes Moorehead's Mrs. Stevenson can only dream of, but that mastery soon becomes a trap. Once she learns that the man she has manipulated so effectively—Henry—is plotting against her, she plunges into panic mode. What Leona realizes with unnerving clarity, as Amy Lawrence points out, is how much hostility is coming her way, not only Henry's but the world's.[55]

Leona's influence over her husband is confident, aggressive, and patronizing. Her domination is conveyed most obviously by her vocalized control. When she recites her wedding vows—"I Leona take thee, Henry"—we know that she has taken ruthless possession of Henry. It is that voice that keeps Henry in his place. The tables are turned on Leona, however, when Henry plots against her authority. Leona is given a heart problem that plays prominently in her husband's scheme to murder her. Heart failure would solve many of his money problems. In debt to his criminal associates, Henry hopes to raise money by collecting the life insurance on Leona, but when he learns that nothing is really wrong with her—Leona is what medical experts call a "cardiac neurotic," the doctor tells Henry—he is forced to take desperate measures. Once Leona learns of Henry's treachery, she realizes to what extent she has been deluded. The foolhardy Henry is not the man she thought he was, the easily manipulated and loving husband. He has been ruthless, defrauding her father's company and plotting murder against her. Shocked by this reversal, Leona loses her most imposing skill, her controlling voice and the ability to command others. Overcome by dread, Leona reels from highborn poise to uncontrolled panic.

In the film's murder sequence, we watch in suspense as the hired killer moves stealthily through the house toward Leona's bedroom. On the phone to the operator, Leona hears the click of the receiver on the other extension, and realizes an intruder is in her apartment. She clasps her hand over her mouth and hangs up, holding back further speech. She stifles herself. The woman with the masterful voice no longer speaks. In her dying struggle, Leona pulls the cover from the night table, sending the radio tumbling to the floor. With the collapse of Leona, radio too takes a fall. Two agents of auditory mastery are momentarily silenced—the drama's protagonist and the very technology that made her possible.

If the demise of Mrs. Stevenson in the radio play was left unclear, Leona's death is easily "read" and disposed of within the codes of film noir. Rather than violating feminine social codes, Leona restores them, heals the wounds provoked by the deviant aurality of Agnes Moorehead's voice. Stanwyck's Leona is just as unsympathetic as Moorehead's Mrs. Stevenson, but she is unlikable for different reasons. Aggressive, domineering, pushy, Stanwyck's Leona is a "nasty dame," as a *New York Times* reviewer complained.[56] She is a nag and (worse) a bossy woman. Henry's resentment at being emasculated by his wife is not only understandable in the viewer's eyes but appropriate, which puts Henry Stevenson in a more sympathetic light than he certainly deserves. In the radio play, Elbert's motives remain a mystery. We know nothing about him. His presence or absence does not factor into our complicated relationship with Moorehead's Mrs. Stevenson. In the film, though, the husband acquires a backstory (he's working-class, with a chip on his shoulder); his father was a heavy drinker; he dropped out of high school to make a living; and he is not very enterprising. Leona has little difficulty pulling Henry's strings, turning this hunk into a trophy husband. She is on the hunt and she bags her game. He might be handsome, but he is a pushover. He is made a vice president of her father's drug company but is mostly miserable, largely because he is not taken seriously. "I'm supposed to follow you around like a pet dog tied to a chain. I'm supposed to like whatever crumbs you throw me," Henry complains to Leona. "You've got me sewed up sixteen different ways for three meals a day and pocket money." In the film, Leona's masculinity is transgressive. Her crime is in turning her husband into a woman, emasculating Henry before our eyes. She is the femme fatale of film noir, a man killer, a "nasty dame."

Well before Stanwyck's Leona is murdered, she is silenced by cinema, her voice absorbed into the narrative logic of the film. The movie is preoccupied with assigning identifiable causes for transgressive actions, Leona's and Henry's. We are meant to view their objectionable acts as a function of class. Leona is a type, the rich bitch, a bossy and spoiled hypochondriac who has been overindulged by a doting father. As she tells Sally Lord, Henry's old flame, "I usually get what I want." Henry is a kept man, a husband whose masculinity has been damaged and who is now reckless and dangerous. "What do I do but keep running back and forth between that rotten office and stuffy house of yours. What do I have, nothing. Nothing of my own. Not even the studs on my shirt or the matches in my pocket." Leona's hysteria is thus less an effect of social malaise (as it is for Moorehead's Mrs. Stevenson in the radio play) than loss of control, but her subsequent frenzy is displaced by the various analeptic turns of the film's visual structure, and with each narrative twist we encounter a disambiguation (she is a "cardiac neurotic") that locates her transgression in the familiar codes of cinema, in film noir. The result is a kind of "aesthetic mainstreaming" of a radical source text that put the voice of a woman front and center.[57]

Screaming Women / Silenced Women

The screaming woman was a recurrent figure in 1940s thriller broadcasts, nearly as indispensable to radio as chiaroscuro was to film noir. She lingered on the air with haunting distress. Her scream, echoing the *Mercury Theatre*'s Martian hum, seemed to originate from elsewhere. Like the wartime sound of Murrow's siren, the screaming woman did not have a simple reference point. Hers was a voice outside the symbolic order of language, whose meaning was a disturbance. *Sorry, Wrong Number* may have been a fiction, but it revealed the gender dynamics at the heart of modernist radio and pointed to the threat of the female voice. Network radio might keep this disorder in check by regulating the broadcast voice, but it could not eliminate it entirely. Prestige programming, which continually explored radio's narrative modes, could not resist the screaming woman.

It was drawn to her distress and the value such disturbance had for modernist storytelling. Ironically, it was cinema that tried to deactivate radio's screaming woman, using its visual codes to master the radiophonic voice.

Anatole Litvak's film is surprisingly self-conscious of its own status as an adaptation. It is particularly aware of itself as one kind of medium (cinema) stealing its thunder from a rival, understanding full well that the status of the original play as a work of radio (without which the movie would not exist) was a significant part of the publicity that surrounded the film. We might even say that the film betrays an unmistakable anxiety of influence, as if it were haunted by other media. The film is, after all, phonophobic and does what it can to erase the audio track it inherited (and profited by), devocalizing the voice that "transfixed" an entire nation. Being overlooked for the lead role in the movie adaptation of *Sorry, Wrong Number* probably did not please Agnes Moorehead. It is said, though, that Barbara Stanwyck repeatedly listened to recordings of the original radio play to get, as she put it, "in the mood" while on the set—to work herself up into a frenzy. Ironically enough, Stanwyck gave herself off camera to what the film could not permit on camera: that voice.

In the economy of radio—there is only so much space for enunciation—someone would have to pay a price for Murrow's discursive power. Betty Wason was one reporter who apparently did. While her expulsion from the airwaves was a small incident, it reflected a much larger concern for network radio, the problem of the speaking woman. As Fletcher's career revealed, a woman might gain access to enunciative space on the air, but radio would remain unsympathetic to female voices, at least for the time being. The volume of the screaming woman's cry was a reliable measure of that antagonism.

The Museum of Jurassic Radio
Sonic Excess in Dylan Thomas and Samuel Beckett

In the Museum of Jurassic Radio, the Shadow stands out as an adventure hero noteworthy for his psychic powers and demented chuckle. His exhibit is around the corner from the 1936 twenty-five-tube Zenith Stratosphere. Just to the right of the crime-fighting star is perched the monocled Charlie McCarthy, the legendary wooden dummy no one actually saw but to whom everyone listened on Sunday evenings at eight. Charlie's top hat sits beside him, along with a playbill from the Rainbow Room. Further down the hall, Marvin the paranoid robot ("I think you ought to know I'm feeling very depressed") is seated on a stainless-steel chair, alongside the Betelgeusian Zaphod Beeblebrox—both from *The Hitchhiker's Guide to the Galaxy*. Just to the left (in room 237) is the creepy raconteur from the BBC's *Appointment with Fear* (1943–55), the Man in Black, who somehow—thanks to the magic of radio—appeared at the same instant on CBS's *Suspense* in New York.[1] Though invisible on air, these dramatis personae play a substantial role in our memory of radio's literary past. They are joined by other memorable characters, from Peter Lorre's Marvelous Barastro to Agnes Moorehead's Screaming Woman. The Museum of Jurassic Radio, however, would be woefully incomplete without two additional transatlantic exhibits: one reserved for Blind Captain Cat, dreaming of long-ago sea voyages, along with the promiscuous Polly Garter, town washerwoman and the subject of much gossip; and the other set aside for the voluble Maddy Rooney and her ill-tempered husband, Dan—all of whom were introduced to listeners by the BBC's Third Programme in mid-century broadcasts by two of modernism's most distinctively voiced authors.

An Aurality of Its Own: *Under Milk Wood*

The entire cast of *Under Milk Wood*, as a matter of fact, merits a spot in our imaginary museum. As originally conceived, *Under Milk Wood* was to be about the certifiably deranged townsfolk of a small Welsh village who are

Dylan Thomas in 1953, one year before the BBC broadcast of *Under Milk Wood*. (Courtesy of Photofest)

on trial for being mad. The original title of Dylan Thomas's play, "The Town That Was Mad," did not last long, nor did its premise. The "barmy" tale, which was set in the small fishing village of Laugharne under "the starless, bible-black sky," follows the comings and goings of the town's sixty inhabitants over the course of a day, from dawn to dusk. Nothing much happens during that time, in conventional terms, but that nothing is expressed in remarkable language. As the English theater critic Kenneth Tynan wrote of the play shortly after its first BBC broadcast in 1954, Thomas "conscripts metaphors, rapes the dictionary and builds a verbal bawdy-house where words mate and couple on the wing, like swifts. Nouns dress up, quite unself-consciously, as verbs, sometimes balancing three-tiered epithets on their heads and often alliterating to boot."[2]

No two voices had a greater impact on literary radio than those of Orson Welles and Dylan Thomas. Welles captivated listeners at a critical moment in the 1930s during the sudden rise of prestige radio with his innovative adaptations and performances. CBS would not have become a forward-sounding radio network without his booming voice or the striking output of *Mercury Theatre on the Air*. In many respects, Dylan Thomas was the BBC's Orson Welles in the following decade. With the incantatory power of his voice, Thomas opened up a unique space in radio for an irrepressibly exuberant lyricism that (like the mercurial dramatizations of Welles) swung back and forth between high and low culture.

Under Milk Wood was as important a defining moment for radio as *War of the Worlds*. The play gave voice to an aurality so extreme that the practice of radio drama struggled to contain it. The intense musicality of the piece, generated by a radical wordplay that called attention to the materiality of language, had less to do with stock BBC recordings than with the sound effects inherent in individual words. It was, in fact, the discovery of the intrinsically radiophonic condition of spoken language that turned *Under Milk Wood* into an extraordinary sonorous event. "I use everything and anything to make my poems work," wrote Thomas, "puns, portmanteau words, paradox, allusion, paronomasia, paragram, catachresis, slang, assonantal rhymes, vowel rhymes, sprung rhythm. Every device there is in language is there to be used if you will."[3] Thomas unleashed the subversive side of language, an anarchic play of meaning triggered by the continual slippage of words, sounds, and meanings. *Under Milk Wood* had, in the words of John Bayley, an "oral vigor" so remarkable one would scarcely believe that English could produce it.[4]

Thomas's earliest attempts at writing dramatic scripts for BBC's Overseas radio section in 1938 were failures, although they succeeded in getting George Orwell to invite Thomas to read his poetry on his *Voice* broadcasts for the Eastern Service.[5] Asked to write war-based verse dramas, the Welsh poet came up empty-handed. Thomas was no MacLeish. The poet discovered his radio voice, as Ralph Maud writes, in the "personal reminiscence."[6] Thomas wrote (and performed) several prose recollections for the BBC before establishing himself as a poet. These were first-person autobiographical narratives that recollected past events but were conceived dramatically as radio plays. Thomas did not invent the genre of the radio memoir, but his resonant voice and imaginative flare defined the "personal reminiscence" as a literary practice. *Reminiscences of Childhood* aired in 1943, featuring bemused recollections of Swansea. It was followed by *Quite Early One Morning* (1944), *Memories of Christmas* (1945), and *Holiday Memory* (1946). *Reminiscences of Childhood* detailed the appeal of the past in Thomas's characteristically vivid way, but in his follow-up "talks" on seaside Welsh towns—*Quite Early One Morning* and *Memories of Christmas*—Thomas pressed the aurality of his radio prose even further, producing unusually surging rhythms and crescendoing word sounds. The incantatory tone of Thomas's seemingly endless sentence, in the following example from *Memories of Christmas*, saturates listeners with sounds far in excess of the story's simple sense, captured in the vivid slice of life from Christmas past:

> All the Christmases roll down the hill towards the Welsh-speaking sea, like a snowball growing whiter and bigger and rounder, like a cold and headlong moon bundling down the sky that was our street; and they stop at the rim of the ice-edged, fish-freezing waves, and I plunge my hands in the snow and bring out whatever I can find: holly or robins or pudding, squabbles and carols and oranges and tin whistles, and the fire in the front room, and bang go the crackers, and holy holy holy ring the bells, and the glass bells shaking on the tree, and Mother Goose, and Struwwelpeter—oh! the baby-burning flames and the clacking scissorman!—Billy bunter and Black Beauty, Little Women and boys who have three helpings, Alice and Mrs Potter's badgers, penknives, teddy-bears—named after a Mr Theodore Bear, their inventor, or father, who died recently in the United States—mouthorgans, tin-soldiers, and blancmange, and Auntie Bessie playing "Pop Goes the Wesel" and "Nuts in May" and "Oranges and Lemons" on the untuned piano in the parlour all through the thimblehiding musical chairing blindmanbuffing party at the end of the never-to-be-forgotten day at the end of the unremembered year.[7]

Like a magician pulling birds out of a hat, Thomas crowds the microphone with fanciful acoustic effects—compound adjectives ("ice-edged, fish-freezing waves"), extravagant alliteration ("thimblehiding musical chairing blindmanbuffing party"), hyperbolic lists ("holly or robins or pudding, squabbles and carols and oranges and tin whistles, and the fire in the front room, and bang go the crackers, and holy holy holy ring the bells")—all of which heighten the nonsemantic aspect of spoken language.[8] To indulge his delight in the musicality of words, Thomas manipulated a variety of literary devices, from wordplay, puns, and paragrams to alliteration, assonance, and onomatopoeia. These effects, which are widespread in Thomas's poetry, are all the more radical in his radio prose where the constraints of the poetic line do not come into play. For Thomas, sound-making was a never-ending process that had priority over sense-making, one consequence of which was a linguistic deviancy sometimes perceived as a challenge to radio's implicit sense of decorum.[9]

By the mid-1940s, Dylan Thomas already had a name based on the strength of his broadcast work for the BBC, which had begun in 1943. In all, Thomas participated in over 150 BBC programs from 1943 to 1953, as writer, speaker, or actor. In 1946, the peak year of his radio work, Thomas had a hand in forty-nine BBC broadcasts, nearly a dozen of which he wrote himself.[10] At war's end, Thomas was an accomplished writer with a national reputation. His wartime collection *Deaths and Entrances*, published in 1946, received enormous praise.

His success on BBC radio, however, had less to do with his celebrityhood as a poet than with the *spokenness* of his radio prose—with his "organ voice," in Louis MacNeice's words. His most interesting broadcasts utilized that spokenness not to charm BBC listeners but to complicate his subjects. This was certainly the case with *Return Journey*, a radio memoir about revisiting Swansea after the war. In February 1941, Swansea was hit hard by German planes and endured three nights of bombing that demolished the town's center. Thomas had grown up in this Welsh port town and returned there in 1947 to gather material for a BBC radio series called *Return Journey*. Notebook in hand, Thomas examined the wreckage done by German air raids, walking the debris-filled streets like a stranger, past buildings and homes no longer there, jotting down the names of the disappeared storefronts, streets, and houses. "Emlyn road badly hit. Teilo Crescent was wiped out."[11] Swansea's clocks still displayed the time the bombs fell, as though paralyzed by their own trauma. Six years later, the town was still in ruins, and as far as Thomas could see old Swansea was gone. It had become another vanished world, already filled with ghosts of lost people and places.[12]

Return Journey presented a series of thirty-minute radio pieces produced by the BBC's Features Department. The idea behind the series was tied to nostalgia: each episode would send a well-known writer back to a place of special significance in his or her past.[13] Along with the poet Stevie Smith's visit to Kingston upon Hull, Dylan Thomas's return to Swansea was deemed the most engaging broadcast during the program's seven-year run (1945–51). While Thomas may revisit his past in *Return Journey to Swansea*, the radio piece is not a simple memoir. Instead, *Return Journey* is a blend of radio genres—part fiction, part drama, part documentary, part talk—that takes the listener to contemporary bombed-out Swansea just after the war.[14] Because the spoken word traversed generic boundaries more easily than the printed word, radio was a more fluid medium that encouraged forms of cross-coding unique to sound-based narratives. For Thomas, the hybrid form of *Return Journey* allowed his nomadic narrator to explore the specter of displacement in ways that cast doubt on the idea of nostalgia behind the BBC series.

The first-person narrator, who never identifies himself as the (by this time) well-known "Dylan Thomas" but only as the "Narrator," returns to Swansea ostensibly in quest of a former self, the eccentric and mischievous "young Thomas," who will only be spoken of in the third person. The trick, for Thomas, is to represent autobiography as something else:

> NARRATOR (*slowly*): He'd be about seventeen or eighteen ... speaks rather fancy; truculent; plausible; a bit of a shower-off; plus-fours and no breakfast, you know; used to have poems printed in the *Herald of Wales* ... a gabbing, ambitious, mock-tough, pretentious young man; and mole-y, too.[15]

The etymology of "nostalgia" contains the root *nostos*, meaning "return home," an idea of such significance for the Greeks that it was elevated to the status of a literary genre. The Greek *nostoi* ("songs of homecoming") were postwar stories describing the troubled journeys home of Greek warriors after the sack of Troy, the *Odyssey* being the only known surviving example. Like the *Odyssey*, Thomas's *Return Journey* is also a postwar *nostos* but an ironic one at best, with the modernist twist that you can never go home. As evident in the characterization of "young Thomas," the narrator takes a dismissive view of his adolescence. Playful as the text may be, a degree of animus survives the jest, as though Thomas were attempting to mark a real break between past and present selves. Splitting his speaking subject into an authorial narrator and the ghost of a past self helps the author distance himself from the flamboyant youngster he once was. This separation, though, is not presented as a psychological trope so much as a casualty of war. The reality of Swansea's wartime destruction, as imagined by Thomas, is largely what defines its radio mise-en-scène. Postwar Swansea is a "hole in space," a void that casts a strange and dark spell over Thomas's radio play:

> NARRATOR: I went out of the hotel into the snow and walked down High Street, past the flat white wastes where all the shops had been. Eddershaw Furnishers, Curry's Bicycles, Donegal Clothing Company, Doctor Scholl's, Burton Tailors, W. H. Smith, Boots Cash Chemists, Leslie's Stores, Upson's Shoes, Prince of Wales, Tucker's Fish, Stead & Simpson—all the shops bombed and vanished. Past the hole in space where Hodges the Clothiers had been, down Castle Street, past the remembered, invisible shops, Price's Fifty Shilling, and Crouch the Jeweller's, Potter Gilmore Gowns, Evans Jeweller's, Master's Outfitters, Style and Mantle, Lennard's Boots, True Form, Kardomah, R. A. Jones's, Dunn's Tailor, David Evans, Gregory Confectioners, Bovega, Burton's, Lloyd's Bank, and nothing.[16]

In an uncharacteristic move for a poet fond of mythologizing his past, Thomas in this exchange historicizes his homecoming, reliving the damage done by German bombing to Swansea's town center. The catalog of destroyed shops (the narrator lists thirty demolished stores) is more rhetorical than documentary. As voiced by Thomas the narrator, the roll call of dead merchants (Eddershaw, Curry, Leslie, Tucker, Hodges) increases in intensity until reaching a climax just before a caesura that accents the "nothing," the final word and emotional point of the list.

This chronicle of destruction casts a pall over the otherwise ludic account of Thomas's Swansea youth. Wherever the Narrator wanders in search of his past, he is met by signs of its wreckage, shops once "squat and tall" now "blitzed flat graves." The Kardomah Café, where the bohemian set drank and conversed over politics, art, and girls, was "razed to the snow," the voices of poets, painters, and musicians "lost in the willy nilly flying of the years and the flakes." The old school was "shattered, the echoing corridors charred where he [young Thomas] scribbled and smudged and yawned in the long green days." All that remained of the School on Mount Pleasant Hill were the carved initials of the dead, twelve names that are saluted (in another ceremonial roll call) by an unidentified voice to the accompaniment of a "funeral bell."[17]

Thomas's homecoming is marked by dead boys and ruined buildings. The Narrator never finds Young Thomas, only traces of a once-beloved past. The shops have vanished, people are gone, including young Thomas, whom the Park-Keeper identifies (in the program's final words) as "Dead... Dead... Dead... Dead... Dead... Dead." Only the names linger. *Return Journey to Swansea* is a catalog of absence, an obituary of vanished shops and boys. The "voices" have died out—"lost in the willy nilly flying of the years and the flakes."[18] All that can be heard are the memento mori sounds of ringing bells ("School bell," "Funeral bell," "Park bell").

For a radio poet admired for his mythopoeic bravura, *Return Journey* is unusual, not only for its bleakness but also for its refusal to mitigate the pervasive sense of loss, an effect often achieved by Thomas's usual romantic eloquence. The radio piece is very much a "requiem" for old Swansea, as Peter Lewis writes.[19] Thomas had become a radio artist whose naturally expansive manner was now up against the ruins of an ugly war. Swansea could not be saved by his trusty bardic magic. Instead, Thomas rendered himself historically homeless. The anti-poetic reality of Luftwaffe bombing had created a void in his imagination as real as the "hole in space" Swansea had become.[20]

As the classically decentered subject of modernism, the Narrator enacts his own separation from the Young Thomas he had come in search of, even foregoing the wish to speak that former self back into being, as he had done in "Poem in October" and "Fern Hill" two years earlier ("Time held me green and dying / Though I sang in my chains like the sea")—as if the void, the story's figurative center, had swallowed up that sonorous voice. The objects of nostalgia are gone, only their names remain, and barely the voice to speak them.

Postwar Swansea was not a place where the swing-boats swam "to and fro like slices of the Moon," as he describes the town in another radio play.[21] For a moment, history had become an impediment to Thomas's lyricism, arresting the flow of unstoppable language. A critical discontinuity had emerged between the imaginable past and the disastrous present, and for this reason *Return Journey* is a very modernist text in which the bereft present mediates a vanishing past. One gets the impression that Thomas is contesting the very idea behind the BBC series *Return Journey* by undercutting the idea of nostalgia.

Thomas's *Return Journey to Swansea* received strong praise from listeners and BBC insiders alike.[22] The reception was so enthusiastic, in fact, that Thomas was inspired to write a much longer play on the topic, as he explained to his parents: "My Swansea broadcast, by the way, has had a great reception: many, many letters, from Swansea people from Welsh exiles, from Mrs Hole, of Mirador, & Mrs Ferguson, the Uplands sweetshop, & Trevor Wignall, the old sporting journalist from Swansea, and several producers on the BBC. Also some good press notices, three of which I enclose. I want very much to write a full-length—hour to hour & a half—broadcast play; & hope to do it, in South Leigh, this autumn."[23] As it turned out, that full-length play would eventually become *Under Milk Wood*. In Milk Wood, Thomas created a world of its own, as if from scratch, to fill the void created by German bombs. Thomas, the radio artist, had little choice but to tear down the Swansea of the Welsh imaginary. This idyllic site—his symbolic home—was now a town in ruins that had not survived the ugly war nor the grim implications of Hiroshima. It would be replaced by the strange and whimsical world of Milk Wood, Thomas's rib-tickling, reimagined book of Genesis.

Thomas had been flirting with ideas of apocalypse and re-creation since the end of the war. He darkly wrote in a 1950 radio broadcast about plans for a new poem, to be called "In Country Heaven." In it, the world as we know it will have ended; what remains is a "submerged wilderness." "The Earth has killed itself," wrote Thomas. "It is black, petrified, wizened, poisoned, burst; insanity has blown it rotten; and no creatures at all, joyful, despairing, cruel, kind, dumb, afire, loving, dull, shortly and brutishly hunt their days down like enemies on that corrupted face."[24] The poem would comprise, Thomas explained to his BBC listeners, the "tellings" of those who knew in their "Edenic hearts" the "beautiful and terrible worth of the Earth." Thomas never completed "In Country Heaven," but he continued to mull over its cosmic dynamics. He even teased himself, less grimly, with the prospect of writing a libretto for Igor Stravinsky that would be set in a post-apocalyptic future. During his last (and fateful) visit to America in 1953, he met with Stravinsky in Boston to discuss collaboration on a hypothetical opera about the aftermath of a nuclear catastrophe. The idea they explored was a "recreation of the world," how the Earth, now utterly in ruins, might be "reborn" thanks to intervention from outer space.[25]

Under Milk Wood is a work that does not fall easily into place in the literary canon. Billed as a "radio play for voices," it is neither drama, poetry, nor prose. It is its very own genre, whatever that might be, in which the line between writing poetry and doing radio has been all but erased. Produced by Douglas Cleverdon, *Under Milk Wood* aired in January 1954 on the Third Programme, with Richard Burton in the role of First Voice.[26] *Under Milk Wood* has often been viewed as one of the great achievements of the BBC, specifically of the Third Programme. Thomas's tale focuses on one day in the lives of the inhabitants of a tiny fishing village in Wales. While the town—Llareggub ("bugger all" spelled backward)—is as imaginary as its people, the language of Milk Wood is remarkably vivid and tangible.

The story is chronicled by the omniscient First Voice, who guides listeners through the memories, dreams, desires, and despairs of the villagers during one day in early spring. The three-part play (dreaming night, waking morning, and sundown) begins on a moonless night just before sunrise while the villagers lie lost in sleep. "Hush, the babies are sleeping," the narrator (First Voice) tells us, "the farmers, the fishers, the tradesmen and pensioners, cobbler, school-teacher, postman and publican, the undertaker and the fancy woman, drunkard, dressmaker, preacher, policeman, the webfoot cocklewomen and the tidy wives" (1).[27] The whole town sleeps, and if we listen closely we can hear "the dew falling, and the hushed town breathing" (2). The intimacy of the all-wise and all-knowing First Voice captures listeners in a conspiratorial spell as we yield to his enticing call to eavesdrop on the drowsy town.

Their dreams mark the villagers as eccentrics who are defined largely by their amusing quirks and foibles. Blind Captain Cat is dreaming of ancient sea voyages and bygone sweethearts; Mary Ann Sailors, of the Garden of Eden; the fastidious Mrs Ogmore-Pritchard, of her dead (henpecked) husbands; the procreative Poly Garter, of breeding a galaxy of children; dressmaker Myfanwy Price, of a "barnacle-breasted" Mog Edwards; Mog Edwards ("I am a draper mad with love"), of the unattainable Myfanwy Price; Jack Black the cobbler, of scaring young lovers; Evans the Undertaker, of his mother's welshcakes; Willy Nilly the postman, of delivering mail; Sinbad Sailors, of the town's quintessential beauty (Gossamer Benyon); Mrs Butcher Benyon (the Butcher's wife), of owl meat, dogs' eyes, and manchop; the Reverend Eli Jenkins, poet and preacher, of Bardic glory; Mr Pugh, of poisoning Mrs Pugh; Mrs Organ Morgan (the wife of a church organist), of silence.

With this collection of types, a poet could build another Earth, so faulty and dysfunctional as to be immune to the virus of perfection, a place of post-lapsarian joy perceptible only in the recombinatory *jouissance* of comic re-creation. The absence of malice or hostility—this troupe could not be more innocuous—would be less remarkable if it were not for the haunting savagery of a war that had scarred Wales and damaged all of England. There is gossip and envy and bittiness aplenty, but even the resentment exchanged between Mr and Mrs Pugh is portrayed as a perverse kind of joy. They would not trade this pleasure for all the happiness under the sky. Thomas's villagers inhabit a bizarre alternate reality that frames the warmongering absurdities of the incipient Cold War. "To begin at the beginning," the First Voice says at the outset of the play, benignly appropriating the mantle of world-maker. "It is Spring, moonless night in the small town, starless and bible-black, the cobblestreets silent and the hunched, courters'-and-rabbits' wood limping invisible down to the sloe-black, slow, black, crowblack, fishingboat-bobbing sea" (1). The narrator's voice emerges from silence out of a brooding darkness that enfolds the dumbfounded town.[28] It emerges into sound, produced by the irrepressibly melodic effects of Thomas's writing, with its wordplay, alliteration, internal rhyming, onomatopoeia, assonance, and euphony.

There is hardly a moment in *Under Milk Wood* that does not call attention to the aurality of language (not to mention the aurality of existence), as if sound-making and world-making were intimately connected. The missing link in this equation is the listener, whom the narrator recruits for his participatory project. "You can hear the dew falling, and the hushed town breathing," the First Voice points out. "And you alone can hear the invisible starfall, the darkest-before-dawn minutely dewgrazed stir of the black, dab-filled sea" (2). Thomas positions the listener as a voyeuristic collaborator, someone who eavesdrops on *Under Milk Wood*'s unsuspecting villagers in the privacy of not only their homes but their dreams, to bear witness to the stirring village by the sea. "Come closer now. Only you can hear the houses sleeping in the streets in the slow deep salt and silent black, bandaged night. Only you can see, in the blinded bedroom, the combs and petticoats over the chars, the jugs and basins, the glasses of teeth" (3). The narrator's invitation lures listeners to advance closer to Milk Wood's sleeping subjects. Only we can hear their dreams.

We are coaxed to come nearer to a world whose existence depends not only on the words of the narrator, but on the hearing of the curious listener as well. This enticement is an irresistible whisper. "Time passes. Listen. Time passes. Come closer now" (3), says the demiurgic First Voice. This triple act of imagining—the bardic word, the villagers' dreams, and our listening (eavesdropping)—is a magic spell that draws all participants into an aural totality, if not ecstasy, made up of, as Thomas would say elsewhere, "the musical mingling of vowels and consonants."[29] "To listen," as Don Ihde writes, "is to be dramatically engaged in a bodily listening that 'participates' in the movement of the music."[30] Milk Wood is exactly the sort of participatory universe in which the extravagant music of language gathers up being out of its own whirling energy. Milk Wood is a place where words—not as command ("Let there be Light") but as pure unstoppable sound—accumulate in defiance of semantic, grammatical, and categorical boundaries. Here we gaze with the all-hearing ear ("you can hear the dew falling"), whose capacity, in such a heightened state, trespasses on the rule of eyesight: "Now the voices round the pump can see somebody coming" (48). Thomas's remade Eden is hospitable not only to drunkards, rogues, malcontents, and promiscuous lovers but to the radical pleasure (and power) of the ear:

> FIRST VOICE: Alone in the hissing laboratory of his wishes,
> Mr Pugh minces among bad vats and jeroboams, tiptoes through spinneys of murdering herbs, agony dancing in his crucibles, and mixes especially for Mrs Pugh a venomous porridge unknown to toxicologists which will scald and *viper* through her until her ears fall off like figs, her toes grow big and black as balloons, and steam comes creaming out of her navel. (69–70)

In this auditory utopia, verbs mutate into nouns and nouns into verbs, while matter and energy remain in such flux that little can be fixed in time or place.

Milk Wood is a volatile world, and its one constant—mutability—is shared by everyone and everything. The town drunk, Cherry Owen, lifts his beer-filled tankard to his mouth only to find that it is alive with gills. "He shakes the Tankard. It turns into a fish. He drinks the fish" (20).[31] On the strength of his "linguistic deviancy," as Gareth Thomas calls it, the poet transforms the persistence of being into continuous, teeter-tottering change.[32] Unlike the biblical creation myth, where the authorial assertion of the *logos* imposes order on chaos in the grammatical form of a monotheistic voice ("Let the earth bring forth grass"), Thomas's story depends on a dialogic realignment that deters the sort of pecking order that prevails in the book of Genesis. In place of categorical codes and referential systems and the work of designation, what we instead find in the Ovidian world of Milk Wood is an ensemble of guiltless human types who, no matter how flawed, participate in the generative work of sound-making, in the incantatory rhythms and inexhaustible handiwork of wordplay.

Under Milk Wood is different from Thomas's other radio broadcasts to the extent that it draws upon what Ihde calls the "dramaturgic voice," a voice in which the musicality of words is amplified rather than silenced.[33] The spoken word does not ordinarily call attention to the sound it makes, to its music.[34] In "ordinary" speech, the sounding remains in the background, as if withdrawing from the *insistence* of meaning, from what is not sounded. When that insistence is checked, as on the stage, it is replaced by a kind of strangeness that wavers in the gap between sound and sense. In his literary exuberance, Thomas played up the musical strangeness of language at the expense of its referential value.[35] He liberated the *logos* from the law.

In Dylan Thomas' *Under Milk Wood*, the BBC had found what it was looking for: an eccentric radio text tuned to the ear. "One had heard nothing like it before, and we may never hear anything like it again," said one of the first reviews.[36] The huge success of Thomas's play seemed to offer the kind of radio experience advocates of the Third Programme had dreamed of from the start and provided evidence that radio drama could, as Mark Cory says, "somehow turn the absence of a visual stimulus into an aesthetic advantage."[37]

Samuel Beckett and the BBC: *All That Fall*

Stirred by the critical success of *Under Milk Wood*, the BBC invited Samuel Beckett to write a drama for radio broadcast the following year. International interest had been roused by the Paris production of *Waiting for Godot*, and the BBC was eager to tap the growing popularity of avant-garde drama. Beckett's involvement with the BBC played a key part in the complex relationship between modernist literature and a powerful new medium. Already a well-published novelist and dramatist, Beckett brought to his radio venture a set of preoccupations that would take him in unexpected directions. Like his earlier work, *All That Fall* reflects on the familiar modernist obsession with paralysis and death. But unlike anything Beckett had written before, his first radio play gave his negativist philosophy an unusual twist, particularly in its representation of female subjectivity, in the guise of his protagonist, Mrs. Rooney, whom Beckett endows with surprising presence. That Beckett should allow one of his characters such a vocalic fullness of being is surprising, especially in light of his radical minimalism, and suggests how writing for radio altered, even if only temporarily, the parameters of his storytelling.

Broadcasting Beckett would have been inconceivable without the Third Programme's push for new abstract and experimental works from the mid-1940s to the late 1950s.[38] In its pursuit of the avant-garde, the BBC provided significant patronage for elite writers. But the benefits were mutual. The practice of legitimizing broadcast radio by associating it with Beckett and other well-known authors with proven reputations resembled the American tradition of "prestige" programming. With CBS's *Columbia Workshop* and *Mercury Theatre on the Air*, American radio had demonstrated ten years earlier that borrowing the cultural cachet of the literary, in which authorship was a marker of value, was a proven strategy for heightening the allure of an emergent medium.[39] The BBC's Third Programme was launched in 1946, and during the first five years it maintained an ambitious schedule. It aired talks by T. S. Eliot, Thomas Mann, Iris Murdoch, Bertrand Russell, Evelyn Waugh, Graham Greene, and E. M. Forster, as well as recitals of the poetry of Donne, Milton, and Keats. There was a reading in four installments from John Hersey's *Hiroshima*, about the survivors of the A-bomb, which had just been published in the *New Yorker*, followed by an hour-long documentary on the science of atomic energy. Other productions included a dramatization of the *Canterbury Tales*, new translations of the *Agamemnon* and Sartre's "Huis Clos," a reading of Virginia Woolf's short story "The Duchess and the Jeweler," an adaptation of *Animal Farm* (scripted for the BBC by Orwell himself), a miscellany of Aristophanes' comedies (acted by Dylan Thomas), and a live broadcast of George Bernard Shaw's *Man and Superman*, which ran for a whopping five hours.[40]

Despite this seeming wealth of programming, a shortage of original material thwarted the new mandate for cutting-edge writing of works specific to radio. As the Controller of the Third Programme wrote in 1949: "Our experience to date has shown that we cannot expect a very substantial flow of worthwhile contemporary radio drama at Third Programme level. We will be lucky if during the year we can find say ten pieces that are suitable. For the rest we must decide what to perform from the corpus of dramatic literature which is written for the theatre."[41] Lofty aims notwithstanding, the Third Programme seemed condemned to the same recycled fare, even if highbrow, of its predecessors. That changed in 1953 with the appointment of Donald McWhinnie as the BBC's assistant head of drama, who led the Third Programme in an aggressive search for original material.[42] McWhinnie, who had a strong predilection for modernist writing, thought that the surrealistic idiom of absurdism, with its interest in interiorized characters, would lend itself to radio.[43]

The partnership between Beckett and the BBC would last for nearly a decade and was valuable to both parties. The first of his four radio plays, *All That Fall*, did not resemble anything Beckett had done before. Writing for sound exclusively, Beckett handled the challenge of the new medium with an intuitive understanding of its unique properties, which he took

Samuel Beckett in the mid-1980s, when his radio plays were produced for American broadcast. (Courtesy of Photofest)

seriously. In later years, Beckett famously refused to allow his radio drama to be staged in the theater:

> *All That Fall* is specifically a radio play, or rather radio text, for voices, not bodies. I have already refused to have it "staged" and I cannot think of it in such terms. A perfectly straight reading before an audience seems to me just barely legitimate, though even on this score, I have my doubts. But I am absolutely opposed to any form of adaptation with a view to its conversion into "theatre." It is no more theatre than *Endgame* is radio and to "act" it is to kill it. Even the reduced visual dimension it will receive from the simplest and most static of readings . . . will be destructive of whatever quality it may have and which depends on the whole thing's coming out of the dark.[44]

For Beckett, radio was its own distinctive medium, one that demanded an emphasis on the voice far beyond anything required in a staged drama.

To create a dense acoustic texture that would help the story come "out of the dark," Beckett endowed the play with rich colloquial dialogue, a loquacious female protagonist, a distinctive (and noisy) setting, a large cast of characters, and a far more developed plot than he typically used.

All That Fall takes place outside of Dublin in early summer and centers on Maddy Rooney, an overweight and outspoken seventy-two-year-old woman who has just hauled herself out of bed after a long bout of illness to trudge down a country road to the Boghill railway station to meet her husband, Dan, on his birthday, a blind and cranky old-timer due back from his office job in Dublin. Maddy's quest is labored and slow, burdened as it is by old age, disappointment, and chance meetings.

Much of Beckett's play documents what goes on in Maddy's head as she meets various characters en route to the station. Her first encounter is with Christy, the dung carrier, who tries to peddle manure from his horse-drawn cart. Next she meets Mr. Tyler on his bicycle, and soon after, Mr. Connelly recklessly hurtles by in his van, nearly running over both Maddy and Mr. Tyler. Lastly, Mr. Slocum, an old flame, motors by and gives Maddy a lift in his automobile, but only after a macabre and comical sequence in which Mr. Slocum tries to stuff the rotund Maddy (with her "two-hundred pounds of unhealthy fat") into the car. Finally, arriving at the Boghill station, Maddy reunites with her husband, whose train arrives an unheard-of fifteen minutes late.[45] The two make their arduous way home together under threatening skies, with Maddy quizzing Dan, who is evasive, about the train's delay. (He is reluctant to reveal that the train was late because a little child fell out and slipped under its wheels.) Maddy and Dan continue homeward in silence, under a *"tempest of wind and rain"* (59).[46]

As unusual as these features of plot and character are in Beckett's work, what is most remarkable about this radio play is its soundscape, meticulously designed by a writer presciently aware of the acoustic properties of his new medium. *All That Fall* begins with a multitrack prelude of animal, human, and musical sounds. Here are Beckett's directions: *"Rural sounds. Sheep, bird, cow, cock, severally, then together. Silence. Mrs Rooney advances along country road towards railway-station. Sound of her dragging feet. Music faint from house by way. 'Death and the Maiden.' The steps slow down, stop."* Beckett's directions make sure that the first noises we hear are farmyard animals—a bucolic quartet of sheep, birds, cows, and roosters— immediately followed by the percussive sound of Mrs. Rooney's dragging feet and the faint music of Schubert's *Death and the Maiden* fading up from the near distance. The dragging feet halt as Mrs. Rooney speaks the first words of the play: "Poor woman. All alone in that ruinous old house" (1). The opening line reveals Maddy's sensitivity to sound, as she responds to the far-off strains of Schubert's string quartet by filling in the emptiness of the unnamed woman's house—the "ruinous" space—with a kind of feminist empathy. The gramophone will replay *Death and the Maiden* again on the return journey Maddy and her husband make, serving the play as both overture and coda.

Maddy's radiophonic life owes much to her heightened acoustic sensibility. She is a character who navigates her journey by listening and whose aural "point of view" frames the story. Present throughout the play, she provides the story's operative, though sorely oppressed, intelligence. As the sound of Schubert's music fades away in the opening moments, Maddy begins to hum the melody herself, picking up where the *lied* left off. In the role of Echo, Maddy identifies herself musically with the lonely woman.[47] Her humming stops with the approach of sightless Christy's horse-drawn wagon, just as the sound of cartwheels breaks the Schubertian spell. "Is that you, Christy?" Maddy asks, as though blind herself, focused as she is on hearing.[48] Maddy Rooney may be a wreck of a woman—"an hysterical old hag"—but she reveals a remarkably astute ear for the acoustic nuances around her (5). In fact it is Maddy's capacity as a listener that mediates the relationship between spoken language and consciousness in the play. She is the acoustic center of the play, both a maker of sound and its hearer, and, as such, enjoys an unusual degree of agency for a Beckett character.

What she does with this agency is to question the very nature of spoken language (if not radio itself). Maddy joins a list of other characters in Beckett's fiction and drama who, suffering through various kinds of linguistic anxiety, question the ability of language to signify reality. In Maddy's case, her linguistic self-consciousness is bound up with a bodily awareness that is marked by comic decrepitude and "speaks" to listeners with a peculiar force. Maddy's form of embodiment is evoked by the various earthy sounds she vocalizes throughout the play (huffing, puffing, heaving, moaning, groaning, nose-blowing, crying, laughing), all of which draw attention to the physicality of language, emphasizing its spoken properties—its soundness.

Maddy has no difficulty reproducing her missing body by means of speech, even if that body is unwieldy, and this would seem to be in defiance of a medium that is essentially acousmatic and thus invisible. But while the space of radio drama inevitably dissolves the body as signifier, that space also allows its return by narrative means as an effect of consciousness or perception of self. Maddy's radio body comes back out of the dark as a signified under the sign of decrepitude, providing her with numerous speaking points. The more Maddy grumbles about the dead weight of her body, the more narrative space her vocalized subjectivity inhabits. Ordinarily, it is the voice that is produced by a body. But voices, especially on radio, can also produce bodies, if only because the radio body is not corporeal but exists virtually in acoustic space. As Steven Connor writes, the vocalic body is a "surrogate or secondary body, a projection of a new way of having or being a body, formed and sustained out of the autonomous operations of the voice."[49] Beckett's intuitive interest in Maddy's radio body is consistent with his recurrent interest in interrogating language, not as the work of cognition so much as a visceral effect of embodied subjectivity. Maddy's perception of occupying space depends entirely on the sounded nature of meaning.

In her aurally defined largeness, Maddy is the exact opposite of her blind husband, Dan, who embodies a diminishing selfhood: "The loss of my sight was a great fillip. If I could go deaf and dumb I think I might pant on to be a hundred," he says late in the play (43). Dan is a typical Beckettian burn-out who does not seek identity so much as flee from it, one more shuffling moribund, as Connor puts it, longing for self-annihilation through a gradual fade-out.[50] Next to her husband, Maddy Rooney is a glorious and extravagant wreck of a woman. Together, the two form the proverbial odd couple, and if anything, the blindness of her husband reminds us how perspicacious Maddy often can be.

Maddy may be spirited and even resilient, but she is no less miserably self-conscious than others in Beckett's tortured drama. A good listener, she overhears herself and senses something awry in her affair with words. For Maddy, each spoken word is a step toward being but also an occasion for distress. Because language (as often in Beckett) is haunted by its own failure, her verbal self-awareness always flirts with its own disappearance. Maddy is as mindful of her own "lingering dissolution" (7), as she calls it, as of anything else in the play, frequently giving voice to a biblical sense of fate: "Let us halt a moment," she says, "and this vile dust fall back upon the viler worms" (8–9). In Maddy's mind, the world is passing, in all of its mechanical violence, beyond the ancient conviviality of oral exchange. Mr. Connolly's van rushes by with a "thunderous rattle," nearly running down the bike-riding Mr. Tyler, while Mr. Slocum in his "great roaring machine" backs over a hen (9). And, of course, the mystery at the heart of the story, what postpones the mail train, hangs on another overheard hit-and-run. Maddy acknowledges her own vulnerability with an aural pun that neatly captures her sense of herself as constructed by language: "It is suicide to be abroad" (7).

Her Rabelaisian instincts embarrass both herself and her neighbors. Early in the play, after the encounter with the bicycling Mr. Tyler, Maddy, wrestling with her girdle, cries out for help: "Oh cursed corset! If I could let it out, without indecent exposure. Mr. Tyler! Mr. Tyler! Come back and unlace me behind the hedge! (*She laughs wildly, ceases.*) What's wrong with me, what's wrong with me, never tranquil, seething out of my dirty old pelt, out of my skull, oh to be in atoms, in atoms!" (11). The bawdy moment, voiced with a kind of bucolic delight, is as rich in sound as it is in absurdity, but Maddy cannot enjoy the Shakespearean moment, tormented as she is by her (or is it Beckett's?) obsession with "dissolution."

That an obese, elderly, rheumatic woman should, even in jest, imagine such an amorous moment—"At my time of life! This is lunacy!" (17)—is a powerful reminder of the body of Maddy Rooney. Technically speaking, Maddy's corporeality (all two-hundred pounds' worth) is invisible. Equipped with only microphones, the broadcast studio would seem to be the vanishing point of the human body. Radio is bodiless, an irreducible fact that Beckett no doubt found irresistible. And yet, like a missing limb, Maddy's body is far more present than absent, thanks to the suggestive power of sound, which has the capacity "to make us believe virtually anything," as Hugh Kenner has put it.[51] Beckett was not only aware of the paradox of the "vocalic body" but went out of his way to play it up, as is evident in the ever-present refrain of Mrs. Rooney's *dragging feet*, an acoustic trope that recurs throughout the play, as though her body itself had a distinctive voice, a voice found not so much in language as in pure sound.

When the BBC received Beckett's script, it knew it was in possession of a remarkable piece of writing; also apparent was that the script called for a rather special understanding of sound effects. Donald McWhinnie spoke with Beckett about the acoustic design of the play, and both agreed that the sound should be treated surrealistically in order to evoke the inner life of Maddy Rooney. McWhinnie took Beckett's opening sound direction (*Rural sounds. Sheep, bird, cow, cock, severally, then together. Silence*) as his cue to provide the production with a consistently stylized soundscape. This is how he later explained his solution to the opening of the play:

> The purpose of this prelude is not primarily to evoke a visual picture, and if it resolves itself into "farmyard noises," it will, in fact, be pointless, since it is not directly linked to the action, although echoes of it are heard during the course of the play, in various contexts. It is a stylized form of scene-setting, containing within itself a pointer

to the convention of the play: a mixture of realism and poetry, frustration and farce. It also demands a strict rhythmic composition; a mere miscellany of animal sounds will not achieve the effect. The author specifies four animals; this corresponds exactly to the four-in-a-bar metre of Mrs. Rooney's walk to the station and back, which is the percussive accompaniment to the play and which, in its later stages, becomes charged with emotional significance in itself.[52]

For McWhinnie, BBC's conventional sound effects would not do. In his reading of Beckett's radio script, *All That Fall*'s sound design required a more avant-garde treatment, something that would move the poetic center of the play toward the purely musical.

The real challenge of producing Beckett's new play, in McWhinnie's mind, would be to avoid the clichéd sounds of realistic drama. Beckett himself had written to John Morris, the Controller of the Third Programme, to say that *All That Fall* called for "a rather special quality of bruitage, perhaps not quite clear from the text."[53] The BBC's handling of Mrs. Rooney was smart and resourceful but took, as McWhinnie admitted, most of its cues from the playwright. Beckett's original idea for *All That Fall* emerged, he explained in a letter to Nancy Cunard in June 1956, out of the imagined sounds produced by an old lady: "Never thought about radio play technique but in the dead of t'other night got a nice gruesome idea full of cartwheels and dragging of feet and puffing and panting which may or may not lead to something."[54]

McWhinnie's inspiration for stylizing the soundscape came from Pierre Schaeffer's experimental sound studio, Club d'Essai at Radio-Television Francaise (RFT) in Paris. McWhinnie himself had visited Schaeffer's studio in the mid-1950s and returned to London with heightened interest in experimental sound. "The Club d'Essai provided," McWhinnie said, "a special approach to actors and radio performance and to aural inventiveness through musique concrète, acoustic effects and the highly imaginative use of sheer sound. It could not fail to prove stimulating to an enthusiast for the medium."[55] McWhinnie urged the BBC to set up a similar studio for the creation of electronic effects, one big enough to house dubbing machines, turntables, tape recorders, echo chambers, oscillators, filters, and space for microphones and two or three actors. The BBC's radiophonic workshop derived from *musique concrète* the idea that all sounds—or noises—could be musicalized.[56] "The principle is simple," McWhinnie explained: "Take a sound—any sound—record it, and then change its nature by a multiplicity of operations. Record it at different speeds, play it backwards, add it to itself over and over again.... By these means, among others, we can create sounds which have never been heard before and which have a unique and indefinable quality of their own. By a lengthy technical process we can compose a vast and subtle harmonic pattern using only one basic sound—say, the noise of a pin dropping."[57] For the BBC sound department, the solution to producing Beckett was to be found in the art of noise and the new technology of the tape machine.[58]

McWhinnie's idea was to musicalize *All That Fall* as much as possible, with the result that the inherently lyrical qualities in Maddy Rooney's character were played up—in particular, her fine ear for eloquent speech. "The footsteps of Mr. and Mrs. Rooney, their real journey," McWhinnie wrote, "must gradually attract poetic and symbolic overtones, so that eventually even the wind and rain which beat against them are almost musical in conception."[59] The job of stylizing Beckett's effects was given to Desmond Briscoe, head of the Radiophonic Workshop. Because the BBC had a large archive of natural sounds, it had been customary for producers to choose their audio from the BBC effects library. But this would not do for Beckett's play. "Beckett's script was remarkable, really remarkable," Briscoe said. "The whole nature of the thing led to experimentation."[60] Briscoe suggested that they do away with natural sounds altogether and in their place use simulated ones, which would help underscore the surreal side of the play as Beckett had suggested.[61] For the sound of Mrs. Rooney walking, for instance, they would introduce a simple drum rhythm, a steady percussive beat that would also be used as the effect of Mr. Rooney's walking stick. Briscoe's approach demonstrated that character could be evoked by any effect within the spectrum of sound, whether realistic or stylized. You are what is heard. In this, Maddy's radiophonic presence bypassed the limitations of the stage body. Free from the gaze of theater, Maddy could be grotesque, vaguely poetic, and immaterial at the same time—a complete paradox that defied the speech-oriented stage. Such a conception fit surprisingly well with Artaud's nonlogocentric theatre of cruelty.[62]

If Briscoe's aim was to augment Beckett's depiction of Maddy as the aural core of the play by suggesting that everything emerges out of her mind, Maddy's presence is the more interesting against the backdrop of the play's numerous absent or disappeared subjects, ghostly beings who never were or who died young: Minnie, for instance, Maddy's unborn daughter, lost after a miscarriage forty years earlier. In her imagination, Maddy tries in vain to reproduce Minnie's body. Minnie, she thinks, by now would be "girding up her lovely little loins" as she passes through menopause. Ironically, Maddy's reverie duplicates Mr. Tyler's earlier news that his daughter has just undergone a hysterectomy: "They removed everything, you know, the whole . . . er . . . bag of tricks. Now I am grandchildless" (10). At the end of the play, Jerry brings the news of a fatal accident, a young child run over by the train. Yet another missing body. With these spectral bodies, Beckett reminds the listener of the memento mori theme evoked at the outset when Maddy overhears the distant notes of Schubert's *Death and the Maiden* on a gramophone.

If the untimely deaths of so many children cast a pall over the Rooney's perseverance, it also emphasizes Maddy's own improbable presence. In the ancient struggle between breath and death, speaking is vital. As always in Beckett, however, language is troubled. With her sensitive ear, Maddy intuits that something is not quite right in the logosphere, puzzling over her words and phrases the way many of Beckett's figures do, condemned to linguistic torment. And so she asks Christy if he finds her speech odd. Her eccentric style, evident soon enough, makes her feel awkward. "Do you find anything . . . bizarre about my way of speaking? (*Pause.*) I do not mean the voice. (*Pause.*) No, I mean the words. (*Pause, more to herself.*) I use none but the simplest words, I hope, and yet I sometimes find my way of speaking very . . . bizarre" (3). It's not clear why Maddy should suddenly feel self-conscious—perhaps she has been bedridden for some time—but her linguistic misgivings are "unspeakably excruciating," as she later confesses.

To be alienated by language from herself and from others is the cause of real anguish for Mrs. Rooney. Her speech is not "bizarre" so much as roundly figurative, which lends her spoken words an extravagance that doesn't fit in. Predicting rain, Maddy says that "soon the first great drops will fall splashing in the dust" (38). Laboring up the long steps of the Boghill train station is worse than scaling "the Matterhorn," she says, and when there, Maddy (with figurative zest) advises her reluctant companion, Miss Fitt, to lean her against the wall "like a roll of tarpaulin." For all this fuss she apologizes: "I'm sorry for all this ramdam, Miss Fitt"— to which Mr. Tyler responds with evident surprise: "(*in marveling aside*). Ramdam!" Mr. Tyler's wonder is Beckett's way of marking Mrs. Rooney's *parole* as if not strange, at least peculiar. Maddy's eloquence, which others view as out-of-date, marks her as different, especially in the post-romantic environment she inhabits so nervously. It is as though Mrs. Rooney had just woken from a long Rip Van Winkle sleep into a hard-edged world of meanness and mechanical violence. Little wonder that Maddy will listen to the archaic language of animals with such sympathy. While Christy does not answer Maddy's original question, her husband, Dan, will later confirm her linguistic misgivings:

> MR. ROONEY: Do you know, Maddy, sometimes one would think you were struggling with a dead language.
> MRS. ROONEY: Yes indeed, Dan, I know full well what you mean, I often have that feeling, it is unspeakably excruciating.
> MR. ROONEY: I confess I have it sometimes myself, when I happen to overhear what I am saying.
> MRS. ROONEY: Well, you know, it will be dead in time, just like our own poor dear Gaelic, there is that to be said.
> (*urgent baa*)
> MR. ROONEY: (*startled*) Good God!
> MRS. ROONEY: Oh, the pretty little wooly lamb, crying to suck its mother! Theirs has not changed, since Arcady. (48)

The rural language of animals may endure (it has since the beginning, as Maddy imagines), but that spoken by the Rooneys is dying. English is not "dead" to the Rooneys, however, the way Old Norse or Gaelic is. It is not extinct. Their struggle is an effect of *overhearing* the sound of spoken English, as Dan suggests. It is a problem of the voice listening to itself. As Dan confesses, language is agonizing "when I happen to overhear what I am saying." For both, speaking enacts a kind of estrangement, provoking slippage between words and things, as if spoken language had trouble lining up with reality. In this estrangement, there is a linguistic torment that points to the declining power of the word, which is something the Rooneys vaguely suspect and which Maddy feels keenly.

The agony of the verbal is a familiar theme in Beckett. Elsewhere, Beckett points to the floating signifier as the basis of linguistic alienation. Watt's encounter with a pot is the classic case in point:

> Looking at a pot, for example, or thinking of a pot, at one of Mr Knott's pots, of one of Mr Knott's pots, it was in vain that Watt said, Pot, pot. Well, perhaps not quite in vain, but very nearly. For it was not a pot, the more he looked, the more he reflected the more he felt sure of that, that it was not a pot at all. It resembled a pot, it was almost a pot, but it was not a pot of which one could say,

Pot, pot, and be comforted. It was in vain that it answered, with unexceptionable adequacy, all the purposes, and performed all the offices, of a pot, it was not a pot. And it was just this hairbreadth departure from the nature of a true pot that so *excruciated* Watt. For if the approximation had been less close, then Watt would have been less anguished. For then he would not have said, This is a pot, and yet not a pot, no, but then he would have said, This is something of which I do not know the name. And Watt preferred on the whole having to do with things of which he did not know the name, though this too was painful to Watt, to having to do with things of which the known name, the proven name, was not the name, any more, for him.[63]

This passage from Beckett's novel carefully traces the instability of the *logos*. Watt is anguished that the word "pot" no longer names the pot, the result of a slippage articulated along the lines of acoustic drift. As the sound of "pot" drifts increasingly away from the thing it represents, thanks to his insistent repetition and comical rhyming with Watt and Knott ("what" and "not"), the signifier's linkage to meaning becomes ever more tenuous. What is important for Watt is not to seize the essence of the idea behind "pot" but to reassure himself that sound and sense are operating according to plan—which they're not: "Watt's need of semantic succour was at times so great that he would set to trying names on things, and on himself, almost as a woman hats."[64]

Watt's linguistic crisis centers on the dysfunction of language, triggered by the gap between sound and sense. "It resembled a pot, it was almost a pot, but it was not a pot of which one could say, Pot, pot, and be comforted." The Rooneys' struggle with acoustic drift is equally vexing, and like Watt they find little "semantic succour" in their auditory relationship with people or things. For Maddy, as for Watt, speaking does not endow words with sense but rather empties them of it. If there is any kind of solace, it is to be found in the nature of sound itself—in *sonority*—in the melancholia of Schubert's *Death and the Maiden* that frames the play or in Maddy's ancient verbal exuberance: "Let us a halt a moment and this vile dust fall back upon the viler worms" (8–9).[65] Or perhaps in the unrestrained hilarity that erupts from the couple on quoting the sermonic text from Psalm 145 scheduled for the following day: "The Lord upholdeth all that fall and raiseth up all those that be bowed down. (*Silence. They join in wild laughter.*)" (56).

The laughter of the Rooneys is at a text they find dubious, if not incredible. It is the laughter of pure irony that doubts even its own meaning, laughter not in the face of absurdity but as an expression of it. The highly stylized animal noises are really no different. As described by McWhinnie, they refer primarily to their own condition as musical sound, not to any farmlike reality, and in this sense they too are an expression of the absurd. More than that, they are nonverbal sounds ("*chirp, moo, baa, bark, cackle*" [43]) that reach beyond language, as does the Rooneys' "wild" laughter, not to mention Maddy's "*Dragging steps, etc.*," the most consistent musical event in the story.

In his first radio play, Beckett effectively challenged the conventional "reading" of sound effects in broadcast drama by minimizing their representational task. No sound effects, Beckett instructed, were to be realistic. The BBC took Beckett at his word. To produce the sound of rainfall, as the BBC's McWhinnie explained, several people stood around the microphone "all going 'tsts tst tssttst tsts' with their lips and this was the rain, of course." Following the lead of Schaeffer and the Club d'Essai in Paris, the Radiophonic Workshop then processed the "tsts" through a high-pass filter, removing all bass frequencies, a distortion that further dissociated the sound from its reference point (rain).[66] "It resembled rain, it was almost rain, but it was not rain of which one could say, Rain, rain, and be comforted." Beckett's interest in stylized sound suggests that he wished to place imaginative demands on listeners by dividing acoustic signals from their signs, making it difficult to identify, in Schaeffer's words, their "sonorous sources." In this way, Beckett was harnessing acoustic drift. By setting sounds at odds with sense—Mrs. Rooney's "*Dragging steps, etc.*" rarely sound like footsteps—Beckett was asking the listener to wonder, "What exactly am I hearing?"[67]

As this question suggests, the sound effects of *All That Fall* were defamiliarized in a way that was consistent with modernism's emphasis on estrangement in art. The Radiophonic Workshop gave Maddy a surreal presence, made evident not only by musicalized dragging feet but also by the actress Mary O'Farrell's proximity to the microphone in her voicing of Maddy's isolation and instability. The decision to position O'Farrell, and no one else, inches from the microphone had the effect of foregrounding her voice and presence. Across the airwaves, Maddy looms large. In contrast with the other, more muted characters, she is heard as an expressive subject who fills the air space. That Maddy should wonder if her words sound "bizarre" is an irony that reflects not only her alienation but also Beckett's awareness of radiophonic practices. Both Beckett and the BBC's sound designers went out of their way to make Mrs. Rooney sound strange.

That strangeness is amplified by her implied body. Her words continually construct it for us: "Oh let me just flop down flat on the road like a big fat jelly out of a bowl and never move again! A great big slop thick with grit and dust and flies, they would have to scoop me up with a shovel" (37). When she isn't busy producing it ekphrastically for the listener, the sound effects—which announce her shambling, panting, and moaning—conjure up her body for us: "*Sound of handkerchief loudly applied*" (20); "*Sounds of her toiling up steps on Miss Fitt's arm*" (26); "*Mrs. Rooney blows her nose violently and long*" (30).[68] Hers is the abject body that, for Julia Kristeva, "disturbs identity, system and order."[69] It is a body that does not respect borders, positions, or rules.

In all its carnivalesque splendor, Mrs. Rooney's body is as elemental as the noise of barnyard animals, and just as surreal.[70] And though it may occupy significant acoustic space, her body is essentially incorporeal—pure sound that refers to nothing, to something that is not there. Hard as Maddy will try to find presence in the Word, it is only through sound—not language—that she can give shape to her existence, however decrepit that might be. If anything, her aural vivacity is a parody of the Christian metaphysics of the *logos*, the divine Word made flesh.

When *All That Fall* aired in 1957, the avant-garde acoustics of the play had their desired effect. As one reviewer noted, the production created "a miraculous web of sound effects" that "penetrat[ed] one's aural imagination": "Donald McWhinnie's production of *All That Fall* was . . . a miraculous web of sound effects and I could listen to Mary O'Farrell for ever in any part whatever. . . . Here she was a wheezing old woman puffing to the station to meet a train which arrived late because it had run over a child. The incident, like a dull bad dream recounted to you by some forcible old bore in a Dublin pub, had a tiresome way of penetrating one's aural imagination all next day. This is a feather in the cap for sound drama, a thing sui generis not at all eclipsed by television, though now wholly ignored by the Press."[71] The play had struck a chord, just as had *Under Milk Wood* three years earlier. The sound of a "wheezing old woman puffing to the station" lingered in the minds of listeners after the broadcast. Rudolf Arnheim may have been right that voices "have neither feet nor ears," and yet, with the help of the BBC, Beckett's first radio play turned the voice of Maddy Rooney into an expressive instrument that could create, from its own private space, not only a body but an entire world.⁷²

As aesthetically different as Dylan Thomas and Samuel Beckett are, their radiophonic work shares a similar interest in resisting the transparency of language-as-word. Turning away from realist conventions, they construct worlds that defer to the disturbing power of sound. For Thomas and Beckett, the voice is not speech but sound, and their radio plays take extreme measures to liberate the word from speech. *Under Milk Wood* dramatizes the arbitrariness of signification through an excess of sound, while *All That Fall* insists that spoken language is of the body, and in embodiment we find new ways to complicate, if not resist, the symbolic order of language—the logocentric. In both instances, radio takes revenge on the *logos* for having devocalized language.⁷³

Radio as Music
Glenn Gould's Contrapuntal Sound

Under the heading of modernist sound art, you will find the names of Luigi Russolo, Antonin Artaud, Pierre Schaeffer, and John Cage, among others, but probably not Glenn Gould, the famous Canadian pianist. That is a surprising omission, given that Gould's efforts to musicalize the human voice took the radio drama of Dylan Thomas and Samuel Beckett to the point of no return.

How did an internationally acclaimed pianist become a sound artist? In 1964, Canadian pianist Glenn Gould, best known for his Bach interpretations, stunned the music world by announcing his retirement from the concert stage. It was a radical move: Gould would perform no more. The most celebrated artist in all of Canada was only thirty-two and at the height of his career when he turned his back on the concert hall, but Gould had developed, as he put it, a love affair with the microphone. He withdrew into the recording studio, where he embraced electronic media with a newfound gusto. Always ahead of his time, Gould dropped out, turned on, and tuned in well before Timothy Leary invented the snappy slogan. Nestled in his studio, Gould became a reclusive tape-head, quoting Marshall McLuhan, speaking to others only by telephone and reassembling his recorded performances (as though a filmmaker) by splicing tape. When Gould died unexpectedly at the early age of fifty—from a stroke—he left behind not only a significant musical legacy of nearly eighty recordings on disk for CBS, but also a small but remarkable body of works composed for radio, the most prominent of which is *The Solitude Trilogy* (1967–77), one of the milestones of late-twentieth-century radio.

A series of three one-hour documentaries on isolation in the northern parts of Canada, *The Solitude Trilogy* is not the kind of work one listens to on the car radio, and not just because of its length. Gould's unusual approach to radio is famous for the demands it puts on the listener. Gould believed that the ear was a greatly underused organ and that there was no particular reason why anyone could not listen to three or more conversations at once.[1] Gould liked to compare his radio work to the music of Bach and often called his unique approach to sound "contrapuntal." In *The Solitude Trilogy*, this meant weaving voices in and out as a composer might write lines of music in a fugue. Gould's relationship with the music of Bach was as significant for his radio work as it was for his concert performances. Applied to a radio documentary, a Bach-like aesthetic's complex and contrapuntal style would seem counterproductive to the kind of didactic clarity required by the genre. But Gould firmly believed that the human voice could be treated as a musical instrument and that spoken words could be integrated into a variety of intricate sonic arrangements.

Gould's approach to radio was closer to European sound art than to the Anglo-American narrative traditions that had given shape to three decades of broadcast programming, and it was aided and abetted by multitrack recording and editing technology. When Gould retired from performance and withdrew into the recording studio, he was opting for a laboratory of sound (the kind dreamed of by Dziga Vertov and his "laboratory of hearing" in the 1920s). For Gould, the studio was not only a refuge from the worries of performance. It was an electronic sanctuary that promised, thanks to the "prospects of recoding," total control over the artistic experience. At the center of Gould's studio practice was the tape splice, the rearranging of sounds.[2]

Despite his renown as a concert pianist, radio was Gould's preferred medium. In his so-called retirement, he produced several works for the CBC in Toronto, including documentary portraits of Leopold Stokowski, Pablo Casals, Arnold Schoenberg, Richard Strauss, and Petula Clark. Gould's most important radio work, however, was *The Solitude Trilogy*, an innovative series of "documentaries" on the Canadian North that, as Richard Kostelanetz has suggested, ranks as one of the greatest achievements in North American radio art.[3]

Outside of Canada, few listeners are familiar with these works. Gould is best remembered as the charmingly mad genius who wore winter coats and gloves all year long, hummed while he performed, and devised oddball alter egos for television. When his obituary appeared on the front page of the *New York Times*, mention of "The Idea of North" (the celebrated first piece in the *Trilogy*) was relegated to the last column of a long tribute to Gould's pianism. One of the most radical texts in radio history had become an afterthought.[4]

Glenn Gould standing in the doorway of a train car in a CBC publicity shot for "The Idea of North," circa 1970. (Courtesy of Herb Nott, the Glenn Gould Estate, and the Canadian Broadcasting Corporation Still Photo Collection / Harold Whyte)

Gould had grown up on radio and had listened with uninterrupted interest to Canadian radio drama, where such genre blurring was common. He was particularly keen on the CBC drama series *Stage*, which ran on Sunday nights from the mid-1940s to the mid-1970s, as well as the popular *CBC Wednesday Night*, which broadcast three hours of original radio plays and adaptations once a week, including related talks and documentaries. "I was fascinated with radio theater," Gould said in an interview, "because it seemed to me somehow more pure, more abstract. . . . A lot of that kind of ostensibly theatrical radio was also, in a very real sense, documentary-making of a rather high order. At any rate, the distinctions between drama and documentary were quite often, it seemed to me, happily and successfully set aside."[5]

Gould's departure from the performance stage opened up new artistic possibilities for the would-be writer and radio producer. No longer tormented by the demands of a live audience, Gould hoped to invent a new radio art in the security of the recording studio, surrounded by microphones, reel-to-reel tape recorders, and audio engineers—a new art that would (as one biographer put it) blend musical and literary form.[6] Whatever it was, he seemed to have devised his very own genre, something he would call "contrapuntal radio."[7]

In 1967, Janet Somerville, the producer of the CBC show *Ideas*, commissioned Gould to make a radio documentary about the North as a special project to mark Canada's first centennial celebration. Having something more literary in mind, however, Gould was little interested in producing a conventional documentary. As he saw it, he had been asked to write "a sort of Arctic 'Under Milk Wood.'"[8] The Dylan Thomas radio play, which had aired a little more than twelve years earlier on the BBC, was an interesting model. Nothing may happen in the play and there is little character development, as early reviewers complained, but the radical lyricism of *Under Milk Wood*, with its poetry consistently on the verge of song, emphasized the relationship between music and spoken language in a way that must have impressed Gould. The result of Gould's effort was "The Idea of North," a program that, as Kevin McNeilly writes, does not propose a concept of *northernism* so much as theorize solitude and creativity in terms that were congenial to Gould himself. Gould's interest was "in the effects of solitude and isolation upon those who have lived in the Arctic or Sub-Arctic."[9] All three parts of the *Trilogy* explore "communities-in-isolation."

An Arctic *Under Milk Wood*: "The Idea of North"

The significance of *The Solitude Trilogy* is complicated as much by its startling form as by its surprising density. The initial program, "The Idea of North," amazed many when it first aired in 1967. Like the subsequent two programs, it is an experimental and provocative text that seems to defy interpretation at every turn. No one was quite sure what to make of it. Billed as a documentary, "The Idea of North" violated nearly every rule of reportage. Gould adopted the unusual strategy of overlapping the voices of his interviewees, with two or three people speaking simultaneously for long stretches of time. Equally strange, Gould allowed ambient sounds and music to interfere with their discourse, which is sometimes silenced by the rattle of a train, the roar of the sea, or the swelling sounds of Sibelius's Fifth Symphony.

What Gould had assembled was not easy to define. Robert Hurwitz called it a "symphony"; Geoffrey Payzant called it a "tape collage."[10] Gould himself referred to his *Solitude* programs as "documentaries" but also called them variously "essays," "dramas," "mood pieces," and "dream documentary."[11] Sometimes he even mixed up his genres: "The Idea of North" may be "technically a documentary," Gould wrote, but one "which thinks of itself as a drama."[12] In Gould's mind, such distinctions were not terribly relevant. Radio was compelling, he suggested, the more so when it mingled (or mangled) its forms. Gould took devilish delight in the prospect of genre blurring. The speakers in his documentaries were not called subjects but "dramatis personae," just as the segments of each broadcast were divided into prologues, acts, scenes, and epilogues. Gould, in fact, liked to think of his radio pieces as a species of literature and was fond of comparing aspects of *The Solitude Trilogy* to a medley of literary works, from Thornton Wilder's *Our Town* and Katherine Anne Porter's *Ship of Fools* to Franz Kafka's *Metamorphosis* and Jorge Luis Borges's short fiction. What "The Idea of North" most resembled, however, was a radio play—a kind of Canadian *Under Milk Wood*—except that the voices were real and unscripted.

As far as Gould was concerned, the North was not an actual place but a complex of tropes basic to the Canadian imaginary. "The north has fascinated me since childhood," he said in the liner notes to the program, "but my notion of what it looked like was pretty much restricted to the romanticized, art-nouveau-tinged Group of Seven paintings which, in my day, adorned virtually every second school-room and which probably served as a pictorial introduction to the north for a great many people of my generation."[13]

Tape recorder in hand, Gould interviewed five people for the "documentary," each of whom had spent significant time in the North. Although in the edited program Gould's subjects appear to be speaking with one another on the Muskeg Express from Winnipeg to Churchill, they were questioned separately and never met. The "drama-like juxtapositions," in Gould's words, are an illusion constructed in the studio, one that Gould repeated in all three programs. The interaction of the characters, Gould wrote, was crucial, and so he cast his subjects with care. "We wanted an enthusiast, a cynic, a government budget-watcher, as well as someone who could represent that limitless expectation and limitless capacity for disillusionment which inevitably affects the questing spirit of those who go north seeking their future," Gould wrote.[14] The interviewees who played these roles (unknown to each other) included Robert Phillips, a government man who had worked in the Department of Northern Affairs; Marianne Schroeder, a nurse who had spent time in the northwest corner of Hudson Bay; Frank Vallee, a professor of sociology in Ottawa; James Lotz, a British anthropologist; and Wally Maclean (who plays the narrator), a retired surveyor who had worked for the Canadian National Railway in Manitoba and a raconteur fond of quoting the classics.[15] Each subject was typecast in post-production so that Gould might play out his story in a way consistent with Anglo-American traditions of radio drama, while at the same time adapting dialogic structures to musical notions.

Gould's unorthodox notion of documentary radio was undeniably radical, but what distinguished his compositional approach to "The Idea of North" was his musical interpretation of voice. Once each character's role was established discursively on tape, the specific meaning of this or that word would become increasingly irrelevant. As in Prokofiev's *Peter and the Wolf*, where each character in the story is represented by a different instrument, in Gould's "Idea of North" each point of view would be represented by a different voice, over and above its content. Gould's understanding of spoken language was radiophonic, stripping a character down to his or her acoustic essence:

> The five people we used as characters in this play-documentary were all people who had experienced isolation in some very special way, and had things to say about it. By the time we were about half-way through that hour, we had a fair notion as to which aspect of isolation had attracted each of them; so, in the second half, we began superimposing conversations or phrases, because by this time our characters had become archetypes and we no longer needed their precise words to identify them and their position. We needed only the sound of each of their voices and the texture of that sound mixing with voices to do this.[16]

Once the interviews were complete and the tapes transcribed, Gould holed up in a motel room in Wawa, Ontario, on the northern shore of

Lake Superior. He knocked off a script in three weeks, returning to his CBC studio in Toronto for the arduous work of splicing. It was quite an operation, observers have noted, as Gould and his CBC crew hovered over Ampex tape machines. "Gould would sit up on the control panel," a *Toronto Star* reporter explained, "his script resting on a music stand, and cue Tulk [Lorne Tulk, the CBC audio engineer] with a vocabulary of gestures not unlike those of an orchestral conductor."[17]

If Gould was less beholden to fact than the ordinary documentarian, that was because he was more interested in a "metaphoric" interpretation of the North than a conventional commentary.[18] In Gould's mind, the "idea" of north was a literary construct that grew out of his fascination with solitude and isolation. His hour-long program was to be a journey not into a terrestrial wilderness but into a mental interiority. To accomplish this on tape required considerable editorial intervention in post-production, when Gould cut, spliced, and layered his interviews into a complex vocal "docudrama."[19] Divided into five scenes (including a prologue and an epilogue), "The Idea of North" opens with Marianne Schroeder's voice, fading up quietly (*pianissimo*): "I was fascinated by the country as such. I flew north from Churchill to Coral Harbor on Southampton Island at the end of September. Snow had begun to fall and the country was partially covered by it. . . . I remember I was up in the cockpit with the pilot, and I was forever looking out, left and right, and I could see ice floes over the Hudson Bay and I was always looking for a polar bear or some seals that I could spot but, unfortunately, there were none."[20]

Schroeder, who plays the "enthusiast" in Gould's cast, narrates her arrival in the North, describing her interest in the strangeness of the landscape. Her heightened expectancy is the suspense of a young woman traveling to a mythic country: "And as we flew along the East coast of Hudson Bay, this flat, flat country frightened me a little, because it seemed endless. We seemed to be going into nowhere, and the further north we went the more monotonous it became. There was nothing but snow and, to our right, the waters of Hudson Bay." In the middle of Schroeder's discourse, the voice of Frank Vallee—the designated "cynic"—cuts into her monologue: "I don't go, let me say this again, I don't go for this northmanship at all. I don't knock those people who do claim that they want to go farther and farther north, but I see it as a game—this northmanship bit . . . as though there's some special merit, some virtue, in being in the North or some special virtue in having been with primitive people: well, you know, what special virtue is there in that?"

Vallee's rant against "northmanship" overlaps with Schroeder's arrival tale, both voices running simultaneously. On first listening to "The Idea of North," the intrusion of Vallee is startling. His is an unexpected voice, as the listener does not yet understand the rules of Gould's program. Vallee's denial of Schroeder's theme ("I don't go, let me say this again, I don't go for this northmanship at all") sounds like interference, as though one channel's signal had just leaked into another. Such "cross talk" is barred from electronic communication or is understood as a glitch when it does occur, as when hearing pieces of other people's conversations on a telephone (which Lucille Fletcher so evocatively played with in *Sorry, Wrong Number*).[21] But it is not a mistake: Schroeder's voice fades down just as Vallee's is boosted, a technical maneuver that authorizes Vallee's intrusion. Vallee (and his crankiness) has the support of the broadcast studio.

It's not long before Vallee's voice, too, is interrupted by another, this time by Robert Phillips, the "government budget-watcher." "Sure, the North has changed my life," says Phillips. "I can't conceive of anyone being in close touch with the north, whether they lived there all the time or simply traveled it month after month and year after year—I can't conceive of such a person as really being untouched by the North." Phillips's voice, literate and mellow, offers temporary relief from the sound of Vallee's grumbling. Less than two minutes into the program, all three "characters" are speaking simultaneously—Schroeder, Vallee, and Phillips—sometimes in harmony, at other times at cross-purposes. While none of them has ever met, they have been placed together in the same scene, like characters in a CBS play. Gould's handling of his performers adapts radio's proximity effect to his own inventive needs, converting documentary subjects, who had been recorded separately in isolation from one another, into dramatic characters sharing the same acoustic stage.

The prologue ends with Schroeder's elegiac comments about her Northern experience. Her voice returns to the foreground, while Vallee and Phillips continue speaking underneath, as though providing background music: "I always think of the long summer nights when the snow had melted and the lakes were open and the geese and ducks had started to fly north. During that time, the sun would set, but when there was still the last shimmer in the sky, I would look out to one of those lakes and watch those ducks and geese just flying around peacefully or sitting on the water, and I thought I was almost part of that country, part of that peaceful surrounding, and I wished that it would never end." There is a wistfulness in Schroeder's words ("I would watch those geese flying around peacefully and I wished that it would never end") that turns on the postcard charm of the North. A nurse who, buoyed by dreamy images of the North as the last vast Canadian frontier, traveled to an Inuit village at Coral Harbour on Hudson Bay when younger, Schroeder adds a plaintive note to the opening sequence. Out of the chorus of voices, Gould isolates this lyrical moment, rather than Vallee's dissent, by privileging Schroeder's text with foregrounded clarity, allowing her to have both the first and the last words of the prologue. Among the three disparate views of northern Canada, the nostalgic voice of Marianne Schroeder will linger longest in the listener's mind.

Marianne Schroeder's idyllic vision will be qualified later in the program by voices of disenchantment (including her own). "I think the North in the future," says Robert Phillips, "is going to look appallingly like the rest of Canada. And that's great as far as I'm concerned. It's going to look like suburbia." And as Schroeder herself admits, after working at Coral Harbour for several hard months, "I just didn't want any part of the North any longer." For now, though, Schroeder's enthusiasm functions as a signpost for Wally Maclean's narrative and the program's journey into complexity, just as her arrival tale will echo through Maclean's narrative about a hypothetical young man's first journey to the North.

Maclean, a surveyor for the Canadian National railroad, was handpicked by Gould to play the role of narrator. Gould had met Maclean on the Muskeg Express while himself traveling by train to Churchill, just before beginning work on "The Idea of North." In Maclean, Gould had met a kindred spirit, or so he tells listeners in his three-minute introduction to the program:

> Several years ago I went North aboard a train known affectionately to Westerners as the Muskeg Express—Winnipeg to Fort Churchill . . . and at breakfast I struck up a conversation with one W. B. Maclean, or as he was known along the line and at all the hamlet sightings where his bunk car would be parked, Wally. Wally Maclean is a surveyor, now retired, and within the first minutes of what proved to be a daylong conversation, he endeavored to persuade me of the metaphorical significance of his profession. He parleyed surveying into a literary tool, even as Jorge Luis Borges manipulates mirrors and Franz Kafka badgers beetles. And as he did so, I began to realize that his relation to a craft, which has as its subject the land, enabled him to read the signs of that land, to find in the most minute measurement a suggestion of the infinite, to

encompass the universal within the particular. And so when it came time to organize this programme and to correlate the disparate views of our four other guests, I invited Wally Maclean to be our narrator and to tell me how, in his view, one can best obtain an idea of North.

Gould was no doubt taken with Maclean's folksy manner but also with the older man's fondness for literary tropes, which resembled his own keenness for bookish analogies. Maclean's allusion to the myth of Sisyphus eleven minutes into the program is a noteworthy case in point. A roundabout way of reimagining his own adventures when younger, Maclean tells the story of a man heading north for the first time, from Winnipeg to Churchill. It is a "long, terrible, trying trip," Maclean says. To pass the time, the hypothetical young man explains his interest in philosophy, singling out the predicament of Sisyphus, the king of Corinth condemned for eternity to roll a boulder uphill, only to watch it tumble back down again and again. The hypothetical traveler is merely perplexed by the absurdity of Sisyphus's ordeal, but Maclean sees the myth as a telling metaphor for the journey to and from the North. "Well, somehow the sameness of the trip in, and the trip out, is part of the endless feeling that we are up against this myth—this business of having to do things for no apparent reason." But he does not share this insight with the young man, only with the listener. "You don't want to smash his dream before it has diminished," he says, darkly.

For Albert Camus, of course, Sisyphus became a trope for the futility of man's search for meaning, and in Gould's documentary the Sisyphus reference conveys a similar message. For Maclean, the challenge of going northward is how to reckon with the failure of an idea (the North as a place of pristine beauty and innocence) often mythologized in the Canadian imaginary.[22] In reflecting on his own past, Maclean suggests that searching for metaphysical uplift may be pointless but that the futility of the journey matters less than the journey itself.[23] Our encounter with the North does not mean meeting the sublime in open space but an encounter with our inner selves. It is an initiation.[24]

As the resident philosopher, Maclean reads Sisyphus in ways that add another layer of meaning to a journey that has become more complex. For Gould, the Camusian Sisyphus pertains less to ultimate questions than to structural mischief. Sentenced to an endlessly futile task, Sisyphus was condemned to roll an immense boulder up a steep hill, only to watch it roll back down. His labor mirrors the struggle of Gould's dramatis personae to produce a dominant narrative that might advance a coherent interpretation of the North. This turns out to be a Sisyphean effort in Gould's radio piece. Instead of building a consensus, after each assertion about the North, Gould splices in a counter-statement (in musical terms, a kind of tonal inversion) that foils the previous remark. A large boulder goes up the hill, only to fall back down. This strategy remains in effect throughout the "documentary," interrupting any effort to build an overarching narrative. For Gould, the North was always a shifting idea, but the program's mischievous ability to backtrack repeatedly on many of the characters' statements indicates that Gould had more in mind than merely exploring alternative ideas of nordicity.

Gould's tonal inversions were a signature part of his "documentary" work, for which he coined the term "contrapuntal radio," a notion that grew out of his interest in Bach's use of counterpoint in keyboard music. Gould approached his documentary radio as if he were composing a fugue in the manner of Bach, creating a verbal equivalent to musical counterpoint by overlapping human voices, ambient sounds, and vocal timbres and repositioning his subjects' comments as dramatic dialogues. As a pianist, Gould thrilled his public with an uncanny ability to maintain with precision the absolute clarity of separate contrapuntal lines in his performances of Bach. Gould's ability to orchestrate human voices in similar ways in his sound documentaries gave his radio work, as Edward Said wrote, "an unexpectedly novel dimension," but it also challenged radio's privileging of human speech.[25]

In Gould's eyes, the banality of straightforward radio was a side effect not only of its predictability but also of its monologic voice, its privileging of the spoken word over anything else. All voices are uniformly important, Gould liked to say: "There are no main voices."[26] Gould's interest in overlapping voices was not a gimmick but an offshoot of his commitment to polyphony. Gould seemed to have been possessed, as Steven Connor writes, of a "multitrack consciousness."[27] When asked about his fugal approach to radio, Gould liked to play up the dialectics integral to counterpoint: "If you examine any of the really contrapuntal scenes in my radio pieces, you'll find that every line stacks up against the line opposite, and either contradicts it or supplements it."[28] For Gould, counterpoint was a mode of composition in which each individual voice carried on a life, as he put it, of its own.[29]

Gould's contrapuntal aesthetic is most radical in "The Idea of North" and is evident in the alternation between idealism and cynicism. With each new tonal inversion, Gould's cast of characters revises its collective notion of the North.[30] It's not so much the spoken word of each character that mediates the meaning of nordicity as the acoustic ironies triggered by Gould's splicing. The real challenge for Gould's listeners is to catch these subtle incongruities, in which one character's words are at variance with another's. Once aware of these ironies, we no longer tune in to their discrete voices but instead listen to their structured relationships.[31] Wally Maclean's digression on Sisyphus, for instance, is first intercut with the stories of Lotz and Phillips, which describe their earliest encounters with the North. Just as Lotz explains his repeated expeditions to the North, outlining the frustrations and disappointments he faced along the way but also emphasizing the lasting sense of meaningfulness the journeys left him with, Gould interposes Maclean's digression on Sisyphus, which seems to come from nowhere. Here is Lotz referring to his expeditions to the North: "Memory of course tends to cast a pall over our worst and best experiences. But looking back at this—a group of men isolated, each trusting the other and each respecting the other, in a small community in isolation—and it's not just a touch of the old nostalgia, it's a feeling of having participated in something very meaningful, both personally and professionally." This is a moment of hard-won conviction for Lotz, and we can hear the import rising crescendo-like in his voice, in an appeal to sincerity. His recurring quest for the North has had its ups and downs, but in retrospect the worth of the search has transformed his life. Gould frames Lotz's moment of moral uplift with a cut to Maclean's story of Sisyphus, that figure doomed to a meaningless task. Gould's edit does not turn Lotz into a deluded character, but it does qualify his declaration of conviction as possibly naive. As tape editor, Gould has gone out of his way to temper Lotz's spoken text, while also casting a shadow over the idealism of the hypothetical traveler. The line between these two personae, the fictional "young fellow" of Maclean's yarn and Lotz the "enthusiast," seems to blur, thanks to the tape-based proximity effect.[32]

For an earlier generation of sound-makers, the proximity effect typically entailed close-miking, a common radiophonic practice during the heyday of radio drama in the 1940s because it was an effective means of emphasizing presence, interiority, and aberrant psychologies.[33] The BBC took advantage of close-miking to play up Beckett's Mrs. Rooney's solipsistic plight; in *Sorry, Wrong Number*, Mrs. Stevenson's crisis is mediated by speaking hysterically and closely into a telephone, which is itself a kind of microphone; Orson Welles and Edward R. Murrow went a step further by thematizing close-miking as a way of narrativizing radiophonic practices.

In Gould's sound work, the proximity effect evolved further, becoming a function of montage that allowed Gould to simulate the dynamics of drama by rearranging documentary voices in a fictional acoustic space. Even though his subjects were interviewed independently, Gould spliced together their comments so that they appear to be in conversation, suggesting an entirely fabricated proximity, one to another.[34]

Gould controlled his splicing with impeccable irony.[35] There is Robert Phillips talking about the government's new commitment to the North followed hard by James Lotz's despondent assertion that Ottawa really didn't give a hoot about the northwest territories. Phillips says: "The end of 1953 was the beginning of an administrative revolution in the North [in which] it was decided to make a new investment in the North." Ten seconds later, Lotz says, "You come from the Ottawa, you go in the North, you write a report, you make a list of recommendations, you bring it back to Ottawa, and nobody pays any attention to it." And there's Marianne Schroeder extolling the North for making known in a new way the fundamental value of human companionship—here in the North, she says, "one could realize the value of another human being"—intercut fifteen seconds later with Phillips's skepticism about intimacy in the North: "What nobody else will ever know is whether you're kidding yourself or not. Have you really made your peace with these other people or have you made a peace because the only alternative to peace is a kind of crack-up?"

James Lotz, the resident idealist, has several expansive moments that are, more often than not, punctured by Gould's impish editing. Here is Lotz describing his own transformation: "The thing about the North, of course, in personal terms is that in the North you feel, it's so big, it's vast, it's so immense, it cares so little. And this sort of diminishes you. And then you think, my God, I am here: I got here, I live here, I live, I breathe, I walk, I laugh, I have companions." Seconds later, Frank Vallee, the voice of cynicism, flatly contradicts Lotz: "I found that the wide open spaces concept isn't quite what it's cracked up to be. I felt cooped-in, because I was so afraid to get lost."

No character in the program escapes irony. Even Wally Maclean, Gould's handpicked narrator, is sabotaged by the negative dialectic of Gould's manic editing. Throughout the program, the train, which Gould called his "basso continuo," is heard continuously in the background. Each character's voice is mediated by that evocative sound, the rhythmic clanking of the wheels rolling northward, as if the entire cast were on board the Muskeg Express bound for Churchill.[36] Thanks to this fictive device, each voice is brought "on board," just as the "young fellow" traveling north for the very first time becomes Wally Maclean's imaginary companion, taking Gould's place. As the soundtrack is linked to Maclean's diegesis, the journey by train frames his meandering narrative with particular emphasis. On trains, people tell stories. Unlike the straight lines of the track, though, Maclean's tale is a winding one, and compared to the less folksy characters in the program his discourse is markedly digressive. If Gould calls attention to Maclean's role as narrator, as he does early in the program in his spoken introduction, it is not so much to invest authority in Maclean's métier as it is to raise the stakes of the narrator's struggle to grasp and then communicate the meaning of the North. What will happen to the young researcher being carried farther and farther north? How will his initiation quest end? Will the North become the young man's nightmare or his dream?

Maclean does little to answer these questions in his nine-minute "soliloquy," which concludes "The Idea of North." Maclean's monologue is layered not over the sound of the train but over the final movement of Sibelius's Fifth Symphony, the only music in the program. Though Sibelius's music is bold and decisive, Maclean's effort to bring resolution to the riddle of the North is hardly conclusive:

> So you begin by saying, oh well, we did—at least what some of us thought was a challenge a while back. Well, surely it's a challenge now. I mean this is the first time he's [the imaginary "young fellow" traveling north for the very first time] been on these rails that run north. Oh yes, you say, but then the challenge was different then. A few years back, certainly in human memory, people thought that this, what we call our "North," presented a real challenge. Well, what form did they take? What form? As if everything must somehow have form that you can sort of put in words. This is hard, this is hard on you. He must notice that you're struggling a bit, see. But what you're really saying then is something like this. That there was a time when the challenge was understandable. What challenge then? Oh well, here you have to take it easy.

Maclean advises caution apparently because the "idea" of North, so complicated and disturbing, is likely to overwhelm the imaginary traveler. But Maclean himself seems to have reached an impasse in parsing the idea of North. As Sibelius drives the story forward to its forceful conclusion, Maclean's voice trails off in a kind of muddled confusion. By the end of "The Idea of North," Wally Maclean's words seem to dissolve before our very ears. "They come," as one of Gould's biographers has observed, "perilously close to gibberish."[37] The triumphant mood of Sibelius is full of certainty and exultation, while Maclean's narrative takes the listener deeper into ambiguity and perplexity. The impression we are unavoidably left with is that words fail Wally Maclean when he most needs them.

As these instances show, Gould constructs a kind of intertextuality in the spaces between speakers, which, thanks to repeated erasures, curiously adds up to zero. Gould goes out of his way, in other words, to neutralize any cumulative meaning. There's conflict but no resolution. With so many mutually exclusive voices, as McNeilly points out, "The Idea of North" produces "a welter of contradiction and incoherence" that turns the North into "a zone of antagonisms."[38] It might be tempting to reduce this friction to the tensions between romantic and realist expressions of the North, but that would be to overlook the provocative nature of Gould's program, behind which it is not hard to see what Theodor Adorno (whom Gould read) called the "disenchantment of the concept," a strategy for battling bewitched ideas.[39] For Gould, the North is a kind of enchanted idea that is put through the wringer of contrapuntal radio. The outcome might seem vexing at first, but Gould's artistry, as Edward Said wrote, was not designed simply to alienate listeners or frustrate expectations, but rather to lure them in by provocation in order to excite new kinds of thinking.[40] Like Stanley Fish's self-consuming artifact, Gould's documentary takes the listener beyond the place where discursive forms can speak to us, as if the totality of meaning were a threat to the pure act of listening.[41]

In lieu of a standard documentary, with pros and cons and authorial warranties, Gould created a rich and textured sound collage that offered little narrative assistance but instead required from listeners a kind of attention radio ordinarily did not demand. Gould was playing out his modernist assumptions about art and the public. Like a Joycean text, "The Idea of North" would call for acute interpretive skills. In the irrepressibly contrapuntal mind of Glenn Gould, "The Idea of North" would not, however, have the last word on the subject of nordicity. The program had captivated listeners, but it also confused a good many, for obvious reasons. Not only was cross talk challenging to decode, but the absence of a reliable narrator, a stabilizing presence in more conventional documentaries, kept listeners off balance. "I thought I was listening to two radio stations," noted one listener.[42] According to Robert Hurwitz in the *New York Times*, hearing a Gould radio program was like "sitting on the IRT during rush hour, reading a newspaper, while picking up snatches of two or three conversations as a portable radio blasts in the background, and the car rattles down the track."[43] Still, the piece was heralded as bold, innovative, and poetic. The Gould broadcast, as the *Montreal Star* noted, was "likely to stand as the forerunner of a new radio art, a wonderfully imaginative striving for a new way to use the only half-explored possibilities of an established form." The *Toronto Star* liked how Gould used "the hypnotic drone of moving train wheels as a bass," weaving the voices of the subjects into a "thick and moody line." "There was no attempt to define a problem," said the newspaper. "Instead Gould used his interviews to create a sound composition about the loneliness, the idealism and the letdowns of those who go North." The *Ottawa Citizen* called the program a "poetic and beautiful montage of the North . . . that was more real and honest than the entire ten-foot shelf of standard clichés about Canada's Northlands."[44]

Modernity and Its Discontents: "The Latecomers" and "The Quiet in the Land"

Keen to develop his notion of contrapuntal radio further, Gould jumped at the opportunity to undertake a follow-up program. In the spring of 1968, the CBC asked him to make a new radio piece in order to inaugurate its national FM stereo service, and this gave him an opportunity for creating a companion piece to "The Idea of North." That summer, Gould took a boat to Newfoundland "in search," as he put it, "of characters for a documentary."[45] With the assistance of a local CBC engineer, Gould interviewed a wider cast of characters this time and before leaving Newfoundland recorded a multitude of ocean sounds. What he found over the course of four weeks were thirteen subjects who had remained in Newfoundland despite government resettlement programs and who were willing to talk about their refusal to comply.

The island province of Newfoundland was the last to join the Confederation, in 1949. At issue was the government effort to move Newfoundlanders from isolated coastal communities, or outports, into larger urban areas. Providing health care, education, transportation, post office support, and other federal amenities could be achieved more cheaply and efficiently, Ottawa believed, if people moved from isolated settlements to Canada's larger towns and cities. (In 1951, only 45 percent of Canada's population lived in cities.)

By the time Gould had begun work on "The Latecomers," the resettlement programs had become increasingly unpopular. This gave Gould's subject an edge, but what most engaged him about Newfoundland was its isolation and "the cost of nonconformity," as he explained in the liner notes to the new program. As in "The Idea of North," Gould interviewed his subjects separately and then overlapped their voices in the studio, using thirteen interviewees this time instead of five. Compared to the cast of "The Idea of North," which had been made up mostly of white urban professionals (there were no Native subjects and only one woman, Marianne Schroeder), the cast of "The Latecomers" was more diverse (although only two women were included, one of whom appears solely in the prologue), featuring a mix of raconteurs and rustics—"old coots" as Gould called them—along with the highly cultivated voices of the educated class that was so dominant in "The Idea of North."[46]

Apart from exploring the idea of isolation, Gould wanted the sound of the sea—lapping waves, crashing surf, pounding rocks—as a signature element in the new program. Once again, there would be a "basso continuo," a line of accompaniment that would run unceasingly behind the speaking Newfoundland characters. Like the continuous sound of the train moving along its tracks in "The Idea of North," the sound of the sea in "The Latecomers" starts off as an indexical sign that, through its persistence, becomes increasingly metaphorical and textual. In the case of the train in Gould's earlier radio piece, we are in motion, moving toward a destination we never reach, partly because the "idea" of the North remains an imaginary—or resisted—construction in Gould's program. If the sound of the train moved the listener through an imaginary landscape, the ocean is a place marker that fixes us in a very specific setting, the island geography of Newfoundland. Here there is nowhere to go, on an island rimmed by the sea. "Newfoundland is an island at the end of the line," notes John Scott sixteen minutes into the documentary. As a continuous sound, the sea develops its own musical language, which reminds us of the isolation of the Newfoundlanders—their remoteness and loneliness.

"The Latecomers" begins where "The Idea of North" ends, with the struggle of voices to be heard.[47] Much of what follows would surely have been lost on those listeners who first tuned into the 1971 CBC broadcast. As the first thing we hear, the thirty-seven-second collage of sea sounds dominates the scene. The waves move back and forth between the left and right stereo channels signaling their pervasiveness. When Gould's subjects do begin talking, they are forced to speak over the rumbling waves and hissing surf.[48] Their voices are lost to noise. Refusing to fade down the sound of the sea had much in common with the extreme use of cross talk in "The Idea of North." In both cases, Gould deliberately flouted broadcast radio's acoustic order (the privileging of the human voice).

As Gould explained in interviews, he did not understand why it was necessary to assign hierarchal value to the sound of spoken language. Why should speech be privileged over music or other sounds? "It is a strange notion—this idea that the respect for the human voice in terms of broadcasting is such that one shuts down all other patterns to an appropriately reverential level. Very often in TV documentaries particularly I get very upset by the fact that the moment any character—the narrator, the subject, or someone talking about the subject—happens to open his mouth, all other activity has to grind to a halt or at any rate come down fifteen decibels to ensure respect. It's nonsense. The average person can take in and respond to far more information than we allot him on most occasions."[49] Gould had already demonstrated his resistance to "respect for the human voice" in "The Idea of North," where the primacy of speech could hardly stand up to his contrapuntal trickery, and would find new ways in each segment of *The Solitude Trilogy* to defy the logocentric imperative inherent in documentary form. Mixed at a relentlessly high level, the ocean in "The Latecomers" competes with the voices of Newfoundland's subjects, intruding into the auditory imagination of the listener, making our work that much harder (by fifteen decibels, as a guess). What is compromised is the intelligibility of the sign, of the word. As implied by Gould, Newfoundland is endangered by *aphonia*, loss of voice. Much of the listener's effort is devoted to rescuing the vocal signal of Newfoundlanders from the natural sound of the sea. What we hear, when we do, is privation and resignation. The sound of the forsaken. Modernity has "robbed" the island of its solitude, and there is little that can be done. "This thing that has happened to you and me has happened to us over a period of a hundred years, you know, the mad rush of this. . . . They robbed us of the solitude, and really the value of life comes from solitude," says the first speaker. "Fifteen years ago I enjoyed life here so much nothing would have induced me to leave," says the second. "Now that I would probably like to leave it's too late." "I suppose I could leave Newfoundland—I don't think I'd be anxious to leave it," says another voice, barely audible over the roar of the ocean. "A man at my age now, you see when you come up to certain age you must stay where you're at," adds another. During the three-and-a-half-minute prologue, we hear ten different voices, which Gould compared to a Greek Chorus, most of whom will not be heard again until the end of the program during the epilogue. What the speakers say matters less than the acoustic contest between islanders and the sea (or as Levi-Strauss would have said, between culture and nature). This is a battle that Gould's Newfoundland speakers, who leave no voiceprint, will lose without the listener's help.

By the end of the prologue, we have either learned how to focus our ears—with patience we can decode not only the vocal signifiers but can also detect the "musical tone" (melancholy) of the speakers—or we have simply turned off the radio. Gould's own ability to eavesdrop on several different conversations at once in a crowded restaurant is part of the lore that now surrounds him. His skill at filtering out ambient noise, as Connor suggests, seemed to stimulate his auditory imagination, and this is what he demands of his listeners in all three segments of his *Trilogy*.[50]

Having learned in the prologue how to "listen" to "The Latecomers," we are rewarded with a lengthy speech that provides useful narrative information about place, time, character, and theme. The speaker is Dr. Leslie Harris, who is identified by Gould in his liner notes as the "narrator." He is like the first violinist, or concertmaster, in an orchestra and is given more airtime than any other speaker in the program. Scene one begins with a long two-minute monologue by Harris:

> There were times of difficulty, admittedly, but we had a comfortable life. It seemed so to us, mind you. By modern standards, I suppose, or by the expectations of people now it wouldn't have been considered so. We were living in virtually complete isolation. There was no telephone. . . . We had a very rigid Methodist grandfather who came to the south coast from the North and who brought with him the idea that the only good on the face of the earth was work, well work and doing one's duty, whatever that meant, and it meant many things at many times. And this was passed on, this zeal for work and for doing one's duty, despite whatever might stand in the way, including personal proclivity and inclination.

Harris is the program's memoirist, filtering the "idea" of Newfoundland through his own personal history. He speaks with painstaking precision and clarity, often qualifying his remarks with rephrasing and afterthoughts. This is a man long used to editing himself:

> The consequence of this [zeal for work and doing one's duty] is that I am basically a very lazy person. And yet I work harder, I think, than most people because I'm driven by this thing about work and duty

Glenn Gould's Contrapuntal Sound

that is bred into me—or at least, I suppose this is not true, it's not a genetic thing, but it was certainly educated into me from my infancy. I mentioned already my grandfather being Methodist, not that this has any theological consequence because he wasn't a theologian—nor had any pretensions to be—but as far as his attitude toward work and life was concerned it had an effect on us. And of course then we grew up in a very puritanical sort of regime.

His voice is a bookish one, cultivated, literate, sophisticated, and tempered by learning.

Harris may be at home with modernity and may belong to a cultural elite—or so his scholarly voice would suggest (he is a college professor)—but Gould grounds his persona in a pretechnological past ("There was no telephone") where restraint and self-reliance give shape to personal histories. One can easily imagine the appeal of such a character, who often speaks on both sides of the issue, for the contrapuntal-minded Gould. As narrators go, Harris is a considerate one, though slightly tormented, measuring his past with a critical eye in one moment and an appreciative one in the next. Rarely does he leave a statement unqualified. It's not that Harris is ambivalent about Newfoundland but that his responses are so studious and deliberate, as if he were composing his thoughts for the page. Harris, for whom speaking and writing seem one and the same, operates on such a high level of linguistic competence that it is hard not to be aware of his scrupulous syntax and the use of the kind of articulated self-analysis that Walter Ong would ascribe to the textual habit of writing.[51]

As a character in a drama, Harris is ear-catching for his highly articulate discourse. In his voice, the world is reproduced as text; his speech is an echo of the page. In his painstaking efforts we hear the order of discourse, as described by Foucault, the disciplinary self-control that rules his voice. If he seems, at first hearing, to inhabit a privileged position in the program, that impression is soon qualified by the debut of an entirely different kind of voice.

In the differential logic of "The Latecomers," the *typographic* voice of Leslie Harris (borrowing a term from Gould's contemporary, McLuhan) is placed in counterpoint to the speaking voice of Eugene Young, the program's resident raconteur, who first "appears" nine minutes into the program:

I had an old friend of mine, a Catholic priest. His name was Father Fitzgerald. He was afterwards Dr. but I think if they made him Pope he'd still be Father Fitzgerald to me. He wrote some wonderful poems of Newfoundland. And he expresses himself to my liking in many ways. I know one verse of a ballad that he wrote, which people might consider to be doggerel, but expresses Newfoundland, oh, so well. The verse is: "And what's a cup of tea to the likes of me? In fancy eggshell china. Hors d'oeuvres or chicken a la mode, or any foreign dish, like noodles, lilac sherbet, aperitifs and bouillon, when all I do so wish is for brews, fresh cod's heads and a bit of watered fish." That's for me. My friend. That's Newfoundland.

For the raconteur, Newfoundland is a land that is as inseparable from its stories, songs, and poems as the island is from the sea. Newfoundland is a culture that exists largely in the language of the people ("all I do so wish is for brews, fresh cod's heads and a bit of watered fish") and is retrievable through oral performance. The idea behind Eugene Young's storytelling role is that meaning is shared rather than constructed (or disciplined). It preexists in the tribal lore of the folk. It is not surprising, in this light, that Young should challenge the theme of the program—isolation. As he says, "We people on this island of Newfoundland do not, for one moment, consider ourselves isolated in any way."

Gould splices the two characters side by side in scenes one and two, with Young's stylized oral flourishes serving as a counterpoint to the introspective, hypotactic, and linear remarks of Harris. Young's bardic role in the program reflects Gould's considerable efforts to structure his program around a theorized and (during the late 1960s) popular tension between the cultures of orality and literacy. The character of Eugene Young is musical and spontaneous. As resident bard, he is given to unscripted riffs full of rhythmic and alliterative turns of phrase, evoking a performative mastery:

> I've been a round considerable lot. But the sights and sounds of Newfoundland are not in these places. You feel like a stranger there. Because you're not getting the same air. You're not getting the same atmosphere. And when I say atmosphere, I'm not talking about buildings and glorious things. I'm talking about, just the air, the aroma, the smell of Newfoundland. I've been as far west as California. Oh, that beautiful weather. The sun, she rises every morning. She goes down every night and comes up in the same blaze of glory. And after being there for a week, you take it from me, I'm looking forward to a foggy day, a rainy day, a little bit a Sou'West wind and a little bit of Northeast wind. Oh, this is Newfoundland.

The garrulous Young is a character who might be more at home in Dylan Thomas's Llareggub than in a study of cultural change in remote Canada, not surprising, since Gould's program has more in common with *Under Milk Wood* than first meets the ear. This is particularly evident in an anecdote about the powerful sense of place evoked by Newfoundland. As Young explains:

> I can remember the time, on a boat called the Old Sagonna. I was going north from Corner Brook. The Captain of that boat was a Captain Gullidge. It was as thick with fog—the likes of which you've never seen before. As a matter of fact, I think you could cut it out in blocks and pass it over the stern to get ahead. I was up on the bridge with Captain Gullidge this day, and, by God, it was some thick [fog]. And he had his nose up in the air and he was sniffing. And I said to him, I said, "Captain Gullidge," I said, "in the name of God," I said, "what are you sniffing for?" He said, "I'm trying to smell the land." . . . So I said to him, I said, "Captain Gullidge," I said, "what are you sniffing for?" "Well," he said, "between Trout River and," he said, "Bon Bay there's a patch of the heather and the wind off here," he said, "from the sou'west." He said, "You gets the smell of it at this time of the year, and when I gets the smell of that Scotch Heather," he said, "I knows where I am." That's what I'm talking about, atmosphere. That kind of ozone. The purity of the air. I'm sure you can't find it in Toronto.

Young's lyricism sparkles throughout the program, and if he does not quite steal the show, Gould repeatedly calls attention to his eccentric and distinctive aurality. As Gould wrote in his liner notes to the program:

> The Newfoundlander is first of all a poet. Spirits of Celtic bards linger on among these people; a sense of cadence, of rhythmic poise, makes their speech a tape editor's delight. Even when caught out with little to say—and that happens rarely—they say it in elegant metrics. But mingling with the urge to turn all observation into verse, a blunt saga like dispatch of detail gives point and purpose to their story. Perhaps the fact of life against the elements—as for the Iceland and Greenland peoples—disciplines their stanzas, gives an underpinning of reality to their ever-ready impulse to fantasize.
>
> In a certain sense, of course, Newfoundland itself is a fantasy—a disadvantaged piece of real estate set adrift between two cultures, unable to forget its spiritual tie to one, unable wholly to accept its economic dependence on the other.[52]

In Gould's "fantasy" of Newfoundland, the Celtic bard is an aural wizard, a lyricist for whom music and story are inseparably joined and conveyed through expressive verse. To fulfill that role, Eugene Young, whose tapes required unusual intervention, had to be revised.

In a debate with pianist Arthur Rubinstein over the virtues of tape-edited performances, Gould explained that he and Lorne Tulk spent nearly 400 hours editing "The Latecomers," adding that one Newfoundland speaker in particular (perhaps either Young or Harris) required a vast amount of editorial labor; he was a loquacious subject whose speech was riddled with "ums" and "uhs," the so-called disfluencies of spoken discourse. As Gould explained, the subject was a delightful man, smart and thoughtful, who was critical to the structure of the program:

> He was very articulate and very perceptive, but he had a habit of saying "um" and "uh" and "sort of" and "kind of" constantly—so constantly, in fact, that you got absolutely sick of the repetitions. I mean every third word was separated by an "um" and an "uh." . . . Well, we spent—this is no exaggeration—we spent three long weekends—Saturday, Sunday, and Monday, eight hours per day—doing nothing but removing "um's" and "uh's" and "sort of's" and righting the odd syntactical fluff in his material. . . . We made a conservative guess that there were sixteen hundred edits in that man's speech alone in order to make him sound lucid and fluid, which he now does. *We made a new character out of him.* You see, I don't really care how you do it. . . . If it takes sixteen hundred splices, that's fine.[53]

Gould's subjects are as real as their concerns, but their pairings and arrangements within each scene are obviously invented: "We made a new character out of him." Cleansing a documentary speaker's discourse of its disfluencies, of his discourse markers, is an especially interesting case in point. Like Chomsky, Gould heard his character's starts and stops, his "ums" and "er's" (what linguists call "neutral vowel sounds"), as performance errors, as though his Newfoundlander had misplayed a note on the keyboard. Having edited out his own imperfections in Bach recordings countless times, Gould applied the same kind of fastidiousness to the recorded words of Young (or Harris). "Superficially, the purpose of the splice," Gould had written, "is to rectify performance mishaps."[54] If Gould's speaker was to become his "Celtic bard" or "typographic man," he had to be put right, in a spirit of "take-twoness."[55]

The structure of "The Latecomers" requires a credible voice whose aurality is its chief appeal. By casting Young in so large a role, Gould calls more attention to the materiality of voice than he did in "The Idea of North," where all five speakers sound more or less alike: as writerly members (like Dr. Leslie Harris) of the intellectual class. Eugene Young is Gould's first "primitive," a nod to McLuhan's "aural man." His large-sounding voice, with its heavy brogue accent, rounded vowels, and orotund timbres, stands out from everyone else's. Gould's contrapuntal approach to "The Latecomers" required a speaker sonorous enough to offset the extreme textuality of Leslie Harris's narration, a voice that would be heard not as speech but as music. As Frances Dyson notes, whenever the materiality of sound becomes the focus of attention, sense begins to unravel.[56] This was the lesson of *Under Milk Wood*, which was not lost on Gould.

Both characters, Eugene Young and Dr. Leslie Harris, are of great use to Gould in his efforts to structure his program around a McLuhanesque dichotomy between orality and literacy, each playing a definitive role as a specific aural "type." Other characters with less airtime in the program also conform (more or less) to the two-culture divide. There's Reverend Burry, for instance, who may lack the Celtic lyricism of Eugene Young but who is no less of a storyteller:

> Now, then, I went and stayed in this chap's home where I had stayed before so many years—in a palace with all the modern conveniences, electric lights, television—I shaved Sunday morning with an electric razor—and all that kind of thing. And I said to the man of the house, "Wallace," I said, "Wallace, what do you think of it all?" "Yes," he said, "I know what you have in mind. You're thinking of the years you came here, the first few years you were here," he said. "Well, of course," he said, "we have this beautiful home and all these conveniences but," he says, "I'd rather go back to the old days. Now then, my children," he says, "they are growing up with it. But," he says, "as far as we're concerned, we'd give up all these things if we could get back to the type of living where we knew each other. We were friendly. We could communicate with each other. We helped one another—but now," he says, "you don't get that kind of thing today. That's all gone, that's what we've lost." Now isn't it tragic—but it's a reflection on our modern civilization. That's what it is, on all of us.

Many are equally nostalgic for an imagined past, but their accord is less interesting than their contrasting "musical" styles, as Gould would say.

McLuhan had taken up the theme of orality and literacy in the early 1950s. As he often argued, literate culture was witnessing the return of orality in the form of escalating electronic media. The new orality was essentially residual, or "secondary," in the words of Walter Ong, and did not conflict with literacy so much as co-exist with it in contemporary culture. Gould's interest in the ideas of McLuhan is not surprising. As some have said, he took McLuhan's writings on electronic media more seriously than McLuhan himself did.[57] Like the media visionary, Gould regarded hearing as a more powerful sense than sight and liked to use McLuhan's notion of wraparound environment when describing his own relationship to sound. Gould is said to have carried a radio with him at all times in order to be immersed in sound: "Radio, in any case, is a medium I've been very close to every since I was a child, that I listen to virtually nonstop: I mean, it's wallpaper for me—I sleep with the radio on, in fact now I'm incapable of sleeping *without* the radio on."[58] In a way, Newfoundland had been transformed into a mediascape by Gould. On tape, the mediascape is an inclusive space, made up of aural participants and performers whose voices are not self-canceling (as in "The Idea of North") but are instead complementary and interdependent. If Gould draws attention to a sense of local identity tied to cultural geography, it is a mediated sense of community that is the result of cutting and pasting. Gould's Newfoundland is a collective intelligence that is networked electronically via the tape splice. The residual irony of "The Latecomers" involves the extent to which Gould himself carries out a program of "resettlement" via tape-splicing, by relocating his subjects editorially in an imaginary community of discourse.

Gould's ability to "move" characters around in virtual space was greatly enhanced by stereo technology, which had been recently added to FM broadcasting by the CBC. In "The Latecomers," Gould approached the chance to work in stereo with zeal.[59] Being able to locate speakers at different points across the stereo spectrum allowed him to dramatize more precisely the location of his characters in relation to one another by manipulating the illusion of depth and width. Gould relished the greater complexity permitted by binaural sound, so much so that he even flirted with the possibility of producing part three of the trilogy, "The Quiet in the Land," in quadraphonic sound. With "The Quiet in the Land," the most technologically complex of the three radio pieces, Gould completed his study of solitude. The program takes listeners to Red River, Manitoba, where in 1971 Gould interviewed both current and lapsed Mennonites and assembled their nine voices in a "documentary" focusing on the effort of a religious people to live outside mainstream society. In the opening prologue, Gould created as intricate and virtuoso a montage as anything he had ever done for radio, layering together the sounds of a church bell, children at play, passing automobiles, birdsong, a Mennonite congregation singing a hymn, a sermon, a cello suite by Bach, Janis Joplin singing "Mercedes-Benz," and the overlapping voices of Mennonite speakers—all in striking counterpoint, driving the tension between worldly materialism and spiritual piety. As Gould told an interviewer after completing the program, what he had accomplished in "The Quiet in the Land" was "going to make everything [he had] done up till the present seem like Gregorian chant by comparison."[60]

Radical Listening

By his final program, Gould had perfected the idea of "contrapuntal radio" to such an extent that the competence of his radio listeners would have to match the skill of an audiophile if they were to follow the documentary. In prioritizing the act of listening, Gould assumed that his public would accept the invitation to tune in as carefully and as raptly to his radio programs as they had to his recordings of Bach's *Goldberg Variations*. Since Gould's "mood-pieces" are too involved to understand in one pass, he was obviously expecting a degree of close listening that would be quite foreign to the drive-time experience of public radio listeners today. Was this presumptuous?[61]

Had it not been for the FM revolution in radio, which set off the underground movement in free-form radio throughout North America, where the host or DJ (who considered his format an audio art) enjoyed complete control over program content with few stylistic or commercial limits, the answer certainly would be yes.[62] Glenn Gould's cubist experiment with radio in the *Solitude Trilogy* coincided precisely with, and was enabled by, the wider bandwidth and free-form radio that peaked in North America in the late 1960s and early 1970s. At the core of these developments was a zealous quest for, as Susan Douglas writes, a deeper, richer, and more nuanced listening experience made possible by technical advances in sound production and transmission.[63] As the underground movement in radio was proving in America, close listening would be defined as the celebration of sound itself, with listeners quickly developing a longing for high fidelity that answered the call of free-form radio's cerebral programming. Whether airing poetry and literature, discussing contemporary politics, or analyzing the deep structure of music, FM radio's underground gurus (like *Radio Unnameable*'s Bob Fass in New York City or Johnny Hyde's *The Gear* in Sacramento) treated their listeners to a heady mix of cultural fare: Buffalo Springfield one moment, a Mozart sonata the next, and in between Beat poetry, stories, essays, social satire, and political monologues, perhaps followed by a Balinese gamelan piece. The dynamics of radio were changing as rapidly as the programming. Even in remote Toronto, Glenn Gould was at the center of an acoustic culture tuned into the subtleties and complexities of a kind of sound art that would redefine an entire generation of radio listeners.

All Things Reconsidered
The Promise of NPR

In recent years, National Public Radio has been criticized for its stodginess. The shows are bland, critics say—or at least too cautious—and its cultural coverage is limited. Its quirkiness level is at an all-time low, and young listeners no longer tune in.[1] Forty-plus years ago, however, NPR was anything but stuffy. The adjectives applied to it—funky, playful, spirited, and edgy—described a network that was young at heart. NPR was not merely nimble back then; it was also better connected to sonic traditions that had prevailed during radio's golden age, such as experimental sound-making and radiophonic literature. When NPR debuted in 1971, cutting-edge American radio drama found its way back onto the air after nearly twenty years of silence, as did avant-garde sound collages, personal essays, surrealistic narratives, and vérité sound documentaries. Given the network's renown as a news-gathering agent today, it is easy to overlook the fact that NPR, as Susan Douglas has observed, almost single-handedly rejuvenated radio in the early 1970s.[2] How NPR engineered such a radiophonic revival, and what happened in its aftermath, is the story of this final chapter.[3]

Founding Mothers

Every Thursday morning, NPR used to invite the public on a tour of its large, wedge-shaped headquarters at 635 Massachusetts Avenue.[4] The tour began in the smartly designed lobby with its fancy high ceilings. If you were early, you could sit in a comfortable leather chair and watch a slide show of NPR personalities projected on a large screen. There you could see Noah Adams and Terry Gross, plus the women with exotic names: Laksmi Singh, Margot Adler, Renée Montagne, Mara Liasson, and Sylvia Poggioli. Also Steve Inskeep, formerly of *Morning Edition*, and Tom and Ray Magliozzi, formerly of *Car Talk*. Gazing at the screen was like celebrity spotting without the trouble of being out and about.

These radio stars were smiling, and why shouldn't they be? While newspapers, magazines, and TV continue to lose ground, NPR's growth has been enviably robust throughout the last decade. NPR now boasts more news bureaus globally than the *Washington Post* or any of the major TV networks, and its listenership rivals Rush Limbaugh's, with 30 million people tuning in each week to its popular news "magazines" *Morning Edition* and *All Things Considered*. Once a small and fledgling alternative network, NPR has turned itself into a renowned organization increasingly independent of federal support.

My lingering in the lobby wasn't for a tour, however, but for an interview with Susan Stamberg, NPR's "founding mother." Susan Stamberg is to NPR what Edward R. Murrow is to CBS, an icon. While just an interview, this encounter felt like a date, maybe because many of a certain age have had a crush on her voice since they were in school. Back then, few were used to hearing a woman on the radio, especially one who was having a good time. As Bob Edwards has said, Stamberg was never afraid to put her personality on the air.

At a small table in NPR's seventh-floor café, where the special is the Honduran Quesadilla, the recorder was on and the questions began. How have things changed over the years? What was the network like during its first decade of broadcast (in the 1970s) when NPR was not the hard-news powerhouse it is today, when it actually aired a good deal of arty fare, including daily doses of literature?

Stamberg herself has interviewed thousands of well-known people, from Luciano Pavarotti to Rosa Parks, but now that she has become a subject of public interest herself, she seems to relish the role reversal. As the first woman to anchor a national news program, Stamberg had to carve out a space for herself without any female role models. In the beginning, she lowered her voice, she said, to sound like a man and spoke in a formal style. Stamberg does a deft impersonation of a male broadcaster, sounding like Laurie Anderson in pitch-shifting mode. It was stressful, she adds, trying to produce that authoritative sound. Bill Siemering, NPR's first program director and creator of *All Things Considered*, "told me to be myself, and that was terrifying to me. And slowly I stopped pretending to be someone else and just began to talk."[5] Stamberg thinks Siemering had found in her "the voice he had heard in his head for the new show," she said. He did not want the tone of *All Things Considered* to resemble the *March of Time*. He wanted something "more chatty, more intimate, more personal." With Stamberg, NPR found a way to become simpatico with post-Vietnam America.

Susan Stamberg in the NPR studio during a broadcast of *All Things Considered*, 1970s. (NPR Photo, courtesy of National Public Radio)

Stamberg shared her job with several male co-hosts during her career at NPR, but there was never any doubt that she defined the style of *All Things Considered*.[6] Listeners heard the news, but that wasn't the only reason they tuned in. The congenial voice of a female anchor brought charm to radioland, signaling a reluctance to abide by old broadcast formulas. Not only that, but the new program included stories that were engaging for their distinctly offbeat character (a report on the hundredth anniversary of the banana) or for their interest in events on the margins of culture (a thirty-minute feature devoted to men and women who grew up in the Appalachian hills of West Virginia).

By design, *All Things Considered* avoided conventional broadcast practices. What Stamberg liked best about the early days at NPR was experimenting with different kinds of storytelling. You know, she said, this was the time of the great cinema verité filmmakers, like D. A. Pennebaker and Frederick Wiseman, whose techniques NPR adopted. NPR watched what film people were doing with their handheld cameras, the way they dodged voice-overs, and did the same with tape recorders. Stamberg recalls these moments with surprise, as if she were remembering the novelty of NPR for the first time. "The idea," Stamberg said, "was to tell a story without telling it—just sound through chunks." That meant going without a narrator, which defied traditional conventions. A gutsy choice for an upstart radio program.

Stamberg's first verité feature focused on the Abbie Hoffman–style lawyer Philip Hirschkop, who defended the 13,000 May Day protesters arrested in the aftermath of the antiwar demonstrations in Washington, D.C., in May 1971. Stamberg spent an entire day with Hirschkop and his assistants, keeping her tape recorder running for five hours. ("Turn that thing off," Hirschkop told her, a sound bite she kept in the report.) Edited down to sixteen minutes, the feature presented a mix of aural snippets portraying an insouciant lawyer consulting with his harried staff over the dull details of an upcoming court case. Perry Mason this was not, but it made for engaging radio.

Not everyone at NPR appreciated the new style. "We had an excellent producer named Josh Darsa," Stamberg said, "who wanted to be the next Edward R. Murrow. Murrow was the big god for all of us, of course, but our work was so different from what he had accomplished. At any rate, Darsa called me over after the Hirschkop report ran and told me the piece was lousy. And I said, 'Why is that, Josh?' 'Well, all those things you put in, they are like sound effects, but you never told us anything, you never told us a story.'" Stamberg pauses for emphasis. "I had to make a real defense for what I was doing, that I was doing the audio version of cinema verité. I was simply telling the story in a different way. That was early in the game, when we wanted to be different from what anyone else in radio was doing. But Darsa said no, no—that's not the way we do it. You have to do a proper narration." Stamberg starts laughing at the producer's obstinacy.[7]

Several years ago, *New York* magazine called Stamberg's sense of humor the best on radio. In person, Stamberg sounds no different than she does on the air. Quizzical yet playful, she does not suffer from the sobriety of the professional class. From across the table, the laughter is infectious. When asked about the commentaries NPR often ran on *All Things Considered*—personal essays, rants, and satires by writers from around the country (Bailey White from rural Georgia, the Romanian-born Andrei Codrescu from Louisiana, Baxter Black from Texas), Stamberg muses for a moment. How did these outliers wind up on the air? Before journalists took over the network, *All Things Considered* was more imaginative about programming, Stamberg says. But honestly, "we were so desperate to fill the air back then. After all, ninety minutes was a long time," she adds, bursting into laughter.

Innovation was written into NPR's founding code. Its mission statement, penned by Bill Siemering, promised listeners an expanded aural experience by speaking "with many voices and many dialects," but also by advancing "the art and the enjoyment of the sound medium." That NPR took such a promise seriously seems remarkable in retrospect. The network has strayed from that mission over the years, as NPR's critics often point out, but that only makes its original achievement more significant.

Critics have not hesitated to take NPR to task for its slide away from creativity. Many see today's NPR as too "mainstream," wrote Scott Sherman in the *Nation*. Above all, "too deferential to power."[8] Even Stamberg, who embodied the adventurous spirit of NPR during its heyday, seems taken aback by the network's predictable sound. With the exception of the car guys, everyone sounds the same. "What do you mean," Stamberg asks, the twinkle gone from her eyes. Sometimes it is difficult to tell who is speaking. Was that Michelle Norris, Michelle Block, or Mara Liasson—or Greg Inskeep or Ari Shapiro? A typical complaint is that the network no longer produces distinctive voices but instead the "NPR drone."[9] Thus Brian Montopoli's gripe: "If you listen to a lot of NPR, you realize how similar it all sounds: no matter who is talking, or what they're talking about."[10]

Obviously, for these critics the network has lost its cutting edge. NPR is particularly sensitive to the graying of its listeners. Its difficulty in reaching the demographic of eighteen- to twenty-five-year-olds is a sore spot in public radio's marketing strategy. Stamberg knits her brow. She has no doubt heard these complaints before. "The main thing that happened to us," Stamberg admits reluctantly, "is that we became professionalized over the years. In those first years, we were inventing ourselves. And that took at least ten years. But in the course of our success, we got more resources, hired more staff, there was more competition for air time, more writers, more journalists, and narrating became a much more efficient way of doing things. When NPR started we only had five reporters. I don't know what it is today, probably over one hundred. Once we got richer, we produced the kind of radio our critics don't necessarily like, and that changed the sound because the listener wasn't hearing great voices anymore. Today NPR is what it is because that's all there is, because of the obligation for news—no one else is providing it—the program has become far more formatted than it's ever been before."[11]

Radio and the Raconteur

Once Edward R. Murrow had moved to television with the documentary series *See it Now* (1951–58), his unique contribution to broadcast literature—the radio essay—was nearly forgotten.[12] It was overshadowed by his television work, best remembered for its probing of Communist witch-hunt hysteria and for its decisive exposé of Joseph McCarthy. As radio's literary achievements faded from memory, the airwaves featured fewer essayists and raconteurs. The art of storytelling had nearly disappeared from American radio in the years after TV's rise in popularity—except for the witty and satirical monologues of Jean Shepherd on New York City's WOR.[13] Shepherd's program, *A Voice in the Night*, which was broadcast from 1956 to 1977, regaled late-night listeners, whom Shepherd called the "night people," with real-life tales of growing up in the gritty mill town of Hammond, Indiana. Shepherd's most enduring stories were drawn from boyhood misadventures in the industrial Midwest and were told in a relentlessly ironic voice that gave full expression to what he saw as the inescapable absurdity of human life.[14] His characters, as the *Wall Street Journal* noted, "flirt valiantly but briefly with victory, only to go down in the end to crushing defeat."[15]

During his twenty-one years on the air, Shepherd spun countless yarns from his childhood in Indiana and his army experience. His rambling monologues are stocked with vivid storylines and zany characters (wedge-shaped Big Al and foul-smelling Wanda Hickey), but they are also packed with searching non-narrative moments, including mock commentaries, playful digressions, and wisecracking observations (an account of H. L. Mencken's four-volume tome *The American Language*, with a digression on American humor, or an autobiographical reading of Samuel Beckett's

Krapp's Last Tape).[16] Such discursive ingenuity turned Shepherd's spiel into a compelling art form that, even while drawing on earlier dramatic broadcast traditions, was unprecedented on radio. Shepherd's improvisatory radio work blurred the lines between "talk radio," essayism, and memoir (not to mention fiction). His was "such a hypnotic voice," as the film critic Kenneth Turan recalls, that "he'd go off on these tangents and he'd somehow bring you back."[17] The meandering genius behind Shepherd's monologues recognized few boundaries and thrived when seeming to go astray. Marshall McLuhan hailed Shepherd as the Montaigne of the airwaves, "the first to use radio as an essay." "The mike," wrote McLuhan, was Shepherd's "pen and paper."[18] Thanks to the appeal of his droll stories, Shepherd's *A Voice in the Night* enjoyed a cult following of "intense proportions," as the *New York Times* put it, that cut across all age groups.[19] He had rekindled a part of radio that still mattered to listeners.

Shepherd may not have been the first radio essayist nor the last, but his eccentric monologues revealed an overlooked demand for idiosyncratic radio voices and storytellers with a knack for personal reflection. NPR did not fail to notice. Public radio was not able to welcome a voice as wild, rambling, and ironic as Shepherd's, but it could invite "fresh" voices from outside the Beltway to supply the network with personal stories, reminiscences, and commentaries that reflected a broader slice of America.[20]

In 1976, listeners were likely to have encountered a voice that seemed to violate most of the formalities of radio. By then, NPR was five years old and *All Things Considered* was widely viewed as the coolest thing on the air.[21] The voice belonged to Kim Williams, a naturalist from Missoula, Montana, who possessed a homespun, cracker-barrel style. What listeners heard was someone describing a new method for making chili featuring half a cup of earthworms: "I'm designing a new recipe for a contest. The main ingredient has to be . . . well . . . here it is: Earthworms!" Williams explained, in a perfectly reasonable way, how natural it was for people in other cultures to acquire protein from insects and lizards. In subsequent essays, Williams spoke in praise of chokecherries, parsnips, dandelion salads, bear grease, cattails, and wild herbs, long before eating weeds became chic. Her monologue was a far cry from the commentaries of Daniel Schorr pondering illegal CIA activities (1976) or the Iran Hostage Crisis (1980). Her subject was as peculiar as her voice.

Kim Williams had aired a weekly radio show about wild plants and herbs on KUFM in Missoula in the mid-1970s. After Montana Public Radio sent a sample tape to Washington, NPR signed Williams in 1976 as a "commentator," code in public radioland for "personal essayist."²² Williams died from cancer in 1986. With the exception of the heavily accented Andrei Codrescu, her ten-year stretch as a guest commentator had been the longest on NPR. The example of Kim Williams is significant for what it says about voice. As Linda Wertheimer has written, in Bill Siemering's vision of public radio, owning a "big bass voice would not be a prerequisite for presenting the news," since he believed that "all kinds of people should speak on the radio."²³

Williams's commentaries began with homey observations but, full of simple wisdom and plenty of wit, often veered unpredictably in the direction of social critique. As a throwback to Thoreau, her appeal to naturalist values was certainly engaging, well in advance of the whole foods movement, but it was the voice in which she delivered her essays more than anything else that captured listeners and made her a radio character. Her voice was so peculiar one had to go searching for metaphors in order to describe it, as it was possessed of an aural strangeness that was partly folksy but also adolescent (a trait later echoed by David Sedaris and Sarah Vowell). One of her longtime fans, Ian Frazier, writing in the *New Yorker*, compared Williams's voice to that of Cindy Lauper. To Susan Stamberg, it was a cross between Edith Bunker and Grandma Moses.²⁴ Williams' success was all the more surprising given that she was working in all but a dead tradition. The radio "commentator," as one might expect, did not survive the arrival of television or radio's own dwindling resources in the 1950s. Commentators like Howard K. Smith and Eric Sevareid, who had worked with Murrow during the war, moved to television in the early 1960s. Like Walter Cronkite, they continued to air short commentaries for radio through the 1970s, but their métier and personae had changed significantly for the camera.²⁵ If not for NPR, the radio commentator would now be all but forgotten, an obscure footnote in the history of the wireless. NPR brought the commentator back to life during its innovative first decade in the 1970s, though in a very different guise. Telling a good story should have little to do with varnishing your vowels or disciplining your diphthongs, NPR thought. Nobody, after all, really wants to sound like Ted Baxter, the pompous newsman on *The Mary Tyler Moore Show*. An unproven entity itself, NPR had the good sense back then to develop the appeal of outliers.

It was in the spirit of outreach that NPR's *All Things Considered* went searching in the 1970s and 1980s for voices with regional or foreign inflections, voices that, like Susan Stamberg's (with its New York accent and giggle), could break through the sound barrier. Member stations had grumbled that contributions by the rank and file were continually rejected by NPR in favor of material produced in Washington.[26] By broadcasting a steady stream of "commentaries" from writers all over the country (Paula Schiller on extreme cold in Fairbanks, Alaska; a rant by Montanan Kim Williams on junk food; Vertamae Grosvenor on the death of John Lennon; raconteur and Floridian Gamble Rogers on fishing), the network replaced the D.C.-centric monotone with a varied sound that was consistent with Siemering's many-voiced vision of public radio while satisfying member stations' desire for a national scope.[27] NPR gave airtime to Andrei Codrescu, a foreign-born poet as renowned for his thick Romanian accent as for his ironic view of American culture; Baxter Black, the "Cowboy Poet" and humorist from Las Cruces, New Mexico, master of the southwestern drawl and homespun essays on cow bloat, barbed wire, manure, and the daily ups and downs of ordinary folks in close proximity to large, messy animals; Bailey White from rural Georgia, who told wry tales about eccentric characters and provided vivid descriptions of small-town southern life, including her oddball mother's recipe for road kill; and Daniel Pinkwater from Hoboken, New Jersey, a writer of children's books turned humorist, who recounted the trials of being fat or weird. These were not detached broadcast voices, orotund and transcendent, but fully embodied voices, incarnated in a talking self that turned its own physicality into an expressive force that was inseparable from the writing. The appeal of NPR's commentators was in the Barthesian "grain of their voice," in what McLuhan called "those gestural qualities that the printed page strips from language" but which return on the radio.[28] So it is with Sarah Vowell, who sounds like a disaffected teenager scheming revenge from the basement of a library; or with David Sedaris, the man-boy whose self-ironic hilarity plumbs the joyful absurdities of his dysfunctional family; or with David Rakoff, whose sardonic, world-weary voice was as droll as that of the snarkiest of bloggers.

As a marginalized genre, the radio essay was unique to NPR and fit perfectly with its programming philosophy of diversity. In his mission statement, Siemering emphasized the cultural side of public radio over mere news-gathering, which was a decisive nod in the direction of the arts and heterogeneity.[29] At its dawn, the network showcased storytellers, artists, and authors, flooding the airwaves with the voices of raconteurs. Susan Stamberg's interviews with prestigious writers—Saul Bellow, John McPhee, Isaac Asimov, Joan Didion, Henry Miller, Susan Sontag, Ivan Doig,

Katha Pollitt, John Irving, Thomas Merton, Paul Theroux, Fran Liebowitz, Donald Hall, and Walter Jackson Bate—became famous over time and marked *All Things Considered* as alternative radio with a literary sensibility.[30] But the idiosyncratic essays that digressed from the day's news stories on both *Morning Edition* and *All Things Considered*, recorded by obscure writers in the underfinanced studios of far-flung member stations, contributed to that sense of "otherness" even more. When an as-yet-unknown Sedaris read excerpts from his diary as a Macy's department store elf on *Morning Edition* in late 1992 ("I wear green velvet knickers, a forest-green velvet smock and a perky little hat decorated with spangles"), listeners heard a thirty-something man with the voice of a young boy chronicling his stint as Santa's helper in the disingenuous retail space of a shopping mall. The essay was full of zany turns, including an impersonation of Billie Holiday singing "Away in the Manger," but also managed to provide a cynical reading of the false cheer of the "holiday spirit" with an ironic air that may have reminded listeners of Jean Shepherd. Crumpet, the gay Elf, was not exactly what Bob and Alice of Dayton, Ohio, were expecting on Christmas Eve, but this was certainly radio with a difference, something prized by the network's interest in acoustic alternatives to commercial media. Such essays helped revive the storytelling side of radio, perhaps even in ways not imagined by Bill Siemering.[31]

Outside of the compelling stories told by Murrow during the London Blitz, the BBC reminiscences of Dylan Thomas, or the talk radio of Jean Shepherd, NPR's short commentaries were unprecedented in radio history. Essay-like elements appeared commonly in the work of Norman Corwin and were encouraged in BBC "features." But the essay had never stood on its own; instead, as though a stepchild, the radio essay always accompanied other genres: poetry, fiction, and drama. Now NPR commentators delivered freestanding essays, personally voiced reflections on the American scene. Their pieces may have been short, but they were self-contained prose works, kin to the kinds of writing that formed part of a literary tradition stretching from Montaigne through Orwell and beyond. Many of NPR's personal essayists, like Kim Williams, had considerable success, and some remained on the air for a quarter century or more (among them, Andrei Codrescu, Baxter Black, Daniel Pinkwater, and Bailey White).[32] They became celebrities in the culture of public radio, buoyed by a loyal audience that followed their careers straight to the bookstore. Bailey White's radio fans kept her first collection, *Mama Makes Up Her Mind* (1995), on the best-seller list for over fifty-five weeks.[33] No essayists, of course, ever became rich airing four-minute commentaries on drive-time radio, but their ever-increasing fan base ensured them multiple book deals.

Not everyone, however, was on board with the cult of eccentricity.[34] Frank Mankiewicz, president of NPR from 1977 to 1983, reportedly cringed every time he heard Kim Williams.[35] Mankiewicz, like many in management following him at NPR, had steered the network in the direction of hard-nosed news, promoting *All Things Considered* as the "New York Times" of radio—an idea that the network, for better or worse, has lived up to.[36]

Contrapuntal Public Radio

The debut of *All Things Considered* in May 1971 was incoherent and bewildering by today's "professional" standards. From a purely acoustic point of view, however, the program was captivating. The inaugural broadcast featured a longish verité audio documentary on antiwar demonstrations in Washington and another lengthy report about a nurse named Janice with a heroine addiction. Both features were drawn out and unfocused. In the case of the antiwar protest, NPR sent reporters onto the streets of Washington equipped with tape recorders and the directive to capture the frenzy of the May Day protests as realistically as possible. It was the largest march against the Vietnam War yet, as Bill Siemering remembers it, all converging on the nation's capital to shut down government business for the day. Nearly 200,000 demonstrators "filled the roads, blocked the bridges, and stalled the morning commuter traffic, all in an effort to shut down the government."[37] Protesters were met by 10,000 federal troops, who moved quickly to various cites in Washington, and another 5,000 Metropolitan Police from D.C. By early evening, over 12,000 demonstrators had been detained in the largest mass arrest in U.S. history. NPR's coverage of the event does not shy away from the bedlam provoked by such intense social conflict.

The resulting twenty-four-minute "sound portrait," as Siemering called it, aired on the debut broadcast of *All Things Considered*. It opens with the first two stanzas of Phil Ochs's folk song "Power and Glory" and then plunges into mayhem. The edited tape sounds rough, edgy, bold, and intense, but it suffers from spatial confusion (jumping from scene to scene, reporter to reporter, with little rhyme or reason) and a muddled point of view (it's unclear who is talking or why). "We wanted to capitalize on the sound quality of radio to tell stories," Siemering later said, "to escape from the sterility of a sound-proof studio, and to give the listener a sense of being present amidst the action."[38] This is NPR's on-the-street reporter Jeff Kamen describing the scene in Washington, speaking above the loud hum of helicopters, the roar of motorcycles, and the shouts of protesters:

> Someone threw a brick at you, officer? "Yes sir." Right here as you were driving through? "Right." One of the motorcycle police officers said someone threw a brick at him. I was here at the time and didn't see anything thrown. Army helicopters coming in low. Keeping constant surveillance, keeping various command posts, military, police, and obviously presidential, advised as to what's going on. One helicopter now is in real low, military police helicopter. Up on the rise of this highway section, young people are holding the American flag upside down. A handful of police officers has succeeded in clearing at least half of this roadway. Traffic is flowing again. A Washington, D.C., bus just arrived. Police officers wearing white riot helmets coming out of the bus. They snap on their helmets. Integrated police team. The demonstrators are fleeing. . . . Two police officers just grabbed two demonstrators. They were just walking. The search is peaceful but unprovoked. Tear gas is being fired outside the Department of Agriculture. There weren't that many demonstrators here, but when the police moved out they grabbed as many long-haired young people as they could find. Grabbed them and searched them, put them up against walls, buses, cars. Searched them. Today in the nation's capital, it is a crime to be young and have long hair.[39]

NPR's reporters, bearing small Sony TC-100 cassette recorders, were clearly overwhelmed by an event that forced President Nixon to call out thousands of federal and National Guard troops in riot gear, arresting over 10,000 protesters. The march was chaotic, and that is exactly what was captured on air: the police, the National Guard, protesters, and news reporters are all clearly swept up in an incident whose social and political meaning transcends them. No single reporter can grasp the political turbulence that is evoked so vividly on tape. The NPR reporters interviewed protesters, police, and office workers, alertly describing the turmoil surrounding them. Above all, they recorded several hours of ambient sound (shouting voices, motorcycles, helicopters).[40] NPR's producers had faith in the power of sound, without any voice-over explanation, to convey the larger meanings of the day. In Susan Stamberg's words, "There was no interfering narrator."[41]

Whether or not NPR's debut story was good news (it certainly was not, by traditional standards), it was interesting radio. The richly textured Vietnam-protest piece is thick with invasive sounds, sirens, motorcycles, army helicopters, traffic, screaming protesters, yelling cops, baffled reporters. These are not background or ambient sounds but the story itself, signifiers of vicious violence and the cracking open of heads. The acoustics of the scene are so powerful they blur the line between subjects and objects, narrators and characters, which is why the reporters sometimes sound like demonstrators and vice versa. The current style of hard news—neat, clean, and controlled—could not be more different.[42] The Vietnam protest feature overwhelmed any effort of the on-location reporters or the host Robert Conley to take narrative control. After twenty-four minutes of on-the-street social turmoil, Conley, a veteran of the *New York Times* and NBC, can only say: "In a moment we'll have a discussion of what the effects are of today's actions."

All Things Considered may have been underfunded, understaffed, and defiant of journalistic conventions, but the program won NPR its first Peabody Award in 1972, a little over a year after its first broadcast.[43] With that kind of national respect, NPR had little reason to alter its unorthodox approach to cultural and journalistic storytelling. Rather than modeling itself on the Walter Cronkite–led *CBS Evening News*, it sought authenticity by decentralizing its reportorial practices and by playing the outsider. There would be no master narrative, no dominant spokesman.[44] So determined was Siemering that NPR would not sound like commercial radio that he refused to hire a star anchor, even one that came gift wrapped. The Ford Foundation promised to support NPR with funding ($300,000), provided that it hire the broadcast journalist Edward P. Morgan as host of *All Things Considered*. Morgan was, as Jack Mitchell explains, ABC-Radio's answer to Edward R. Murrow, an authoritative broadcast journalist with recognizable stature who would bring to the fledgling network necessary credibility and legitimacy. With a style that mimicked Murrow, Morgan was, in the eyes of the Ford Foundation, a reliable narrator and a commanding presence. The consummate insider, Morgan had worked with Howard K. Smith and had even been a participant in the second presidential debate in 1960. Ever the populist, Siemering vetoed the idea, despite the interest of others in Morgan's prestige, fearing that a commentator with such a weighty style would foil his quest for the alternative (nondomineering) voices he hoped to cultivate on the new program.[45]

Siemering's position at NPR was short lived, but the network remained faithful to his anti-authoritarian model of storytelling for two decades, and this included a steady interest in marginal events and characters. There was coverage of the National Headache Conference in Washington; a report on a Velcro orchestra; cartoonist Gahan Wilson on his trip to Transylvania; an interview with pole-sitter Vernon Woodrich while atop a thirty-foot flagpole in Los Angeles (Stamberg: "How do you go to the bathroom?" Woodrich: "Well, I have a chemical toilet"); a monologue by Bob Kingsley (a safecracker who did eight years in prison) describing his criminal vocation as an art form; and a feature with Ira Flatow recording penguins at the South Pole. NPR's enthusiasm for inconsequential news manifested itself in any number of ways, from the quest for the perfect hamburger to Stamberg's conversation with a man in Montana who grew the world's largest pumpkin.

New York magazine, the cradle of New Journalism and radical chic, was impressed by the fact that *All Things Considered* would devote fifteen prime-time minutes to stories of so little consequence.[46] One such story involved Michael Meyers, an art teacher in Kansas City, who undertook a peculiar project called the "Audio Encyclopedia of Personal Knowledge." Meyers had sent a tape to NPR in Washington, and Stamberg interviewed the Kansas City art teacher on *All Things Considered* in March 1979. Meyers's off-the-wall project was random and vague. The art teacher had asked people of different ages to sit down in a quiet room and write responses to a simple question: "After all of these years, what do you know?" Meyers asked his participants to begin each sentence with the phrase "I know." "I didn't know what I was going to get," he explained to Stamberg. What people wrote and said sounded like poetry, Meyers said. "I know my body is dying," wrote one speaker. "I know that spoken words can't be trusted," said another. "I know the following about the external world: Asparagus makes one's urine smell. Babe Ruth hit 714 home runs. Hank Aaron hit more.... I know that wealthy people make me nervous." These were voices of strangers, entirely anonymous, speaking intimately about their fears and desires ("I know I'll always long to be somewhere else.... I know my father died in the morning"). The simple rules of Meyers's experiment provoked an unexpected lyricism that occasionally became profound. There was nothing newsworthy about this, and it is hard to define the cultural value of such an experiment. What the segment suggested was that NPR was interested in listening to its listeners, ordinary people with little or no claim to political or cultural significance, as if their voices mattered.[47]

The following year (1980), *All Things Considered* aired a documentary on the New Hampshire primary during the presidential campaign. The twenty-minute program included predictable moments from Edward Kennedy, Governor Jerry Brown, George H. W. Bush, Howard Baker, and John B. Anderson, along with "actuality" from the town of Claremont, New Hampshire (traffic sounds, cameras clicking, high school bands, the singing of the Rotary Club). What made the radio piece unorthodox was its narrator. Rather than assigning its own field reporter, *All Things Considered* invited David Puksta (who wrote his own copy), the seventeen-year-old son of Claremont's mayor, to narrate the story. A news "reporter" (not one of NPR's) can be heard in the background, but his role is peripheral to the story. Instead, young David Puksta, in a regional dialect so strong he sounds like an actor auditioning for *Our Town*, guides the listener through the field of candidates:

> About this time during primary season, most people who want to become president feel some kind of urge to visit this little town of Claremont. About 14,000 people live here. It's called the city where the work gets done. It's pretty much a factory town—textiles, steel, paper, that sort of stuff. On Tremont Square is the city hall and chamber of commerce. We got a pet shop and a bookstore, a place to buy shoes. We renovated the old opera house. Years ago they had midget wrestling in there, but now they have jazz groups, ballet, operettas. We know a lot about hard work, low wages, and long winters here. We know a lot about politics, too. . . . Over there is the Congregational Church; across the street's the Presbyterian. Methodist and Unitarian are over there. . . . Here's the grocery store and here's Mr. Morgan's drugstore.[48]

Throughout the piece, the smooth voices of professional politicians (Edward Kennedy and George Bush, for instance) are juxtaposed with the strong dialect of the amateur Puksta, whose non-rhoticity (r-dropping) and broad-a sounds call as much attention to the young man's vocalic persona as to the putative event. It is the sound of Puksta's New Hampshire voice, in other words, that is put forward as the source of meaning, as if it were his job to play a particular sonic role. Glenn Gould had demonstrated the advantages of such an approach in *The Solitude Trilogy*, in which human voices were portrayed as sonic "types" whose "tonality" had greater weight than any spoken word. By eluding the obvious, Gould showed, radio content could be subtle and indirect.

NPR's primary story was influenced by Gould's idiosyncratic radio style in other ways as well. Gould's *The Solitude Trilogy* was exceptional for its unusual technique of playing the voices of two or more speakers simultaneously. For Gould, the use of cross talk was an effective way of erasing, or at least humbling, the authoritative discourse of professional talkers.[49] In NPR's primary story, David Puksta's voice is superimposed over the voice of Jerry Brown, who can be heard expressing opposition to the proposed licensing of the Seabrook Nuclear Power Plant. Brown's speech suddenly fades down, relegated to background sound, while Puksta takes charge of the issue. "Energy is probably one of the biggest issues our candidates want to latch onto this year," says Puksta—we can barely hear Brown stumping in the background ("Well, I oppose the licensing of Seabrook, and my position is quite different from Carter's. I've been working to provide an alternative to . . ."). Puksta: "Last primary about 10% of people had wood stoves; this time it's about 65%. Cost of home heating oil doubled in the last year, and it's still rising. One guy in town figured out how to heat a furniture factory by using the sawdust from the machines." Puksta's lack of textual authority, along with the foregrounding of ambient sounds (traffic noise, cameras clicking, marching band, whistling, gas pump clamor, applause, high school band), effectively moves the story away from the media-savvy candidates and their message toward the boy narrator and the acoustic realities of his small town. Puksta concludes by poking fun at politicians, something the entire story does from start to finish. In an ordinary world filled with ordinary people, early winter's mess is a problem for all. But not so for the politicians: (*Fade to band music/background noises/traffic/cameras clicking.*) "So that's what it's like in Claremont, during the primary season. Very busy here. Lots of things to see for a few weeks. Interesting things. Like, you notice the black limousines never get slush on them. The TV camera crew cars, they get slush on 'em; police cars get slush on 'em. Ordinary cars, they get slush on 'em. Politicians' cars, they never get slush on 'em." (*High school band/cheering to end.*)[50]

If politicians lived in a less-contrived world, maybe they too would get a little messy, Puksta concludes, promoting the humble realties of Claremont, New Hampshire, the real winner in this primary. Even Edward R. Murrow, a great advocate of the "little people," would never have thought to transfer his microphone (and authorial control) to a bystander—to a high-school kid. David Puksta was NPR's Wally Maclean, Gould's friendly, down-home narrator in *The Solitude Trilogy*, who attempts to guide listeners to Canada's north country. The way NPR's campaign story swerves from its apparent newsworthy content to a different tale about ordinary people, canceling out certain sounds to the advantage of others, harks back to the radical sound aesthetic of Gould's *Trilogy*, where various voices are played off of one another to great effect. In the case of the NPR story, professional/national voices are drowned out by amateur/local sounds, thanks to what Gould called "contrapuntal" storytelling.[51]

Experimental Storytellers: Joe Frank and Ken Nordine

NPR's attention to marginal stories fed its interest in human-interest radio genres such as commentaries, essays, and contrapuntal documentaries, which allowed the network to sustain its commitment to sound as an artistic medium. This pledge was in keeping with Siemering's aim of revitalizing radio as a whole. While NPR's approach to nonfiction may have diverged from typical broadcast practices in the 1970s and 1980s, its efforts were hardly radical and cannot be said to have tested the medium. But this did not mean that the network was deaf to more experimental forms of storytelling that would put radio to the test.

One year after its debut broadcast, on Sunday, 30 April 1972, NPR aired an unusual sound piece called *Rivers of the Skull*, the seventh in a series of thirteen experimental radio works produced by member station WFCR in Amherst, Massachusetts. Billed as an "abstract surrealistic sound painting," *Rivers of the Skull* challenged listeners with a peculiar montage of acoustic elements, including selections read from the *Tibetan Book of the Dead* and audio clips from various NASA space shots, all of which were mixed with the reverberated sound of dripping water. Not your typical Sunday programming.

The twenty-eight-minute collage is strange, grandiloquent, and ironic. Voiced by a female speaker, the selections from the *Tibetan Book of the Dead* are striking, owing partly to the elevated style of the text but also to the arresting sense of afterlife ("On the third day, the primal form of the element earth will shine forth as a yellow light") conjured up in Buddhist thought. The female narrator captures the heightened quality of the prose without ever relinquishing its strangeness. Intercut with this sublime voice we hear the crackly voices of Apollo astronauts and ground control: "This is Apollo/Saturn launch control. We have go for Apollo 11."

The *Tibetan Book of the Dead* is a funerary text that describes the experience of consciousness after death, during the interval after the cessation of life and the next rebirth. Traditionally, the book was read aloud by the living to the dead, to help them find their way to rebirth. The grand style of the *Tibetan Book of the Dead*, its Dantesque vision of the hereafter, could not be more at odds with the fragments of NASA-speak we hear in *Rivers of the Skull*. The ironies are made all the more conspicuous by parallel editing:

> TIBETAN BOOK OF THE DEAD: During this time no relative or fond mate should be allowed to weep or to wail as such is not good for the deceased, and so restrain them. Oh nobly born, thy breathing is about to cease. Thy guide hath set thee face to face with a clear light.
>
> APOLLO 11, NASA PUBLIC AFFAIRS OFFICER: 30 seconds and counting. Astronauts report it feels good. T minus 25 seconds. 20 seconds and counting. T-minus 15 seconds. Guidance is internal. 12, 11, 10, 9, ignition sequence starts, 8, 7, 6, 5, 4, 3, 2, 1, 0. All engines running. Lift off. We have a lift off. 32 minutes past the hour. Lift off on Apollo 11. Tower cleared.
>
> TIBETAN BOOK OF THE DEAD: The Lord of Death will place around thy neck a rope and drag thee along. He will cut off thy head, pull out thy intestines, lick up thy brain, drink thy blood, eat thy flesh, and gnaw thy bones. But thou wilt be incapable of dying. Dusts of wind and icy blasts, hail storms and darkness, and impressions of being pursued by many people will come upon thee. Rock caverns and deep holes in the earth, cliffs and mists interlock therein.
>
> APOLLO 11, BUZZ ALDRIN: Hey, Houston, that may have seemed like a very long final phase. The AUTO targeting was taking us right into a football-field sized crater, with a larger number of big boulders and rocks for about one or two crater diameters around it, and it required a P66 and flying manually over the rock field to find a reasonably good area.[52]

The program's effects were limited to the echoing sound of water drips, which refer to the scene of death in the program's opening selection from *Tibetan Book of the Dead* (Narrator: "Bodily sensation of pressure, earth sinking into water. Clammy coldness, as though the body were immersed in water, which gradually emerges into that of feverish heat. Water sinking into fire"). As the voice of the *Tibetan Book of the Dead*, the female narrator sustains the eerie spirit of the afterlife ritual, beside which the normally banal sounds of NASA seem strange and otherworldly—as though spaceflight had recovered its proper voice.[53]

Today, supporters of public radio probably think of Sunday programming in terms of Lynne Rossetto Kasper's *The Splendid Table* or Ira Glass's *This American Life*. In all likelihood, a work of surrealistic sound art like *Rivers of the Skull* would set NPR's fund-raising drive back a few dollars. Were we more adventurous listeners back then? Have we lost our sense of acoustic curiosity? In the 1970s, when NPR's producers made decisions without regard for Arbitron ratings, a sense of adventure informed the young network's attitude toward storytelling that harked back to the golden years of radio. During that time, NPR surprised even itself by hiring Joe Frank (1978) and by picking up Ken Nordine's eccentric *Word Jazz* (1980). Fabulists who later developed cult followings, Frank and Nordine were a good match for NPR's experiment with novel forms of storytelling that, like *Rivers of the Skull*, tested the boundaries of listening.

Joe Frank's radio shows, a collage of essay, fable, drama, and improvisation, are renowned for their ironic forays into the dark side of human experience. Frank developed his unique style during the heyday of freeform radio, getting his start with a late-night show in 1977 at WBAI in New York, the home of the FM revolution. He was hired a year later to co-anchor NPR's weekend edition of *All Things Considered*. Over the course of the next two decades, he produced and developed hundreds of essays, monologues, and plays at NPR and later at KCRW in Santa Monica. Frank's third-person narratives, mixed to repetitive electronic music (from Brian Eno's ambient tracks to Steve Reich's loops), are mesmerizing, intellectually probing, funny, and disturbing. As Susan Emerling writes, Joe Frank conjures up the bad dreams that *This American Life* and *A Prairie Home Companion* have when they leave the radio station at night.[54] Imagine Rod Serling reprogrammed by Antonin Artaud. Frank himself felt a bit out of place anchoring the weekend edition of *All Things Considered*, closing the show with his manic, Dostoyevsky-inspired five-minute essays, and he moved to *NPR Playhouse* before his one-year contract with NPR (which was not renewed) ran out.[55] Frank continued producing his hybrid radio plays as an independent before he was hired by NPR's Santa Monica affiliate, KCRW, and given his own hour-long slot.

It was at Santa Monica's KCRW that Frank earned his reputation as the "Apostle of Noir Radio," airing highly produced one-hour shows every week. What exactly Frank was broadcasting is hard to say, but it emerged out of a pastiche of different sound genres: carefully scripted monologues voiced by Frank, group discussions by mock experts, improvised dramatic narratives performed by his actors and friends, and always the moody, looping ambient music—all of which was meticulously edited into a composite mix of fantasy and factual autobiography. Frank's work is essentially indefinable. Even Frank himself has difficulty describing what he does. To find kindred examples of his KCRW opus—*Work in Progress*, *In the Dark*, or *The Other Side*—you would need to look at the history of Hörspiele, experimental German radio drama, but even here you would come up short since Hörspiele rarely involves the probing autobiographical focus that is a trademark of Frank's unusually personal art.[56] Like Jean Shepherd, Frank walked the line between fact and fiction with his obsessive monologues.

An iconic example is Frank's *A Call in the Night*, a mercurial mix of monologue, melodrama, and mock talk show that fluctuates between autobiography and burlesque, which aired on *NPR Playhouse* in 1979. The piece opens with Frank's soliloquy recounting a traumatic moment from childhood, highlighted by recollections of a dying father and a crippling condition that confined the narrator to a wheelchair, and then shifts to bizarre scenes in which a woman (Jo, from the city) tries to seduce a stranger (Ed, from the country) during an outbreak of the bubonic plague. Episodes from the Jo and Ed play are then critiqued by a panel of mock theater critics, who (though largely self-parodic) nevertheless manage to articulate relevant themes—dread, loss, and affliction—that resonate throughout the hour-long piece.

These three formats seem at first hearing only vaguely related. After close listening, however, the linkage becomes apparent: the awkward seduction scene in Frank's second monologue mirrors the clumsy melodramatic romance of Jo and Ed; the theater critics in the mock talk show refer to "Malka" as author of the play under review (which is also the narrator's assumed surname in the monologues). Illness and paralysis are disturbing conditions that ripple through all segments. Like the club-footed and fatherless narrator, Ed too has bad feet and is searching for a long-lost parent.

In addition to these correspondences, the dreamlike monologues also contain literary patterns of meaning. The first begins suggestively in a garden, and the last ends ominously in a cemetery, evoking a symbolic sense of beginning and ending. In the opening text, the young boy intuits the death of his father in the form of a mirage (a "huge bloated hand") before the fact of his demise is revealed:

> We were in the garden. I sat in my wheelchair. A nurse massaged my feet. Another brought me tea with lemon and sugar. A third finished reading to me from a children's book. My mother, as manager of the troupe, was auditioning a new clown. Above him, the huge bloated hand of my father hung limply from his window, the vein pulsing. One of the nurses rolled me down to the beach. We watched the waves, seagulls drifting in the wind above the water. Then she said, one night, years ago, a great fish beached itself right here on the shore. People came with a net and dragged it out to sea, but it swam back and again threw itself on the sand.[57]

The monologue is delivered without modulation and in a manic style, as if the speaker were possessed by a harrowing event.

The final monologue returns to the scene of agony, the memory of the wheelchair-bound five-year-old's loss of his father, but also flashes forward to a picnic in a cemetery, where the narrator—now an adult—suddenly discovers he has been paralyzed from the waist down. "My father died when I was five. I was about to undergo a corrective operation for club feet. It was important that the surgery be performed as soon as possible. So my mother explained my father's absence by telling me that he had gone to Boston on business." In this finale, Frank repeats the scenario three times. ("My father died when I was five. . . . Years later I traveled to Boston to meet a friend. . . . On the last day of my visit, I persuaded her to picnic with me at a local cemetery. . . . But when we decided to leave, I found I was paralyzed from the neck down.") With each iteration, the paralysis becomes more grotesque and hallucinogenic, as though the narrator were trapped in a nightmare. ("But when it was time to leave I found I was buried under six feet of earth.") The electronic music pulsates over and over again like a heartbeat behind Frank's recursive monologue, which has become itself a kind of loop from which the narrator cannot escape. What was once a physical handicap (club feet) in Frank's narrative has become, by the fiftieth minute, a haunting form of psychic infirmity.

Frank's voice, angst-ridden and mesmerizing, draws the listener into a hypnotically bizarre world full of strange pathos and irony. His shows are alternately dark, weird, and very funny, the *Wall Street Journal* noted, "but always hard to turn off."[58] As Harry Shearer said when he first heard Joe Frank, "It was like a fist coming out of the radio."[59] Frank's unnerving dramas revisit the classic world of noir radio, inhabited by screaming women, shady stalkers, and helpless subjects, only to internalize those disturbing voices of the 1940s in his narrator's own mind. That narrator may not produce a literal scream when he finds himself buried six feet underground in his father's cemetery, but the listener can still hear his spiritual cry of pain.

The kind of radio Joe Frank produced cannot be listened to casually. Like Glenn Gould's contrapuntal radio, Frank's psychodramas require an attentive ear to catch the bizarre play of sounds and words: the mesmerizing beats of the electronic loop, the soap-opera themes of Jo and Ed, the affected intonations of the mock theater critics, the hypnotic and clipped voice of the narrator. Together, these radiophonic strains create a network of acoustic tensions that lure the listener in while destabilizing the listening experience.

An absurdist in another vein, Ken Nordine is the Calvino to Frank's Kafka, comic where Frank was bleak. Nordine is a Chicago-based spoken-word artist who began recording his legendary radio show *Word Jazz* in the late 1950s.[60] Known for his baritone voice-overs more than for his sound art, Nordine attracted wide interest with his *Word Jazz* and *Son of Word Jazz* recordings on Dot Records. Set to hipster music, Nordine's offbeat stories and aural vignettes are like thought experiments conducted in the solipsistic region of the brain—silly, charming, and fanciful.[61] Nordine's narratives usually feature oddball characters absorbed by strange fixations. A good example is the temporal fanatic in the classic story "What Time Is It?" from the first *Word Jazz* album, backed by the Chico Hamilton Quintet performing jazz cellist Fred Katz's compositions scored especially for Nordine.[62] The story masquerades as an etiological account of the origin of "time-tellers" used by Time of Day services.[63] We first encounter Nordine's everyman as a drone going through the motions of a repetitive middle-class existence, trapped in a dreary routine. "There was this guy who was a regular guy who lived a regular life," says the narrator, who "woke up 7:30 every morning, ate the same breakfast, kissed the same wife goodbye every morning. Went to the same office. He did this Monday through Friday." Awakened at two in the morning one night by a practical joker asking for the time, he is jolted from routine and becomes so possessed by computing the correct time that he surrounds himself with clocks and consumes all kinds of books on the subject, eventually becoming omniscient. "He knew what time it was on Arcturus, and the Pleiades, and the Milky Way." This mastery, however, proves to be a curse, leading only to another form of meaningless toil. In the end, the not-so-regular guy is confined to a little room as an official time-teller, a functionary of the state, who repeats the time of day to anyone who calls.[64] The gift of knowing thus becomes an affliction, much in the manner of Borges's story "Funes the Memorious," where absolute memory is agonizing. Like someone in a Kafka-style universe, Nordine's timekeeper cannot escape the absurd, locked in a small room indefinitely. There is for him no exit.

However grim that message might seem, the jazzy score lifts the fable above the weight of the world with, as Italo Calvino might say, the "secret of lightness."[65] Listeners follow the protagonist from one form of drudgery to another, an outcome that is thematically bleak, but the musicality evokes a liveliness and intelligence that is entirely upbeat. The Fred Katz jazz composition, marked by its loose tempos, sprightly tone, and atmospheric style, guarantees a certain levity, even with its dead-end message. It is, in fact, this tension between sound and sense that makes Nordine's radio work so persistently interesting.

Some of Nordine's stories are straight-up third-person narratives, while others resemble short radio plays made up of interior dialogues of the pondering self in conversation with a bemused inner self, as if the mind were an infinite regress of rambling voices. "Multiphrenic" is the neologism Nordine has applied to his bi-vocal storytelling. In "The Ish Fish," for instance, Nordine tells the story of a whale that was so hungry it ate all the fish in the ocean, except for the Ish Fish, which spoke to the whale secretly about forbidden food. In addition to the narrator, Nordine's fable contains a wisecracking voice, presumably the narrator's alter ego or subconscious, who occasionally interjects (represented in italics in the selection below) with quips that ricochet off the narrative, sometimes in a parodic way:

> I gotta tell you about this whale. [*Whale?*] A very pale whale. [*Laughter*] He was always hungry. [*A pale*] He'd eat star fish [*whale*] and gar fish crab and dab, place and dace, skate and his mate, and mackerel and pickerel. And he loved the twirly whirly eel. [*I like eel myself*] anything he could eat that was fishy the whale, this pale whale would love. [*Dover sole is one of my favorites.*] There was only one fish left, [*Almondine*] an Ish Fish, a very small fish that hid just behind the whale's right ear so he could talk to him in confidence. [*Ish Fish*] The whale stood on his tail and said I'm hungry [*Ish Fish*]

and the Ish Fish said, "You should try . . . man. Have you ever tasted man? [*What kind of fish is thish?*].⁶⁶

How exactly the listener is meant to understand the second voice ("I like eel myself") isn't always clear—is this "other" voice supplementary or mischievous?—but we can be certain that Nordine's double-voiced storytelling triggers an irony that brackets the entire enunciative act.

An Aesopian fable about talking fish, Nordine's whimsical story focuses on the transgressive appetite of the whale, whose rash act of eating a man comes back to haunt him. His Jonah-like victim, who turns out to be the narrator himself, provokes a disturbance inside the whale, scratching and scuffing his gullet. Afterward, the whale wants only to expel the man. Having suffered lasting abrasions, the whale can no longer eat large fish, not to mention another human. "And that's the reason why whales nowadays never eat men," says the narrator, as a favor to those in need of a moral to his story. And, "Oh yes," he remembers, "the suspenders I left behind" in the whale's mouth, the narrator adds playfully, should also be mentioned so as not to confuse this Jonah with the biblical one. The clever electronic music, which simulates vocalized whale songs and feeding calls, surrounds Nordine's fable in an ocean of unearthly sounds suggestive of a time before time—even though Nordine's story world is continuous with the ordinary world of department stores and the Chicago rapid transit system.

The narrator's is not the lone voice in Nordine's story, however. The "other" voice, that of the alter ego, is cheeky and digressive. It is a submerged voice that, compared to the full frequency range of the narrator's deep baritone, seems to come out of a small speaker. Nordine pioneered what musicians today call the "phone effect," filtering his alter ego's voice by reducing its high and low frequencies, with the result that it sounds as if it were spoken on a telephone. Essentially, the voice has been shrunk and loses authorial presence, which licenses it to be parenthetical and even mischievous. While the narrator seems not to hear its wisecracking asides ("What kind of fish is thish?"), listeners relish its unsupervised remarks and its sarcastic detachment, even if not sure how to situate that voice in relation to the story.

Nordine's double-voiced radio challenges the ear to hear what it normally does not: the mind speaking to itself. Because these interior voices do not always behave, they often interfere subtly with our ability to decipher the narrative. In "The Ish Fish," the parenthetical voice may be inside the mind of the narrator, but it remains outside of the story proper, indifferent to the lure of the fabulist style, where its asides raise doubts about the speaker's narrative mastery. These tensions require from listeners an ability to listen ironically.

Even if Nordine's best stories do not take themselves seriously, they do evoke a charm that is just ambiguous enough to make the listener wonder if something serious isn't going on. There is the lighthearted fabulist voice of the narrative, the ludic baritone of Nordine's voice, the Borgesian strangeness of the plot, the Kafkaesque predicament at the end, and the fanciful sound textures and diverting jazz mix, which transforms whatever hint of desperation that informs the text into something else, though we cannot be sure what that is.

Ending an Era

Joe Frank and Ken Nordine may have enjoyed a devoted listenership, but their time on NPR was short lived. As cultural programming lost ground to hard news coverage, NPR's acoustic adventures in storytelling eventually began to seem irrelevant, a postscript to an aural culture that no longer existed. The network's original idea for a many-voiced network may have been doomed from the start for the simple reason that, by the late 1980s, this is not what the newsy people on the payroll prized, nor is it what the average public radio listener wanted, then or now.[67] Given the choice between expansive radio programming and terrific reporting, NPR's listeners chose the latter.[68]

When Susan Stamberg was hired to host *All Things Considered* in 1972, NPR faced serious complaints from member stations in the heartland. It was not long before station managers in the Midwest objected that her voice was too New York for their listeners. They wanted her off microphone. They wanted a patriarch. Little did they know that Stamberg was radiogenic precisely because she was not Walter Cronkite.[69] What's more, she broke the law of solemnity—she giggled into her microphone.[70]

Reactions were mixed. *New York* magazine called Stamberg's the "best giggle in broadcasting."[71] For some, Stamberg's sense of humor was a refreshing break from the traditionally unsmiling sound of newscasting. For others, especially those with a vested interest in the masculine orthodoxy of broadcast news, it was less welcome. In that context, female laughter was an aberrant sound. Like the laughter of Sarah in the Old Testament, Stamberg's giggle was an affront to power, a slight.[72]

Compared to the discursive sobriety of network anchors like Walter Cronkite, Eric Sevareid, and Chet Huntley at the *CBS Evening News*, her signature laughter raised questions about the authority of narration in the truth-seeking culture of the news. From the vantage point of the patriarchy, Stamberg was the unreliable narrator in modern fiction, her laughter a diversionary tactic that rerouted her line of inquiry away from the blandness of coolly objective journalism. In the discursive formation of the news, her laugh functioned as an excess (or even waste) that contaminated the meaning-making operation of news as observational knowledge, posing a challenge to the order of discourse. Laughter belonged to the world of leisure, not of work, and Stamberg's whimsy uncomfortably blurred the boundaries between the two. Stamberg's laughter was a cultural technique, as Michel de Certeau would understand it, a swerve that was an implicit critique of the "oracular voice" of masculine modernity.[73]

The problem of the speaking woman that *Sorry, Wrong Number* had so famously explored three decades earlier did not disappear from radio in the age of TV, but it did play out in a venue that was philosophically and artistically engaged by forms of sonic deviance. That NPR's debut—and the hiring of Susan Stamberg—coincided with the advent of feminism only made the issue more poignant. For a brief spell, NPR rejuvenated a vital form of broadcast culture with strong ties to literary practice not evident (with the exception of Glenn Gould and Jean Shepherd) since the late 1940s. What NPR contributed to that tradition was a diversity not only of sound and voice but a mix of acoustic genres that nudged radio in new directions, from the radio essay and documentary to psychodrama, fables, and collage. Eager to test the boundaries of the broadcast medium, NPR was not shy about loading more voices and sounds into the heads of listeners than they might reasonably bear, disrupting conventional radio and journalistic practices. The network, it seemed, was on a mission to reeducate the American ear.

Today, it is hard to imagine an NPR that once took substantial risks on behalf of innovative programming. Nevertheless, although the once-feisty network is now part of the mainstream, its concern for reaching younger listeners (the median age of NPR's listeners is fifty-six) has revived an interest in creative sound-making and storytelling. NPR syndicated the widely acclaimed *Radiolab*, a math, science, and philosophy show with an elaborate acoustic style, that has drawn a devoted following since 2005 for its engaging mix of science, art, and theater (with episodes on laughter, time, randomness, and ghosts). In 2010, the network partnered with the Public Radio Exchange (PRX) to launch Glynn Washington's *Snap Judgment*, a show that has been a huge success with more diverse listeners and that quickly made Washington the first African American host to join the league of extraordinary radiomen. *Snap Judgment*'s stories are shorter, edgier, and more acoustically rich than *This American Life* broadcasts, and they feature an ethnically wider range of voices.

Despite NPR's revived storytelling interest, much of the creative work currently heard on radio is found elsewhere. Best known is *This American Life*, a weekly radio program hosted by Ira Glass that was until recently distributed by Public Radio International (it is currently self-distributed through a partnership with PRX). Since its debut broadcast in 1995, *This American Life* has aired radio features made up primarily of first-person stories, essays, memoirs, and documentaries. Broadcast on nearly 600 radio stations across the country and one of the top podcasts on Apple's iTunes, *This American Life* has triggered a near-obsession with radio storytelling that sparked not only *Radiolab* (which airs on 500 radio stations), but several other shows that began filling the narrative void on public radio created by the mainstreaming of NPR.

Thanks to *This American Life* and its many offshoots, long-form radio storytelling seems alive once again, whether in the form of radio broadcasts or of Internet podcasts. When Jay Allison launched *The Moth Radio Hour* in 2009, a weekly podcast featuring unscripted "true" stories told live, he was assuming that the appetite for narrative radio was keen enough for the Moth storytelling movement to reach a wider audience online. The outburst of story-driven podcasts in the past few years suggests that Allison may have been right and that we are perhaps seeing a renaissance of acoustic storytelling reminiscent of radio in the 1930s and 1940s.

Story-driven podcasts aired on traditional radio have surfaced so rapidly that it's hard to keep count. Jonathan Goldstein's *WireTap*, produced at CBC radio, delivers an idiosyncratic mix of monologue and phone conversation that is often funny and pointed. Roman Mars's *99% Invisible*, another PRX show, features personal stories geared toward architecture and design (including an episode on the broadcast clock in radio control rooms as a design challenge). In 2013, KCRW in Santa Monica partnered with McSweeney's, the literary publishing house, to launch a new monthly storytelling podcast, *The Organist*. There's even a podcast about launching a podcast, Alex Blumberg's *StartUp*.

The list could go on. The Latino version of *This American Life*, *Radio Ambulante*, took off in 2012 as a Spanish-language podcast featuring journalists and storytellers from around the Americas, thanks to a Kickstarter campaign (the show raised $46,000). Launched by the Peruvian-born novelist Daniel Alarcón, *Radio Ambulante* pursues stories that are, according to Alarcón, "uniquely Latin American." Among the show's more memorable tales have been a Peruvian's twenty-six-day trip to New York as a stowaway ("The Stowaways," 15 May 2012), the Argentinian mafia ("Another Country," 12 April 2013), and a Colombian shaman caught up in a scandal because he couldn't stop the rain ("The Shaman," 13 May 2013). Drawing on *Radiolab*'s example of meticulous sound design, the new program takes advantage of highly crafted audio, with evocative ambient tracks and layered voices and music.

Just recently, PRX launched a new podcast network to promote digital-first audio programming. Supported with a $200,000 grant, the new network, Radiotopia, is an online warehouse of story-driven radio shows: *Benjamin Walker's Theory of Everything* (a mix of philosophy, fiction, and journalism); *Radio Diaries* (first-person stories about ordinary life); *99% Invisible*; Lea Thau's *Strangers* (encounters with new acquaintances); *Mortified* (humiliating stories); and the Kitchen Sisters' *Fugitive Waves* (on lost and found sound).

As these and other storytelling shows have multiplied, listeners have steadily migrated to online venues. Given the thousands of niche programs on the web, it would seem that alternative radio (no news, talk, or music) is moving toward a post–mass-media culture, a state in which individuals and groups have access to numerous channels and powerful expressive tools.

With Sarah Koenig's *Serial* (2014), a podcast throwback to serialized broadcasts of old-time radio, we have come full circle. Telling one true-crime story over the course of its first season, *Serial* (which has been downloaded 68 million times) attracted an audience that became obsessed with the narrator's (Koenig's) detective skills and meandering style. Like the devoted fans of *Ma Perkins* seventy-five years ago, today's listeners cannot wait to hear what happens next: did Adnan Syed, her ex-boyfriend, really strangle Hae Min Lee?

There are, of course, crucial differences between the new wave and the old. Unlike the voices of radio's past, from Orson Welles and Norman Corwin to Jean Shepherd and Joe Frank, today's storytellers are well-trained, schooled in the art of personal narrative and Pro Tools, but also restrained. Gone from radio are the overwrought screams and tormented voices, the manic monologues and sweeping narrations, through which writers once gave voice to the dreams and nightmares of their listeners—to the trauma of modernity.

The new storytelling is a literature of post-dramatic radio. The old genres, including fiction and poetry, are largely absent from the new mix. Radio's new wave cannot take its ear off of reality, as though it is an acoustic branch of literary journalism. Podcast storytelling today is largely fact-based; it is what John Biewen and Alexa Dilworth call "reality radio."[74] Today's listeners do not project themselves into imaginary worlds so much as empathize with sympathetic narrators who document contemporary social manners and mores. In modernist broadcast culture, radio was mesmerized by its own image, by the tension between word and sound, and it turned that fascination into a new radiophonic grammar. Like modernism itself, that fascination has faded, leaving behind a fitfully and nostalgically remembered legacy of innovation that radio itself still has yet to come to terms with.

Notes

Introduction

1. John Cage was first approached by CBS to suggest an author he would like to compose for. Initially, Cage suggested Henry Miller, without, however, having read any of his books. After doing so, he instead suggested Kenneth Patchen, whose *The Journal of Albion Moonlight* he had read and enjoyed. See Cage, *Conversing with Cage*, 157.

2. See Kahn, *Noise, Water, Meat*, 137.

3. As Seán Street notes, Cage took advantage of the *Columbia Workshop*'s sound technology, using turntables as a modern DJ would to augment the live performance of percussive instruments with variable frequency sounds and generator whines. See Street, *The Poetry of Radio*, 122.

4. See the letters sent to CBS and Cage himself following the broadcast, in Cage, John Cage Correspondence Collection.

5. "Middletown" was actually Muncie, Indiana. See Lynd and Lynd, *Middletown*, 269; and Brown, *Manipulating the Ether*, 3.

6. Holter, "Radio among the Unemployed," 166–67.

7. Ackermann, "Dimensions of American Broadcasting," 7.

8. "Radio: Money for Minutes," 46.

9. Barnouw, *Golden Web*, 63.

10. The drama critic John Gassner, for instance, noted that with the start of prestige programming the "air waves are no longer completely monopolized by Pollyanna and her laxative-sponsored cousins." See Gassner, *Twenty Best Plays of the Modern Theatre*, xx–xxi.

11. "Theatre: Fall of the City," 60.

12. Lewty, "What They Had Heard Said Written," 200.

13. McLuhan, *Understanding Media*, 306.

14. For the notion of a "sonic regime," see Sterne, *Audible Past*, 33.

15. The popularity of auteur theory in film studies reinforced academic prejudices against radio, as did the Frankfurt School's censure of radio's role in shaping mass culture. See Hilmes, "Rethinking Radio," 1–19.

16. Ibid., 2.

17. Other important books on sound poetics, in addition to those cited above, include Bernstein, *Close Listening*; Kahn, *Noise, Water, Meat*; Labelle, *Background Noise*; Neumark, Gibson, and van Leeuwen, *Voice*; Jacob Smith, *Vocal Tracks*; Strauss, *Radiotext(e)*; Suisman and Strasser, *Sound in the Age of Mechanical Reproduction*; Weiss, *Experimental Sound and Radio*; and Verma, *Theater of the Mind*.

18. See Altman, *Sound Theory, Sound Practice*; Augoyard and Torgue, *Sonic Experience*; Cavarero, *For More Than One Voice*; Chion, *Voice in Cinema*; Connor, *Dumbstruck*; Dolar, *A Voice and Nothing More*; Ihde, *Listening and Voice*; Nancy, *Listening*; Schafer, *The Soundscape*; and Voegelin, *Listening to Noise and Silence*.

19. On the social and cultural history of radio, see Barlow, *Voice Over*; Douglas, *Listening In*; Heyer, *The Medium and the Magician*; Hilmes, *Radio Voices*; Hilmes and Loviglio, *Radio Reader*; Keith, *Radio Cultures*; Lenthall, *Radio's America*; Loviglio, *Radio's Intimate Public*; Savage, *Broadcasting Freedom*; and Squire, *Communities of the Air*. On broadcast history, see Blue, *Words at War*; Cloud and Olson, *The Murrow Boys*; Hilmes, *Network Nations*; MacDonald, *Don't Touch That Dial*; Miller, *Emergency Broadcasting and 1930s American Radio*; Razlogova, *The Listener's Voice*; and Sterling and Keith, *Sounds of Change*. On the political and economic tensions in radio history, see Allen, *Speaking of Soap Operas*; Cox, *Frank and Anne Hummert's Radio Factory*; Goodman, *Radio's Civic Ambition*; McChesney, *Telecommunications, Mass Media, and Democracy*; Newman, *Radio Active*; and Smulyan, *Selling Radio*. On the history of public radio, see Looker, *The Sound and the Story*; McCauley, *NPR*; Mitchell, *Listener Supported*; Roberts et al., *This Is NPR*; and Stamberg, *Talk*.

20. In addition to these studies, for the relationship between radio and modern literature, see also Crisell, *Understanding Radio*; Fisher, *Ezra Pound's Radio Operas*; and Guralnick, *Sight Unseen*.

21. Poizat, *The Angel's Cry*, 65; Artaud, *Theater and Its Double*, 40.

22. In 1935, CBS's president, William Paley, suggested that unsold airtime might provide a timely opportunity for experimentation. Irving Reis, a CBS studio engineer and playwright who had suggested the idea of an experimental radio series months earlier, now got a shot. The name of the series, *Columbia Workshop*, was his. See Barnouw, *Golden Web*, 65.

23. As CBS executive Douglas Coulter said, when *The Columbia Workshop* debuted, few models existed for radio art: "There was no show on the air without many limitations, taboos, and sacred cows. The way was clear for the inauguration of a radio series without precedents, one that would experiment with new ideas, new writers, new techniques; a series that would stand or fall by the impression made on a public of unbiased listeners, with no restriction save the essential and reasonable one of good taste" (Coulter, *Columbia Workshop Plays*, vi).

24. Corwin, *Thirteen by Corwin*, vii, ix. *Thirteen by Corwin* was a collection of the writer's radio plays broadcast by the *Columbia Workshop*.

25. Callow, *Orson Welles*, 371.

26. Along with crime and mystery programs, the thriller was one of the fastest-growing radio genres during the war. See McCracken, "Scary Women and Scarred Men," 183.

27. Insofar as the scream conjures up the unthinkable, as Michel Chion suggests (*Voice in Cinema*, 77), it refers to that which cannot be said, to the unspeakable. For Antonin Artaud (*Theater and Its Double*, 10), the scream was vital to disturbing the illusion of meaning evoked by representational art. The scream

called attention to the materiality of language and created mischief between signifier and signified.

28. The problem of "devocalization" was introduced to sound studies by Adriana Cavarero. She argues in *For More Than One Voice* (42): "It is rather strange that Plato's readers have rarely taken the trouble to reflect on the phenomenon of the devocalization on logos, which follows from its reduction to the visual as the guarantor of truth as presence. Put simply, this probably could also be described as a subordination of speaking to thinking that projects onto speech itself the visual mark of thought. The result is the firm belief that the more speech loses its phonic component and consists in a pure chain of signifieds, the closer it gets to the realm of truth. The voice thus becomes the limit of speech—its imperfection, its dead weight."

29. Displacement here refers to the substitution of one activity for another: watching for listening.

30. Elsewhere in Canada, England, and Europe, a different story unfolds, one based on continuity rather than disruption.

31. Murrow, "Preparation of the Documentary Broadcast," 380 (cited in Hilmes, *Network Nations*, 140).

32. Underground radio and its free-form style were, of course, deeply connected to countercultural habits of mind, especially in its advocacy of undisciplined sound. For some, free-form radio evoked the magic of radio during its so-called golden years, when the individual human voice was as compelling as it was unpredictable. Discussions of progressive developments in 1960s radio can be found in Downing, *Radical Media*; Engelman, *Public Radio and Television in America*; Keith, *Voices in the Purple Haze*; Lasar, *Pacifica Radio*; and Walker, *Rebels on the Air*.

33. Bernstein, *Close Listening*, 4 and 17.

Chapter 1

1. According to *Fortune* magazine, NBC hardly made a cent on radio in 1929, despite selling great amounts of airtime (see Smulyan, *Selling Radio*, 63). In a few years' time, however, the economic prospects of radio changed radically for all players.

2. Under Goebbels's direction, German radio manufacturers built the Volksempfänger (the "People's Radio"). Using only three tubes, the Volksempfänger was a simple radio receiver and therefore cheap enough (seventy-six Reichsmarks) to make radio reception affordable for a mass audience. As it was limited to shortwave signals, however, the People's Radio could not tune in foreign broadcasts, making it an ideal propaganda tool.

3. As Shawn Vancour notes, Arnheim had already begun a serious discussion of sound art in his earlier work on cinema, *Film as Art* (1932), which included considerable analysis of radio in terms of spatial and temporal manipulation (see "Arnheim on Radio," 180–81).

4. Arnheim, *Radio*, 14, 137–38.

5. Ibid., 28.
6. Ibid., 27–28.
7. Kahn, *Noise, Water, Meat*, 11.
8. Cantril and Allport, *Psychology of Radio*, 25.
9. Goodman, "Distracted Listening," 34–37.
10. Arnheim, "To the American Reader of the New Edition," in *Radio*, 8–9.
11. See *Speech and Phenomena*, 80, where Derrida writes: "Ideally, in the teleological essence of speech, it would then be possible for the signifier to be in absolute proximity to the signified aimed at in intuition and governing the meaning. The signifier would become perfectly diaphanous due to the absolute proximity to the signified. This proximity is broken when, instead of hearing myself speak, I see myself write or gesture."
12. See *Of Grammatology*, where Derrida argues that "the formal essence of the signified is *presence*, and the privilege of its proximity to the logos as *phonē* is the privilege of *presence*" (18). For Derrida, the *logos* designates not only speech (the word) but the entire conceptual system of Western metaphysics.
13. Attali, *Noise*, 27.
14. Dolar, *A Voice and Nothing More*, 43–44. As Michel Poizat notes, opera may not exist without the libretto, but its expressive force is quite contrary to the rule of language. In opera, "what the dramatic situation signifies counts for nothing in the outbreak of emotion, and one of the primordial preconditions for the occurrence of this emotional upheaval resides in the destruction of signification" (see *The Angel's Cry*, 31).
15. Voegelin, *Listening to Noise and Silence*, 5.
16. Kristeva, *Revolution in Poetic Language*, 28.
17. Or, as Don Idhe says, "the foreign tongue is first a kind of music before it becomes a language" (see *Listening and Voice*, 157).
18. Linguists speculate that we have two distinguishable ways of listening based on speech and non-speech modes of aural perception, which follow different paths in our neural system. We seem to be tuned normally to the non-speech mode of listening. Reuven Tsur, in his study of cognitive poetics, suggests that language users will often switch back and forth between auditory (non-speech) and phonetic (speech) modes of listening (see "Onomatopoeia: Cuckoo-Language and Tick-Tocking").
19. Chion, *Audio-Vision*, 28–29.
20. Milutis, "Radiophonic Ontologies and the Avantgarde," 59.
21. Although this distinction, introduced by Ihde in *Listening and Voice*, 149, has not received much critical interest, I have found it highly useful in discussing the literary turn in radio history.
22. Alexander Pope, "An Essay on Criticism," 29. John Locke similarly urged: "For let us consider this proposition as to its meaning (for it is the sense, and not the sound, that is and must be the principle or common notion)" (see Locke, *Philosophical Works of John Locke*, 172). Conventional wisdom held that the auditory had no purpose in the absence of the signifying order. Not only that, but sound unregulated by sense was dangerous, if not demonic.

23. Dolar, *A Voice and Nothing More*, 43.
24. Plato, *The Republic*, III, 391a-d, 636.
25. Ibid., X, 601a-c, 825–26.
26. Barker, *Greek Musical Writings*, 4–14.
27. Sophocles, *Ajax*, 1204.
28. Plato, *Symposium*, 176e.
29. Aristotle, *Politics*, VIII, 1341a17–b19. Aristotle writes: "There is a meaning also in the myth of the ancients, which tells how Athene invented the flute and then threw it away. It was not a bad idea of theirs, that the Goddess disliked the instrument because it made the face ugly; but with still more reason may we say that she rejected it because the acquirement of flute-playing contributes nothing to the mind, since to Athene we ascribe both knowledge and art." See ibid., 1341b, 1314.
30. Marsh, *Music and Society in Early Modern England*, 20.
31. Butler, "By Instruments Her Powers Appeare," 357.
32. Shakespeare, *Richard III*, 1.1.12–13. Plato warns in *The Republic*, III, 411b, of the enfeebling effects of the *aulos*:

> Now when a man abandons himself to music to play upon him and pour into his soul as it were through the funnel of his ears those sweet, soft, and dirge-like airs of which we were just now speaking, and gives his entire time to the warblings and blandishments of song, the first result is that the principle of high spirit, if he had it, is softened like iron and is made useful instead of useless and brittle. But when he continues the practice without remission and is spellbound, the effect begins to be that he melts and liquefies till he completely dissolves away his spirit, cuts out as it were the very sinews of his soul and makes of himself a "feeble warrior."

33. Achilles' terrible war cry occurs in Book 18 of the *Iliad*, ll. 251–76:

> So there he rose and loosed an enormous cry
> and off in the distance Pallas shrieked out too
> and drove unearthly panic through the Trojans.
> Piercing loud as the trumpet's battle cry that blasts
> from murderous raiding armies ringed around some city—
> so piercing now the cry that broke from Aeacides.
> And Trojans hearing the brazen voice of Aeacides,
> all their spirits quaked—even sleek-maned horses,
> sensing death in the wind, slewed their chariots round
> and charioteers were struck dumb when they saw that fire,
> relentless, terrible, burst from proud-hearted Achilles' head,
> blazing as fiery-eyed Athena fueled the flames. Three
> times the brilliant Achilles gave his great war cry over the trench,
> three times the Trojans and famous allies whirled in panic—
> and twelve of their finest fighters died then and there,
> crushed by chariots, impaled on their own spears.

Artaud's idea of the "theater of cruelty" struck at the heart of classic representation, with its call to replace language with gestures, cries, screams, noises, and glossolalia in order to reveal the "true spectacle of life" (*Theater and Its Double*, 12). As he wrote in *Here Lies*, "All true language is incomprehensible, like the chatter of a beggar's teeth" (549).

34. The demonic voice, as Anne Carson has observed, is often gendered female: "Madness and witchery as well as bestiality are conditions commonly associated with the use of the female voice in public, in ancient as well as modern contexts." Carson continues: "For example there is the heart chilling groan of the Gorgon, whose name is derived from a Sanskrit word, *garg*, meaning 'a guttural animal howl that issues as a great wind from the back of the throat through a hugely distended mouth.' There are the Furies whose highpitched and horrendous voices are compared by Aiskhylos to howling dogs or sounds of people being tortured in hell (*Eumenides*). There is the deadly voice of the Sirens and the dangerous ventriloquism of Helen (*Odyssey*) and the incredible babbling of Kassandra (Aiskhylos, *Agamemnon*) and the fearsome hullabaloo of Artemis as she charges through the woods (*Homeric Hymn to Aphrodite*)." See Carson, "Gender of Sound," 120.

35. See Weiss, "Radio, Death, and the Devil," 269–307.

36. Ihde, *Listening and Voice*, 150.

37. Heyer, *The Medium and the Magician*, 37.

38. Hersh, "Now Hear This," 1.

39. All references to Orson Welles's *The War of the Worlds* are to the *Mercury Theatre on the Air* broadcast of 30 October 1938 and are from my transcription. The radio play is available on *The War of the Worlds* CD and at http://sounds.mercurytheatre.info/mercury/381030.mp3.

40. Merleau-Ponty, *Phenomenology of Perception*, 4.

41. Nancy, *Listening*, 7.

42. Voegelin, *Listening to Noise and Silence*, 27, notes: "Sound is the solitary edge of the relationship between phenomenology and semiotics, which are presumed to meet each other in the quarrel over meaning."

43. In Chapter 3, I discuss how "interrupting the message" shapes the entirety of the *Mercury Theatre's* version of Welles's *War of the Worlds*.

44. Cavarero, *For More Than One Voice*, 12; Nancy, *Listening*, 2. For a useful discussion of Cavarero's ideas, see Dohoney, "An Antidote to Metaphysics," 70–85.

45. Dolar, *A Voice and Nothing More*, 20.

46. See Newman, *Radio Active*, 109–38.

47. Thurber, *The Beast in Me*, 231 and 209.

48. As Poizat makes clear, opera would fight back against the mastering effect. In such instants, when language disappears and is gradually superseded by the cry, an emotion arises that can be expressed only by the eruption of the sob that signals absolute loss; finally a point is reached where the listener himself is stripped of all possibility of speech (*The Angel's Cry*, 37).

49. Dolar, *A Voice and Nothing More*, 21.

50. Stedman, *The Serials*, 307, 256–57; "Radio: Hummerts' Mill."

51. Allen writes: "Our knowledge of the world of the soap opera may be always limited, but it is never problematic" (*Speaking of Soap Operas*, 84).

52. Cox, *Frank and Anne Hummert's Radio Factory*, 22. By 1947, according to an article in the *Milwaukee Journal* (13 July 1947), the Hummerts were producing sixty-seven daytime serials each week. It has been estimated that at its peak the Hummerts controlled 12.5 percent of the entire network radio schedule. See Dunning, *On the Air*, 58; and "Radio: Hummerts' Mill."

53. Thurber, *The Beast in Me*, 231.

54. Higby, *Tune in Tomorrow*, 129–30.

55. "Oxydol's Own Ma Perkins" was the official title of the soap. Procter and Gamble's ownership and investment in the fictional mom—America's "mother of the airwaves," as she came to be known—was taken seriously, as if listeners might forget the connection between the story and its sponsors.

56. As Allen writes, the soap announcer's "narrational role went well beyond merely framing the soap opera story and relating it to the commercial message. He frequently intervened in the diegesis, mediating between characters and reader, and in doing so, firmly established the norms of the narrator's voice as those atop the soap's perspectival hierarchy" (*Speaking of Soap Operas*, 157).

57. Written by Lee Gebhart, this 1935 episode of *Ma Perkins* was printed in full in James Whipple's *How to Write for Radio*, 115–24. My references are to this version of the script.

58. Newman, *Radio Active*, 110.

59. Connor, *Dumbstruck*, 24. Connor writes: "In a culture of writing, in which words come to take on the quality of objects, voices will tend increasingly to be modeled upon and to be assimilated to the condition of written words, which is to say as seemingly manipulable forms and quasi-spatial objects. The ephemerality and uncontrollability of oral language, deriving largely from the fact that it comes and goes so unpredictably in time, means that it is more apt than writing to suggest a world of powers and powerful presences."

60. So overdetermined was the Hummerts' conception of spoken drama that they went outside for reassurance that their radio scripts were sufficiently transparent, asking the readability expert Rudolf Flesch at nearby New York University to test mathematically for clarity. The Hummerts were hoping for a high Flesch score, which they got (see Higby, *Tune in Tomorrow*, 140).

61. On the popularity of the Chiquita jingle, see Newman's insightful analysis in *Radio Active*, 42–44.

62. It is worth noting that similar distinctions between highbrow and lowbrow culture were being drawn by the industry itself. *Variety* pointed out in 1937: "As regards daytime programs—a change has taken place here, too. . . . The daytime programs are now nearly all serials. This development is one of salesmanship, not showmanship. The serial for the housewife, like the serial for the child, is designed to sustain interest in a continued story, day by day, and with it bring sales. Crude, perhaps, as compared to the evening program, it nonetheless has not yet burned itself out" (Grunwald, "Program-Production History," 28; quoted in Hilmes, *Radio Voices*, 151). As Hilmes observes, broadcast radio contained

deep-seated contradictions owing to its highbrow ambitions and mass-market dependency: "Negotiations of high and mass culture played a large role in the development of radio. Broadcasting maintained a deeply conflicted social status as a public institution upholding official 'high' culture, yet given over to selling products for private profit to a mass audience. Its mass/private/feminine base constantly threatened to overwhelm its 'high'/public/masculine function" (*Radio Voices*, 153). If daytime radio became the refuge of pop-narrative serials, nighttime programming would play host to prestigious literary adaptations.

63. "Prestige" radio shows were "sustaining" (that is, noncommercial) programs intended to attain goals of cultural uplift and win broadcasters increased cultural stature.

64. The trend toward serious drama did not end with this outburst. Adaptations of such canonical writers as Ibsen, Marlowe, Gogol, Corneille, Eliot, and Tolstoy were broadcast by the end of the 1930s. According to *Variety Radio Directory*, 164 adaptations of stage plays, 60 adaptations of prose and poetry, and 208 plays written specifically for radio aired in 1938 alone (see *Variety Radio Directory*, 254–62).

65. See Nachman, *Raised on Radio*, 313–14.

66. *Time* magazine was amused by the *Workshop*'s obsession with sound design: "Original director of the *Workshop* was Irving Reis, a swarthy, jittery onetime control-room engineer who thought the production, not the play, was the thing, and who sweated with oscillators, electrical filters, echo chambers to produce some of the most exciting sounds ever put on the air—Gulliver's voice, the witches in *Macbeth*, footsteps of gods, the sound of fog, a nuts-driving dissonance of bells, the feeling of going under ether" (17 July 1939).

67. *Oakland Tribune* (18 July 1936). As Hilmes points out, Reis's innovative ideas about experimental drama were partly inspired by "his travels to Great Britain and Germany, where he observed radio producers using studio techniques that mixed drama and fact, recorded sound and live studio production." See Hilmes, *Only Connect*, 111.

68. All references to *The Hitch-Hiker* are to the published version of the script in Fletcher, *Sorry, Wrong Number and The Hitch-Hiker*, 23–39. The radio play was first performed on 17 November 1941 by Welles and the Mercury Theatre group on CBS's *Orson Welles Show*. Welles repeated his performance for CBS's *Suspense* on 2 September 1942. The *Suspense* broadcast is available at https://archive.org/details/Suspense-TheHitchhiker.

69. Verma, *Theater of the Mind*, 98.

70. Rod Serling adapted Fletcher's radio play for *The Twilight Zone* in 1960. Ronald Adams became Nan Adams, played by Inger Stevens. As Serling explains in his opening narration: "Her name is Nan Adams. She's twenty-seven years old. Her occupation: buyer at a New York department store, at present on vacation, driving cross-country to Los Angeles, California, from Manhattan. Minor incident on Highway 11 in Pennsylvania, perhaps to be filed away under accidents you walk away from. But from this moment on, Nan Adams's companion on a trip to California will be terror, her route fear, her destination quite unknown."

71. "People listened in those days, and the voices of Agnes Moorehead and Orson Welles set the complete mood for a half hour. And along with the marvelous sound effects and music, I mourn the passing of good radio drama," Lucille Fletcher recalled to columnist Robert Wahls in 1972 (quoted in Grams, *The Twilight Zone*, 233).

72. Fletcher, *Sorry, Wrong Number and The Hitch-Hiker*, quotations from 23 and 25, respectively.

Chapter 2

1. Corwin, *On a Note of Triumph*, 9. Norman Corwin, the unofficial poet laureate of American broadcast culture, wrote more plays for the *Columbia Workshop* than any other writer and was widely recognized for his ability to adapt radio art to the literary imagination.

2. As Spinelli observes, Corwin walks a fine line in *On a Note of Triumph* between popular and experimental radio forms, moving from vernacular to linguistically novel (difficult) locutions repeatedly and with remarkable precision, as if luring the listener into a trap (see "Masters of Sacred Ceremonies," 77–78).

3. Corwin, *On a Note of Triumph*, 69.

4. Roth, *I Married a Communist*, 40.

5. According to a 1939 *Fortune* poll (cited by Brown, *Manipulating the Ether*, 3).

6. "Radio: Money for Minutes," 46.

7. "Radio Broadcasting," 117.

8. Holter, "Radio among the Unemployed," 163–69.

9. Palter, "Radio's Attraction for Housewives," 141.

10. The next year, Crosley would debut a fifty-eight-inch-tall cabinet radio called the "Super-Power Receiver," which included thirty-seven tubes (the Stratosphere had only twenty-five) and produced seventy-five watts of power.

11. Robert Allen writes that "by the end of 1935 Procter and Gamble was the largest user of network radio in the world and NBC's most important client. On that network alone, Procter and Gamble sponsored 778 program hours in 1935—664 of which were daytime programs. By 1937 its radio advertising expenditures were $4,456,525 with over 90 percent going to daytime programming" (*Speaking of Soap Operas*, 117).

12. Goodman, *Radio's Civic Ambition*, xiii.

13. Rorty, *Order on the Air*, 7. See Newman's summary of Rorty's relationship with the medium (*Radio Active*, 58–63).

14. Tom Lewis, "'A Godlike Presence,'" 30.

15. "The Week."

16. Mencken, "Radio Programs."

17. Cited by Barnouw, *Golden Web*, 24.

18. Ibid., 25.

19. Smulyan, *Selling Radio*, 126.

20. Rorty, *Our Master's Voice*, 266.

21. Also called "sustaining" programs, prestige productions (quality-based unsponsored programming that earned networks respect rather than dollars) were financed out-of-pocket by the networks themselves, with the tacit understanding that their value lay largely in serving the public interest. Thus, in 1937, David Sarnoff brought Arturo Toscanini to NBC as resident maestro (at some cost), creating a house orchestra and weekly broadcasts; in later years, General Motors would pick up the bill. See Barnouw, *Golden Web*, 71.

22. For extensive analysis of the reform movement's critique of commercial broadcasting, see McChesney, *Telecommunications, Mass Media, and Democracy*. As McChesney suggests, the consequences of the failed amendment were enormous. Had Wagner-Hatfield, which found an astonishing degree of support in 1934, become law, it would "have established precedents that may well have been carried over to television in the 1940s and 1950s. At the very least [it] would have accomplished an important task for the reform movement of the 1930s by making nonprofit (and noncommercial) broadcasting a viable prospect for millions of American listeners, and given the notion of broadcast reform an immediacy that it lacked throughout its existence" (260). The reform movement may have failed in Washington, but its reach did not end there. As Goodman writes, American radio in the second half of the 1930s was "profoundly shaped by broadcaster anxiety about possible reform," and, as the industry magazine *Broadcasting* warned in 1936, "alertness rather than smugness" was the order of the day (*Radio's Civic Ambition*, 6–7).

23. For several months, Irving Reis, the *Workshop*'s first director, had lobbied CBS to produce cutting-edge programming. At last, someone listened (see Barnouw, *Golden Web*, 65).

24. Written in 1936, the year of the *Workshop*'s debut, Rudolf Arnheim's discussion of multitrack mixing in his analysis of radio drama reads like a blueprint of what the *Columbia Workshop* was to become (see Arnheim, *Radio*, 95–132).

25. Dunning, *On the Air*, 170.

26. In its first broadcast, the *Workshop* was introduced with pizzazz by the announcer, who situated the program's novelty within the broader social history of modern technologies, boasting that "radio has reduced the area of the world to a split second of time for the transmission of human thought and feelings, of a man's literature, his music, his spoken word. In the five centuries that bridge the year since Gutenberg invented movable type and gave the world the store of man's knowledge through the printed word, no discovery has promised greater potentialities for shaping the world's culture than the slim swift path of the electric wave. With the speed of light, it cuts through the barriers of boundary, class, race, and distance. While these words, electrically amplified one hundred trillion times from the microphone to the transmitters which hurl them on the air, are being sent to you on broadcast bands, a hundred other bands of the radio spectrum are busily engaged performing useful functions for man." See *Columbia Workshop*, "A Comedy of Danger" and "The Finger of God."

27. Ever radio's prescient theorist, Arnheim wrote: "Most important of all is the distance of the microphone from the source of sound, because the relative

distance of the sound not only serves the listener as spatial orientation of the scene of action, but at the same time has strong expressive content" (*Radio*, 52).

28. Ruttman's sound piece, a radio collage that captures the fleeting sounds of daily urban life, documents a weekend in the city of Berlin. The piece transitions from work to the countryside and then back to the grind on Monday. A filmmaker, Ruttman recorded his ambient sounds optically on film stock, well before the invention of audio tape, which he cut and spliced together in a montage of street sounds and end-of-day work noises: clocks, typewriters, telephone bells, cash registers, hammers, factory sirens, along with pastoral acoustics (train whistles, roosters crowing, bird song, cowbells, children singing). Ruttman, best remembered for his 1927 documentary *Berlin, Symphony of a City*, called *Weekend* a "blind film." See Gilfillan, *Pieces of Sound*, 3–6.

29. Russolo, "The Art of Noises," 10.

30. "Broadcast Gives 'Sight' to the Ears," 131A. Just a year later, however, Douglas Coulter, who had become CBS vice president in charge of broadcast, singled out *Broadway Evening* in his preface to *Columbia Workshop Plays: Fourteen Radio Dramas* as an exemplar of the *Workshop*'s new radio aesthetic. It was "noisy" and difficult to take in, Coulter wrote, but that was essentially what made it so significant as radio drama. "Broadway Evening really sounded the keynote of the Workshop. It gave an impression of the Broadway scene with its milling crowds, the roar of the subways, the pitchmen on the curbs, the barkers in front of the movie palaces, the sirens of the fire engines and ambulances, bits of conversation overheard at juice stands, the inevitable street brawl—a kaleidoscopic *effect* produced by brief scenes of what the average observer would take in on a stroll from Forty-second Street to Central Park. It was a noisy job, at times incoherent and hard to listen to, but it demonstrated conclusively that a new day for radio drama had arrived and that, with laboratory experimentation *on the air*, new techniques and ideas could be developed that would raise the standards of all radio programs" (vii).

31. Attali, *Noise*, 26–27.

32. Broadcast radio might be viewed as a form of popular entertainment, given its ability to reach large audiences, but that accessibility did not prevent the emergence in the 1930s and 1940s of challenging radio "texts" whose difficulty coincided with modernist practices in other media. *Broadway Evening* challenged conventional listeners nearly as much as would a work of John Cage decades later. The fact that CBS set out on a quest for legitimacy indicates that the boundary between "high" and "low" culture is generally more fuzzy than we think, as Lawrence Levine observes in *Highbrow/Lowbrow*, 234.

33. The media consistently responded with enthusiasm to the *Columbia Workshop*'s programming. The endorsement by the *New York Times* writer John K. Hutchens was typical. Observing the rise of the prestige movement in radio, Hutchens writes: "It was as recently as 1936 that the Columbia Broadcasting system led the way with the *Columbia Workshop*, training writers, developing techniques that would satisfy the demands peculiar to a new form and a new audience. That the writers and methods developed by Columbia and later by

other networks were successful, and that the five brief years were rich in accomplishment, there can be no doubt" ("Drama on the Air," X12). See also "Broadcast Gives 'Sight' to the Ears," 90: "After a year's work, the *Columbia Workshop* has more than accomplished its aim. In fact, according to many of its critics, it has become the radio drama of the future itself."

34. Arnheim writes: "This is the great miracle of wireless. The omnipresence of what people are singing or saying anywhere, the overleaping of frontiers, the conquest of spatial isolation.... [You] make countries tumble over each other by a twist of your hand, and listen to events that sound as earthly as if you had them in your own room, and yet as impossible and far-away as if they had never been" (*Radio*, 14 and 20). The introduction of the velocity or ribbon microphone brought with it the "proximity effect," an increase in bass or low-frequency response when a sound source is close to a microphone.

35. Fussell, *Wartime*, 181.

36. Arnheim, *Film as Art*, 215–16.

37. "Broadcast Gives 'Sight' to the Ears," 131A.

38. "Radio: Prestige Programs."

39. My transcription.

40. Network radio provided listeners with comment cards, soliciting feedback from the audience. Response to the inaugural broadcast of the *Workshop* was promising, as the announcer for one episode noted: "Good evening, ladies and gentlemen. Tonight the *Columbia Workshop* is about to present a second program dedicated to you and the magic of radio. Before we do, we wish to thank you for your generous response to our request for your opinions on the experiment we demonstrated in our experiment on radio technique versus stage technique. During long rehearsals of the stage play with a parabolic microphone, we learned a great many things which, added to your opinions of the broadcast, have led us to decide to continue the investigation into the use of the parabolic microphone for radio drama. More than 80 percent of the letters told us that the stage play, presented exactly as it would be in the theater, allowing the artists freedom of movement, enhanced the illusion of dramatic reality. Because of your interest in response, we're planning further experiments along this line with modified equipment which will enable us to overcome some of the difficulties we encountered and with dramatic scripts which will be shaped especially for the scope of the parabolic microphone. The first will be ready in a few weeks." See *Columbia Workshop*, "Broadway Evening" (from author's transcription).

41. The *Workshop*'s third episode included a long demonstration on microphone technology, in which the program's announcer called various radio actors for assistance: "We're now going to show you the difference in pick up perspective between the dynamic microphone, which was the latest type before the velocity was perfected, and the velocity. Ms. Francis, it's your turn to help. Ladies and gentlemen, Ms. Arlene Francis, one of radio's best-known actresses. Suppose you do Lincoln's Gettysburg address for us. Start on this dynamic microphone over here and walk around it in a circle."

42. Derrida, *Of Grammatology*, 156.

43. Barthes, *S/Z*, 75. For Barthes, the dilatory space was the essence of narrative evasion.

44. "Radio: Radio Revolution?"

45. Corwin, *Thirteen by Corwin*, ix. *Thirteen by Corwin* was a collection of the writer's radio plays broadcast by the *Columbia Workshop*; the preface was by Carl Van Doren.

46. Coulter, *Columbia Workshop Plays*, viii.

47. "We do not plan to abide by any preordained concept of radio drama," Reis liked to say. "We plan to do almost anything that lends itself to unique treatment and interesting experiments with sound effects and voices" (Reis, quoted in the *Oakland Tribune* [18 July 1936]). During his tenure as director of the *Workshop*, Reis remained steadfast to the cause of innovation, which was supported by CBS's bosses who embraced the idea of doing a radio series, in Coulter's words, "without precedents" (Coulter, *Columbia Workshop Plays*, vi).

48. MacLeish, *Reflections*, 119.

49. That the *Workshop*'s theme (radio itself is the story) was reaching a public can be glimpsed in Louis Untermeyer's review of MacLeish's play: "The effectiveness of this verse play is increased by Mr. MacLeish's recognition of the resources of the radio and his employment of the Announcer as a combination of Greek Chorus and casual commentator. Writing for the radio, he has indicated a new power for poetry in the use of the word in action, without props or settings, the allusively spoken word and the 'word-excited imagination.' It is an exciting prospect, this new appeal directly to the ear, the ear which is 'already half poet,' and it is an experiment which is also a distinguished accomplishment" (Untermeyer, "New Power for Poetry," 7).

50. "Theatre: Fall of the City."

51. MacLeish, *Fall of the City*, 3-4.

52. Ibid., 8-9.

53. Ibid., 10.

54. Ibid., 21-22.

55. MacLeish, *Reflections*, 106-7.

56. Welles's Announcer is inseparable from his microphone. He is a media extension, in McLuhan's sense. Throughout the speech-making, the Announcer shifts from one discourse to the next, powerless to gauge the relative meaning of each, as though interpretation was not a part of his job. Not until the end does the Announcer awaken to the larger significance of what has happened. For much of the play, he functions much like the Chorus in a Greek play, reproducing (like a tape recorder) what is said by civic leaders. By the end, though, he has awakened to meaning.

57. MacLeish, Foreword, *Fall of the City*, ix-x.

58. MacLeish, *Reflections*, 111.

59. MacLeish thought of his subsequent radio play, *Air Raid*, which was broadcast by CBS just days before the *Mercury Theatre* production of *War of the Worlds*, as a "journalistic opera" (*Reflections*, 119).

60. In 1941, MacLeish praised Edward R. Murrow at a Washington dinner honoring "the voice of London." Murrow, MacLeish said, made real and urgent

to men and women far away from London what they had not known. He had "burned the city of London in our houses and we felt the flames that burned it." Without rhetoric, Murrow had destroyed "the superstition of distance and of time—of difference and of time" (quoted in Fang, *Those Radio Commentators*, 304).

61. These lines are borrowed, with modification, from Murrow's first broadcast from Vienna, 13 March 1938 (see Bliss, *In Search of Light*, 4–5).

62. Cited in Dunning, *On the Air*, 171.

63. MacLeish's example inspired an outpouring of written work for radio by many well-known writers, partly owing to the critical success of *Fall of the City* but also partly owing to the preface penned by the poet for the printed version of the radio play, which pitched radio drama as an overlooked venue for poets and writers with experimental ambitions.

64. MacLeish's radio trope should not be confused with the formula adopted by *The March of Time* news show, which began as a radio broadcast in 1931. *The March of Time* re-created selected news events with professional actors and impersonators (Agnes Moorehead, Art Carney, Arlene Francis, Frank Readick, Porter Hall, Joseph Cotton, and Orson Welles), using elaborate sound effects and a full studio orchestra. The "news" show was immensely popular, in part because it so effectively dramatized major news stories.

65. Denison, "Radio and the Writer," 370.

66. "Theatre: Fall of the City."

67. Matthews, "Radio Plays as Literature," 48.

68. MacLeish, *Fall of the City*, x, ix.

69. See Hilmes, *Hollywood and Broadcasting*, 78–115.

70. Coulter, *Columbia Workshop Plays*, v.

71. MacLeish described what he thought was most interesting about his verse plays in radio terms: "The really inventive technical development is the use of the natural paraphernalia of the ordinary broadcast, that is to say, an announcer in the studio and a reporter in the field. I used that in both *Fall of the City* and in *Air Raid*, and a very successful device it turned out to be. It give you a Greek chorus without the rather ridiculous self-consciousness involved in carting a chorus in and standing them against the wall and having them recite. These people have a function; they are recognized by large audiences of nonliterary people as being proper participants" (*Reflections*, 119).

72. Although Edward R. Murrow would not begin broadcasting from London until the following summer, MacLeish had of course tuned in to CBS's coverage of the Munich Crisis in March 1938, when he would have heard Murrow's and Kaltenborn's live reports and analysis.

73. In both *Fall of the City* and *Air Raid*, MacLeish anticipated the work of Edward R. Murrow with extraordinary accuracy. MacLeish's rooftop radio announcers may speak in verse while Murrow the essayist will speak in elegant prose, but Murrow's penchant for metaphors and lyrical imagery tightens the eerie connection between fact and fiction.

74. As MacLeish later wrote, he was particularly interested in erasing the acoustic edge between the human voice and the air-raid siren, in order to

complicate the relationship between sound and sense: "Take the woman's voice—at its shrillest it parodies the rise and fall of a wartime siren. It also relates to a song which rises and falls. It relates to fear, to ecstasy. It has all these possibilities, and it's used thematically as a sort of base to come back to emotionally. Incidentally, it's my impression (I don't listen to radio plays very much but I listen to television plays occasionally) that neither radio nor television has made much progress over where we were in the middle thirties. In fact, we got off to a better start than I think we're getting off to a finish" (*Reflections*, 120). It is equally (if not more) likely that the wartime siren "parodies" the woman's singing voice. That the listener can hear both meanings can be attributed to acoustic drift.

75. Denning describes the "air-raid genre" in the context of the Popular Front movement and antifascist radio art in the late 1930s (see *The Cultural Front*, 383).

76. Corwin, *They Fly through the Air*, 97–119, at 109.

77. Ibid., 118–19.

78. As R. LeRoy Bannerman writes in *Norman Corwin and Radio*, even though broadcast radio was fast becoming a very big business by the mid-1930s, "only about a third of the network schedule was sponsored" (33).

79. Alan Lomax went on to produce several music ethnography programs for CBS from 1935 to 1950 (see Denning, *The Cultural Front*, 91).

80. Corwin, *Thirteen by Corwin*, vii, ix.

81. "Millions *Hear* Their *Columbia Broadcasting System*," 66. The CBS advertisement comes after the bibliographic article "The Literature that Radio Produces" (65).

Chapter 3

1. "W. S. Paley, Against 'Forced' Programs," 26. To support his point, Paley told the Federal Communications Commission in Washington that listeners were turning from jazz to symphony and opera—as if the change from an ethnically black to a white musical genre was a step up the educational ladder. CBS, he testified, "has carefully refrained from imposing on its audience any small personal concepts of what that audience ought to receive. Rather has it sought so far as possible to act as editors and directors of a great news and educational and entertaining service."

2. Reith, *Broadcast over Britain*, 34. As David Goodman points out, apologists for American radio were in the habit of reminding the public that, unlike British radio, American broadcasting gave the people what they wanted (*Radio's Civic Ambition*, 78).

3. As Michele Hilmes writes, the networks were at best divided about their mission: "Placed in the hands of large, government-endorsed corporations, whose early assurances of quality and high cultural standards conflicted with their need for economic support, radio became a commercialized medium with one foot in the vulgar popular and one foot on the ladder of social hierarchy (*Radio Voices*, 187).

4. The DuPont Company sponsored *The Cavalcade of America*, hoping to hide its sins behind the program's prestige. In the years after World War I, the company had been branded a "merchant of death" because of the huge profits DuPont had made from gunpowder. It was heavily criticized for profiteering in wartime, especially after the publication of *The Merchants of Death* by H. C. Engelbrecht and F. C. Hanighen in 1934 about the weapons industry. Because of its immense unpopularity, DuPont sought the help of the advertising firm BBDO, which advised taking cover behind "educational" programming. See Christiansen, *Channeling the Past*, 53–99.

5. In 1937, just a year after the debut of the *Columbia Workshop*, Columbia University began offering classes in radio drama for its students, taught by Erik Barnouw, the broadcast historian. Textbooks and anthologies on radio drama appeared in rapid succession, among them Barnouw, *Radio Drama in Action*; Krulevitch and Krulevitch, *Radio Drama Production*; Whipple, *How to Write for Radio*; Wylie, *Radio Writing*; and Levenson, *Teaching through Radio*.

6. Callow, *Orson Welles*, 371.

7. Michael Denning argues that the rhetoric of fascism and antifascism runs throughout Welles's career and across different media (see *The Cultural Front*, 375).

8. "The Theatre: Marvelous Boy."

9. For Hugo's narrator, the point—it would seem—is not to stick to the point. In a typical discursive entry, Hugo writes: "This book is a drama in which the hero is the Infinite. The second character is Manuotes" (*Les Misérables*, 322).

10. Vargas Llosa, *Temptation of the Impossible*, 158.

11. See Rippy, *Orson Welles and the Unfinished RKO Projects*, 22.

12. "First Person Singular: Welles Innovator on Stage," 25.

13. *Radio Annual* (1939) (cited in Callow, *Orson Welles*, 373).

14. Houseman, *Run-Through*, 363.

15. Houseman, *Unfinished Business*, 177–79.

16. Welles transforms the panoramic narrator of Hugo's novel into someone far more intimate in his radio adaptation. Rather than being detached, Welles's narrator is implicated in the world of the story, if only by voice alone, through close-miking and a lower pitch. Welles understood how to control narrative voice in radio through the *proximity effect*, how to create an aural close-up, often achieved by microphone placement. As Rick Altman has explained, Welles's radio practice was "placed in the service of radio's overall narrative/discursive tension," and that often included drawing attention to his narrator's mastery ("Deep Focus Sound," 14).

17. All references to Welles's *Dracula* are to the *Mercury Theatre on the Air* broadcast of 11 July 1938 and are from my transcription. The radio play is available on *The Mercury Theatre on the Air, Vol. 1*, CD.

18. Genette, *Narrative Discourse*, 256.

19. Stoker, *Dracula*, 308.

20. Ibid., 28.

21. See Wicke, "Vampiric Typewriting," 470.

22. Stoker, *Dracula*, 43.

23. Ibid., 355 and 368.

24. Kittler, "Dracula's Legacy," 71, 73. As Kittler observes, *Dracula* is not so much a vampire novel as a "written account of our bureaucratization" (73).

25. Stoker, *Dracula*, 348. Rebecca Pope emphasizes the novel's concern with the process of its own textual production in "Writing and Biting in Dracula," 211.

26. *Variety*, 1938.

27. As the *Florence Times* of Alabama reported on 2 November 1938: "So realistic was the Welles production of the utterly imaginative tale of a descent upon earth of monstrous people from Mars, that radio listeners from New York to San Francisco and Canada to the Gulf of Mexico believed a catastrophe was really happening. Many were injured in the widespread panic that ensued" (3). Reports of panic in the wake of the CBS broadcast seemed to develop their own narrative impetus. "FAKE RADIO 'WAR' STIRS TERROR THROUGH U.S." ran the *New York Daily News* front-page headline for Monday, 31 October 1938. "A wave of mass hysteria seized thousands of radio listeners throughout the nation," reported the *New York Times* on the same day. The broadcast, the *Times* goes on to say, "disrupted households, interrupted religious services, created traffic jams and clogged communications systems." Recent critics have suggested that the so-called mass hysteria provoked by the CBS broadcast may have been stirred more by media hype than by listener panic (see Socolow, "The Hyped Panic"; and W. Joseph Campbell, *Getting It Wrong*, 26–44).

28. Rorty, "Radio Comes Through," 372.

29. Kathy Newman sees Rorty's tenacious criticism of commercial radio as an important incitement behind Roosevelt's creation of the Federal Communications Commission (see *Radio Active*, 63).

30. Radio receiver sales soared. More sets were sold in September 1938 than in any other month in history (see Culbert, *News for Everyman*, 73).

31. Barnouw, *Golden Web*, 80.

32. Rorty, "Radio Comes Through," 372.

33. Kaltenborn, *I Broadcast the Crisis*, 3.

34. McLuhan, "Radio," 299.

35. Kaltenborn, *I Broadcast the Crisis*, 3.

36. Knoll, "Demise of the Radio Commentator," 359.

37. Fang, *Those Radio Commentators*, 8.

38. Brown, *Manipulating the Ether*, 172.

39. Lazarfeld, *Radio and the Printed Page*, 141–43.

40. Listeners imagined all sorts of things, from little green men to menacing German soldiers. As Howard Koch later wrote: "In the course of forty-five minutes of actual time . . . the invading Martians were presumably able to blast off from their planet, land on the earth, set up their destructive machines, defeat our army, disrupt communications, demoralize the population and occupy whole sections of the country. In forty-five minutes!" (*The Panic Broadcast*, 11–12).

41. Barnouw, *Golden Web*, 87–88.

42. Cantril, *Invasion from Mars*, 53.

43. All references to *War of the Worlds* are to the 30 October 1938 broadcast and are from my transcription. The play is available on the *War of the Worlds* CD and at http://sounds.mercurytheatre.info/mercury/381030.mp3.

44. Heyer, *The Medium and the Magician*, 87.

45. Spinelli compares Welles's achievement in *War of the Worlds* to Artaud's Theatre of Cruelty in the program's ability to deconstruct the listener's confidence in radio, in its modernist assault on the scene of listening (see Spinelli, "Masters of Sacred Ceremonies," 76). After looking at some 2,000 letters from listeners of the original broadcast, A. Brad Schwartz concludes that listeners were less concerned with invading Martians than with the sudden unreliability of radio (see *Broadcast Hysteria*).

46. The example set by Welles made such self-reflexive moments popular on radio. There would be many imitators, such as Peter Lorre, who narrated and starred in *Mystery in the Air* (1947).

Chapter 4

1. Quoted in Stansky, *First Day of the Blitz*, 31–32.
2. Ziegler, *London at War*, 113.
3. Nixon, *Raiders Overhead*, 13.
4. Stansky, *First Day of the Blitz*, 42.
5. Mack and Humphries, *London at War*, 40.
6. Douglas, *Listening In*, 175.
7. Ihde, *Listening and Voice*, 4.
8. Cantril and Allport, *Psychology of Radio*, 232.
9. For many modern journalists, for whom Murrow is the undisputed patron saint of American broadcasting, the memory of the London Blitz is forever tied to the image of Murrow perched dangerously on the rooftop of the BBC, heroically broadcasting his dramatic reports back to the United States. At the center of Murrow hagiography lie such words as "integrity," "honesty," "courage," as Gary Edgerton notes in "The Murrow Legend as Metaphor," 76. These lofty impressions retain their force, even if they do not always match the facts. When Murrow applied for a job with CBS in 1935, he added five years to his résumé, claimed to have majored in international relations, and listed a master's degree from Stanford University among his credentials. In truth, Murrow had been a speech major at Washington State University. Luckily for him, the con was not detected. Even though we may have lost sight of the historical Murrow in the process of reification, few seem eager to relinquish the legend. As David Halberstam has noted, Murrow was "one of those rare legendary figures who was as good as his myth" (*The Powers That Be*, 38).
10. Sevareid, *Not So Wild a Dream*, 177–78.
11. Murrow, *This Is London*, 158–59.
12. Stanley Cloud and Lynne Olson suggest that Murrow's talents were uniquely tailored not just to wartime writing but to the trauma of the London Blitz in particular (see *The Murrow Boys*, 89).

13. As Ted Koppel remembers, it was the voice of Murrow that inspired his career: "By the time I was 9 years old, living in England, listening to this rich, deep baritone on BBC, I had already decided that this is what I wanted to be, a foreign correspondent—it was all based on this image of Murrow" (quoted in Edgerton, "The Murrow Legend as Metaphor," 89). It has become a trope of broadcast journalists to project Murrow as a universal mentor—often it is Murrow's voice that sets careers in motion.

14. MacLeish, *Air Raid*, 101. MacLeish's Announcer in *Air Raid* anticipates the rooftop broadcasts of Murrow with eerie accuracy: "Anti-aircraft! . . . We can't see it: we hear it. . . . Wait. There's a burst. There's another. . . . They follow each other like footsteps. The steel stamps on the sky: the Heel hits. . . . They hang like Quills driven in sky: The quarry invisible . . . (*An explosion is clearly heard*)" (118–19).

15. Sevareid, the most self-conscious member of the "Murrow Boys," not only produced his own Murrowesque essays for broadcast but seems to have perceived the significance of Murrow's craft early on as something new and influential that gave "not just the bones of the news, not an editorial by itself, nor a descriptive 'color' story by itself, but in a few minutes putting it all in one package—the 'hard news' of the day, the feel of the scene, the quality of the big or little men involved, and the meaning and implications of whatever had happened." The result was that "all the rigid, traditional formulae of news writing had to be thrown out of the window, and a new kind of pertinent, contemporary essay became the standard form" (see Sevareid, *Not So Wild a Dream*, 178).

16. Fang, *Those Radio Commentators*, 6.

17. Ibid., 97.

18. Father Coughlin's anti-Semitism, among other things, so concerned radio's establishment that in 1939 the National Association of Broadcasters adopted new rules setting increasingly severe limitations on the sale of radio time to controversial spokesmen. Over forty radio stations dropped Father Coughlin's broadcasts as a result of the new code (Barnouw, *Golden Web*, 135–38; see also Warren, *Radio Priest*).

19. It is ironic to note that Kaltenborn's highly composed broadcasts were actually ad-libbed during the Munich Crisis. As he later explained: "Every one of these talks was entirely unprepared, being an analysis of the news as it was occurring. The talks were made under a pressure I have not experienced in seventeen years of broadcasting. . . . Earphones clamped over my head as I broadcast brought me the voice of the speakers abroad whose words I followed with my commentary. At times, while I talked, my attention had to focus on four things at once in addition to the words I was speaking" (quoted in Fang, *Those Radio Commentators*, 31–32).

20. Ibid., 40. For the *Mercury Theatre*'s radio adaptation of *Julius Caesar* in September 1938, Welles invited Kaltenborn to provide narrative commentary on the political dynamics of Shakespeare's Roman play, which included the reading of passages from *Plutarch's Lives*. To do so, Kaltenborn had merely to walk downstairs from Studio Nine to Studio One (see Heyer, *The Medium and the Magician*, 66–67).

21. Cantril and Allport, *Psychology of Radio*, 232.

22. See Creamer and Hoffman, *Radio Sound Effects*, 8; and Turnbull, *Radio and Television Sound Effects*, 7–15.

23. Quoted in R. Franklin Smith, *Edward R. Murrow*, 56.

24. The moment may not have been newsworthy, but its "atmosphere" (Murrow's favorite word for ambience) was rich and complex, which Murrow hoped to render for listeners. Judging by the memorable words of Archibald MacLeish at a New York dinner honoring Murrow in 1941 ("You destroyed the most obstinate superstition of all the superstitions—the superstition against which poetry and all the arts have fought for centuries, the superstition of distance and time"), Murrow did in fact achieve such an effect. See MacLeish, Paley, and Murrow, *In Honor of a Man and an Ideal*, 6.

25. Murrow, *This Is London*, 178. The experiential condition of writing was, as Orwell repeatedly observed, crucial to modern prose. As Orwell wrote in *Homage to Catalonia*, for instance, it was not enough to merely observe the Spanish Civil War from the sidelines. One had to be involved. "I had come to Spain with some notion of writing newspaper articles, but I had joined the militia almost immediately, because at that time and in that atmosphere it seemed the only conceivable thing to do." Unlike Hemingway, who was in Spain as a famous "writer," Orwell was immersed in the stench and dirt of the front (and was even shot by a sniper). See Orwell, *Homage to Catalonia*, 4.

26. Olson, *Citizens of London*, 39.

27. Nachman, *Raised on Radio*, 406.

28. It is of little surprise that Murrow was put off by Kaltenborn's pompous and didactic style. See Nimmo and Newsome, *Political Commentators*, 136; see also Sperber, *Murrow*, 140–41, for Murrow's spat with Kaltenborn during coverage of the Munich Crisis.

29. Ida Lou Anderson, Murrow's college drama teacher, reportedly suggested the opening line and advised him to pause just after the pronoun: "This—is London" (Sperber, *Murrow*, 184–85).

30. Ibid., 233–34.

31. Murrow, *This Is London*, 141.

32. Quoted in Kendrick, *Prime Time*, 206.

33. Murrow, *This Is London*, 146–47.

34. Notable exceptions were Ernie Pyle, Vincent Sheehan, and of course the Murrow Boys.

35. Quoted in Kurth, *American Cassandra*, 318. The speech was later reprinted by *Life* magazine under the title of "There Was a Man" (27 January 1941).

36. Murrow, *This Is London*, 170–71.

37. As Murrow would later complain, he could not see "why there is no time to tell the greatest story of lifetime without being cluttered up with these ill-informed bastards in New York" (quoted in Kendrick, *Prime Time*, 221). He especially frowned on the news establishment's efforts to tell *his* story. Far from the raging fires of London, studio-based commentators could not be expected to get it right, to tell the story of the bombing as it was actually experienced by Londoners (Murrow, *This Is London*, 174–75).

38. Not all commentators were censured by Murrow. In a 21 July 1940 report, he summarized a BBC broadcast by the English radio commentator J. B. Priestley on social conflict in England without any sign of irony. Unlike Thompson, Priestley was not far from the action. See Murrow, *This Is London*, 136.

39. Ibid., 177–78.

40. He may have been critical of her commentary, but Murrow and Thompson were friends. Murrow would, in fact, try later to bring her on board with CBS as a member of the "Murrow Boys."

41. Quoted in Cull, *Selling War*, 102.

42. Murrow, *This Is London*, 134.

43. As the BBC has recently noted, Charles Gardner's report on the pilot bailing out of his German plane—the climax of the dogfight broadcast—was not accurate. The German pilot was really an RAF pilot (Officer Michael Mudie), who died of his injuries the following day. See http://www.bbc.co.uk/archive/battleofbritain/11431.shtml.

44. Shortly after the broadcast of *War of the Worlds*, CBS apologized in the press "that some listeners to the Orson Welles *Mercury Theatre on the Air* program last night mistook fantasy for fiction. . . . Naturally it was neither Columbia's nor *Mercury Theatre*'s intention to mislead anyone . . . and when it became evident that a part of the audience had been disturbed by the performance, five announcements were read over the network later in the evening to reassure those listeners" (see *New York Times*, 31 October 1938, 2).

45. "Radio 'Invasion' Throws Listeners into Hysteria," 1–2.

46. An article appearing in *Variety* in 1939 warned of radio's dangers as follows: "While it does not create the tensions of the day, radio elongates the shadows of fear and frustration. We are scared by the mechanized columns of Hitler. We are twice-scared by the emotionalism of radio. Radio quickens the tempo of the alternating waves of confidence and defeatism which sweep the country and undermine judgment. Radio exposes nearly everybody in the country to a rapid, bewildering succession of emotional experiences. Our minds and our moral natures just cannot respond to the bombardment of contradiction and confusion" (quoted in Kendrick, *Prime Time*, 234).

47. Quoted in Sperber, *Murrow*, 133.

48. Perisco, *Edward R. Murrow*, 159.

49. Murrow, *London after Dark*. My transcription. All references are to the complete 24 August 1940 broadcast, available online at http://www.otr.com/londonafterdark.shtml.

50. For an analysis of war sounds, see Goodale, *Sonic Persuasion*, 106–10.

51. Cited in Seib, *Broadcasts from the Blitz*, 3.

52. Douglas, *Listening In*, 183.

53. Sevareid, *Not So Wild a Dream*, 178.

54. Murrow's keen sense of hearing allowed him to channel what to American listeners was an unseen world—a phantom world. As Salomé Voegelin writes, "Sounds are like ghosts. . . . The spectre of sound unsettles the idea of visual

stability and involves us as listeners in the production of an invisible world" (*Listening to Noise and Silence*, 12).

55. Augoyard and Torgue, *Sonic Experience*, 123–26.

56. Murrow, *This Is London*, 172.

57. In film, the synecdoche effect would be equivalent to a zoomed-in close-up.

58. We might even look at Murrow's project as a continuation of the *Columbia Workshop*'s early efforts (1936–37) in educating the listening public about the nature of sound, which I discuss in Chapter 2. Murrow and the *Workshop* shared a vested interest in the acoustic competence and auditory sensitivity of the listener. Murrow extended this interest in acoustic competence to his own radio texts, often metaphorically creating effects utilized by the *Workshop*'s sound effects staff.

59. Murrow, *This Is London*, 179–80.

60. Ibid., 138.

61. Murrow, 16 August 1940, ibid., 140. The imaginary sense of the air war over England became a motif in Murrow's early broadcasts, often linked to the remoteness of Luftwaffe bombers. Murrow, sounding like the Orwell of *Homage to Catalonia*, reported on 25 August 1940: "The strongest impression one gets of these bombings is a sense of unreality. Often the planes are so high that even in a cloudless sky you can't see them. I stood on a hill watching an airdrome being bombed two miles away. It looked and sounded like farmers blasting stumps in western Washington. You forget entirely that there are men down there on the ground. Even when the dive bombers come down looking like a duck with both wings broken and you hear the hollow grunt of their bombs, it doesn't seem to have much meaning" (ibid., 147).

62. The endless nighttime bombing was baffling, and Murrow, like a character in a Beckett play, could see little and understand less. But these limitations only seemed to sharpen his hearing. As in modernist texts such as Faulkner's *Absalom, Absalom!* (1936), even a limited kind of knowing must first be grounded in epistemological doubt (see McHale, *Postmodernist Fiction*, 8).

63. Murrow, *This Is London*, 173.

64. Ibid., 209–10.

65. Murrow, *In Search of Light*, 70–91.

66. Murrow, *This Is London*, 148.

67. Murrow's efforts to call attention to sound in a sound-based medium lent his essays a reflexive quality that resonated with the programming of the *Columbia Workshop*. That Murrow's sound descriptions came to resemble sound cues in a *Columbia Workshop* broadcast—the "bestial grunt of bombs," the "uneven screaming" of an air-raid siren, the "mumbling" of big German bombers, the "rumble of guns," the "thunder of gunfire," the "harsh, grating sound" of broken glass, "the roar of motors"—points to a continuum that existed between avant-garde drama on CBS and broadcast news during the formative years of radio. Radio tropes crossed generic boundaries as easily as voice actors.

68. Susan Douglas notes that while the technical difficulties of shortwave transmission undercut the reliability of foreign broadcasts, the effect back home was quite the opposite: "This actually heightened the romance of hearing the New York announcer's voice imploring the ether with 'America calling Prague; America calling Berlin; come in, London' and to hear Shirer answer, 'Hello, America, hello, CBS, this is Berlin,' as if the announcer embodied the city itself." The imperfections of shortwave made foreign reports seductive. "You were inclined to lean closer," writes Douglas, "to try to use your body to help pull him in yourself. And listeners came to understand a semiotics of sound, as different sound quality itself signified the genre, the urgency, and the importance of the broadcast." See her *Listening In*, 178.

Chapter 5

1. As Anne Carson points out in "Gender of Sound," 121.
2. Funk, "The Tumbling Box," lines 25–28.
3. Bulfinch, *Greek and Roman Mythology*, 80.
4. Echo was no longer capable of an originary voice. She was limited strictly to counterpoint. "I am Echo, the nymph who repeats all she hears," says the unhappy nymph in Aristophanes, *Thesmophoriazusae*, 389.
5. Ovid, *Metamorphoses*, 67–73.
6. Freud's "On Narcissism: An Introduction" led the way. What Narcissus "projects before him as his ideal is the Ersatz of the lost narcissism of his childhood, in which he was his own idea." See Freud, *The Standard Edition*, 4:93.
7. McLuhan, "The Gadget Lover," 41.
8. Ibid., 46.
9. Ovid, *Metamorphoses*, 72.
10. Silverman argues that in classical cinema female speech is often rendered meaningless and that woman's enunciative power has been repeatedly withheld from her. As an "acoustic mirror," her role is limited to reflecting back (echoing) to patriarchy the illusion of its discursive primacy. Consequently, woman's speech is often reduced to hysterical bantering, gossip, and prattle. See Silverman, *Acoustic Mirror*, 42–80.
11. In *Echo and Narcissus*, Amy Lawrence shows how the female voice in film continually manifests itself as a "problem" for male authority. Her discussion of *Sorry, Wrong Number* focuses on Anatole Litvak's 1948 film adaptation of the radio play and the extent to which the narrative authority of Mrs. Stevenson's cinematic counterpart (Leona) poses a threat to the ocular imperatives of classical cinema (131–45).
12. Cavarero, *For More Than One Voice*, 165–72.
13. As Michele Hilmes explains, the debate over the desirability of women's voices on air dates back to the mid-1920s and was argued in public venues. Ten years later, "non-performing women's voice had virtually disappeared from nighttime schedules and could be heard only during daytime hours devoted specifically to 'women's' concerns" (see *Radio Voices*, 141–43).

14. Quoted in Hosley, "As Good as Any of Us," 154.

15. She found one, a man in the American Embassy who served as her voice, saying "I'm Phil Brown speaking for Betty Wason" (see ibid.).

16. Listeners, of course, were more accustomed to the female voice on daytime radio. Mary Margaret McBride, for instance, pioneered a talk show format featuring unscripted interviews with hundreds of significant political and cultural figures of the day. From 1934 to 1954, McBride was, as Susan Ware writes, the Oprah Winfrey of daytime radio, with millions of devoted fans tuning in to her daily program. Nevertheless, despite her immense popularity, the media dismissed McBride as a "chatterbox." She was a woman on radio who had little right to command a microphone, her critics assumed, even if her listeners responded far differently (see Ware, *It's One O'clock and Here Is Mary Margaret McBride*).

17. As another foreign correspondent confessed, CBS "did not favor women on the air, especially from foreign points." According to Harry W. Flannery, who replaced Shirer in Berlin, most listeners "preferred male voices and had no confidence in women for such assignments, even though some of them... were as good reporters as any of us." Flannery, *Assignment to Berlin*, 109. Wason, at least, could produce a script for her dummies, but that was hardly consoling. "I knew that I was an excellent reporter, and yet they said my voice did not come across. Well, I have done so much broadcasting since then that I know my voice was good, and it was just the objection to a woman's voice giving news." Whatever Wason thought of her skills, the network saw her as discursively insufficient. She was the sexual other (being "frail and feminine") of classic Hollywood cinema, someone denied entry into the symbolic order. No matter how authorial Betty's role was in the airing of her reports, CBS went out of its managerial way to mask that process, overdubbing her voice with that of a vocal dummy. She may have gotten the last word in, but like the girl doomed to repetition, that word was never her own. See Hosley, "As Good as Any of Us," 154.

18. Along with crime and mystery programs, the thriller was one of the fastest-growing radio genres during the war; see McCracken, "Scary Women and Scarred Men," 183.

19. *The Whole Town's Sleeping*, written by Ray Bradbury, first appeared in *McCall's* in September 1950. It was adapted for CBS's *Suspense* in 1955 by Antony Ellis and then rebroadcast in 1958. Jeanette Nolan played Lavinia Nebbs in 1955; Agnes Moorehead played the role in 1958. All quotations from *The Whole Town's Sleeping* are from my transcription.

20. Silverman, *Acoustic Mirror*, 69.

21. *The Screaming Woman* aired on *Suspense* on 25 November 1948. The thirty-minute play, starring Margret O'Brien as the young girl and Agnes Moorehead (who else) as the screaming woman, was adapted by Sylvia Richards. In all, CBS purchased three stories by Bradbury for radio adaptation on *Suspense*. Bradbury's first foray into radio had occurred two years earlier when NBC bought the rights to *Killer, Come Back to Me*, which had first appeared in the July 1944 issue of *Detective Tales* magazine. It was adapted for NBC's radio thriller *Mollé Mystery Theater* in May 1946. See Weller, *Bradbury Chronicles*, 139–40. All

quotations from *The Screaming Woman* in the following discussion are from my transcription of this broadcast.

22. Dippy, Margaret's friend, tags along to hear the screaming woman who has been described with such urgency. At first, Dippy thinks Margaret is playing a ventriloquist trick. Margaret persists in revealing the mysterious voice, and after some digging Dippy too hears the screaming. "Hey, there really is a woman buried down there," Dippy says, but still cannot wrap his mind around the idea of the screaming woman. "What if it's just a radio buried down there?" he wonders (with profound insight).

23. Chion, *Voice in Cinema*, 21–22. Chion writes that radio, being acousmatic by definition, "cannot play with showing, partially showing, and not showing," unlike film (21). But that is precisely what makes Bradbury's screaming woman so fascinating. Radio is "playing" with that which is not there: the body. Arguably, we might even say that Mrs. Nesbitt's missing body, of which Margaret takes such great heed, endows the ten-year-old with a kind of presence that transcends radio as a medium, through Margaret's role as listener.

24. Ibid., 77–79.

25. Connor, "Panophonia."

26. A burst of non-semanticized phonemes, the scream dissolves the linguistic sign and its system, as Julia Kristeva explains in connection with Artaud's glossolalia; see "The Subject in Process," 118. For Artaud, the scream (and other anti-linguistic sounds) is crucial in its capacity to disrupt the semantic structures obscuring the "forces above and beyond papyrus"; see *Theater and Its Double*, 10.

27. Artaud, *Theatre and Its Double*, 71 and 111.

28. Weiss, "Radio, Death, and the Devil," 295.

29. Cited in ibid., 278.

30. MacLeish's sound cue calls for a crossfade that blends two contradictory sounds, a lyrical female voice and the brute sound of war: "A crazy stammering of machine guns hammers above the rising roar. . . . Over it the voice of the Singing Woman rising in a slow screaming scale of the purest agony broken at last on the unbearably highest note. The diminishing drone of the planes fades into actual silence." MacLeish, *Air Raid*, 123.

31. Fletcher's story is widely understood to be one of the most critically acclaimed plays in radio history; see Grams, *Suspense*, 21–22.

32. By its fourth broadcast in 1945, *Sorry, Wrong Number* had become an urban legend. After each broadcast the phone company was besieged by callers complaining about the "insensitivity of its operators." See Dunning, *On the Air*, 699.

33. This and subsequent quotations are from my transcription of Fletcher's *Sorry, Wrong Number*, broadcast on CBS's *Suspense* on 25 May 1943. The radio play is available at https://archive.org/details/Suspense-SorryWrongNumber.

34. McCracken, "Scary Women and Scarred Men," 189.

35. "Radio: Repeat Performance."

36. White, "Queer Career of Agnes Moorehead," 100–101.

37. Ibid., 100.

38. Fletcher, Preface, *Sorry, Wrong Number*, 5.

39. Just as the Count is excluded from Mina's mediatory network in Bram Stoker's *Dracula*; see Kittler, "Dracula's Legacy."

40. See Rakow, "Women and the Telephone."

41. Artaud, cited in Weiss, "Radio, Death, and the Devil," 276.

42. Crane, "Projections and Intersections," 93.

43. "Sorry, Wrong Number," 91.

44. Fletcher, Preface, *Sorry, Wrong Number*, 3.

45. Barthes, "Grain of the Voice," 182.

46. Silverman, *Acoustic Mirror*, 61.

47. Connor, *Dumbstruck*, 35. Connor describes the vocalic body as a side effect of the embodying power of voice. "Voices are produced by bodies: but can also themselves produce bodies. The vocalic body is the idea—which can take the form of dream, fantasy, ideal, theological doctrine, or hallucination—of a surrogate or secondary body, a projection of a new way of having or being a body, formed and sustained out of the autonomous operations of the voice.... It may then appear that the voice is subordinate to the body when in fact the opposite is experientially the case; it is the voice which seems to colour and model its container" (35).

48. Dolar, *A Voice and Nothing More*, 45.

49. Jewell, "Hollywood and Radio," 126.

50. See Hilmes, *Hollywood and Broadcasting*, 78-115.

51. Already Stanwyck's Leona is invested with considerably more agency than Moorehead's Mrs. Stevenson. Though bedridden, as Amy Lawrence writes, Leona has quite a reach, in effect "organizing the narrative through what she hears. She is the one who makes sense of the narrative, and as such becomes our surrogate, an auditing spectator within the text." Lawrence, *Echo and Narcissus*, 131.

52. See ibid., 142-44; and Solomon, "Adapting 'Radio's Perfect Script,'" 30-32.

53. Leona's narrative stance in the story is determined more by her ability to hear than to see. Lawrence observes that "Leona occupies and demonstrates the position of the radio listener, sitting in his or her home, overhearing others speaking yet unable to intervene or make herself heard." Lawrence, *Echo and Narcissus*, 137.

54. Silverman, *Acoustic Mirror*, 79.

55. Lawrence, *Echo and Narcissus*, 139.

56. Crowther, "Sorry, Wrong Number."

57. The phrase "aesthetic mainstreaming" is borrowed from Stam, "Introduction," 43.

Chapter 6

1. The BBC's "Man in Black" (played by Valentine Dyall, a Shakespearean actor who later voiced the part of Gargravarr in *The Hitchhiker's Guide to the Galaxy*) was imported from CBS's *Suspense* in 1942. The Man in Black was the announcer for *Suspense*, and as a spokesman for the horror genre it was his job to pitch the story of the evening, identify the actors (usually Hollywood celebrities), reaffirm

the formal properties of the program, and then plug the sponsor, Roma Wines. Although he stood outside the frame of the story, he created a secondary order of fiction by casting himself as the incumbent voice of psychological horror: "This is The Man in Black, here again to introduce Columbia's program, *Suspense*. . . . If you've been with us on these Tuesday nights, you will know that *Suspense* is compounded of mystery and suspicion and dangerous adventure. In this series are tales calculated to intrigue you, to stir your nerves, to offer you a precarious situation and then withhold the solution, until the last possible moment." Impresario, commentator, and actor, the Man in Black was played by George Kearnes, in addition to others, and served as gatekeeper to a genre in great demand.

2. Tynan, "Under Milk Wood: A True Comedy of Humours," *Observer* (26 August 1956), reprinted in *Curtains*, 145.

3. Thomas, "Preface: Notes on the Art of Poetry," xx.

4. Bayley, *Romantic Survival*, 214.

5. *Voice* was Orwell's monthly radio magazine focusing on literary topics broadcast by the BBC's Eastern Service. As Orwell explained in an essay about his program, the fact that the BBC had little hope of reaching young and educated adults in India with its typical propaganda provided an excuse to broadcast something more "highbrow" than was generally possible; see Orwell, "Poetry and the Microphone," 857.

6. Thomas, *On the Air with Dylan Thomas*, ix.

7. Thomas, *Memories of Christmas*, 22–23.

8. As Thomas wrote in his letters, "I've got to get nearer to the bones of words, & to a Matthew Arnold's hell with the convention of meaning & sense" (Thomas, *Collected Letters*, 195).

9. The fact that Thomas's irrepressible *jouissance* maximized the baroque sound effects of his radio prose may have disturbed the Talks Department. Thomas's BBC producer in Wales, an enthusiastic supporter, lobbied the Director of Talks in London to broadcast the poet's seaside essays. But G. R. Barnes at first balked at the prospect, grumbling that Thomas's "breathless poetic voice" was inappropriate for a national talk. The English Home Service would also initially resist attempts to broadcast *Under Milk Wood*, which it viewed as a work of obscenity. See Thomas, *On the Air with Dylan Thomas*, 9.

10. The possibility that Thomas might join the BBC as a staff contributor arose in 1950, as Ralph Maud notes, but never quite panned out. See ibid., viii.

11. Ibid., 177. *Return Journey* was commissioned by the BBC and first broadcast in June 1947. Thomas returned to Swansea a few months earlier in February 1947 on a fact-finding trip, going out of his way to compile this formidable list of vanished shops. Interested from the beginning in Swansea's wartime destruction, Thomas wrote to a town official seeking the names of all the shops destroyed by German bombing. He also contacted an old teacher to learn of the extent of the damage. More than anything else, perversely or not, the ruin of Swansea was on the writer's mind when commissioned to contribute to the BBC's *Return Journey*. See Lycett, *Dylan Thomas*, 240.

12. "Our Swansea is dead," Thomas had lamented on a return visit in 1941, shortly after the bombing; cited in Ferris, *Dylan Thomas*, 177.

13. Peter Lewis, "The Radio Road to Llareggub," 92.

14. Such hybridity was typical of the BBC Features Department throughout the 1940s, as it was of Norman Corwin's commemorative radio pieces and CBS's more innovative programming.

15. Thomas, *Return Journey*, 180.

16. Ibid., 181.

17. Ibid., 184 and 185.

18. Ibid., 189.

19. Peter Lewis, "The Radio Road to Llareggub," 94.

20. Thomas borrowed the phrase "hole in space" for *Return Journey* from an apocalyptic poem written in 1933, "Not Forever Shall the Lord of the Red Hail": "A hole in space shall keep the shape of thought, / The lines of earth, the curving of the heart, / And from this darkness spin the golden soul." Thomas, *Notebook Poems*, 191.

21. Thomas, *Holiday Memory*, 144.

22. Douglas Cleverdon, the BBC producer of *Under Milk Wood*, wondered "whether there has ever been a better thirty-minute radio piece" than *Return Journey to Swansea*; see Cleverdon, *The Growth of Milk Wood*, 15.

23. Letter to D. J. and Florence Thomas (19 July 1947), in Thomas, *Collected Letters*, 653–54.

24. Thomas, *Poems*, 302.

25. Ferris, *Dylan Thomas*, 291.

26. Thomas had premiered *Under Milk Wood* in a reading at the Poetry Center in New York a few months earlier (14 May 1953), performing a number of roles (including First Voice and Reverend Eli Jenkins, among others). In a shocking turn of events, Thomas died six months later during a return trip to New York, two months before the BBC's famous broadcast of the play. The director of the Poetry Center, John Malcolm Brinnin, described the 14 May reading:

> The stage was dim until a soft breath of light showed Dylan's face.... One by one, the faces of the other actors came into view as the morning light of Milk Wood broadened and Dylan's voice, removed and godlike in tone, yet pathetically human in the details upon which it dwelt, made a story, a mosaic and an *aubade* of the beginning movements of a village day. Expectant, hushed, and not at all prepared to laugh, the audience seemed as deep in concentration as the actors on stage until, finally, unable not to recognize the obvious bawdy meaning of some of the play's early lines, two or three people laughed outright. But still there was a general uneasiness, an incomprehension, as if these outbursts had been mistaken laughter. Then, as soon as it became evident that this story of a village was as funny as it was loving and solemn, a chain of laughter began and continued until the last line.
>
> When the lights slowly faded and the night had swallowed up the last face and muffled the last voice in the village, there was an unexpected

silence both on stage and off. The thousand spectators sat as if stunned, as if the slightest handclap might violate a spell. But within a few moments the lights went up and applause crescendoed and bravos were shouted by half the standing audience while the cast came back for curtain call after curtain call until, at the fifteenth of these, squat and boyish in his happily flustered modesty, Dylan stepped out alone. (Brinnin, *Dylan Thomas in America*, 209–10)

27. All quotations are from Thomas, *Under Milk Wood*.

28. While composing *Under Milk Wood*, Thomas imagined his work, as he wrote in a letter, as an "entertainment coming out of darkness." What he was hoping to write was "an impression for voices, an entertainment out of the darkness, of the town I live in, and to write it simply and warmly and comically with lots of movement and varieties of moods, so that, at many levels through sight and speech, description and dialogue, evocation and parody, you come to know the town as an inhabitant of it." Thomas, *Collected Letters*, 813.

29. Cited in Holbrook, *Dylan Thomas*, 67. Writing for the *Adelphi* in 1934, Thomas goes on to question the optical bias of the modernism of the eye, lamenting the decline of spoken-word art: "'The Death of the Ear' would be an apt subtitle for a book on the plight of modern poetry.... It would be possible to explain this lack of aural value and this debasing of an art that is primarily dependent on the musical mingling of vowels and consonants by talking of the effect of a noisy, mechanical civilization on the delicate mechanism of the human ear. But the reason is deeper than that. Too much poetry to-day is flat on the page, a black and white thing of words created by intelligences that no longer think it necessary for a poem to be read and understood by anything but the eyes." Cited in ibid., 67.

30. Ihde, *Listening and Voice*, 155–56.

31. Thomas's noun-derived participles reveal traces of the kind of linguistic crossbreeding—young girls are "bridesmaided by glowworms" and the boys are dreaming of the "jollyrodgered sea"—that blurs the line between thingness (or states of being) and action as becoming, in which agency is decentered both grammatically and ontologically. That Thomas should mix an archaic or "bardic" style with such destabilizing poetic techniques has long angered critics of his poetry.

32. Gareth Thomas, "A Freak User of Words," 80.

33. Ihde, *Listening and Voice*, 167.

34. Thomas often wrote of the priority of sound in his writing. As he explained in his "Notes on the Art of Poetry," first published as "Poetic Manifesto" in the *Texas Quarterly*, what words meant did not matter nearly as much as their sonic properties: "I wanted to write poetry in the beginning because I had fallen in love with words. The first poems I knew were nursery rhymes, and before I could read them for myself I had come to love just the words of them, the words alone. What the words stood for, symbolized, or meant, was of very secondary importance. What mattered was the sound of them as I heard them for the first time on the lips of the remote and incomprehensible grown-ups who seemed, for

some reason, to be living in my world. And these words were to me, as the notes of bells, the sounds of musical instruments, the noises of the wind, sea, and rain, the rattle of milkcarts, the clopping of hooves on cobbles, the fingering branches on a window pane, might be to someone deaf from birth, who has miraculously found his hearing." Reprinted in Thomas, *Poems*, xv.

35. Robert Graves's famous complaint is a case in point. Graves grumbled that Thomas was "drunk with melody, and what the words were he cared not. He was eloquent, and what cause he was pleading, he cared not. . . . He kept musical control of the reader without troubling about the sense." See Graves, *The Crowning Privilege*, 138–39.

36. Cited in Peter Lewis, "The Radio Road to Llareggub," 72.

37. Cory, "Soundplay," 335.

38. The partnership between Beckett and the BBC would last for nearly a decade and was valuable to both parties. As Everett C. Frost writes, "The association with Beckett made a significant contribution to the BBC, one that prompted the development of a center to figure out how best to use the new technologies in the service of broadcast. But it also had a profound effect on Samuel Beckett, making him an increasingly astute and innovative writer for not only radio but, subsequently, film and television as well." See Frost, "Meditating On," 311.

39. See Bignell, *Beckett on Screen*, 88–90.

40. For the original broadcast listing of these programs in *Radio Times*, see T. S. Eliot, "Paul Valery," Third Programme, 27 December 1946, *Radio Times* 1212 (20 December 1946), 30; Thomas Mann, "Germany: Her Character and Destiny," Third Programme, 4 June 1947, *Radio Times* 1246 (29 August 1947), 16; Iris Murdoch, "The Novelist as Metaphysician," Third Programme, 26 February 1950, *Radio Times* 1376 (24 February 1950), 19; Bertrand Russell, "Science and Democracy," Third Programme, 5 January 1947, *Radio Times* 1214 (3 January 1947), 8; Evelyn Waugh, "Half In Love with Easeful Death," Third Programme, 15 May 1948, *Radio Times* 1282 (7 May 1948), 21; Graham Greene, "The Crisis," 16 February 1947, *Radio Times* 1220 (14 February 1947), 8; E. M. Forster, "American Impressions," Third Programme, *Radio Times* 1252 (10 October 1947), 4; John Donne, "A Selection of Poetry" (read by George Rylands), Third Programme, 2 January 1946, *Radio Times* 1213 (27 December 1946), 24; John Milton, "On the Morning of Christ's Nativity" and "An Eclogue for Christmas" (read by Robert Harris and Reginald Beckwith), Third Programme, 24 December 1946, *Radio Times* 1212 (20 December 1946), 18; Keats, A Selection of Poetry (read by Dylan Thomas), Third Programme, 17 October 1946, *Radio Times* 1202 (11 October 1946), 20; John Hersey, "Hiroshima," Light Programme, 30 November 1946, *Radio Times* 1208 (22 November 1946), 31; Chaucer, "The Canterbury Tales," Third Programme, 21 October 1946, *Radio Times* 1203 (18 October 1946), 8; Aeschylus, "The Agamemnon," Third Programme, 29 October 1946, *Radio Times* 1204 (25 October 1946), 12; Jean-Paul Sartre, "Huis Clos," Third Programme, 4 October 1946, *Radio Times* 1200 (27 September 1946), 24; Virginia Woolf, "The Duchess and the Jeweller" (read by James McKechnie), Third Programme, 27 November 1946, *Radio Times* 1208 (22 November 1946), 20; George Orwell, "Animal Farm,"

Third Programme, 14 January 1947, *Radio Times* 1215 (10 January 1947), 16; and George Bernard Shaw, "Man and Superman," Third Programme, 1 October 1946, *Radio Times* 1200 (27 September 1946), 12.

41. Cited by Drakakis, "Introduction," 13–14.

42. As Kate Whitehead explains, McWhinnie's appointment in 1953 is generally regarded as the turning point in the Drama Department's new preference for the avant-garde; see her *The Third Programme: A Literary History*, 139.

43. The breakthrough at the BBC with the plays of Thomas, Giles Cooper, and Beckett corresponds to the second stage of radio art, as outlined by Mark Cory in his survey of the tradition of German *Hörspiele*: "The experimental nature of the new technology itself, plus the remarkable pluralism characteristic of Weimar culture, gave rise to at least three distinct types of radio art before the war. The first was a logical extension of the stage, radio perceived as a theater of the blind. The second took radio 'drama' beyond the staging of works for the blind and sought to develop an imaginative literature written expressly for the new medium. The third understood something even broader: radio art as acoustical art, a radical and short-lived breaking away from literary conventions that was to signal the debut of the avant-garde tradition resurrected with such success in the 1960s." See Cory, "Soundplay," 334.

44. Cited in Frost, "Fundamental Sounds," 367.

45. Beckett, *All That Fall*, 41. All quotations are from this edition.

46. The original BBC broadcasts of Beckett's radio plays (1956–76) are available from the British Library (Beckett, *Works for Radio*, CD); the 1986 American production of Beckett's *All That Fall* is available from *Evergreen Review*.

47. Ulrika Maude suggests that Maddy is "transported by sound alone into the 'ruinous old house' in which *Death and the Maiden* is played"; see her *Beckett, Technology, and the Body*, 51. The possibility that sound might transcend the limits of realist space is consistent with the idea that sound is not fixed by referentiality, which is the gist of acoustic drift.

48. Self-referential moments such as this (on BBC radio, Maddy is indeed blind) are common in the play, where Beckett reminds listeners that this story is mediated by a broadcast medium.

49. Connor, *Dumbstruck*, 35.

50. Connor, *Samuel Beckett*, 1.

51. Kenner, *Samuel Beckett*, 173. As Kenner observes, even though Mrs. Rooney is an illusion produced on radio, her physical gestures "make her at the same time vastly substantial" (171).

52. McWhinnie, *The Art of Radio*, 133.

53. Beckett, *The Letters of Samuel Beckett, Volume II: 1941–1956*, 656.

54. Letter to Nancy Cunard, 5 June 1956; quoted in Knowlson, *Damned to Fame*, 428.

55. McWhinnie, *The Art of Radio*, 27.

56. Emilie Morin discusses the relationship between Pierre Schaeffer's theory of *musique concrète* and its influence on Beckett, noting that the playwright's sophisticated approach to acoustic design in *All That Fall* was shaped in part by

Schaeffer's interest in sounds removed from visual sources. See Morin, "Beckett's Speaking Machines." While the BBC hoped to emulate the techniques of *musique concrète* for radio drama, it was also suspicious of the movement's more experimental side, which seemed unwelcoming to narrative concerns.

57. McWhinnie, *The Art of Radio*, 85–86.

58. This was not lost on the radio-minded Beckett, whose experience with the BBC partly inspired *Krapp's Last Tape* the following year (1958). He had seen the new technology in person at the BBC studio in Paris—he would become fascinated by tape—and later asked McWhinnie to send him a tape recorder manual in order to understand exactly how it worked. It did not hurt that the BBC production of *All That Fall* was an unequivocal success. See Knowlson, *Damned to Fame*, 398.

59. McWhinnie, *The Art of Radio*, 85.

60. Briscoe, *BBC Radiophonic Workshop*, 18–19.

61. Like McWhinnie, Briscoe was also engaged by *musique concrète*, and in particular by the works of Schaeffer and Stockhausen; see Niebur, *Special Sound*, 14–25.

62. "There is nothing more useless than an organ," Artaud wrote in 1947. In a strange way, Maddy's vocalic body approximates Artaud's curious notion of the "body without organs," as formulated in *Theatre and Its Double* but also expressed with tremendous violence and noise in his censored radio play *To Have Done with the Judgment of God*, recorded ten years before the broadcast of *All That Fall*. For Artaud, the body is not simply an accumulation of behaviors and articulations, which for him would be a body *with* organs—a discursive body—but something else.

63. Beckett, *Watt*, 81 (my emphasis).

64. Ibid., 83.

65. Beckett's Molloy, who like Maddy is acoustically sensitized, joins Watt and Mrs. Rooney in their linguistic agony, finding "semantic succour" only in "pure sounds, free of all meaning"; see Beckett, *Three Novels*, 45.

66. Cited in Niebur, *Special Sound*, 23.

67. As Pierre Schaeffer writes, when a sound is removed from its original context, it is the listening itself that becomes significant. It is no longer a question of knowing what the sound points to, what it indicates. Rather, it is a question of "'What am I hearing?' . . . What exactly are you hearing'—in the sense that one asks the subject to describe not the external references of the sound it perceives but the perception itself." See Schaeffer, "Acousmatics," 77.

68. Maddy's disruptive body is perhaps most evident in the hilarious predicaments Beckett scripts for her, as when Mr. Slocum, who offers her a ride to the Boghill station, struggles mightily to squeeze the enormous woman into his motor car:

> MR. SLOCUM: (*In position behind her.*) Now, Mrs. Rooney, how shall we do this?
>
> MRS. ROONEY: As if I were a bale, Mr. Slocum, don't be afraid. (*Pause. Sounds of effort.*) That's the way! (*Effort.*) Lower! (*Effort.*) Wait! (*Pause.*)

No, don't let go! (*Pause.*) ... There! ... Now! ... Get your shoulder under it ... Oh! ... (*Giggles.*) Oh glory! ... Up! Up! ... Ah! ... I'm in! (13-14)

69. Kristeva, *Powers of Horror*, 4.

70. In the words of Katherine Worth, Mrs. Rooney surprises listeners with her "overwhelmingly capacious female presence." See Worth, "Women in Beckett's Radio and Television Plays," 237.

71. Hope-Wallace, Review of *All That Fall*, 155-56.

72. Arnheim, *Radio*, 191.

73. Cavarero critiques philosophy's "devocalization" of the *logos* at length in *For More Than One Voice*. In her view, Plato's legacy is that the "voice becomes not only the reason for truth's ineffability, but also the acoustic filter that impedes the realm of signified from presenting itself to the noetic gaze. This is not simply a privileging of sight or the subordination of speaking to thinking, but rather a precise strategy of devocalizing the logos that relegates the voice to the status of those things that philosophy deems unworthy of attention.... Stripped of a voice that then gets reduced to a secondary role as the vocalization of signified, logos is thus taken over by sight and gravitates increasingly toward the universal" (42-43).

Chapter 7

1. See Ostwald, *Glenn Gould*, 233.

2. See Gould, "The Prospects of Recording," 337-39. Tim Hecker calls Gould's studio-based editorial practices the aesthetics of "total control." Hecker, "Glenn Gould, the Vanishing Performer," 78.

3. Kostelanetz, "Glenn Gould as a Radio Composer," 557.

4. In his study of Gould, Geoffrey Payzant noted that Gould's "contrapuntal radio documentaries are less widely known than might be expected, considering his international renown as an innovative recording artist. They have been broadcast outside Canada, but not extensively, and there has been very little published criticism of them." See Payzant, *Glenn Gould*, 137.

5. Gould, "Radio as Music," 374.

6. Ostwald, *Glenn Gould*, 230-31.

7. Payzant describes "The Idea of North" as a hybrid of "music, drama, and several other strains, including essay, journalism, anthropology, ethics, social commentary, contemporary history." Payzant, *Glenn Gould*, 131.

8. Bazzana, *Wondrous Strange*, 294.

9. McNeilly, "Listening, Nordicity, Community," 104-5.

10. Hurwitz, "Towards a Contrapuntal Radio," 256; Payzant, *Glenn Gould*, 130.

11. As Gould remarked in an interview in 1968, "The Idea of North" was ostensibly a program about isolation. "What it was really about, as a friend of mine kindly said, was 'the dark night of the human soul.' It was a very dour essay on the effects of isolation upon mankind." See Gould, *Glenn Gould: Concert Dropout* (disc).

12. Gould's thoughts about his own radio work were consistently framed in literary/musical terms; see Gould's letter to Elving Shantz, in Gould, *Glenn Gould:*

Selected Letters, 194. Soliciting interviewees for the final program in his *Trilogy* ("The Quiet in the Land"), Gould explained his approach in ethereal terms: "What I hope to achieve, primarily, is a 'mood-piece'—a radio-essay dealing with the degree to which, as one of my interviewees put it, the Mennonites are able to remain 'in the world but not of the world.' It is, in short, a reflective and, I believe, rather poetic program and, if it succeeds, will, I hope, capture the essence of the Mennonite communities and the life style of the peoples involved more faithfully than any recitation of historical facts possibly can."

13. Gould, "The Idea of North: An Introduction," 391.

14. Ibid., 392.

15. Gould met Maclean on the train to Churchill. A garrulous conversationalist, as Bazzana explains, Maclean was a modern-day cracker-barrel philosopher quoting Shakespeare, Kafka, and Thoreau who engaged Gould in a captivating eight-hour conversation. This chat would later supply Gould with the conceit of the journey by train. See Bazzana, *Wondrous Strange*, 292–300.

16. Gould, *Glenn Gould: Concert Dropout* (disc).

17. Quoted in Friedrich, *Glenn Gould*, 187.

18. "Glenn Gould Interviews Glenn Gould about Glenn Gould," in Gould, *Glenn Gould Reader*, 325. Gould said he created "The Idea of North" as a "metaphoric comment and not as a factual documentary."

19. As Bazzana notes, to achieve a more universal and literary impact, Gould deliberately edited most topical references out of his interviews in "The Idea of North" (*Wondrous Strange*, 299).

20. Gould, *Solitude Trilogy*. All quotations are taken from these recordings of the *Trilogy*; the transcriptions are my own.

21. Indeed, when the program first aired, it was flagged for cross talk. Hearing multiple voices speak simultaneously was so unfamiliar that something seemed wrong.

22. Peter Davidson writes that the "persistent myth of the north in our own time is that the exploration of the Arctic is morally pure" (*The Idea of North*, 51).

23. As Camus observes, "One must imagine Sisyphus happy," as it is only the struggle that really matters (*The Myth of Sisyphus and Other Essays*, 123).

24. I have given Maclean the benefit of the doubt in my summary of his account. How the reference to Sisyphus contributes to the invented story of the "young fellow" is a bit sketchy. Any conventional "documentary" maker would have left this digression on the cutting-room floor. Maclean's vagueness did not apparently trouble the splice-happy Gould, who was more interested in the literary implications of a philosophical idea than in the coherence of Maclean's discourse.

25. Said, "The Music Itself," 49.

26. Quoted in Bazzana, *Glenn Gould*, 144.

27. Connor, "Beside Himself."

28. Gould, "Radio as Music."

29. The compositional rigor of Gould's *Solitude Trilogy* is thought to be especially interesting in light of Gould's lack of success as a music composer. As Bazzana writes, "Creating successful works in a new genre of radio art took much

of the sting out of his failure as a composer." *Wondrous Strange*, 313. As a compensatory activity, that rigor also indicated to what extent Gould never doubted that his "contrapuntal radio" was all about making music.

30. The term "counterpoint" comes from the Latin—*punctus contra punctum*—meaning "point against point."

31. Listening to Gould's sound work is perplexing and demanding. As Payzant notes, "With each new hearing one learns more of the rules of the piece, and allows it to reveal its many details, layer upon layer, as one would do with a fugue by J. S. Bach." *Glenn Gould*, 129.

32. On listening to the edited version of "The Idea of North" on radio, James Lotz "became a little irritated at the absence of a coherent series of statements." Quoted in Friedrich, *Glenn Gould*, 198. Like Lotz, others interviewed during the ten-year making of *Solitude Trilogy* expressed their frustration with Gould's apparent manipulations.

33. As audio engineers explain it, "close-miking" refers to the practice of situating a microphone very near the source being recorded in order to emphasize a more direct sound and to minimize the incidence of ambient effects. In close-miking, the microphone is usually fewer than twelve inches from the source.

34. Gould was keenly aware of how recording technologies opened the door to virtual space in sound-making and how the illusion of movement in acoustic space dramatized human thought. As he explained in an interview with John Jessop, electronic recording technologies provided new opportunities for sound-makers: "You see, the sense of area, the sense of space and proximity in the technology, is just not being used at all. But it is used the moment you say to someone, 'But this has dramatic significance.' Even in the earliest days of radio, back beyond those 'Sunday Night Stages' we spoke of earlier, you would find very sophisticated mike placement, I'm sure." Gould, "Radio as Music," 382.

35. Gould himself did not do the tape splicing on "The Idea of North" but did conduct the editing. Peter Shewchuk, one of several CBC editors who worked with Gould and Lorne Tulk on the program, recalls how specific and detailed Gould's instructions were during the process. Gould knew exactly what every voice was doing at any given moment: "Glenn gave the editors diagrams showing where the voices would go—we all had our own page which we worked on in isolation—and I was struck by how carefully everything had been scripted. People didn't understand the complex relationship of the voice to the music, this concept of contrapuntal radio. In fact, when the program was first aired, it was logged as crosstalk and there was much criticism over the fact that voices were sounding simultaneously. On the contrary, however, you really have to listen very carefully and be quite intelligent and astute." See Johnson, "Stories Untold."

36. Bazzana suggests that Gould's metaphor of the train journey drew on Katherine Anne Porter's *Ship of Fools*, which was published just a few years earlier in 1962. It was a favorite of Gould's, and he told others that Porter's novel had partly influenced his conception of "The Idea of North." See Bazzana, *Wondrous Strange*, 297–98.

37. Friedrich, *Glenn Gould*, 205.

38. McNeilly, "Listening, Nordicity, Community," 89.

39. Adorno, *Negative Dialectics*, 12–13. As Adorno explains it, the disenchantment of the concept is an antidote to idealism and is recommended as a means of liberating the "nonconceptualities" inherent in the concept that are normally masked by "enchantment." On Gould's reading of Adorno, see Cavell, *McLuhan in Space*, 163.

40. Said, *On Late Style*, 117.

41. Fish, *Self-Consuming Artifacts*, 3.

42. Gould, "Radio as Music," 380.

43. Hurwitz, "The Glenn Gould Contrapuntal Radio Show." Hurwitz was borrowing Gould's own idea of eavesdropping on multiple sounds. As Gould explained in a 1968 interview: "It's amazing to me . . . why one shouldn't be able to comprehend, clearly and concisely, two or three simultaneous conversations. Some of our most aware experiences are gleaned from sitting in subways, in dining-cars on trains, in hotel lobbies—simultaneously listening to several conversations, switching our point of view from one to another, picking out strands that fascinate us." Cited in Payzant, *Glenn Gould*, 131.

44. The quotations from the *Montreal Star*, the *Toronto Star*, and the *Ottawa Citizen* are cited in Friedrich, *Glenn Gould*, 189.

45. Gould, "'The Latecomers': An Introduction," 394.

46. Gould, "Radio as Music," 378.

47. Just as Wally Maclean's words are nearly drowned out by Sibelius's Fifth Symphony in the epilogue of "The Idea of North," the voices of Gould's Newfoundlanders are silenced by the sea in the prologue of "The Latecomers."

48. Bazzana notes that in his radio art Gould liked to avoid conventional "foreground-background distinctions," even if that put an enormous burden on the listener to do the work of separating out the voice from background music and ambient noise. *Wondrous Strange*, 301.

49. Ibid., 380.

50. Connor, "Beside Himself."

51. Ong, *Orality and Literacy*, 55, 101.

52. Gould, "'The Latecomers': An Introduction," 394–95.

53. Gould, "Rubinstein," 288 (my emphasis).

54. Gould, "The Prospects of Recording," 337.

55. One of Gould's favorite terms, "take-twoness" referred to his preferred editorial practice of splicing a second take into a studio tape recording. It became a metaphor for repeated intervention (as a form of electronic invention). See Gould, "The Prospects of Recording," 331–53.

56. Dyson, *Sounding New Media*, 8.

57. See Kostelanetz, "Glenn Gould," 126.

58. Gould, *Conversations with Glenn Gould*, 103.

59. See Bazzana, *Wondrous Strange*, 306.

60. Quoted in Friedrich, *Glenn Gould*, 198.

61. Gould was, as Matthew McFarlane observes, "supremely confident in his ideal audience" and suggested that listeners were rarely challenged enough by

radio: "The average person can take in and respond to far more information than we allot him on most occasions." See McFarlane, "Glenn Gould, Jean Le Moyne, and Pierre Teilhard de Chardin," 74. For Gould, that meant listening to more than one voice or conversation at the same time. Gould, "Radio as Music," 380.

62. Tom McCourt notes that the number of educational FM radio stations swelled from 29 in 1948 to 326 in 1967. See his *Conflicting Communication Interests in America*, 42. For a detailed discussion of the explosion in FM broadcasting, see Sterling and Keith, *Sounds of Change*.

63. Douglas, *Listening In*, 257. The extent to which Gould was appealing to what Douglas calls a "masculine, hi-fi aesthetic" (268) is hard to chart, but the participants in the high-fidelity craze during the 1960s and 1970s were largely middle-class males.

Chapter 8

1. After nearly two decades of admiration, listeners in the 1990s began to sour on public radio's aesthetic mainstreaming, critiques of NPR's politics and programming emerging on both the left and the right. See, for instance, Aufderheide, "Will Public Broadcasting Survive"; Husseini, "The Broken Promise of Public Radio"; Logivlio, "Sound Effects: Gender, Voice, and the Cultural Work of NPR"; Marcus, "Public Radio Hosts Drop In and Maybe Stay Too Long"; Montopoli, "All Things Considerate"; Porter, "Has Success Spoiled NPR"; and Sherman, "Good, Gray NPR."

2. As Douglas writes, not only did NPR provide access to long-excluded voices (as Murrow would say, the voices of "the little people") but it "revitalized radio as a highly suggestive aural medium in which the calculated use of sound could create powerful mental images in listeners' minds." *Listening In*, 286. Unlike the prevailing commercial radio programmers, NPR saw great value in sound as an artistic medium.

3. The creation of NPR makes a compelling story, one that has been told several times. See Looker, *The Sound and the Story*; McCauley, *NPR*; McCourt, *Conflicting Communication Interests in America*; Mitchell, *Listener Supported*; Roberts et al., *This Is NPR*; and Stamberg, *Every Night at Five*.

4. Since my visit to interview Susan Stamberg in July 2010, NPR has moved into a new 400,000-square-foot complex (or "palace," as some critics grumble) on North Capitol Street, with soaring ceilings, an employee gym, and a gourmet café. The $200 million building was mostly funded from donations, private funds, and tax dollars and was said, according to the *Washington Post*, to draw the ire of some. See "A Look Inside NPR's New Headquarters." The tours have become so popular that they now take place daily.

5. Siemering wanted the NPR sound to be casual, Stamberg recalls in a recent reminiscence: he wanted it to sound conversational. This meant no deep-voiced announcers. "We're going to talk to our listeners just the way we talk to our friends—simply, naturally," he said. "We don't want to be the all-knowing voices from the top of the mountain." Roberts et al., *This Is NPR*, 13.

6. As Siemering wrote, Stamberg's voice was vital to the identity of the new network: "Susan Stamberg, more than anyone else, became the voice of NPR. Listeners responded to her authenticity and genuine engagement with people. She listened. She asked the questions listeners would ask and more. She knew how to tell stories, skillfully using sound in the telling. Susan still has one of the most expressive voices on radio." See Siemering, "My First Fifty Years in Radio and What I Learned."

7. In the beginning, the sound people at NPR kept staffers at bay from print journalism and their reliance on heavily narrated stories. In the battle between orality and literacy, the former had the edge. This would soon change.

8. Sherman, "Good, Gray NPR."

9. The phrase is borrowed by Scott Sherman from NPR staffers.

10. Montopoli, "All Things Considerate." Sarah Vowell makes a similar charge in *Radio On*, 13.

11. Unless attributed to other sources, the information in the preceding paragraphs comes from my interview with Susan Stamberg in the old NPR headquarters, Washington, D.C., on 19 July 2010.

12. Before moving to television, Murrow (now a CBS executive) helped form the network's new Documentary Unit (1946–48). On Murrow's role in CBS's postwar documentary efforts, see Ehrlich, *Radio Utopia*, 48–59.

13. As Douglas notes, by the 1960s, narrative forms had vanished from radio. *Listening In*, 34.

14. Shepherd began his show during what Gerald Nachman calls the "era of the wise-guy DJ." *Seriously Funny*, 278.

15. Pinkerton, "The Talker."

16. The Mencken commentary aired in April 1960; Shepherd's discussion of *Krapp's Last Tape* aired on 21 July 1968.

17. Quoted in Nachman, *Seriously Funny*, 269.

18. McLuhan, "Radio," 303.

19. Ramirez, "Jean Shepherd, a Raconteur and a Wit of Radio, Is Dead."

20. Unlike his closest radio heir, Garrison Keillor, Shepherd was a cynic whose stories often come to grips with, as Shepherd's obituary in the *Los Angeles Times* explains, "the total absurdity of life on earth." *Los Angeles Times*, 17 October 1999.

21. In Jules Feiffer's words, it was "the most comprehensive, thoughtful, good-humored, analytical show on the air." Quoted in Piantadosi, "Stamberg Considered," 90.

22. Shepherd preferred to call himself a "commentator."

23. Wertheimer, *Listening to America*, xix.

24. To my ears, Kim Williams sounded like Thelma Ritter (Stella in Hitchcock's *Rear Window*) on uppers.

25. Fang, *Those Radio Commentators*, 333–34. With the exception of NPR's short commentaries, which were really personal essays, the tradition of the broadcast commentator was more or less replaced by the new "talk-radio" format during the 1970s. See Douglas, *Listening In*, 284–327.

26. Shortly after Congress passed the Public Broadcasting Act in 1967, which created the Corporation for Public Broadcasting, the new board of directors overseeing NPR often split, as Michael P. McCauley has written, over the question of centralized program production. Those with strong ties to college radio stations (the backbone of National Educational Radio) argued for locally produced radio content. Centralization would win out over more populist models, but NPR would remain particularly sensitive during its first ten years to the call for regional content and voices. See McCauley, *NPR*, 24.

27. In his "National Public Radio Purposes," a lofty manifesto adopted by NPR's board as its mission statement, Siemering emphasized the educational importance of public radio: "Because National Public Radio begins with no identity of its own it is essential that a daily product of excellence be developed. This may contain some hard news, but the primary emphasis would be on interpretation, investigative reporting on public affairs, the world of ideas and the arts. The program would be well paced, flexible, and a service primarily for a general audience. It would not, however, substitute superficial blandness for genuine diversity of regions, values, and cultural and ethnic minorities which comprise American society; it would speak with many voices and many dialects. The editorial attitude would be that of inquiry, curiosity, concern for the quality of life, critical, problem-solving, and life loving."

28. McLuhan, "Radio," 303.

29. Before being hired by NPR in 1970, Siemering spent eight years in Buffalo as the general manager of the student radio station WBFO. While there, he listened to Canadian Broadcasting Corporation programs (including *Ideas*, the show that first aired Glenn Gould's "The Idea of North" in 1967), which were broadcast from Toronto seventy miles away. The CBC, Siemering has said, helped give shape to his idea of progressive radio as practiced in Buffalo and refined in Washington at NPR.

30. *Time* magazine called *All Things Considered* the "most literate" news program on radio in 1979. "All the News Fit to Hear," 70.

31. When Sedaris's essay was first broadcast, as Ira Glass (who produced the tape and pitched the recording to NPR) notes, it generated more tape requests than any other story in *Morning Edition*'s history.

32. NPR's loyalty to its commentators—to its "other" voices—has sometimes faltered. In a 1995 Christmas essay on *All Things Considered*, Andrei Codrescu poked fun at fundamentalist Christians who believed in the idea of the "rapture": "The evaporation of 4 million who believe this crap would leave the world an instantly better place," the acerbic writer said with characteristic irony. Having received some 40,000 complaints from listeners, NPR straightaway aired an apology, which did not sit well with Codrescu. See "NPR Apologizes for Codrescu's Remark."

33. Conciatore, "Rodeo Clowns and Radio Poets."

34. Mankiewicz had brought to NPR's loose culture a sense of high-minded professionalism and was intent on upgrading its sound. To his ears, Williams may have come across like a bumpkin. Doug Bennet, Mankiewicz's successor in the mid-1980s, may have agreed. He called the network's non-news features from the early counterculture days "cutesy." See Looker, *The Sound and the Story*, 129 and 114.

35. Stamberg, *Talk*, 272.

36. As early as 1979, NPR's Linda Wertheimer acknowledged tension between the arts backers and the news people at the network. "The cultural people in the beginning were a little upset about Mankiewicz's evident leanings toward the news side," she was quoted as saying. "But what Frank has is just a refined instinct for quality." Cited in Piantadosi, "Stamberg Considered," 94. In another ten years, the "news side" would successfully colonize the network.

37. Roberts et al., *This Is NPR*, 25.

38. Ibid.

39. From my transcription. The debut broadcast of *All Things Considered* can be heard at http://www.npr.org/sections/thetwo-way/2013/11/19/246193689/robert-conley-first-host-of-all-things-considered-dies.

40. See Oney, "The Philosopher King," 3.

41. As she said of her own vérité piece on the lawyer Philip Hirschkop (from my interview notes).

42. In *Listening to America*, 7, Wertheimer writes: "As I listen to the tape of that first day's broadcast, it sounds rough. Listeners had no way of knowing who was speaking, reporters and the people they talked to were almost all nameless. In some cases, we didn't say where the conversations were taking place, or where the events we listened to happened. Sound indulgent in some places, overlong in others. We wouldn't do it that way now, and yet, we would. For all its unedited, sprawling, confusing quality, we did what Conley said we would on that first day. We put our listeners out there, in the middle of everything. We served up sound and texture, shouts and sirens. Even the confusion is a reflection of that day."

43. Ironically, as Jack Mitchell has written, Siemering was fired by the network a few months before *All Things Considered*—the show he created—won the Peabody Award. Mitchell, who worked with Siemering at NPR, credits the radioman for having encouraged the network to "innovate and defy convention." See Mitchell, *Listener Supported*, 75.

44. During one review session in 1971, NPR's reporters and producers listened to a documentary produced by Stamberg for WAMU, her former employer. The piece, of which Stamberg was quite proud, featured a male narrator anchoring the story with the obligatory authority of the CBS broadcast voice. Siemering said pointedly to his staff, "This is exactly what we don't want to sound like." Quoted in Oney, "The Philosopher King," 12.

45. See Mitchell, *Listener Supported*, 62.

46. After eight years on the air, *All Things Considered* had attracted a cult-like following and a steadily increasing listenership. Other media were paying attention. What *New York* magazine liked most about the show was its eccentric approach to storytelling: "The show seems to find many of its most loyal fans in artists—cartoonists in particular—partly, perhaps, because [*All Things Considered*] shares the cartoonist's way of looking at the news in an amused, confounded manner." See Piantadosi, "Stamberg Considered," 94.

47. Stamberg, *Every Night at Five*, 206–8.

48. A transcript of the story is included in ibid., 21–25. Stamberg herself makes the analogy to Thornton Wilder's play when summarizing the appeal of David

Puksta's narration (ibid., 20). An MP3 version of "Primary Season in Claremont" can be heard online at *Hearing Voices* (http://hearingvoices.com/stories.php?currentPageNum=5&fID=42&fidType=subject).

49. All but Marianne Schroeder and Wally Maclean are professional talkers in "The Idea of North." The other speakers, James Lotz, Frank Valee, and Bob Phillips, are writers and experts whose voices are continually qualified by counterpoint and overlap. For the most part, Maclean is protected from cross talk, and Gould often rescues Schroeder from the extreme effects of overlapping.

50. Stamberg, *Every Night at Five*, 25.

51. By 1980, all three hour-long segments of Gould's *Trilogy* had aired at least once, and his avant-garde radio aesthetic was beginning to catch on with American sound-makers.

52. My transcription. *Rivers of the Skull* is available in the National Public Radio Collection of the Library of Congress.

53. Steve Butterfield, the producer of *Rivers of the Skull*, may have intended his collage to serve a more politically satiric end. Richard Nixon's phone call to Apollo 11 ("Because of what you have done, the heavens have become a part of man's world") is noticeably small-minded in this context. That cannot be said, however, of the astronaut-speak, which, however unimaginative, acquires an unexpected bizarreness in proximity to the *Tibetan Book of the Dead*.

54. Emerling, "Public Radio's Bad Dream," 1.

55. *NPR Playhouse*, NPR's drama series, ran from 1981 to 2002.

56. From its beginnings in the 1930s, German Hörspiele, unlike the Anglo-American tradition of radio drama, laid greater emphasis on the acoustic exploitation of the medium. As Everett C. Frost writes: "The major tendency in the evolution of radio drama in Germany over the last half century is the successful and increasingly sophisticated attempt to define and develop a radiophonic art form in its own terms, fully exploiting the possibilities of the medium, equivalent to, but independent of the genres of literature and drama out of which it emerged." See Frost and Herzfeld-Sander, *German Radio Plays*, ix; and Cory, "Soundplay," 331–71. Hörspiele artists, as Cory explains, were particularly keen on probing the "problematical nexus of verbal and nonverbal elements that has been the most vexing and yet most exciting stimulus for radio art." Cory, "Soundplay," 331.

57. My transcription. Frank's *A Call in the Night* is available on his website (https://www.joefrank.com/shop/call-in-the-night-a/).

58. Hughes, "Radio's Prince of Darkness."

59. Quoted in Diamond, "Radio Noir."

60. Backed up by a three-piece combo, Nordine first performed his spoken-word narratives in a Chicago nightclub (the Offbeat Room) in 1956. In all, Nordine recorded over twelve albums of *Word Jazz*. Sound artists rarely become household names, but Nordine's whimsical narratives have left their mark on a number of popular artists, including Leonard Cohen, Tom Waits, and Lori Anderson, who all point to *Word Jazz* as a source of inspiration.

61. Nordine was commissioned by NPR to produce sixty-five *Word Jazz* shows; see Langer, "Will Ken Nordine Ever Grow Up?"

62. Ford, *Dig*, 145.

63. Since the 1920s, phone companies have provided notification of the time to callers, and before the Time of Day Service was automated, live operators—called "time-tellers"—read the time off clocks on walls.

64. "What Time Is It?" was first recorded on *Word Jazz* (Dot Records, 1957). Nordine is accompanied by the Chico Hamilton Quintet performing Fred Katz jazz compositions. Quotations from Nordine's skit are from my transcription.

65. In an essay titled "Lightness," Calvino attributes the "secret of lightness" to an ability to "make language into a weightless element that hovers above things like a cloud or better, perhaps, the finest dust or, better still, a field of magnetic impulses." *Six Memos for the Next Millennium*, 15. In Nordine's best aural fables, an otherwise sober message is conveyed through a musicality that, thanks to the cool jazz of Fred Katz, seems weightless, so much so that the meaning itself, as Calvino suggestively indicates, takes on a similar buoyancy.

66. From my transcription. Nordine's "Ish Fish" was released on *Bits & Pieces of Word Jazz*, audio CD.

67. As McCourt writes, NPR has always appealed to the idea of "public interest," even while moving in a not-so-public direction: "Although NPR invokes the 'public' to differentiate itself from commercial competitors, the system increasingly behaves like a commercial enterprise. This commercialism did not appear overnight; it has been creeping into NPR since the early 1980s." *Conflicting Communication Interests in America*, 63.

68. As Douglas points out, by 1995, *Morning Edition* was the top-rated radio program in highly progressive cities like Boston and San Francisco. *Listening In*, 319.

69. When Jack Mitchell was appointed director of *All Things Considered* in 1972, his first act was to hire Stamberg as co-host of the program, along with Mike Waters. As Mitchell explains in *Listener Supported*, Waters's "voice and style complemented hers well. He was as laid back as she was energetic. He was as marvelous a monologist as she was a conversationalist. They shared, however, a relatively low level of interest in news. Stamberg turned her relative lack of knowledge into an asset by asking the naïve questions a lay person might ask" (70).

70. It is worth pointing out that when Stamberg pitched Tom and Ray Magliozzi's car repair call-in show to unenthusiastic managers at NPR in the mid-1980s, she sang the praises of their sense of humor. "These guys are fabulous," she told the skeptics. "Everybody loves cars, they have those incredible accents, and they laugh all the time—we're putting them on the air" (http://www.scpr.org/programs/offramp/2014/11/05/40177/susan-stamberg-welcomed-ray-and-the-late-tom-magli/).

71. Piantadosi, "Stamberg Considered," 90.

72. For an insightful discussion of the gendered voice of NPR, see Loviglio, "Sound Effects."

73. See de Certeau, "The Laugh of Michel Foucault," 193–98.

74. See the essays in Biewen and Dilworth, *Reality Radio*, including those by Glass and Abumrad.

Bibliography

Ackermann, William C. "The Dimensions of American Broadcasting." *Public Opinion Quarterly* 9, no. 1 (1945): 1–18.
Adorno, Theodor W. *Negative Dialectics*. Translated by E. B. Ashton. New York: Continuum, 1973.
Allen, Robert C. *Speaking of Soap Operas*. Chapel Hill: University of North Carolina Press, 1985.
"All the News Fit to Hear." *Time*, 27 August 1979.
Altman, Rick. "Deep Focus Sound: Citizen Kane and the Radio Aesthetic." *Quarterly Review of Film and Video* 15, no. 3 (1994): 1–33.
———, ed. *Sound Theory, Sound Practice*. New York: Routledge, 1992.
Aristophanes. *Thesmophoriazusae*. In *The Greek Classics: Aristophanes, Eleven Plays*, edited by James H. Ford, 359–95. El Paso: El Paso Norte Press, 2006.
Aristotle. *Politics*. Translated by Benjamin Jowett. In *The Basic Works of Aristotle*. Edited by Richard McKeon. New York: Random House, 1941.
Arnheim, Rudolf. *Film as Art*. Berkeley: University of California Press, 1957.
———. *Radio*. Translated by Margaret Ludwig and Herbert Read. London: Faber and Faber, 1936.
Artaud, Antonin. *Here Lies*. In *Antonin Artaud: Selected Writings*, edited by Susan Sontag, 537–54. Berkeley: University of California Press, 1976.
———. *The Theater and Its Double*. Translated by Mary Caroline Richards. New York: Grove, 1958.
Attali, Jacques. *Noise: The Political Economy of Music*. Translated by Brian Massumi. Minneapolis: University of Minnesota Press, 1985.
Aufderheide, Pat. "Will Public Broadcasting Survive?" *Progressive*, 20 March 1995, 19–21.
Augoyard, Jean-François, and Henry Torgue. *Sonic Experience: A Guide to Everyday Sounds*. Translated by Andrea McCartney and David Paquette. Montreal: McGill-Queen's University Press, 2008.
Avery, Todd. *Radio Modernism: Literature, Ethics, and the BBC, 1922–1938*. Aldershot, UK: Ashgate, 2006.
Bannerman, R. LeRoy. *Norman Corwin and Radio: The Golden Years*. Tuscaloosa: University of Alabama Press, 1986.
Barber, Stephen. *Artaud: The Screaming Body*. N.p.: Creation Books, 1999.
Barker, Andrew, ed. *Greek Musical Writings: The Musician and His Art*. London: Cambridge University Press, 1989.
Barlow, William. *Voice Over: The Making of Black Radio*. Philadelphia: Temple University Press, 1998.

Barnouw, Erik. *The Golden Web, 1933–1953.* Vol. 2 of *A History of Broadcasting in the United States.* New York: Oxford University Press, 1968.

———, ed. *Radio Drama in Action: Twenty-five Plays of a Changing World.* New York: Rinehart, 1945.

Barthes, Roland. "The Grain of the Voice." In *Image, Music, Text*, translated by Stephen Heath, 179–89. New York: Hill and Wang, 1977.

———. *S/Z: An Essay.* Translated by Richard Miller. New York: Hill and Wang, 1975.

Bayley, John. *The Romantic Survival: A Study in Poetic Evolution.* London: Constable, 1960.

Bazzana, Kevin. *Glenn Gould: The Performer in the Work.* New York: Oxford University Press, 1997.

———. *Wondrous Strange: The Life and Art of Glenn Gould.* New York: Oxford University Press, 2004.

Beckett, Samuel. *All That Fall.* New York: Grove, 1957.

———. *The Letters of Samuel Beckett, Volume II: 1941–1956.* Edited by George Craig, Martha Dow Fehsenfeld, Dan Gunn, and Lois More Overbeck. Cambridge: Cambridge University Press, 2011.

———. *Three Novels: Molloy, Malone Dies, The Unnamable.* New York: Grove, 2009.

———. *Watt.* New York: Grove, 1953.

Bernstein, Charles. *Close Listening: Poetry and the Performed Word.* Oxford: Oxford University Press, 1998.

Bignell, Jonathan. *Beckett on Screen: The Television Plays.* Manchester: Manchester University Press, 2009.

Bliss, Edward, Jr., ed. *In Search of Light: The Broadcasts of Edward R. Murrow.* New York: Knopf, 1967.

Blue, Howard. *Words at War: World War II Era Radio Drama and the Postwar Broadcasting Industry Blacklist.* Lanham, Md.: Scarecrow, 2002.

Bogdanovich, Peter. *This Is Orson Welles.* 1992; New York: Da Capo Press, 1998.

Bradbury, Ray. *The Whole Town's Sleeping.* 14 June 1955. Generic Radio Script Library, http://www.genericradio.com. 7 June 2015.

Brinnin, John Malcolm. *Dylan Thomas in America: An Intimate Journal.* Boston: Little, Brown, 1955.

Briscoe, Desmond. *The BBC Radiophonic Workshop.* London: BBC, 1983.

"Broadcast Gives 'Sight' to the Ears." *Popular Mechanics*, January 1938.

Brown, Robert J. *Manipulating the Ether: The Power of Broadcast Radio in Thirties America.* Jefferson, N.C.: McFarland, 1998.

Bulfinch, Thomas. *Bulfinch's Greek and Roman Mythology: The Age of Fable.* New York: Dover, 2000.

Butler, Katherine. "'By Instruments Her Powers Appeare': Music and Authority in the Reign of Queen Elizabeth I." *Renaissance Quarterly* 65 (2012): 353–84.

Cage, John. *Conversing with Cage.* Edited by Richard Kostelanetz. New York: Limelight Editions, 1988.

———. The John Cage Correspondence Collection. Northwestern University Music Library, Evanston, Ill.

Callow, Simon. *Orson Welles, Volume 1: The Road to Xanadu*. London: Penguin Books, 1995.
Calvino, Italo. *Six Memos for the Next Millennium*. Translated by Patrick Creagh. New York: Vintage, 1993.
Campbell, Timothy. *Wireless Writing in the Age of Marconi*. Minneapolis: University of Minnesota Press, 2006.
Campbell, W. Joseph. *Getting It Wrong: Ten of the Greatest Misreported Stories in American Journalism*. Berkeley: University of California Press, 2010.
Camus, Albert. *The Myth of Sisyphus and Other Essays*. Translated by Justin O'Brien. New York: Vintage, 1991.
Cantril, Hadley. *The Invasion from Mars: A Study in the Psychology of Panic*. Princeton: Princeton University Press, 1940.
Cantril, Hadley, and Gordon W. Allport. *The Psychology of Radio*. 1935; New York: Arno Press, 1971.
Carpenter, Humphrey. *The Envy of the World: Fifty Years of the BBC Third Programme and Radio 3*. London: Phoenix House, 1997.
Carson, Anne. "The Gender of Sound." In *Glass, Irony & God*, 119–37. New York: New Directions, 1995.
Cavarero, Adriana. *For More Than One Voice: Toward a Philosophy of Vocal Expression*. Stanford: Stanford University Press, 2005.
Cavell, Richard. *McLuhan in Space: A Cultural Geography*. Toronto: University of Toronto Press, 2002.
Chion, Michel. *Audio-Vision: Sound on Screen*. Translated by Claudia Gorbman. New York: Columbia University Press, 1994.
———. *The Voice in Cinema*. Translated by Claudia Gorbman. New York: Columbia University Press, 1999.
Christiansen, Erik. *Channeling the Past: Politicizing History in Postwar America*. Madison: University of Wisconsin Press, 2013.
Cleverdon, Douglas. *The Growth of Milk Wood*. London: J. M. Dent, 1954.
Cloud, Stanley, and Lynne Olson. *The Murrow Boys: Pioneers on the Front Lines of Broadcast Journalism*. Boston: Houghton Mifflin, 1996.
Cohen, Debra Rae, Michael Coyle, and Jane Lewty, eds. *Broadcasting Modernism*. Gainesville: University Press of Florida, 2009.
The Columbia Workshop. "Broadway Evening." 25 July 1936. Online audio. Internet Archive, https://archive.org/details/Columbia.Workshop_174.
———. "A Comedy of Danger." 18 July 1936. Generic Radio Script Library, http://www.genericradio.com. 7 June 2015.
———. "The Finger of God." 18 July 1936. Generic Radio Script Library, http://www.genericradio.com. 7 June 2015.
Conciatore, Jacqueline. "Rodeo Clowns and Radio Poets." *Current*, 23 October 1995.
Connor, Steven. "Beside Himself: Glenn Gould and the Prospects of Performance." BBCRadio 3, 4 November 1999. www.stevenconnor.com/gould.htm. 7 June 2015.
———. *Dumbstruck: A Cultural History of Ventriloquism*. New York: Oxford University Press, 2000.

———. "Panophonia." http://www.stevenconnor.com/panophonia. 7 June 2015.
———. *Samuel Beckett: Repetition, Theory, and Text*. Oxford: Blackwell, 1988.
Corwin, Norman. *On a Note of Triumph*. New York: Simon and Schuster, 1945.
———. *They Fly through the Air*. In *Columbia Workshop Plays*, edited by Douglas Coulter, 97–119. New York: McGraw-Hill, 1939.
———. *Thirteen by Corwin: Radio Dramas by Norman Corwin*. Preface by Carl Van Doren. New York: Henry Holt, 1942.
Cory, Mark E. "Soundplay: The Polyphonous Tradition of German Radio Art." In *Wireless Imagination: Sound, Radio, and the Avant-Garde*, edited by Douglas Kahn and Gregory Whitehead, 331–71. Cambridge: MIT Press, 1992.
Coulter, Douglas, ed. *Columbia Workshop Plays*. New York: McGraw-Hill, 1939.
Cox, Jim. *Frank and Anne Hummert's Radio Factory*. Jefferson, N.C.: McFarland, 2003.
Crane, David. "Projections and Intersections: Paranoid Textuality in *Sorry, Wrong Number*." *Camera Obscura* 51 (2002): 71–113.
Creamer, Joseph, and William B. Hoffman. *Radio Sound Effects*. New York: Ziff-Davis Publishing, 1945.
Crisell, Andrew. *Understanding Radio*. New York: Routledge, 1994.
Crowther, Bosley. "Sorry, Wrong Number." *New York Times*, 2 September 1948.
Culbert, David Holbrook. *News for Everyman*. Westport, Conn.: Greenwood, 1976.
Cull, Nicholas John. *Selling War: The British Propaganda Campaign against American "Neutrality" in World War II*. Oxford: Oxford University Press, 1995.
Davidson, Peter. *The Idea of North*. London: Reaktion Books, 2005.
De Certeau, Michel. "The Laugh of Michel Foucault." In *Heterologies: Discourse on the Other*, translated by Brian Massumi, 193–98. Minneapolis: University of Minnesota Press, 1986.
Denison, Merrill. "Radio and the Writer." *Theatre Arts Monthly* 22, no. 5 (May 1938).
Denning, Michael. *The Cultural Front: The Laboring of American Culture in the Twentieth Century*. London: Verso, 1998.
Derrida, Jacques. *Of Grammatology*. Translated by Gayatri C. Spivak. Baltimore: Johns Hopkins University Press, 1976.
———. *Speech and Phenomena, and Other Essays on Husserl's Theory of Signs*. Translated by David B. Allison. Evanston: Northwestern University Press, 1973.
Diamond, Jamie. "Radio Noir." *Los Angeles Times Magazine*, 22 November 1987.
Dohoney, Ryan. "An Antidote to Metaphysics: Adriana Cavarero's Vocal Philosophy." *Women and Music: A Journal of Gender and Culture* 15 (2011): 70–85.
Dolar, Mladen. *A Voice and Nothing More*. Cambridge: MIT Press, 2006.
Douglas, Susan. *Listening In: Radio and the American Imagination*. New York: Times Books, 1999.
Downing, John D. H., ed. *Radical Media: Rebellious Communication and Social Movements*. Thousand Oaks, Calif.: Sage, 2001.
Drakakis, John. "Introduction." In *British Radio Drama*, edited by John Drakakis, 1–36. Cambridge: Cambridge University Press, 1981.

Dunning, John. *On the Air: The Encyclopedia of Old-Time Radio*. New York: Oxford University Press, 1998.
Dyson, Frances. *Sounding New Media: Immersion and Embodiment in the Arts and Culture*. Berkeley: University of California Press, 2009.
Edgerton, Gary. "The Murrow Legend as Metaphor: The Creation, Appropriation, and Usefulness of Edward R. Murrow's Life Story." *Journal of American Culture* 15 (1992): 75–91.
Ehrlich, Matthew C. *Radio Utopia: Postwar Audio Documentary in the Public Interest*. Urbana: University of Illinois Press, 2011.
Emerling, Susan. "Public Radio's Bad Dream." *Salon*, 7 March 2000.
Engelman, Ralph. *Public Radio and Television in America: A Political History*. Thousand Oaks, Calif.: Sage, 1996.
Fang, Irving E. *Those Radio Commentators*. Ames: Iowa State University Press, 1977.
Ferris, Paul. *Dylan Thomas: The New Biography*. Washington, D.C.: Counterpoint, 2000.
"First Person Singular: Welles Innovator on Stage, Experiments on the Air." *Newsweek*, 11 July 1938.
Fish, Stanley. *Self-Consuming Artifacts: The Experience of Seventeenth-Century Literature*. Berkeley: University of California Press, 1972.
Fisher, Margaret. *Ezra Pound's Radio Operas: The BBC Experiments, 1931–1933*. Cambridge: MIT Press, 1993.
Flannery, Harry W. *Assignment to Berlin*. New York: Knopf, 1942.
Fletcher, Lucille. *Sorry, Wrong Number and The Hitch-Hiker*. Rev. ed. New York: Dramatists Play Service, 1952.
Ford, Phil. *Dig: Sound and Music in Hip Culture*. New York: Oxford University Press, 2013.
Freud, Sigmund. *The Standard Edition of the Complete Psychological Works of Sigmund Freud*. Edited by James Strachey. 24 vols. London: Hogarth, 1953–74.
Friedrich, Otto. *Glenn Gould: A Life and Variations*. New York: Random House, 1989.
Frost, Everett C. "Fundamental Sounds: Recording Samuel Beckett's Radio Plays." *Theatre Journal* 43 (1991): 361–76.
———. "Meditating On: Beckett, *Embers*, and Radio Theory." In *Samuel Beckett and the Arts: Music, Visual Arts, and Non-Print Media*, edited by Lois Oppenheim, 311–31. New York: Garland, 1999.
Frost, Everett C., and Margaret Herzfeld-Sander, eds. *German Radio Plays*. New York: Continuum, 1991.
Funk, Allison. "The Tumbling Box." In *The Tumbling Box*, 13–14. Chattanooga: C&R Press, 2009.
Fussell, Paul. *Wartime: Understanding and Behavior in the Second World War*. New York: Oxford University Press, 1989.
Gassner, John, ed. *Twenty Best Plays of the Modern Theatre*. New York, Crown, 1939.
Genette, Gérard. *Narrative Discourse: An Essay in Method*. Translated by Jane E. Lewin. Ithaca: Cornell University Press, 1983.
Gilfillan, Daniel. *Pieces of Sound: German Experimental Radio*. Minneapolis: University of Minnesota Press, 2009.

Goodale, Greg. *Sonic Persuasion: Reading Sound in the Recorded Age*. Urbana: University of Illinois Press, 2011.
Goodman, David. "Distracted Listening: On Not Making Sound Choices in the 1930s." In *Sound in the Age of Mechanical Reproduction*, edited by Susan Strasser and David Suisman, 15–46. Philadelphia: University of Pennsylvania Press, 2010.
———. *Radio's Civic Ambition: American Broadcasting and Democracy in the 1930s*. New York: Oxford University Press, 2011.
Gould, Glenn. *Conversations with Glenn Gould*. Edited by Jonathan Cott. New York: Little, Brown, 1984.
———. *Glenn Gould: Concert Dropout*. Disc. Columbia, BS 15 (1968).
———. *Glenn Gould: Selected Letters*. Edited by John P. L. Roberts and Ghyslaine Guertin. Toronto: Oxford University Press, 1992.
———. *The Glenn Gould Reader*. Edited by Tim Page. New York: Knopf, 1984.
———. "The Idea of North: An Introduction." In *The Glenn Gould Reader*, edited by Tim Page, 391–94. New York: Knopf, 1984.
———. "'The Latecomers': An Introduction." In *The Glenn Gould Reader*, edited by Tim Page, 394–95. New York: Knopf, 1984.
———. "The Prospects of Recording." In *The Glenn Gould Reader*, edited by Tim Page, 331–53. New York: Knopf, 1984.
———. "Radio as Music: Glenn Gould in Conversation with John Jessop." In *The Glenn Gould Reader*, edited by Tim Page, 374–88. New York: Knopf, 1984.
———. "Rubinstein." In *The Glenn Gould Reader*, edited by Tim Page, 283–90. New York: Knopf, 1984.
———. *The Solitude Trilogy: Three Sound Documentaries* ("The Idea of North," 1967; "The Latecomers," 1969; "The Quiet in the Land," 1977). CBC PSCD 2003-3, 1992.
Grams, Martin, Jr. *Suspense: Twenty Years of Thrills and Chills*. Kearney, Nebr.: Morris Publishing, 1997.
———. *The Twilight Zone: Unlocking the Door to a Television Classic*. Churchville, Md.: OTR Publishing, 2008.
Graves, Robert. *The Crowning Privilege: Collected Essays on Poetry*. New York, 1956.
Grunwald, Edgar A. "Program-Production History, 1929–1937." *Variety Radio Directory, 1937–1938*. New York: Variety, 1937.
Guralnick, Elissa. *Sight Unseen: Beckett, Pinter, Stoppard, and Other Contemporary Dramatists on Radio*. Athens: Ohio University Press, 1995.
Halberstam, David. *The Powers That Be*. New York: Knopf, 1979.
Hecker, Tim. "Glenn Gould, the Vanishing Performer, and the Ambivalence of the Studio." *Leonardo Music Journal* 18 (2008): 77–83.
Hersh, Amy. "Now Hear This . . . Turning Up the Volume on Radio Theatre." *Back Stage*, 19 February 1993.
Heyer, Paul. *The Medium and the Magician: Orson Welles, the Radio Years, 1943–1952*. New York: Rowman and Littlefield, 2005.
Higby, Mary Jane. *Tune in Tomorrow*. New York: Ace Books, 1968.
Hilmes, Michele. *Hollywood and Broadcasting: From Radio to Cable*. Urbana: University of Illinois Press, 1990.

———. *Network Nations: A Transnational History of British and American Broadcasting*. New York: Routledge, 2012.

———. *Only Connect: A Cultural History of Broadcasting in the United States*. Belmont, Calif.: Wadsworth, 2002.

———. *Radio Voices: American Broadcasting, 1922–1952*. Minneapolis: University of Minnesota Press, 1997.

———. "Rethinking Radio." In *Radio Reader: Essays in the Cultural History of Radio*, edited by Michelle Hilmes and Jason Loviglio, 1–19. New York: Routledge, 2002.

Hilmes, Michelle, and Jason Loviglio, eds. *Radio Reader: Essays in the Cultural History of Radio*. New York: Routledge, 2002.

Holbrook, David. *Dylan Thomas: The Code of Night*. London: Athlone Press, 1972.

Holter, Frances. "Radio among the Unemployed." *Journal of Applied Psychology* 23 (1939): 163–69.

Homer. *Iliad*. Translated by Robert Fagles. New York: Penguin, 1998.

Hope-Wallace, Philip. Review of *All That Fall*. *Time and Tide*, 19 January 1957.

Hosley, David H. "As Good as Any of Us: American Female Radio Correspondents in Europe, 1938–1941." *Historical Journal of Film, Radio, and Television* 2, no. 2 (1982): 141–56.

Houseman, John. *Run-Through*. New York: Simon and Schuster, 1972.

———. *Unfinished Business*. New York: Applause Theatre Books, 1989.

Hughes, Kathleen A. "Radio's Prince of Darkness Rules the Freeways." *Wall Street Journal*, 15 March 1988.

Hugo, Victor. *Les Misérables*. Translated by Charles E. Wilbour. New York: Modern Library, 1992.

Hurwitz, Robert. "The Glenn Gould Contrapuntal Radio Show." *New York Times*, 5 January 1975.

———. "Towards a Contrapuntal Radio." In *Glenn Gould Variations: By Himself and His Friends*, edited by John McGreevy, 253–63. Toronto: Doubleday, 1983.

Husseini, Sam. "The Broken Promise of Public Radio." *Humanist*, September/October 1994, 26–29.

Hutchens, John K. "Drama on the Air." *New York Times*, 2 November 1941.

Ihde, Don. *Listening and Voice: Phenomenologies of Sound*. 2nd ed. Albany: State University of New York Press, 2007.

Jewell, Richard B. "Hollywood and Radio: Competition and Partnership in the 1930s." *Historical Journal of Film, Radio, and Television* 4, no. 2 (1984): 125–41.

Johnson, Penny. "Stories Untold: An Interview with *The Idea of North* editor, Peter Shewchuk." Glenn Gould Foundation (April 2010). http://glenngould.ca/home/2010/4/12/stories-untold-an-interview-with-the-idea-of-north-editor-pe.html.

Kahn, Douglas. *Noise, Water, Meat: A History of Sound in the Arts*. Cambridge: MIT Press, 1999.

Kahn, Douglas, and Gregory Whitehead, eds. *Wireless Imagination: Sound, Radio, and the Avant-Garde*. Cambridge: MIT Press, 1992.

Kaltenborn, H. V. *I Broadcast the Crisis*. New York: Random House, 1938.

Keith, Michael C. *Voices in the Purple Haze: Underground Radio and the Sixties*. Westport, Conn.: Praeger, 1997.

———, ed. *Radio Cultures: The Sound Medium in American Life*. New York: Peter Lang, 2008.

Kendrick, Alexander. *Prime Time: The Life of Edward R. Murrow*. Boston: Little, Brown, 1969.

Kenner, Hugh. *Samuel Beckett: A Critical Study*. New York: Grove, 1961.

Kittler, Friedrich A. "Dracula's Legacy." In *Literature, Media, Information Systems: Essays*, edited by John Johnson, 50–84. Amsterdam: G+B Arts International, 1997.

Knoll, Steve. "Demise of the Radio Commentator: An Irreparable Loss to Broadcast Journalism." *Journal of Radio Studies* 6, no. 2 (1999): 356–70.

Knowlson, James. *Damned to Fame: The Life of Samuel Beckett*. New York: Grove, 1996.

Koch, Howard. *The Panic Broadcast*. New York: Avon Books, 1970.

Kostelanetz, Richard. "Glenn Gould: Back in the Electronic Age." In *Glenn Gould Variations: By Himself and His Friends*, edited by John McGreevy, 125–41. Toronto: Doubleday, 1983.

———. "Glenn Gould as a Radio Composer." *Massachusetts Review* 29 (1988): 557–70.

Kristeva, Julia. *Powers of Horror: An Essay on Abjection*. Translated by Leon S. Roudiez. New York: Columbia University Press, 1982.

———. *Revolution in Poetic Language*. Translated by Margaret Waller. New York: Columbia University Press, 1984.

———. "The Subject in Process." In *Antonin Artaud: A Critical Reader*, edited by Edward Scheer, 116–24. London: Routledge, 2004.

Krulevitch, Walter, and Rome C. Krulevitch. *Radio Drama Production: A Handbook*. New York: Rinehart, 1946.

Kurth, Peter. *American Cassandra: The Life of Dorothy Thompson*. Boston: Little, Brown, 1990.

Labelle, Brandon. *Background Noise: Perspectives on Sound Art*. New York: Continuum, 2006.

Langer, Adam. "Will Ken Nordine Ever Grow Up?" *Chicago Reader*, 12 July 1990.

Lasar, Matthew. *Pacifica Radio: The Rise of an Alternative Network*. Philadelphia: Temple University Press, 2000.

Lawrence, Amy. *Echo and Narcissus: Women's Voices in Classical Hollywood Cinema*. Berkeley: University of California Press, 1991.

Lazarfeld, Paul F. *Radio and the Printed Page*. New York: Duell, Sloan and Pearce, 1940.

Lenthall, Bruce. *Radio's America: The Great Depression and the Rise of Modern Mass Media*. Chicago: University of Chicago Press, 2007.

Levenson, William B. *Teaching through Radio*. New York: Rinehart, 1950.

Levine, Lawrence. *Highbrow/Lowbrow: The Emergence of Cultural Hierarchy in America*. Cambridge: Harvard University Press, 1988.

Lewis, Peter. "The Radio Road to Llareggub." In *British Radio Drama*, edited by John Drakakis, 72–110. Cambridge: Cambridge University Press, 1981.

Lewis, Tom. "'A Godlike Presence': The Impact of Radio on the 1920s and 1930s." *OAH Magazine of History* 6, no. 4 (1992): 26–33.

Lewty, Jane. "'What They Had Heard Said Written': Joyce, Pound, and the Cross-Correspondence of Radio." In *Broadcasting Modernism*, edited by Debra Rae Cohen, Michael Coyle, and Jane Lewty, 199–220. Gainesville: University Press of Florida, 2009.

Locke, John, *The Philosophical Works of John Locke*. Vol. 1 of *The Works of John Locke*. Edited by James Augustus St. John. London: Henry G. Bohn, 1854.

Looker, Thomas. *The Sound and the Story: NPR and the Art of Radio*. Boston: Houghton Mifflin, 1995.

"A Look Inside NPR's New Headquarters." *Washington Post*, 18 June 2013.

Loviglio, Jason. *Radio's Intimate Public: Network Broadcasting and Mass-Mediated Democracy*. Minneapolis: University of Minnesota Press, 2005.

———. "Sound Effects: Gender, Voice, and the Cultural Work of NPR." *Radio Journal: International Studies in Broadcast and Audio Media* 5, nos. 2–3 (2007): 67–81.

Lycett, Andrew. *Dylan Thomas: A New Life*. London: Phoenix, 2004.

Lynd, Robert, and Helen Lynd. *Middletown: A Study in Contemporary American Culture*. New York: Harcourt Brace Jovanovich, 1929.

MacDonald, J. Fred. *Don't Touch That Dial! Radio Programming in American Life from 1920 to 1960*. Chicago: Nelson-Hall, 1991.

Mack, Joanna, and Steve Humphries. *London at War: The Making of Modern London, 1939–1945*. London: Sidgwick and Jackson, 1985.

MacLeish, Archibald. *Air Raid*. In *Six Plays*. Boston: Houghton Mifflin, 1980.

———. *Archibald MacLeish: Reflections*. Edited by Bernard A. Drabeck and Helen E. Ellis. Amherst: University of Massachusetts Press, 1986.

———. *The Fall of the City: A Verse Play for Radio*. New York: Farrar and Rinehart, 1937.

MacLeish, Archibald, William S. Paley, and Edward R. Murrow. *In Honor of a Man and an Ideal: Three Talks on Freedom.* New York: Columbia Broadcasting System, 1941.

Marcus, Greil. "Public Radio Hosts Drop In and Maybe Stay Too Long." *New York Times*, 16 March 1998.

Marsh, Christopher. *Music and Society in Early Modern England*. Cambridge: Cambridge University Press, 2013.

Matthews, William. "Radio Plays as Literature." *Hollywood Quarterly* 1 (October 1945): 40–50.

Maude, Ulrika. *Beckett, Technology, and the Body*. Cambridge: Cambridge University Press, 2009.

McCauley, Michael P. *NPR: The Trials and Triumphs of National Public Radio*. New York: Columbia University Press, 1994.

McChesney, Robert W. *Telecommunications, Mass Media, and Democracy: The Battle for Control of U.S. Broadcasting, 1928–1935*. New York: Oxford University Press, 1993.

McCourt, Tom. *Conflicting Communication Interests in America: The Case of National Public Radio*. Westport, Conn.: Praeger, 1999.

McCracken, Allison. "Scary Women and Scarred Men: Suspense, Gender Trouble, and Postwar Change, 1942-1950." In *Radio Reader: Essays in the Cultural History of Radio*, edited by Michelle Hilmes and Jason Loviglio, 183-207. New York: Routledge, 2002.

McFarlane, Matthew. "Glenn Gould, Jean Le Moyne, and Pierre Teilhard de Chardin: Common Visionaries." *Glenn Gould* 8, no. 2 (2002): 70-77.

McGreevy, John, ed. *Glenn Gould Variations: By Himself and His Friends*. Toronto: Doubleday, 1983.

McHale, Brian. *Postmodernist Fiction*. New York: Routledge, 1987.

McLuhan, Marshall. "The Gadget Lover: Narcissus as Narcosis." In *Understanding Media: The Extensions of Man*, 41-47. Cambridge: MIT Press, 1994.

———. "Radio: The Tribal Drum." In *Understanding Media: The Extensions of Man*, 297-307. Cambridge: MIT Press, 1994.

———. *Understanding Media: The Extensions of Man*. Cambridge: MIT Press, 1994.

McNeilly, Kevin. "Listening, Nordicity, Community: Glenn Gould's 'The Idea of North.'" *Essays on Canadian Writing* 59 (1996): 87-105.

McWhinnie, Donald. *The Art of Radio*. London: Faber and Faber, 1959.

Mencken, H. L. "Radio Programs." *Baltimore Sun*, 29 June 1931.

Merleau-Ponty, Maurice. *The Phenomenology of Perception*. Translated by Colin Wilson. London: Routledge and Kegan Paul, 1962.

Miller, Edward. *Emergency Broadcasting and 1930s American Radio*. Philadelphia: Temple University Press, 2003.

"Millions *Hear* Their *Columbia Broadcasting System*." *Broadcasting*, 11 May 1942.

Milutis, Joe. "Radiophonic Ontologies and the Avantgarde." In *Experimental Sound and Radio*, edited by Allen S. Weiss, 57-72. Cambridge: MIT Press, 2001.

Mitchell, Jack W. *Listener Supported: The Culture and History of Public Radio*. Westport, Conn.: Praeger, 2005.

Montopoli, Brian. "All Things Considerate: How NPR Makes Tavis Smiley Sound Like Linda Wertheimer." *Washington Monthly*, January/February 2003.

———. "Ira Glass on Working in Television, Public Radio's Struggle for Innovation, and Hanging Up on People." *Columbia Journalism Review*, 12 August 2005.

Morin, Emilie. "Beckett's Speaking Machines: Sound, Radiophonics, and Acousmatics." *Modernism/Modernity* 21 (2014): 1-24.

Morris, Adelaide, ed. *Sound States: Innovative Poetics and Acoustical Technologies*. Chapel Hill: University of North Carolina Press, 1997.

Murrow, Edward R. "Preparation of the Documentary Broadcast." In *Education on the Air 1947*, 377-90. Institute for Education by Radio. Columbus: Ohio State University Press, 1947.

———. *In Search of Light: The Broadcasts of Edward R. Murrow, 1938-1961*. New York: Knopf, 1967.

———. *This Is London*. New York: Schocken Books, 1989.

Nachman, Gerald. *Raised on Radio*. Berkeley: University of California Press, 2000.

———. *Seriously Funny: The Rebel Comedians of the 1950s and 1960s*. New York: Pantheon, 2003.

Nancy, Jean-Luc. *Listening*. Translated by Charlotte Mandell. New York: Fordham University Press, 2007.

Neumark, Norie, Ross Gibson, and Theo van Leeuwen, eds. *Voice: Vocal Aesthetics in Digital Arts and Media*. Cambridge: MIT Press, 2010.

Newman, Kathy M. *Radio Active: Advertising and Consumer Activism, 1935–1947*. Berkeley: University of California Press, 2004.

Niebur, Louis. *Special Sound: The Creation and Legacy of the BBC Radiophonic Workshop*. New York: Oxford University Press, 2010.

Nimmo, Dan, and Chevelle Newsome. *Political Commentators in the United States in the 20th Century*. Westport, Conn.: Greenwood, 1997.

Nixon, Barbara. *Raiders Overhead: A Diary of the London Blitz*. London, Scolar Press, 1980.

"NPR Apologizes for Codrescu's Remark That 'Crossed a Line of Tolerance.'" *Current*, 15 January 1996.

Olson, Lynne. *Citizens of London: The Americans Who Stood with Britain*. New York: Random House, 2010.

Oney, Steve. "The Philosopher King and the Creation of NPR." Shorenstein Center on Media, Politics, and Public Policy. Discussion Paper Series, no. D-87, July 2014, 3.

Ong, Walter. *Orality and Literacy: The Technologizing of the Word*. New York: Routledge, 1982.

Orwell, George. *Homage to Catalonia*. New York: Harcourt, 1980.

———. "Poetry and the Microphone." In George Orwell, *Essays*, selected and introduced by John Carey, 857–65. New York: Everyman's Library, 2002.

Ostwald, Peter. *Glenn Gould: The Ecstasy and Tragedy of Genius*. New York: W. W. Norton, 1997.

Ovid. *Metamorphoses*. Translated by Rolfe Humphries. Bloomington: Indiana University Press, 1960.

Palter, Ruth. "Radio's Attraction for Housewives." *Hollywood Quarterly* 3, no. 3 (1948): 248–57.

Patchen, Kenneth. *The Journal of Albion Moonlight*. New York: New Direction Books, 1941.

Payzant, Geoffrey. *Glenn Gould: Music and Mind*. Toronto: Key Porter Books, 1992.

Persico, Joseph E. *Edward R. Murrow: An American Original*. New York: McGraw-Hill, 1988.

Piantadosi, Roger. "Stamberg Considered." *New York* magazine, 22 October 1979.

Pinkerton, W. Stewart, Jr. "The Talker." *Wall Street Journal*, 8 December 1971.

Plato. *Plato: The Republic*. Translated by Paul Shorey. Loeb Classical Library. Cambridge: Harvard University Press, 1956.

———. *Plato in Twelve Volumes: Volume 9 (Phaedrus)*. Translated by Harold N. Fowler. Cambridge: Harvard University Press, 1925.

———. *Plato's Symposium*. Translated by Michael Joyce. New York: Everyman's Library, 1935.

Poizat, Michel. *The Angel's Cry: Beyond the Pleasure Principle in Opera*. Translated by Arthur Denner. Ithaca: Cornell University Press, 1992.

Pope, Alexander. "An Essay on Criticism." In *The Major Works*, edited by Pat Rogers, 17–39. Oxford: Oxford University Press, 2009.

Pope, Rebecca. "Writing and Biting in Dracula." *LIT: Literature, Interpretation, and Theory* 1, no. 3 (1990): 199–216.

Porter, Bruce. "Has Success Spoiled NPR? Becoming Part of the Establishment Can Have Its Drawbacks." *Columbia Journalism Review*, September/October 1990, 26–32.

"Radio: Hummerts' Mill." *Time*, 23 January 1939.

"Radio: Money for Minutes." *Time*, 19 September 1938.

"Radio: Prestige Programs." *Time*, 17 July 1939.

"Radio: Radio Revolution?" *Time*, 25 May 1942.

"Radio: Repeat Performance." *Time*, 10 September 1945.

"Radio Broadcasting." *Fortune*, May 1938.

"Radio 'Invasion' Throws Listeners into Hysteria." *Seattle Post-Intelligencer*, 31 October 1938.

Rakow, Lana F. "Women and the Telephone: The Gendering of a Communications Technology." In *Technology and Women's Voices: Keeping in Touch*, edited by Cheris Kramarae, 207–28. New York: Routledge, 1988.

Ramirez, Anthony. "Jean Shepherd, a Raconteur and a Wit of Radio, Is Dead." *New York Times*, 18 October 1999.

Razlogova, Elena. *The Listener's Voice: Early Radio and the American Public*. Philadelphia: University of Pennsylvania Press, 2011.

Reith, J. C. W. *Broadcast over Britain*. London: Hodder and Stoughton, 1924.

Rippy, Marguerite H. *Orson Welles and the Unfinished RKO Projects: A Postmodern Perspective*. Carbondale: Southern Illinois University Press, 2009.

Roberts, Cokie, et al. *This Is NPR: The First Forty Years*. New York: Chronicle Books, 2010.

Rorty, James. *Order on the Air*. New York: John Day, 1934.

———. *Our Master's Voice: Advertising*. New York: John Day, 1934.

———. "Radio Comes Through." *Nation*, 5 October 1938.

Roth, Philip. *I Married a Communist*. New York: Houghton Mifflin Harcourt, 1998.

Russolo, Luigi. "The Art of Noises: Futurist Manifesto." In *Audio Culture: Readings in Modern Music*, edited by Christopher Cox and Daniel Warner, 10–14. New York: Continuum, 2004.

Said, Edward. *On Late Style: Music and Literature against the Grain*. New York: Vintage, 2006.

———. "The Music Itself: Glenn Gould's Contrapuntal Vision." In *Glenn Gould Variations: By Himself and His Friends*, edited by John McGreevy, 45–54. Toronto: Doubleday, 1983.

Savage, Barbara Dianne. *Broadcasting Freedom: Radio, War, and the Politics of Race, 1938–1948*. Chapel Hill: University of North Carolina Press, 1999.

Schaeffer, Pierre. "Acousmatics." Translated by Daniel W. Smith. In *Audio Culture: Readings in Modern Music*, edited by Christopher Cox and Daniel Warner, 76–81. New York: Continuum, 2004.

Schafer, R. Murray. *The Soundscape*. New York: Knopf, 1977.
Schwartz, A. Brad. *Broadcast Hysteria: Orson Welles's War of the Worlds and the Art of Fake News*. New York: Hill and Wang, 2015.
Seib, Richard. *Broadcasts from the Blitz: How Edward R. Murrow Helped Lead America into War*. Washington, D.C.: Potomac Books, 2006.
Sevareid, Eric. *Not So Wild a Dream*. New York: Knopf, 1946.
Shakespeare, William. *Richard III*. In *The Norton Shakespeare*, edited by Stephen Greenblatt, 515–600. New York: W. W. Norton, 1997.
Sherman, Scott. "Good, Gray NPR." *Nation*, 23 May 2005.
Shirer, William L. *Berlin Diary: The Journal of a Foreign Correspondent, 1934–1941*. Rev ed. Baltimore: Johns Hopkins University Press, 2002.
Siemering, Bill. "My First Fifty Years in Radio and What I Learned." *Transom Review*, 1 March 2003, http://transom.org/2003/bill-siemering-part-1.
———. "National Public Radio Purposes." http://www.current.org/2012/05/national-public-radio-purposes/. 7 June 2015.
Silverman, Kaja. *The Acoustic Mirror: The Female Voice in Psychoanalysis and Cinema*. Bloomington: Indiana University Press, 1988.
Smith, Jacob. *Vocal Tracks: Performance and Sound Media*. Berkeley: University of California Press, 2008.
Smith, R. Franklin. *Edward R. Murrow: The War Years*. Kalamazoo, Mich.: New Issues Press, 1978.
Smulyan, Susan. *Selling Radio: The Commercialization of American Broadcasting, 1920–1934*. Washington, D.C.: Smithsonian Institution Press, 1994.
Socolow, Michael J. "The Hyped Panic over 'War of the Worlds.'" *Chronicle of Higher Education* 55, no. 9 (2008): B16–17.
Solomon, Matthew. "Adapting 'Radio's Perfect Script': 'Sorry, Wrong Number' and *Sorry, Wrong Number*." *Quarterly Review of Film and Video* 16, no. 1 (1997): 23–40.
Sophocles. *Ajax*. Translated by John Moore. In *Sophocles II: Ajax, The Women of Trachis, Electra, and Philoctetes*, edited by David Grene and Richmond Lattimore, 1–62. Chicago: University of Chicago Press, 1969.
"Sorry, Wrong Number." *Life*, 24 September 1945.
Sperber, A. M. *Murrow: His Life and Times*. New York: Freundlich Books, 1986.
Spinelli, Martin. "Masters of Sacred Ceremonies: Welles, Corwin, and a Radiogenic Modernist Literature." In *Broadcasting Modernism*, edited by Debra Rae Cohen, Michael Coyle, and Jane Lewty, 68–88. Gainesville: University Press of Florida, 2009.
Squire, Susan Merrill, ed. *Communities of the Air: Radio Century, Radio Culture*. Durham: Duke University Press, 2003.
Stam, Robert. "Introduction: The Theory and Practice of Adaptation." In *Literature and Film: A Guide to the Theory and Practice of Film Adaptation*, edited by Robert Stam and Alessandra Raengo, 1–52. London: Wiley-Blackwell, 2004.
Stamberg, Susan. *Every Night at Five: Susan Stamberg's All Things Considered Book*. New York: Pantheon, 1982.

———. *Talk: NPR's Susan Stamberg Considers All Things*. New York: Random House, 1993.
Stansky, Peter. *The First Day of the Blitz*. New Haven: Yale University Press, 2007.
Stedman, Raymond. *The Serials: Suspense and Drama by Installment*. Norman: University of Oklahoma Press, 1977.
Sterling, Christopher H., and Michael C. Keith. *Sounds of Change: A History of FM Broadcasting in America*. Chapel Hill: University of North Carolina Press, 2008.
Sterne, Jonathan. *Audible Past: Cultural Origins of Sound Reproduction*. Durham: Duke University Press, 2003.
Stoker, Bram. *Dracula*. Edited by Maurice Hindle. New York: Penguin Classics, 2003.
Strauss, Neil, ed. *Radiotext(e)*. Semiotext(e)16 (1993): 1–350.
Street, Seán. *The Poetry of Radio: The Colour of Sound*. London: Routledge, 2013.
Suisman, David, and Susan Strasser, eds. *Sound in the Age of Mechanical Reproduction*. Philadelphia: University of Pennsylvania Press, 2010.
"Theatre: *Fall of the City*." *Time*, 19 April 1937.
"The Theatre: Marvelous Boy." *Time*, 9 May 1938.
"'There Was a Man.'" *Life*, 27 January 1941.
Thomas, Dylan. *The Collected Letters*. Edited by Paul Ferris. London: J. M. Dent, 1985.
———. *Holiday Memory*. In *On the Air with Dylan Thomas: The Broadcasts*, edited by Ralph Maude, 137–44. New York: New Directions, 1992.
———. *Notebook Poems: 1930–1934*. Edited by Ralph Maud. London: Everyman, 1999.
———. "Preface: Notes on the Art of Poetry." In *The Poems of Dylan Thomas*, edited by Daniel Jones, xv–xxii. New York: New Directions, 2003.
———. *On the Air with Dylan Thomas: The Broadcasts*. Edited by Ralph Maud. New York: New Directions, 1992.
———. *The Poems of Dylan Thomas*. Edited by Daniel Jones. New York: New Directions, 2003.
———. *Return Journey*. In *On the Air with Dylan Thomas: The Broadcasts*, edited by Ralph Maude, 177–89. New York: New Directions, 1992.
———. *Under Milk Wood*. New York: New Directions, 1954.
Thomas, Gareth. "A Freak User of Words." In *Dylan Thomas: Craft or Sullen Art*, edited by Alan Bold, 65–88. New York: St. Martin's Press, 1990.
Thurber, James. *The Beast in Me and Other Animals*. New York: Harcourt, Brace, 1948.
Tsur, Reuven. "Onomatopoeia: Cuckoo-Language and Tick-Tocking: The Constraints of the Semiotic Systems." http://www.trismegistos.com/IconicityInLanguage/Articles/Tsur/default.html. 7 June 2015.
Turnbull, Robert B. *Radio and Television Sound Effects*. New York: Rinehart, 1951.
Tynan, Kenneth. *Curtains: Selections from the Drama Criticism and Related Writings*. New York: Atheneum, 1961.
Untermeyer, Louis. "New Power for Poetry." *Saturday Evening Post*, 22 May 1937.

Vancour, Shawn. "Arnheim on Radio: *Materialtheorie* and Beyond." In *Arnheim for Film and Media Studies*, edited by Scott Higgins, 177–94. New York: Routledge, 2010.

Vargas Llosa, Mario. *The Temptation of the Impossible: Victor Hugo and Les Misérables*. Translated by John King. Princeton: Princeton University Press, 2007.

Verma, Neil. *Theater of the Mind: Imagination, Aesthetics, and American Radio Drama*. Chicago: University of Chicago Press, 2012.

Voegelin, Salomé. *Listening to Noise and Silence: Towards a Philosophy of Sound Art*. New York: Continuum, 2010.

Vowell, Sarah. *Radio On: A Listener's Diary*. New York: St. Martin's Griffin, 1996.

"W. S. Paley, Against 'Forced' Programs." *New York Times*, 18 October 1934.

Walker, Jesse. *Rebels on the Air: An Alternative History of Radio in America*. New York: New York University Press, 2001.

Ware, Susan. *It's One O'clock and Here Is Mary Margaret McBride: A Radio Biography*. New York: New York University Press, 2005.

Warren, Donald. *Radio Priest: Charles Coughlin, the Father of Hate Radio*. New York: Free Press, 1996.

"The Week." *New Republic*, 4 March 1931.

Weiss, Allen S., ed. *Experimental Sound and Radio*. Cambridge: MIT Press, 2001.

———. "Radio, Death, and the Devil: Artaud's pour en finir avec le jugement de dieu." In *Wireless Imagination: Sound, Radio, and the Avant-Garde*, edited by Douglas Kahn and Gregory Whitehead, 269–307. Cambridge: MIT Press, 1992.

Weller, Sam. *The Bradbury Chronicles: The Life of Ray Bradbury*. New York: Harper Perennial, 2006.

Welles, Orson. *Dracula*. Mercury Theater on the Air, 11 July 1938. Generic Radio Script Library, http://www.genericradio.com. 7 June 2015.

Wertheimer, Linda, ed. *Listening to America: Twenty-five Years in the Life of a Nation, as Heard on National Public Radio*. Boston: Houghton Mifflin, 1995.

Whipple, James. *How to Write for Radio*. New York: McGraw-Hill, 1938.

White, Patricia. "The Queer Career of Agnes Moorehead." In *Out in Culture: Gay, Lesbian, and Queer Essays on Popular Culture*, edited by Corey K. Creekmur and Alexander Doty, 91–114. Durham: Duke University Press, 1995.

Whitehead, Kate. *The Third Programme: A Literary History*. Oxford: Oxford University Press, 1989.

Wicke, Jennifer. "Vampiric Typewriting: *Dracula* and Its Media." *English Literary History* 59 (1992): 467–93.

Worth, Katherine. "Women in Beckett's Radio and Television Plays." In *Women in Beckett: Performance and Critical Perspectives*, edited by Linda Ben-Zvi, 236–42. Urbana: University of Illinois Press, 1990.

Wylie, Max. *Radio Writing*. New York: Farrar and Rinehart, 1939.

Ziegler, Philip. *London at War*. New York: Knopf, 1995.

Index

Acoustic close-up, 99–103. *See also* Proximity effect
Acoustic drift, 8–9; Beckett and, 151, 152, 241 (n. 47); *Columbia Workshop* and, 33, 35, 43, 44; effects of, 18–19; MacLeish and, 224–25 (n. 74); mastering effect and, 26–31; phonophobia and, 17–22; radio's ability to exploit, 19, 22, 36, 43, 44; soap operas and, 30–31, 217 (n. 59); Welles utilization of, 22–26, 81–82. *See also* Sound
Acoustic mirrors, 106, 233 (n. 10)
Adams, Noah, 182
Adler, Margot, 182
Adorno, Theodor, 169, 246 (n. 39)
Agamemnon (Aeschylus), 53, 141
Agee, James, 38
Air Raid (MacLeish), 53, 56–58; announcer in, 88, 229 (n. 14); critic's view of, 223 (n. 59); screaming woman in, 111, 235 (n. 30); sound effects in, 57–58, 224 (n. 71)
Air-raid genre, 58, 225 (n. 75)
Alarcón, Daniel, 209
Allen, Fred, 3
Allen, Gracie, 121
Allen, Robert, 27, 217 (nn. 51, 56), 219 (n. 11)
Allison, Jay, 208
Allport, Gordon W., 17, 84–85, 89
All That Fall (Beckett), 11, 140, 141–54, 241 (nn. 47–48, 51), 242–43 (nn. 65, 68, 70); sound effects in, 143–44, 146–47, 148, 152–53
All Things Considered, 12, 183, 189–90, 196, 200; complaints about, 249 (n. 32); literary sensibility of, 190–91, 249 (n. 30); storytelling in, 195, 250 (n. 46); style and techniques of, 184–85; Williams and, 188–89. *See also* National Public Radio (NPR)
Altman, Rick, 5, 226 (n. 16)
American School of the Air, 3
Amos 'n' Andy Show, 2, 60
Anderson, Ida Lou, 230 (n. 29)
Anderson, Maxwell, 62
Apollo 11, 199–200, 251 (n. 53)
The Arabian Nights, 104
Archer, Thomas, 32
Aristophanes, 3, 141
Aristotle, 18, 21, 25
Arnheim, Rudolf, 153, 220 (n. 24); about radio and distance, 45, 84, 220–21 (n. 27), 222 (n. 34); about sound, 15–17, 213 (n. 3)
Artaud, Antonin, 16, 21, 155; on the scream, 110, 212–13 (n. 27), 235 (n. 26); "theater of cruelty" idea of, 148, 216 (n. 33), 242 (n. 62); *To Have Done with the Judgment of God* soundpiece, 22
Asimov, Isaac, 190
Attali, Jacques, 18
Auden, W. H., 4, 6, 42, 55
Augoyard, Jean-François, 5, 98
Aulos, 21, 26, 215 (n. 29)
Aurality. *See* Sound
Auteur theory, 211 (n. 15)
Avery, Todd, 6
Aylesworth, M. H., 60

Bach, Johann Sebastian, 155, 156, 165, 180
Bankhead, Tallulah, 32

Bannerman, R. LeRoy, 225 (n. 78)
Barnes, G. R., 237 (n. 9)
Barnouw, Erik, 75, 226 (n. 5)
Barrymore, John, 3, 32
Barthes, Roland, 49, 119
Bate, Walter Jackson, 190–91
Battle of Britain. *See* London Blitz
Bayley, John, 130
Bazzana, Kevin, 244–45 (nn. 19, 29, 36), 246 (n. 48)
BBC, 15, 62; *All That Fall* aired on, 141–54; Beckett and, 140–54, 240 (n. 38); close-up miking by, 160; coverage of London Blitz by, 85–86, 94–95, 96, 231 (n. 38); Man in Black of, 128, 236 (n. 1); radiophonic workshop of, 147–48, 152–53, 242–43 (n. 56); *Return Journey* aired on, 132–36, 237 (n. 11), 238 (nn. 20, 22); Third Programme on, 128, 136, 140, 141; Thomas as radio announcer for, 130–32, 237 (nn. 9–10); *Under Milk Wood* aired on, 128–30, 136–40; *Voice* radio magazine of, 130, 237 (n. 5)
Beckett, Samuel, 4; and BBC, 140–54, 240 (n. 38); on dysfunction in language, 149, 150–51, 242 (n. 65)
—works: *All That Fall*, 11, 140, 141–54, 241 (nn. 47–48, 51), 242–43 (nn. 65, 68, 70); *Krapp's Last Tape*, 187–88, 242 (n. 58)
Bellow, Saul, 190
Benet, Stephen Vincent, 3, 42; *John Brown's Body*, 63
Benjamin Walker's Theory of Everything (radio show), 209
Bennet, Doug, 249 (n. 34)
Benny, Jack, 3
Bergen, Edgar, 3, 15, 63
Bernstein, Charles, 13–14
Biewen, John, 210
Black, Baxter, 186, 190, 191
Blast magazines, 6
Blitzstein Marc, 65
Block, Michelle, 186

Blumberg, Alex: *StartUp* podcast, 208
Borges, Jorge Luis, 159, 163, 204
Bradbury, Ray, 109, 234 (nn. 19, 21)
Breckinridge, Mary Marvin, 85, 106
Brice, Fanny, 15
Brinnin, John Malcolm, 238–39 (n. 26)
Briscoe, Desmond, 148, 242 (n. 61)
Broadcasting magazine, 61, 220 (n. 22)
Broadcasting Modernism (Cohen, Coyle, and Lewty, eds.), 6
Broadcasting technology, 44–45, 48, 245 (n. 34)
Broadway Evening (radio program), 10, 43–44, 221 (nn. 30, 32)
Burns, George, 121
Burns and Allen, I Bet Your Life, 40
Burry, Reverend, 178
Burton, Richard, 136
Butler, Katherine, 21
Butterfield, Steve, 251 (n. 53)

Cage, John, 5, 42, 63, 155, 221 (n. 32); musical score by, 1, 211 (nn. 1, 3)
A Call in the Night (Frank), 201–2
Calvino, Italo, 204, 252 (n. 65)
Campbell, Timothy C., 6–7
Campbell Playhouse, 113
Camus, Albert, 164, 244 (n. 23)
Canadian Broadcasting Corporation (CBC), 15, 157–58, 249 (n. 29); broadcasts from London by, 92, 96; Gould relationship to, 156, 161; "The Latecomers" aired on, 170–79, 246 (n. 47); "Quiet in the Land" aired on, 179–80
Canterbury Tales (Chaucer), 141
Cantril, Hadley, 17, 84–85, 89
Carney, Art, 224 (n. 64)
Carroll, Lewis: *Alice in Wonderland*, 63
Carson, Anne, 216 (n. 34)
Carter, Boake, 76, 88
Cartwheel (Knight), 44–45
Casals, Pablo, 156
The Cavalcade of America (radio series), 62, 226 (n. 45)

270 *Index*

Cavarero, Adriana, 5, 25, 213 (n. 28); on devocalization, 106, 243 (n. 73)
CBS: *The City Wears a Slouch Hat* aired on, 1, 211 (n. 1); *Columbia Workshop* programs, 9–10, 37–61, 212 (n. 22); *Mercury Theatre on the Air* programs, 22–26, 30, 33, 36, 63, 65–81; Murrow documentaries on, 8, 83–103, 248 (n. 12); power of, 2; prestige-programming decision by, 3–4, 10, 44, 62, 221 (n. 32); *Shakespeare Cycle* of, 3, 32; *Suspense* anthology of, 11, 34, 107–8, 111–19; *War of the Worlds* apology by, 231 (n. 44)
Certeau, Michel de, 207
The Chase and Sanborn Hour, 2
Chion, Michel, 5, 19; about radio, 109, 235 (n. 23); about screams, 110, 117
Chomsky, Noam, 177
Churchill, Winston, 92
The City Wears a Slouch Hat for the Workshop (Patchern), 1, 63
Clark, Petula, 156
Cleverdon, Douglas, 136, 238 (n. 22)
Close listening, 13–14
Close-miking, 160, 166–67, 245 (n. 33)
Cloud, Stanley, 228 (n. 12)
Club d'Essai, 147, 152
Codrescu, Andrei, 186, 189, 190, 191, 249 (n. 32)
Cohen, Debra Rae, 6
Collins, Ray, 44–45
Columbia University, 226 (n. 5)
The Columbia Workshop, 37–61; aim of, 9–10, 222 (n. 23); critical and popular acclaim for, 32, 44, 49, 221–22 (n. 32); debut of, 9, 42, 212 (n. 22), 220 (n. 26); impact on radio culture of, 31–32, 42–49, 60–61; innovations of, 36, 43, 44, 45, 49, 50, 54, 63, 223 (n. 47); listener feedback to, 48, 222 (n. 40); Murrow and legacy of, 232 (n. 58); narrator's role in, 47–49; number of works aired by, 10, 219 (n. 1), 223 (n. 47); as prestige-programming standard, 32, 55, 141; Reis conception of, 42, 212 (nn. 22–23), 223 (n. 47); sound effects in, 33, 45–46, 60, 218 (n. 66); success of, 3, 7
—works aired by, 42, 62–63; *Air Raid*, 53, 56–58, 88, 111, 223 (n. 56), 229 (n. 14), 235 (n. 30); *Broadway Evening*, 10, 43–44, 221 (nn. 30, 32); *Cartwheel*, 44–45; *Fall of the City*, 9–10, 44, 49–55, 223 (nn. 49, 56), 224 (n. 63); *On a Note of Triumph*, 37–38, 219 (n. 2); *The San Quintin Breakout*, 46–47, 50
A Comedy of Danger, 45
Commercials, 31
Communications Act of 1934, 41
Communities of the Air (Squire), 5
Conley, Robert, 194, 250 (n. 42)
Connor, Steven, 5, 31, 217 (n. 59); on Gould, 165, 173; on vocalic body, 110, 120, 145, 236 (n. 47)
Contrapuntal radio: Gould and, 12, 156, 158, 165–66, 169–72, 174–75, 180, 196–97, 246 (n. 43); NPR and, 196–97, 251 (n. 49); term, 245 (n. 30)
Cooper, Giles, 241 (n. 43)
Corneille, Pierre, 3, 218 (n. 64)
Corporation for Public Broadcasting, 249 (n. 26)
Corwin, Norman, 36, 41, 61; and *Columbia Workshop*, 9, 42; literary imagination of, 3, 219 (n. 1); narrative voice emphasis of, 63; and NPR, 191
—works: *On a Note of Triumph*, 37–38, 219 (n. 2); *They Fly through the Air*, 55, 58–60
Cory, Mark, 241 (n. 43)
Cotton, Joseph, 224 (n. 64)
Coughlin, Father, 88, 229 (n. 18)
Coulter, Douglas, 49, 212 (n. 23), 221 (n. 30)
Coyle, Michael, 6
Cradle Will Rock (Blitzstein), 64
Crane, David, 118
Crane, Stephen, 10
Cronkite, Walter, 189, 194, 207

Index 271

Crosby, Bing, 121
Crosley radios, 219 (n. 10)
Cross talk, 162, 196–97, 244 (n. 21), 251 (n. 49)
Cunard, Nancy, 147

Dada, 16, 22, 25
The Dark (*Lights Out* episode), 32
Darsa, Josh, 185
Davidson, Peter, 244 (n. 22)
Davis, Elmer, 88–89
Deaths and Entrances (Thomas), 132
De Mille, Cecil B., 121
Denison, Merrill, 54
Denning, Michael, 225 (n. 75), 226 (n. 7)
Derrida, Jacques, 18, 48–49, 214 (nn. 11–12)
Didion, Joan, 190
Dilworth, Alexa, 210
"Disenchantment of the concept," 169, 246 (n. 39)
Displacement hypothesis, 12–13, 213 (n. 29)
Distracted listeners, 17, 18
Doig, Ivan, 190
Dolar, Mladen, 5, 19, 25–26, 120
Donne, John, 141
Douglas, Susan, 5, 180, 233 (n. 68), 247 (n. 63); and NPR, 182, 247 (n. 2), 252 (n. 68)
The Downbeat on Murder (*Columbia Workshop* broadcast), 45–46
Dracula (Stoker novel), 66–67, 68–69, 70, 71–72, 227 (n. 24)
Dracula (Welles radio adaptation), 66–73; narration in, 68, 69, 73; sound effects in, 30, 33
DuPont Company, 226 (n. 4)
Dyall, Valentine, 236 (n. 1)
Dyson, Frances, 178

Echo, 104–6, 233 (n. 4)
Edgerton, Gary, 228 (n. 9)
Eliot, T. S., 4, 141, 218 (n. 64); *The Four Quartets*, 63

Ellis, Anthony, 234 (n. 19)
Emerling, Susan, 200
Engelbrecht, H. C., 226 (n. 4)
Euripedes, 3

Fables in Verse (poetry show), 3
Fact-fiction border, 47; Frank and, 201; Murrow and, 95, 224 (n. 73); Welles and, 74, 80–82, 86, 231 (n. 44)
The Fall of the City (MacLeish), 49–55; announcer's role in, 51–52, 53, 54, 223 (n. 56); cost of producing, 55; critical acclaim for, 55, 65, 223 (n. 49), 224 (n. 63); crowd in, 44, 50–51, 53; foreword to printed edition of, 55, 224 (n. 63)
Fascism, 49, 52, 226 (n. 7)
Fass, Bob, 181
Faulkner, William: *Absalom, Absalom!*, 232 (n. 62)
Federal Communications Commission (FCC), 62, 81
Federal Radio Commission, 41
Feiffer, Jules, 248 (n. 21)
Female voice, 11; as acoustic mirror, 106, 233 (n. 10); banned from radio airwaves, 106–7, 127; on daytime radio, 234 (n. 16); debate over desirability of, 233 (n. 13); depicted as threat, 21–22, 126, 216 (n. 34); and Echo and Narcissus myth, 104–6; in film, 233 (n. 11); in *The Screaming Woman*, 107–11; in *Sorry, Wrong Number*, 111–16, 119–20; Stamberg and, 207; in *The Whole Town's Sleeping*, 107–9
Film: and radio, 120–21; *Sorry, Wrong Number* in, 121–26, 127, 233 (n. 11), 236 (nn. 51, 53)
The Finger of God (*Columbia Workshop* broadcast), 42–43
The Firestone Hour, 40
Fish, Stanley, 169
Flatow, Ira, 195
Flesch, Rudolf, 217 (n. 60)

Fletcher, Lucille, 42, 113, 219 (n. 71)
—works: *The Hitch-Hiker*, 9, 11, 34, 36, 113; *Sorry, Wrong Number*, 11, 111–26
FM radio, 181, 200, 247 (n. 62)
Ford Foundation, 194
Forster, E. M., 141
Fortune, 39
Foucault, Michel, 174
Francis, Arlene, 222 (n. 41), 224 (n. 64)
Frank, Joe, 12, 200–203
Frankfurt School, 5, 211 (n. 15)
Frazier, Ian, 189
Free-form movement, 13, 213 (n. 32)
Freud, Sigmund, 105, 233 (n. 6)
Frost, Everett C., 240 (n. 38)
Fugitive Waves (radio show), 209
Fussell, Paul, 45

Gabel, Martin, 37, 38
Gardner, Charles, 94–95, 231 (n. 43)
Gassner, John, 211 (n. 10)
Glass, Ira, 200, 249 (n. 31)
Goebbels, Joseph, 15, 213 (n. 2)
Goldstein, Jonathan, 208
Goodman, David, 40, 220 (n. 22), 225 (n. 2)
Gould, Glenn, 155–81; challenge to listeners provided by, 166, 245 (n. 31), 246–47 (nn. 48, 61); contrapuntal aesthetic of, 12, 156, 158, 165–66, 169–72, 174–75, 180, 196–97, 246 (n. 43); editing of interviews by, 160–61; on hearing and listening, 11–12, 155–56, 179; literary works drawn on by, 159, 245 (n. 36); as musical composer, 244–45 (n. 29); radio as medium for, 156, 179; on recording technologies, 245 (n. 34); relationship to CBC, 156, 161; retirement from concert stage by, 155, 158; *Solitude Trilogy* conception of, 11–12, 159, 243–44 (n. 12); sound effects used by, 167–68; studio practice of, 156, 243 (n. 2); tape-edited performances by, 155, 177; tape splicing by, 155, 156, 161, 166, 167, 175, 179, 245 (n. 35), 246 (n. 55); *Under Milk Wood* influence on, 158, 159, 176, 178
—works: "The Idea of the North," 156, 158–70, 243 (nn. 7, 11), 244 (nn. 18, 21), 251 (n. 49); "The Latecomers," 170–79, 246 (n. 47); "The Quiet in the Land," 179–80
Grass, Günter, 21
Graves, Robert, 240 (n. 35)
Great Plays, 3
Greek Chorus, 50, 53, 172–73
Greene, Graham, 141
Green Hornet, 15
Gross, Terry, 182
Grosvenor, Vertamae, 190

Halberstam, David, 228 (n. 9)
Hall, Donald, 190–91
Hall, Porter, 224 (n. 64)
Hamlet (Shakespeare), 32, 44–45, 64
Hanighen, F. C., 226 (n. 4)
Harris, Leslie, 173–74, 178
Hatfield, Henry, 41
Hecker, Tim, 243 (n. 2)
Hermann, Bernard, 11, 34, 37
Hersey, John: *Hiroshima*, 141
Hi-fi radio, 247 (n. 63)
Higby, Mary Jane, 28–29
Hilmes, Michele, 5, 218 (n. 67), 233 (n. 13); about broadcast radio, 217–18 (n. 62), 225 (n. 3)
Hindenburg disaster, 78–79
Hirschkop, Philip, 185
The Hitchhiker's Guide to the Galaxy, 128
The Hitch-Hiker (Fletcher), 9, 11, 34, 36, 113; Welles production of, 34–36, 218 (n. 68)
Hitler, Adolf, 54, 55, 74–75, 85, 92
Holiday Memory (Thomas), 131
Hollywood, 120–21
Hollywood Quarterly, 55
Homage to Catalonia (Orwell), 86, 230 (n. 25), 232 (n. 61)

Homer: *The Iliad*, 20, 215 (n. 33); *The Odyssey*, 133; Plato's antipathy to, 8, 20–21
Hope, Bob, 3
Hörspiele, 201, 241 (n. 43)
Houseman, John, 65–66
Hugo, Victor: *Les Misérables*, 3, 64, 226 (n. 9)
Hummert, Anne and Frank, 9, 27–31, 217 (nn. 52, 60)
Huntley, Chet, 207
Hurwitz, Robert, 159, 169–70, 246 (n. 46)
Husserl, Edmund, 18
Huston, Walter, 3, 32
Hutchens, John K., 221–22 (n. 33)
Huxley, Aldous: *Brave New World*, 63
Hyde, Johnny, 181

Ibsen, Henrik, 3, 218 (n. 64)
"The Idea of the North" (Gould), 158–70, 243 (n. 7); cross talk in, 162, 197, 244 (n. 21), 251 (n. 49); Gould description of, 159–60, 243 (n. 11), 244 (n. 18); radical nature of, 156, 158–59
Ihde, Don, 5, 138, 139, 214 (n. 17)
The Iliad (Homer), 20, 215 (n. 33)
Inskeep, Greg, 186
Inskeep, Steve, 182
Internet, 12–13
Irving, John, 190–91
"The Ish Fish" (Nordine), 204–6

The Jack Benny Show, 40
Jessop, John, 245 (n. 34)
Jolson, Al, 3
Joplin, Janis, 180
Joyce, James: *Ulysses*, 6
Julius Caesar (Shakespeare), 229 (n. 20)

Kafka, Franz, 73, 159, 163
Kahn, Douglas, 5, 17
Kaltenborn, H. V., 75–76, 85, 229 (n. 20); eyewitness news coverage by, 15, 89, 229 (n. 19); and Murrow, 90, 230 (n. 28)
Kamen, Jeff, 193
Kasper, Lynne Rossetto, 200
Katz, Fred, 203, 204, 252 (n. 64)
Kearnes, George, 237 (n. 1)
Keats, John, 141
Keillor, Garrison, 248 (n. 20)
Kenner, Hugh, 146, 241 (n. 51)
King, Steven, 32
Kingsley, Bob, 195
Kittler, Friedrich, 71, 227 (n. 24)
Klauber, Ed, 96
Klein, Adelaide, 45
Knight, Vic, 44–45
Koch, Howard, 227 (n. 40)
Koenig, Sarah, 209
Koppel, Ted, 229 (n. 13)
Kostelanetz, Richard, 156
Krapp's Last Tape (Beckett), 187–88, 242 (n. 57)
Kreymborg, Alfred, 3, 42
Kristeva, Julia, 18, 153, 212 (n. 27), 235 (n. 26)

Lancaster, Burt, 121, 123
Language: Beckett on, 144, 149, 150–51, 154, 242 (n. 65); devocalizing of, 154, 243 (n. 73); Gould on, 160, 172; and human speech, 18, 110, 214 (n. 14); and meaning, 11, 24; and music, 7, 158, 214 (n. 17); and noise, 19, 60; and sound, 7–8, 22, 25; spoken vs. written, 11
"The Latecomers" (Gould), 170–79, 246 (n. 47); sound effects in, 171–72; structure of, 178
Lawrence, Amy, 124, 233 (n. 11), 236 (nn. 51, 53)
Lawrence, D. H., 6
Leary, Timothy, 155
The Legionnaire and the Lady (*Columbia Workshop* broadcast), 55
Les Misérables (Hugo novel), 3, 64, 226 (n. 9)

Les Misérables (Welles radio adaptation), 3, 22-23, 64-65, 89
LeSueur, Larry, 85
Levine, Lawrence, 221 (n. 32)
Levi-Strauss, Claude, 17
Lewis, Peter, 135
Lewis, William, 63
Lewty, Jane, 4, 6
Liasson, Mara, 182, 186
Liebowitz, Fran, 190-91
Life, 119
Lightness, 204, 252 (n. 65)
Lights Out (radio show), 32-33
Limbaugh, Rush, 183
Lincoln Journal and Star, 32
Listening: Gould challenges to, 166, 245 (n. 31), 246-47 (nn. 48, 61); and meaning, 24; speech vs. non-speech, 19, 214 (n. 18). See also Sound
Listening (Nancy), 25
Listening in (Douglas), 5
Little Review, 6
Litvak, Anatole, 121, 127
Locke, John, 214 (n. 22)
Logocentrism, 18, 19, 25, 44, 110, 172
Lomax, Alan, 42, 60, 225 (n. 79)
London after Dark, 96-98
London Blitz, 8, 10, 85-99, 228 (nn. 9, 12), 230 (n. 37); facts of, 83
Long, Huey, 88
Lorentz, Pare, 38, 42, 63
Lorre, Peter, 32, 128, 228 (n. 46)
Lotz, James, 160, 166, 167, 245 (n. 32), 251 (n. 49)
Loy, Mina, 6
Lux Radio Theatre, 55, 63, 120-21

Macbeth (Shakespeare), 3, 63-64
Maclean, Wally, 197-98; Gould interviewing of, 160, 163-64, 166, 167, 168-69, 244 (nn. 15, 24), 251 (n. 49)
MacLeish, Archibald, 4, 13, 39, 81; and Columbia Workshop, 9-10, 42; interest in sound effects, 224-25 (n. 74); and Murrow, 55-56, 223-24 (n. 60, 73), 230 (n. 24)
—works: Air Raid, 53, 56-58, 88, 111, 223 (n. 59), 229 (n. 14), 235 (n. 30); Fall of the City, 9-10, 44, 49-55, 223 (nn. 49, 56), 224 (n. 63); Panic, 53
MacNeice, Louis, 132
Magliozzi, Tom and Ray, 182
Mama Makes Up Her Mind (White), 191
Mankiewicz, Frank, 192, 249 (n. 34), 250 (n. 36)
Mann, Thomas, 141
Ma Perkins (soap opera), 29-30, 217 (nn. 55-57)
The March of Time (news series), 78, 116, 224 (n. 64)
Marinetti, F. T., 16
Marlowe, Christopher, 218 (n. 64); Tamburlaine, 3
Mars, Roman, 208
Marx, Groucho, 40
Mastering effect, 44; Poizat on, 26, 216 (n. 48); and radio, 81; and soap operas, 27-31; term, 8
Matthews, William, 55
Maud, Ralph, 130, 237 (n. 10)
Maude, Ulrika, 241 (n. 47)
May Day protest (1971), 185, 192-93, 250 (n. 42)
McBride, Mary Margaret, 234 (n. 16)
McCarthy, Charlie (wooden dummy), 15, 63, 128
McCarthy, Joseph, 187
McCauley, Michael P., 249 (n. 26)
McChesney, Robert W., 220 (n. 22)
McCourt, Tom, 247 (n. 62), 252 (n. 67)
McCracken, Allison, 116
McFarlane, Matthew, 246-47 (n. 61)
McLuhan, Marshall, 155, 188, 190; about radio, 4, 75; about Narcissus, 105-6; about orality and literacy, 174, 178, 179
McNeilly, Kevin, 158, 169
McPhee, John, 190

Index 275

McWhinnie, Donald, 141, 241 (n. 42); and *All That Fall*, 146–48, 153
Memories of Christmas (Thomas), 131–32
Mencken, H. L., 40, 187
The Merchants of Death (Engelbrecht and Hanighen), 226 (n. 4)
Mercury Theatre on the Air, 65–66, 141; *Dracula* aired on, 30, 33, 66–73, 227 (n. 24); *The Hitch-Hiker* aired on, 34; innovative sound effects of, 30, 33, 36; sponsorship of, 81; *War of the Worlds* aired on, 9, 22–26, 33, 73–81, 126; Welles and, 10, 63, 65, 130
Meredith, Burgess, 3, 32
Meridian 7-1212 (*Columbia Workshop* broadcast), 10, 49
Merleau-Ponty, Maurice, 24
Merton, Thomas, 190–91
Metamorphosis (Kafka), 159
Meyers, Michael, 195
Microphone technology, 44–45, 48
Miller, Arthur, 4, 42, 62
Miller, Henry, 190, 211 (n. 1)
Milton, John, 141
Milutis, Joe, 19
Mitchell, Jack, 194, 250 (n. 43), 252 (n. 69)
Modernism, 87, 135, 140, 152, 210, 239 (n. 29); MacLeish and, 53, 54; Murrow and, 100, 101; and narrative, 27, 33, 66, 87, 135; and noise, 23, 25, 43–44, 60, 94; radio's interplay with, 4, 6–7, 8–9; techniques of, 11, 32; Welles and, 63, 66, 73, 74, 81
Montagne, Renée, 182
Montreal Gazette, 32
Montreal Star, 170
Moore, Marianne, 6
Moorehead, Agnes, 11, 72, 107, 121, 219 (n. 71), 224 (n. 64); in *The Screaming Woman*, 109–10, 234–35 (nn. 21–23); in *Sorry, Wrong Number*, 111–13, 115–17, 119, 127

More Than One Voice (Cavarero), 25, 213 (n. 28)
Morgan, Brewster, 32
Morgan, Edward P., 194–95
Morin, Emilie, 241–42 (n. 56)
Morning Edition, 12, 183, 191, 252 (n. 68)
Morris, Adelaide, 5
Morris, John, 147
Morrison, Herb, 78–79
Mortified (radio show), 209
The Moth Radio Hour, 208
Mr. Smith Goes to Washington, 89
Munich Crisis (1938), 74–75, 76, 77, 89, 229 (n. 19)
Murdoch, Iris, 141
Murrow, Edward R., 3, 76, 83–103, 119, 248 (n. 10); acoustic vigilance by, 9, 99, 100, 102, 232 (nn. 58, 62); background of, 228 (n. 9); backtracking on sonic innovation by, 13; and danger, 91–92; and Kaltenborn, 90, 230 (n. 28); *London after Dark* broadcasts by, 96–98; and MacLeish, 56–57, 223–24 (nn. 60, 73), 230 (n. 24); as mentor and role model, 85, 88, 185, 189, 228 (n. 9), 229 (n. 13); metaphors of, 87, 88, 98, 102; novel by, 98; and proximity effect, 23, 90, 99–103, 166–67, 197; sonic innovation by, 10, 85–89, 86; sound imagery used by, 8, 94–98, 100–101, 102, 232 (n. 67); *See It Now* TV series of, 187; and Thompson, 92–94, 231 (n. 40)
Music: counterpoint in, 165; Gould as composer of, 244–45 (n. 29); Gould as performer of, 155, 158, 177; in Homer's poetry, 20–21; and human voice, 12, 139, 155, 156, 160, 172, 178; and language, 7, 158, 214 (n. 17); Murrow's use of, 8, 13, 90; NPR and, 203, 204, 205, 209; radio airing of, 2, 3, 4, 34; radio productions' use of, 1, 33, 34, 74, 77, 122, 123, 143–44, 159,

276 *Index*

168, 211 (nn. 1, 3); and sound, 7, 19, 147–48, 156
Musique concrète, 147–48, 241–42 (n. 56), 242 (n. 61)

Nancy, Jean-Luc, 5, 24, 25
Narcissus, 104, 105–6, 233 (n. 6)
Narrators. *See* Radio commentators and announcers
Nation, 74, 186
National Public Radio (NPR), 182–210; commentators on, 189, 190, 196, 249 (n. 32); as contrapuntal radio, 196–97, 251 (n. 49); criticisms of, 182, 186, 247 (n. 1); cultural vs. news tension in, 192, 206, 250 (n. 36); and female voice, 207; and Ford Foundation, 194; Frank and, 12, 200–203; innovation by, 186, 189, 194, 207; listenership of, 12, 183; and locally produced material, 190, 249 (n. 26); mainstream and commercial evolution of, 13, 207–8, 252 (n. 67); and May Day protest, 185, 192–93, 250 (n. 42); mission statement of, 249 (n. 27); *Morning Edition*, 12, 183, 191, 252 (n. 68); Nordine and, 12, 203–6; offices of, 182, 247 (n. 4); Peabody Award for, 194, 250 (n. 43); and radio essay genre, 187, 190–92, 207; revitalization of radio by, 182, 198, 207, 247 (n. 2); *Rivers of the Skull* series on, 198–200, 251 (n. 53); Stamberg and, 183–87; storytelling approach of, 195, 197–98, 206, 248 (n. 7), 250 (n. 46); Williams and, 188–89. See also *All Things Considered*
Nazi Germany, 15, 50, 55, 87, 213 (n. 2)
NBC, 2, 113, 213 (n. 1), 219 (n. 11), 234 (n. 21); CBS rivalry with, 3, 32, 44, 62, 63; news coverage by, 74, 75; prestige programming by, 3, 4, 32–33, 41–42, 46; and Toscanini, 3, 220 (n. 21)

Negro Theater Federal Project, 63–64
Networks: growth and power of, 2; prestige radio calculation by, 60, 62; and sponsors, 219 (n. 11), 225 (n. 78); threats to control of, 41, 220 (n. 22). *See also* BBC; Canadian Broadcasting Corporation; CBS; NBC
Newfoundland, 170–79
Newman, Kathy, 5, 30
Newsweek, 54
New Yorker, 26, 141, 189
New York magazine, 195, 206, 250 (n. 46)
New York Times, 125, 156, 169–70, 188
New Zealand Broadcasting Service, 15
99% Invisible, 208, 209
Nixon, Richard, 193, 251 (n. 53)
Noise: filtering out ambient, 173; modernism and, 23, 25, 43–44, 60, 94; reigning, 43–44; and spoken word, 19, 60
Noise, Water, Meat (Kahn), 5
Nordine, Ken, 12, 200–206, 251 (nn. 60–61)
Norman Corwin's Words without Music, 3
Norris, Michelle, 186
NPR Playhouse, 201–2

Oboler, Arch, 31, 36; and *Columbia Workshop*, 9, 42; *Lights Out* horror show of, 32–33
O'Brien, Margaret, 234 (n. 21)
Ochs, Phil, 192
The Odyssey (Homer), 133
O'Farrell, Mary, 152
Olson, Lynne, 228 (n. 12)
On a Note of Triumph (Corwin), 37–38, 219 (n. 2)
Ong, Walter, 4, 174
Opera, 24, 26, 216 (n. 48)
Orality-literacy dichotomy, 175, 178, 179, 248 (n. 7)

The Organist (podcast), 208
Orwell, George, 10, 87; *Animal Farm*, 141; *Homage to Catalonia*, 86, 230 (n. 25), 232 (n. 61); *Voice* radio magazine of, 130, 237 (n. 5)
Ottawa Citizen, 170
Ovid, 104–5

Paley, William S., 91, 212 (n. 22); commitment to prestige programming, 3, 60, 62, 225 (n. 1)
Paramount Pictures, 120
Parker, Dorothy, 42
Patchen, Kenneth, 42, 211 (n. 1); *The City Wears a Slouch Hat*, 1, 63
Payzant, Geoffrey, 159, 243 (nn. 4, 7), 245 (n. 31)
Pennebaker, D. A., 185
Phillips, Robert, 160, 162, 163, 167, 251 (n. 49)
Phonophobia, 17–22
Pinkwater, Daniel, 190, 191
Plato, 25, 215 (n. 32); antipathy to Homer by, 8, 20–21; legacy of, 213 (n. 28), 243 (n. 73)
Podcasts, 208–10
Poe, Edgar Allen, 46
Poetry, 20, 22, 55, 223 (n. 49); radio recitals of, 3, 141, 180; Thomas and, 130, 132, 136, 158, 239–40 (nn. 29, 34)
Poggioli, Sylvia, 182
Poizat, Michel, 214 (n. 14); on mastering effect, 8, 26, 216 (n. 48)
Pollitt, Katha, 190–91
Pope, Alexander, 19
Popular Mechanics, 39, 44, 45
Porter, Katherine Anne, 159, 245 (n. 36)
Pound, Ezra, 6–7; "In the Metro" poem of, 98
Prestige movement: about, 220 (n. 21); CBS and, 3–4, 10, 44, 62, 221 (n. 32); *Columbia Workshop* standard in, 32, 55, 141; demand for, 41–42; goals of, 31, 218 (n. 63); impact of, 3, 9–10, 36, 211 (n. 10); NBC and, 3, 4, 32–33, 41–42, 46; Paley commitment to, 3, 60, 62, 225 (n. 1); pragmatic calculations around, 60, 62; Third Programme and, 140–41
Priestley, J. B., 85–86, 96, 231 (n. 38)
Procter and Gamble, 217 (n. 55), 219 (n. 11)
Production costs, 55
Prokofiev, Sergei: *Peter and the Wolf*, 160
Proximity effect, 109, 222 (n. 34); Gould and, 162, 166–67; Murrow and, 23, 90, 99–103, 166–67, 197; Welles and, 226 (n. 16)
Public radio. *See* National Public Radio (NPR)
Public Radio Exchange (PRX), 207–8, 209
Public Radio International, 208
Puksta, David, 196, 197–98
Pyle, Ernie, 87, 230 (n. 34)

"The Quiet in the Land" (Gould), 179–80
Quite Early One Morning (Thomas), 131

Radio (medium): abolition of distance by, 45, 75, 84, 85, 222 (n. 34); acoustic deviance ability of, 19, 22, 36, 43, 44; as art, 15–16, 60, 158, 241 (n. 43); Beckett view of, 142; as business, 40, 219 (n. 11); contrapuntal, 12, 156, 158, 165–66, 169–72, 174–75, 180, 196–97, 246 (n. 43), 251 (n. 49); cultural impact of, 3–4, 5, 13, 38; displacement hypothesis on, 12–13; fact-fiction dichotomy in, 47, 74, 80–82, 86, 95, 201, 224 (n. 73), 231 (n. 44); and film, 120–21; FM, 181, 200, 247 (n. 62); genre hybridity in, 86, 133, 159, 238 (n. 14); as Gould's preference, 156, 179; hi-fi, 247 (n. 63); highbrow vs. lowbrow, 31, 217–18 (n. 62), 221 (n. 32); international growth of, 15; listenership of, 2, 39–40,

48, 90, 222 (n. 40); literary turn of, 31–36, 61; and mastering effect, 81; McLuhan view of, 4, 75; modernism's interplay with, 4, 6–7, 8–9; music compared to, 7, 19, 156; networks' control of, 2; and newspapers, 83–85; NPR's rejuvenation of, 182, 198, 207, 247 (n. 2); perceived dangers from, 96–97, 231 (n. 46); and popular entertainment, 44, 221 (n. 32); and proximity effect, 23, 89–90, 99–103, 162, 166–67, 197, 226 (n. 16); reform movement view of, 40–41, 42, 220 (n. 22); scholarship on, 5–7, 211 (n. 15); sponsors of, 15, 81, 213 (n. 1), 217 (n. 55), 219 (n. 11), 225 (n. 78); Welles conception of, 65
Radio Active (Newman), 5
Radio Ambulante, 208–9
Radio commentators and announcers: as cultural hero, 74–76; as embodiment of agency, 48–49; in *Fall of the City*, 51–52, 53, 54, 223 (n. 56); in *Ma Perkins*, 29; Murrow as mentor of, 85, 88, 185, 189, 228 (n. 9), 229 (n. 13); Murrow breaking with tradition of, 85–89; NPR resurrection of, 189, 190, 196, 249 (n. 32); in *On a Note of Triumph*, 36, 37; opposition to women as, 106–7, 127, 233 (n. 13); in *They Fly through the Air*, 58–59; Thomas as, 130–32, 237 (nn. 9–10); trustworthiness of, 76, 77, 80; in *War of the Worlds*, 74, 76–78, 80–81; Welles emphasis on, 63, 86
Radio Daily, 89
Radio Diaries, 209
Radio essay: Murrow and, 85, 88, 90–91, 94, 95, 99, 102; NPR and, 187, 190–92, 207
Radiolab show, 207, 208
Radio memoir, 131, 132
Radio Modernism (Avery), 6

Radios: models of, 40, 219 (n. 10); numbers in use, 2, 39, 227 (n. 30)
Radio-Television Française (RFT), 147
Radio Voices (Hilmes), 5
Rakoff, David, 190
Raquello, Ramon, 73
RCA, 120
Readick, Frank, 78, 80, 224 (n. 64)
"Reality radio," 210
Red River, Manitoba, 179–80
Reis, Irving, 44, 220 (n. 23); and *Columbia Workshop* conception, 42, 212 (nn. 22–23), 223 (n. 47); and sound effects, 33, 45–46, 218 (nn. 66–67)
Reith, John, 62
Reminiscences of Childhood (Thomas), 131
Return Journey (Thomas), 132–36, 237 (n. 11), 238 (nn. 20, 22)
Richards, Sylvia, 234 (n. 21)
Rivers of the Skull (radio series), 198–200, 251 (n. 53)
RKO Pictures, 120
Robinson, Edward G., 3, 32
Robson, William, N., 46–47
Rogers, Gamble, 190
The Romance of Helen Trent (soap opera), 27
Rorty, James, 40, 41, 74, 75
Rosten, Norman, 62
Roth, Philip: *I Married a Communist*, 38–39
Royal, John, 42
Rubinstein, Arthur, 177
Russell, Bertrand, 141
Russolo, Luigi, 16, 43–44, 155
Ruttman, Walter, 43, 221 (n. 28)

Said, Edward, 169
Sandburg, Carl, 3, 62
The San Quentin Breakout (*Columbia Workshop* broadcast), 46–47, 50
Sarnoff, David, 120, 220 (n. 21)
Saroyan, William, 42

Index 279

Sartre, Jean-Paul: "Huis Clos," 141
Schaeffer, Pierre, 5, 97, 147, 155; *musique concrète* of, 16, 241–42 (n. 56); on sounds, 152, 242 (n. 67)
Schafer, R. Murray, 5
Schiller, Paula, 190
Schoenberg, Arnold, 156
Schroeder, Marianne, 160, 161, 162–63, 167, 251 (n. 49)
Schwartz, A. Brad, 228 (n. 46)
Schwitter, Kurt: "Ursonate," 22
The Screaming Woman (Bradbury), 109–10, 111, 234 (n. 21)
Screams, 116–17; in *Air Raid*, 111, 235 (n. 30); Artaud on, 110, 212–13 (n. 27), 235 (n. 26); Chion on, 110, 117; and female hysteria, 11, 107, 111, 112, 115–16, 119, 120, 123, 126; in *The Screaming Woman*, 109–10, 111; in *Sorry, Wrong Number*, 11, 112–16; symbolism of, 110, 235 (n. 26); *in War of the Worlds*, 126; in *The Whole Town's Sleeping*, 108–9
Sedaris, David, 189, 190, 191, 249 (n. 31)
See It Now (documentary series), 187
Serial (Koenig), 209
Serling, Rod, 218 (n. 70)
Sevareid, Eric, 88–89, 189, 207; during London Blitz, 96, 98; about Murrow radio essays, 85, 88, 229 (n. 15)
The Shadow (radio show), 60, 64, 78, 116
Shakespeare, William, 21, 39; CBS radio series on, 3, 32; *Hamlet*, 32, 44–45, 64; *Julius Caesar*, 229 (n. 20); *Macbeth*, 3, 63–64
Shapiro, Ari, 186
Shaw, George Bernard, 3; *Man and Superman*, 141
Shearer, Harry, 202
Sheehan, Vincent, 96, 230 (n. 34)
Shepherd, Jean, 12, 248 (n. 20); *A Voice in the Night* program of, 187–88
Sheridan, Richard Brinsley, 3
Sherman, Scott, 186

Sherwood, Robert, 62
Shewchuk, Peter, 245 (n. 35)
Ship of Fools (Porter), 159, 245 (n. 36)
Shirer, William, 76, 85
Shortwave, 56–57, 75, 92, 233 (n. 68)
Sibelius, Jean, 168–69
Siemering, Bill, 189, 194–95, 198, 249 (n. 29); on May Day protest, 192–93; and NPR innovation, 186, 194, 250 (n. 43); on NPR mission, 249 (n. 27); and Stamberg, 183, 247–48 (nn. 5–6), 250 (n. 44)
Silverman, Kaja, 106, 233 (n. 10)
Singh, Laksmi, 182
Sisyphus, 164–65, 244 (nn. 23–24)
Smith, Howard K., 189, 194
Smith, Kate, 121
Smith, Stevie, 133
Smulyan, Susan, 41
Snap Judgment (Washington), 208
Soap operas, 26, 36, 217–18 (n. 62); Allen view of, 27, 217 (n. 51); commercials aired during, 31; Hummerts' production of, 27–31, 217 (n. 52); *Ma Perkins*, 29–30, 217 (nn. 55–57); primacy of spoken word in, 30–31
Socrates, 8
The Solitude Trilogy (Gould), 155–56, 197, 198, 251 (n. 51); Gould description of, 159, 243–44 (n. 12); "Idea of the North," 156, 158–70, 243 (nn. 7, 11), 244 (nn. 18, 21), 251 (n. 49); "The Latecomers," 170–79, 246 (n. 47); "Quiet in the Land," 179–80
Somerville, Janet, 158
Sontag, Susan, 190
Sophocles, 104
Sorry, Wrong Number (Fletcher): film version of, 121–26, 127, 233 (n. 11), 236 (nn. 51, 53); narrative voice in, 123; radio performance of, 11, 111–20, 235 (nn. 31–32)
Sound: ambient, 43, 94–95, 96, 159, 165, 173, 193, 194, 197, 221 (n. 28);

Arnheim on, 15–17, 213 (n. 3); and language, 7–8, 22, 25; and loss of voice, 172; and meaning, 7, 8, 9, 17, 18–19, 22, 24, 139–40, 216 (n. 42); Murrow imagery from, 8, 94–98, 100–101, 102, 232 (n. 67); and music, 7, 19, 147–48, 156; in opera, 24, 26, 216 (n. 48); as phantom world, 98, 231–32 (n. 54); Plato and Aristotle on, 21, 25, 215 (n. 32); Schaeffer on, 152, 242 (n. 67); and sense, 19, 214 (n. 22); and spoken word, 13, 16–17, 18, 25; Thomas on priority of, 139–40, 239–40 (nn. 34–35). *See also* Acoustic drift

Sound effects: in *All Things Considered*, 185; Beckett and, 143–44, 146–47, 148, 152–53; Cage and, 1, 211 (n. 3); *Columbia Workshop* innovations in, 33, 42–43, 45–46, 60, 218 (n. 66); in *Dracula*, 30, 33; Gould and, 167–68, 169–70, 171–72; in *The Hitch-Hiker*, 34–36; in *Les Misérables*, 89; MacLeish and, 50–51, 57–58, 224–25 (nn. 71, 74); *Mercury Theatre on the Air* innovations in, 30, 33, 36; Murrow and, 8, 10, 94–96, 97–98, 100–101, 102; Reis and, 33, 45–46, 218 (nn. 66–67); Thomas and, 131–32; in *War of the Worlds*, 9, 22–26, 33, 126; Welles interest in, 22–23, 32–33

Sound States (Morris), 5
Spanish Civil War, 15, 87
Speech and Phenomena (Husserl), 18
Spinelli, Martin, 219 (n. 2), 228 (n. 45)
Sponsors: DuPont Company, 226 (n. 4); of *Mercury Theatre on the Air*, 81; networks and, 225 (n. 78); Procter and Gamble, 217 (n. 55), 219 (n. 11); selling of airtime to, 15, 213 (n. 1)
Squire, Susan, 5
Stage, 157–58
Stamberg, Susan, 195, 252 (n. 70); about, 183–87; humor and laughter by, 186, 189–90, 206–7, 252 (n. 70); and Siemering, 183, 247–48 (nn. 5–6), 250 (n. 44)
Stanwyck, Barbara, 121–22, 125–26, 127, 236 (n. 51)
Stein, Gertrude, 6
Stereophonic sound, 13
Sterne, Jonathan, 5
Stevenson, Robert Louis: *Treasure Island*, 66
Stoker, Bram: *Dracula*, 66–67, 68–69, 70, 71–72, 227 (n. 24)
Stokowski, Leopold, 156
Storytelling: *Columbia Workshop* innovation in, 42–43; development of radio, 3–4, 39; disappearance of from radio, 187, 248 (n. 13); modernism and radio, 6; NPR approach to, 195, 197–98, 206, 248 (n. 7), 250 (n. 46); NPR revival of, 191; podcast, 208–10; radio's relationship to, 8–9; word-centered vs. sound-centered, 7–8
Stout, Bob, 76
Strauss, Richard, 156
Stravinsky, Igor, 136
Stream-of-consciousness, 32
Street, Seán, 211 (n. 3)
Suspense (radio program), 11, 34, 212 (n. 26), 234 (n. 18); *The Hitch-Hiker* aired on, 113, 218 (n. 68); Man in Black as announcer for, 128, 236–37 (n. 1); *The Screaming Woman* aired on, 109–11; *Sorry, Wrong Number* aired on, 111–19; *The Whole Town's Sleeping* aired on, 107–9, 234 (n. 19)
Swing, Raymond Gram, 88, 90
Synecdoche effect, 23, 98, 232 (n. 57)
Synge, John Millington, 3

"Take-twoness," 177, 246 (n. 55)
Talk radio, 13, 188, 191, 248 (n. 25)
Tape recorders: Beckett and, 242 (n. 58); Gould and, 158, 159; NPR and, 185, 192

Telephony, 123, 124
Television, 5, 172, 187
The Tell-Tale Heart (Poe), 46
Theater Guild on the Air, 62
Theatre and Its Double (Artaud), 110, 235 (n. 26)
Theroux, Paul, 190–91
They Fly through the Air (Corwin), 55, 58–60
Third Programme (BBC), 128, 136, 140, 141
This American Life (Glass), 208
Thomas, Dylan: as BBC announcer, 130–32, 237 (nn. 9–10); on modernism's optical bias, 239 (n. 31); poetry of, 130, 132, 136, 158, 239–40 (nn. 29, 34); on priority of sound, 139–40, 239–40 (nn. 34–35)
—works: *Deaths and Entrances*, 132; *Return Journey*, 132–36, 237 (n. 11), 238 (nn. 20, 22); *Under Milk Wood*, 11, 128–30, 136–40, 238–39 (nn. 26, 28)
Thomas, Gareth, 139
Thomas, Lowell, 76, 88
Thompson, Dorothy, 76, 85, 88, 90, 106; and Murrow, 92–94, 231 (n. 40)
Thurber, James, 26, 28
Tibetan Book of the Dead, 198–200
Time, 27, 46, 61, 64, 116, 249 (n. 30); about *Columbia Workshop*, 49, 218 (n. 66); about *Fall of the City*, 51, 54, 55; about radio's impact, 2, 4, 38
"Time-tellers," 203, 252 (n. 63)
The Tin Drum (Grass), 21
To Have Done with the Judgment of God (Artaud), 22
Tolstoy, Leo, 218 (n. 64)
Torgue, Henry, 5, 98
Toronto Star, 161, 170
Toscanini, Arturo, 3, 220 (n. 21)
Tsur, Reuven, 214 (n. 18)
Tulk, Lorne, 161, 177
Turan, Kenneth, 188

The Twilight Zone, 218 (n. 70)
Tynan, Kenneth, 129–30
Typographic voice, 174

Underground radio, 180–81, 213 (n. 32)
Under Milk Wood (Thomas): aurality of, 11, 128–30, 138–40; Gould influenced by, 158, 159, 176, 178; premiere of, 238–39 (n. 26); story line of, 137–38; Thomas envisioning of, 239 (n. 28)
Untermeyer, Louis, 223 (n. 49)

Vallee, Frank: person interviewed by Gould, 160, 161–62, 167, 251 (n. 49)
Vancour, Shawn, 213 (n. 3), 216 (n. 42)
Van Doren, Carl, 49, 61, 223 (n. 45)
Vargas Llosa, Mario, 64
Variety, 72, 97, 217 (n. 62), 231 (n. 46)
Variety Radio Directory, 218 (n. 64)
Verma, Neil, 35
Vertov, Dziga, 156
Vocalic body: Beckett and, 145, 146; Connor on, 110, 120, 145, 236 (n. 47)
Voegelin, Salomé, 5, 18, 231–32 (n. 54)
Voice: devocalization of, 106, 120, 127, 213 (n. 28); gendering of, 119–20; loss of, 172; as musical instrument, 12, 139, 155, 156, 160, 172, 178; narrative, 69, 123, 226 (n. 16). *See also* Female voice
A Voice and Nothing More (Dolar), 25–26
A Voice in the Night (radio program), 187–88
Voice (radio magazine), 130, 237 (n. 5)
Vowell, Sarah, 189, 190, 248 (n. 10)

Wagner-Hatfield amendment, 41, 42, 220 (n. 22)
Wall Street Journal, 187, 202
Ware, Susan, 234 (n. 16)
The War of the Worlds (Welles radio adaptation), 10, 73–81; fiction-fact

blurring in, 80–81, 228 (n. 45), 231 (n. 44); preposterousness of story in, 76, 227 (n. 40); role of radio announcer in, 74, 76–78, 80–81; sound effects in, 9, 22–26, 33, 126; wave of terror caused by, 74, 76–77, 95–96, 227 (n. 27)
The War of the Worlds (Wells novel), 25, 77
Washington, Glynn, 208
Wason, Betty, 11, 106–7, 127
Waugh, Evelyn, 141
Weekend (Ruttman), 43, 221 (n. 28)
Weiss, Mark, 110
Welles, Orson, 9, 39, 62–82, 130; close-miking by, 166–67; *Dracula* production by, 10, 30, 33, 66–73; fact-fiction blurring by, 80–81, 86; as *Fall of the City* announcer, 51–52, 64, 223 (n. 56); *The Hitch-Hiker* production by, 34–36, 218 (n. 68); interest in sound effects, 22–23, 32–33; left-wing leanings of, 63, 226 (n. 7); *Les Misérables* production by, 3, 22–23, 64–65, 89; *Macbeth* production by, 3, 63–64; and *Mercury Theatre on the Air*, 10, 63, 65, 130; narratorial emphasis of, 63, 65, 86; and proximity effect, 226 (n. 16); signs with Hollywood, 121; sound-sense tension of, 22–26, 81–82; *War of the Worlds* production by, 9, 22–26, 33, 73–81, 227 (nn. 27, 40), 228 (n. 45), 231 (n. 44)
Wells, H. G., 25, 77
Wertheimer, Linda, 189, 250 (n. 36, 42)
White, Bailey, 186, 190, 191
Whitehead, Gregory, 5
Whitehead, Kate, 241 (n. 42)
Whitman, Walt, 3, 38
The Whole Town's Sleeping (*Suspense* drama), 107–9, 234 (n. 19)
Wilder, Thornton, 42; *Our Town*, 159
Williams, Kim, 188–89, 190, 191, 192
Wilson, Gahan, 195
Wireless Imagination (Kahn and Whitehead), 5
Wireless Writing in the Age of Marconi (Campbell), 6–7
WireTap (Goldstein), 208
Wiseman, Frederick, 185
Wolfe, Thomas, 3
Wood, Maurice, 83
Woodrich, Vernon, 195
Woolf, Virginia: "The Duchess and the Jeweler," 141
Word Jazz, 12, 200, 203, 251 (nn. 60–61)
Worth, Katherine, 243 (n. 70)

Young, Eugene, 174–77, 178

Zenith, 40
Zukor, Adolph, 120